Reinforced Concrete
Design Theory and Examples

Reinforced Concrete

Design Theory and Examples

Second edition

T.J. MACGINLEY
Nanyang Technological Institute, Singapore

B.S. CHOO
Nottingham University, UK

Chapter 14, Tall Buildings, contributed by
Dr J.C.D. Hoenderkamp, Formerly of Nanyang
Technological Institute, Singapore

E. & F.N. SPON
An imprint of Chapman and Hall
London • New York • Tokyo • Melbourne • Madras

UK	Chapman and Hall, 11 New Fetter Lane, London EC4P 4EE
USA	Chapman and Hall, 29 West 35th Street, New York NY10001
JAPAN	Chapman and Hall Japan, Thomson Publishing Japan, Hirakawacho Nemoto Building, 7F, 1-7-11 Hirakawa-cho, Chiyoda-ku, Tokyo 102
AUSTRALIA	Chapman and Hall Australia, Thomas Nelson Australia, 480 La Trobe Street, PO Box 4725, Melbourne 3000
INDIA	Chapman and Hall India, R. Sheshadri, 32 Second Main Road, CIT East, Madras 600 035

First edition 1978
Reprinted 1981
Second edition 1990

© 1978 T.J. MacGinley
© 1990 T.J. MacGinley and B.S. Choo

Typeset in 10/12 Times by
Best-set Typesetter Ltd, Hong Kong
Printed in Great Britain by
St Edmundsbury Press Ltd, Bury St Edmunds, Suffolk

ISBN 0 419 13830 7 (PB)

British Library Cataloguing in Publication Data

MacGinley, T.J. (Thomas Joseph) *1930–*
    Reinforced concrete. – 2nd. ed.
    1. Reinforced concrete structures. Designs
    I. Title II. Choo, B. S.
    624.1′8341

ISBN 0-419-13830-7 pbk

Library of Congress Cataloging-in-Publication Data

MacGinley, T.J. (Thomas Joseph)
    Reinforced concrete : design theory and examples / T.J. MacGinley,
    B.S. Choo. — 2nd ed.
        p.   cm.
    Includes bibliographical references.
    ISBN 0-419-13830-7 (pbk.)
    1. Reinforced concrete construction. I. Choo, B. S. II. Title.
    TA683.2.M33 1990
    624.1′8341—dc20   89-70743
                                                                              CIP

Contents

vi   Contents

x   Contents

List of Examples

Preface

The second edition of the book has been written to conform to BS 8110, the new version of the limit state code for structural concrete design. The aim remains as stated in the first edition: to set out design theory and illustrate the practical applications by the inclusion of as many useful examples as possible. The book is written primarily for students on civil engineering degree courses to assist them to understand the principles of element design and the procedures for the design of concrete buildings.

The book has been extensively rewritten. A chapter has been added on materials and durability. Other chapters such as those on columns and buildings have been extended and the design of walls in buildings has been given a separate chapter. A special chapter on the analysis and design of very tall buildings has also been added. This should give students an appreciation of the way in which these buildings are modelled for computer analyses and the design problems involved.
design problems involved.

The importance of computers in structural design is recognized. Computer programs for design of concrete elements are included. In these sections, the principles and steps involved in the construction of the programs are explained and the listings are given.

Acknowledgements

Extracts from BS 8110: Part 1:1985 and Part 2:1985 are produced with the permission of the British Standards Institution. Complete copies of the code can be obtained by post from BSI Sales, Linford Wood, Milton Keynes, Bucks MK14 6LE UK.

1

Introduction

1.1 REINFORCED CONCRETE STRUCTURES

Concrete is arguably the most important building material, playing a part in all building structures. Its virtue is its versatility, i.e. its ability to be moulded to take up the shapes required for the various structural forms. It is also very durable and fire resistant when specification and construction procedures are correct.

Concrete can be used for all standard buildings both single storey and multistorey and for containment and retaining structures and bridges. Some of the common building structures are shown in Fig. 1.1 and are as follows:

1. The single-storey portal supported on isolated footings;
2. The medium-rise framed structure which may be braced by shear walls or unbraced. The building may be supported on isolated footings, strip foundations or a raft;
3. The tall multistorey frame and core structure where the core and rigid frames together resist wind loads. The building is usually supported on a raft which in turn may bear directly on the ground or be carried on piles or caissons. These buildings usually include a basement.

Complete designs for types 1 and 2 are given. The analysis and design for type 3 is discussed. The design of all building elements and isolated foundations is described.

1.2 STRUCTURAL ELEMENTS AND FRAMES

The complete building structure can be broken down into the following elements:

Beams	horizontal members carrying lateral loads
Slabs	horizontal plate elements carrying lateral loads
Columns	vertical members carrying primarily axial load but generally subjected to axial load and moment
Walls	vertical plate elements resisting vertical, lateral or in-plane loads
Bases and foundations	pads or strips supported directly on the ground that spread the loads from columns or walls so that they can be supported by the ground without

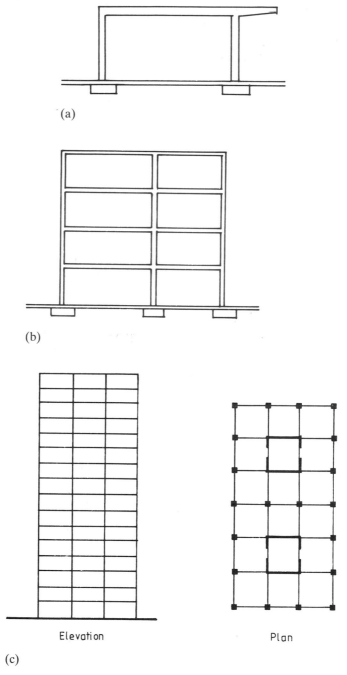

(a)

(b)

Elevation   Plan

(c)

Fig. 1.1 (a) Single-storey portal; (b) medium-rise reinforced concrete framed building; (c) reinforced concrete frame and core structure.

excessive settlement. Alternatively the bases may be supported on piles.

To learn concrete design it is necessary to start by carrying out the design of separate elements. However, it is important to recognize the function of the element in the complete structure and that the complete structure or part of it needs to be analysed to obtain actions for design. The elements listed above are illustrated in Fig. 1.2 which shows typical cast-*in-situ* concrete building construction.

A cast-*in-situ* framed reinforced concrete building and the rigid frames and elements into which it is idealized for analysis and design are shown in Fig. 1.3. The design with regard to this building will cover

1. one-way continuous slabs
2. transverse and longitudinal rigid frames
3. foundations

Various types of floor are considered, two of which are shown in Fig. 1.4. A one-way floor slab supported on primary reinforced concrete frames and secondary continuous flanged beams is shown in Fig. 1.4(a). In Fig. 1.4(b) only primary reinforced concrete frames are constructed and the slab spans two ways. Flat slab construction, where the slab is supported by the columns without beams, is also described. Structural design for isolated pad, strip and combined and piled foundations and retaining walls (Fig. 1.5) is covered in this book.

1.3 STRUCTURAL DESIGN

The first function in design is the planning carried out by the architect to determine the arrangement and layout of the building to meet the client's requirements. The structural engineer then determines the best structural system or forms to bring the architect's concept into being. Construction in different materials and with different arrangements and systems may require investigation to determine the most economical answer. Architect and engineer should work together at this conceptual design stage.

Once the building form and structural arrangement have been finalized the design problem consists of the following:

1. idealization of the structure into loadbearing frames and elements for analysis and design
2. estimation of loads
3. analysis to determine the maximum moments, thrusts and shears for design
4. design of sections and reinforcement arrangements for slabs, beams, columns and walls using the results from 3
5. production of arrangement and detail drawings and bar schedules

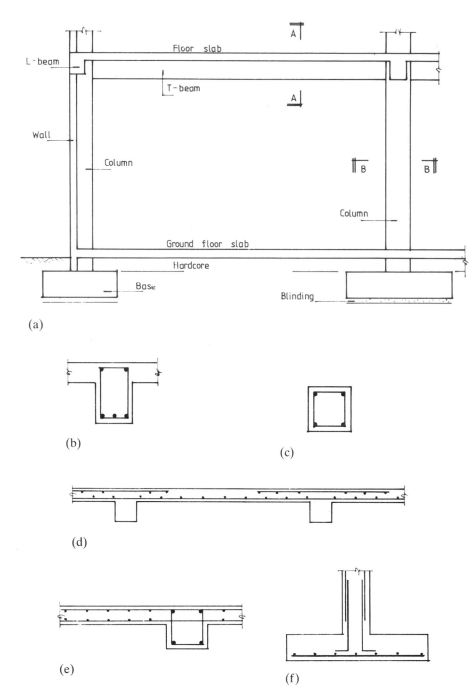

(a)

(b)

(c)

(d)

(e)

(f)

Fig. 1.2 (a) Part elevation of reinforced concrete building; (b) section AA, T-beam; (c) section BB, column; (d) continuous slab; (e) wall; (f) column base.

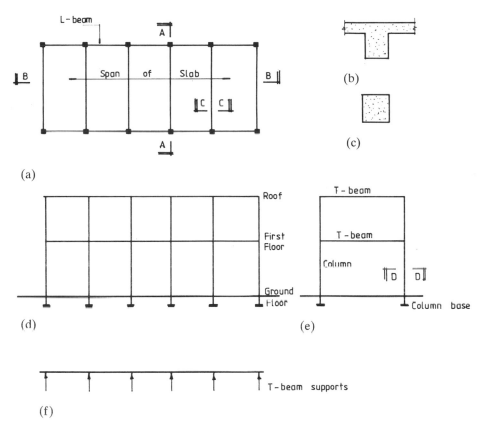

Fig. 1.3 (a) Plan roof and floor; (b) section CC, T-beam; (c) section DD, column; (d) side elevation, longitudinal frame; (e) section AA, transverse frame; (f) continuous one-way slab.

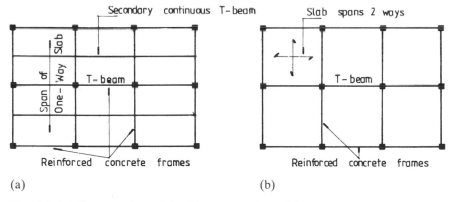

Fig. 1.4 (a) One-way floor slab; (b) two-way floor slab.

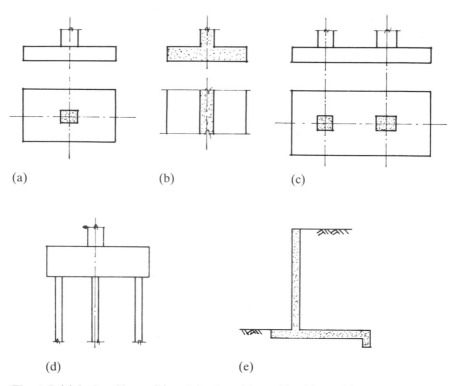

Fig. 1.5 (a) Isolated base; (b) wall footing; (c) combined base; (d) pile foundation; (e) retaining wall.

1.4 DESIGN STANDARDS

In the UK, design is generally to limit state theory in accordance with

> BS 8110: 1985: *Structural Use of Concrete*
> Part 1: *Code of Practice for Design and Construction*

The design of sections for strength is according to plastic theory based on behaviour at ultimate loads. Elastic analysis of sections is also covered because this is used in calculations for deflections and crack width in accordance with

> BS 8110: 1985: *Structural Use of Concrete*
> Part 2: *Code of Practice for Special Circumstances*

The loading on structures conforms to

> BS 6399: 1984: *Design Loading for Building*
> Part 1: *Code of Practice for Dead and Imposed Loads*

CP 3: 1972: Chapter V: *Loading*
Part 2: *Wind Loads*

The codes set out the design loads, load combinations and partial factors of safety, material strengths, design procedures and sound construction practice. A thorough knowledge of the codes is one of the essential requirements of a designer. Thus it is important that copies of these codes are obtained and read in conjunction with the book. Generally, only those parts of clauses and tables are quoted which are relevant to the particular problem, and the reader should consult the full text.

Only the main codes involved have been mentioned above. Other codes, to which reference is necessary, will be noted as required.

1.5 CALCULATIONS, DESIGN AIDS AND COMPUTING

Calculations form the major part of the design process. They are needed to determine the loading on the elements and structure and to carry out the analysis and design of the elements. Design office calculations should be presented in accordance with *Model Procedure for the Presentation of Calculations*, Concrete Society Technical Report No. 5 [1].

The examples in the book do not precisely follow this procedure because they are set out to explain in detail the steps in design. The need for orderly and concise presentation of calculations cannot be emphasized too strongly.

Design aids in the form of charts and tables are an important part of the designer's equipment. These aids make exact design methods easier to apply, shorten design time and lessen the possibility of making errors. Part 3 of BS 8110 consists of design charts for beams and columns, and the construction of charts is set out in this book, together with representative examples.

The use of computers for the analysis and design of structures is standard practice. In analysis exact and approximate manual methods are set out but computer analysis is used where appropriate. Computer programs for element design are included in the book. However, it is essential that students understand the design principles involved and are able to make manual design calculations before using computer programs.

1.6 DETAILING

The general arrangement drawings give the overall layout and principal dimensions of the structure. The structural requirements for the individual elements are presented in the detail drawings. The output of the design calculations are sketches giving sizes of members and the sizes, arrangement, spacing and cut-off points for reinforcing bars at various sections of the structure. Detailing translates this information into a suitable pattern of reinforcement for the structure as a whole. Detailing is presented in accordance with the *Joint Committee Report on Standard Method of Detailing Structural Concrete* [2].

It is essential for the student to know the conventions for making reinforced concrete drawings such as scales, methods for specifying bars, links, fabric, cut-off points etc. The main particulars for detailing are given for most of the worked exercises in the book. The bar schedule can be prepared on completion of the detail drawings. The form of the schedule and shape code for the bars are to conform to

BS 4466: 1981: *Specification of Bending Dimensions and Scheduling of Bars for the Reinforcement for Concrete*

It is essential that the student carry out practical work in detailing and preparation of bar schedules prior to and/or during his design course in reinforced concrete.

Computer detailing suites are now in general use in design offices. Students should be given practice in using the software during their degree course.

2

Materials, structural failures and durability

2.1 REINFORCED CONCRETE STRUCTURES

Reinforced concrete is a composite material of steel bars embedded in a hardened concrete matrix; concrete, assisted by the steel, carries the compressive forces, while steel resists tensile forces. Concrete is itself a composite material. The dry mix consists of cement and coarse and fine aggregate. Water is added and this reacts with the cement which hardens and binds the aggregates into the concrete matrix; the concrete matrix sticks or bonds onto the reinforcing bars.

The properties of the constituents used in making concrete, mix design and the principal properties of concrete are discussed briefly. A knowledge of the properties and an understanding of the behaviour of concrete is an important factor in the design process. The types and characteristics of reinforcing steels are noted.

Deterioration of and failures in concrete structures are now of widespread concern. This is reflected in the increased prominence given in the new concrete code BS 8110 to the durability of concrete structures. The types of failure that occur in concrete structures are listed and described. Finally the provisions regarding the durability of concrete structures noted in the code and the requirements for cover to prevent corrosion of the reinforcement and provide fire resistance are set out.

2.2 CONCRETE MATERIALS

2.2.1 Cement

Ordinary Portland cement is the commonest type in use. The raw materials from which it is made are lime, silica, alumina and iron oxide. These constituents are crushed and blended in the correct proportions and burnt in a rotary kiln. The clinker is cooled, mixed with gypsum and ground to a fine powder to give cement. The main chemical compounds in cement are calcium silicates and aluminates.

When water is added to cement and the constituents are mixed to form cement paste, chemical reactions occur and the mix becomes stiffer with time and sets. The addition of gypsum mentioned above retards and controls the setting time. This ensures that the concrete does not set too quickly before it can be placed or too slowly so as to hold up construction. Two stages in the setting process are defined in

> BS 12: 1978: *Specification for Ordinary and Rapid Hardening Portland Cement*

These are an initial setting time which must be a minimum of 45 min and a final set which must take place in 10 h.

Cement must be sound, i.e. it must not contain excessive quantities of certain substances such as lime, magnesia, calcium sulphate etc. that may expand on hydrating or react with other substances in the aggregate and cause the concrete to disintegrate. Tests are specified in BS 12 for soundness and strength of cement mortar cubes.

Many other types of cement are available some of which are

1. rapid hardening Portland cement – the clinker is more finely ground than for ordinary Portland cement
2. low heat Portland cement – this has a low rate of heat development during hydration of the cement
3. sulphate-resisting Portland cement

2.2.2 Aggregates

The bulk of concrete is aggregate in the form of sand and gravel which is bound together by cement. Aggregate is classed into the following two sizes:

1. coarse aggregate – gravel or crushed rock 5 mm or larger in size
2. fine aggregate – sand less than 5 mm in size

Natural aggregates are classified according to the rock type, e.g. basalt, granite, flint.

Aggregates should be chemically inert, clean, hard and durable. Organic impurities can affect the hydration of cement and the bond between the cement and the aggregate. Some aggregates containing silica may react with alkali in the cement causing the concrete to disintegrate. This is the alkali–silica reaction. The presence of chlorides in aggregates, e.g. salt in marine sands, will cause corrosion of the steel reinforcement. Excessive amounts of sulphate will also cause concrete to disintegrate.

To obtain a dense strong concrete with minimum use of cement, the cement paste should fill the voids in the fine aggregate while the fine aggregate and cement paste fills the voids in the coarse aggregate. Coarse and fine aggregates are graded by sieve analysis in which the percentage by weight passing a set of standard sieve sizes is determined. Grading limits for each size of coarse and fine aggregate are set out in

BS 882: 1983: *Specification for Aggregates from Natural Sources for Concrete*

The grading affects the workability; a lower water-to-cement ratio can be used if the grading of the aggregate is good and therefore strength is also increased. Good grading saves cement content. It helps prevent segregation during placing and ensures a good finish.

2.2.3 Concrete mix design

Concrete mix design consists in selecting and proportioning the constituents to give the required strength, workability and durability. Mixes are defined in

BS 5328: 1981: *Methods of Specifying Concrete including Ready-mixed Concrete*

The types are

1. designed mix, where strength testing forms an essential part of the requirements for compliance
2. prescribed mix, in which proportions of the constituents to give the required strength and workability are specified; strength testing is not required

The water-to-cement ratio is the single most important factor affecting concrete strength. For full hydration cement absorbs 0.23 of its weight of water in normal conditions. This amount of water gives a very dry mix and extra water is added to give the required workability. The actual water-to-cement ratio used generally ranges from 0.45 to 0.6. The aggregate-to-cement ratio also affects workability through its influence on the water-to-cement ratio, as noted above. The mix is designed for the 'target mean strength' which is the characteristic strength required for design plus the 'current margin'. The value of the current margin is either specified or determined statistically and depends on the degree of quality control exercised in the production process.

Several methods of mix design are used. The main factors involved are discussed briefly for mix design according to *Design of Normal Concrete Mixes* [3].

1. Curves giving compressive strength versus water-to-cement ratio for various types of cement and ages of hardening are available. The water-to-cement ratio is selected to give the required strength.
2. Minimum cement contents and maximum free water-to-cement ratios are specified in BS 8110: Part 1, Table 3.4, to meet durability requirements. The maximum cement content is also limited to avoid cracking due mainly to shrinkage.

3. Tables giving proportions of aggregate to cement to give a specified workability are available. For example, Table 1 in BS 5328 gives the mass of dry aggregate to be used with 100 kg of cement for a given grade and workability. Table 2 in the same code gives the mass of fine aggregate to total aggregate. In *Design of Normal Concrete Mixes* [3] the selection of the aggregate-to-cement ratio depends on the grading curve for the aggregate.

Trial mixes based on the above considerations are made and used to determine the final proportions for designed mixes.

2.2.4 Admixtures

Admixtures are discussed in BS 8110: Part 1, section 6.1.5. The code defines admixtures as substances added to concrete mixes in very small amounts to improve certain properties by their chemical and/or physical effects.

Admixtures covered by British Standards are as follows:

1. hardening or setting accelerators or retarders
2. water-reducing admixtures which give an increase in workability with a lower water-to-cement ratio
3. air-entraining admixtures, which increase resistance to damage from freezing and thawing
4. superplasticizers, which are used for concrete in complicated sections

The code warns that the effect of new admixtures should be verified by trial mixes. It states that admixtures should not impair durability and the chloride ion content in particular should be strictly limited (section 2.7.5(a)).

2.3 CONCRETE PROPERTIES

The main properties of concrete are discussed below.

2.3.1 Compressive strength

The compressive strength is the most important property of concrete. The characteristic strength that is the concrete grade is measured by the 28 day cube strength. Standard cubes of 150 or 100 mm for aggregate not exceeding 25 mm in size are crushed to determine the strength. The test procedure is given in

BS 1881: 1983: *Methods of Testing Concrete*
Part 108: Method for Making Test Cubes from Fresh Concrete
Part 111: Method of Normal Curing of Test Specimens

Part 116: Method for Determination of Compressive Strength of Concrete Cubes.

2.3.2 Tensile strength

The tensile strength of concrete is about a tenth of the compressive strength. It is determined by loading a concrete cylinder across a diameter as shown in Fig. 2.1(a). The test procedure is given in BS 1881.

2.3.3 Modulus of elasticity

The short-term stress–strain curve for concrete in compression is shown in Fig. 2.1(b). The slope of the initial straight portion is the initial tangent

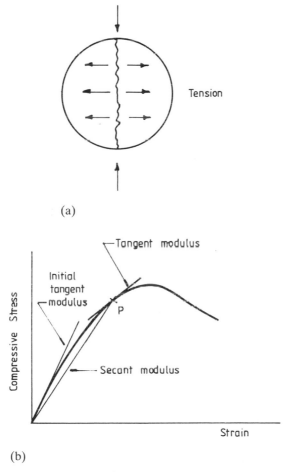

(a)

(b)

Fig. 2.1 (a) Cylinder tensile test; (b) stress–strain curve for concrete.

modulus. At any point P the slope of the curve is the tangent modulus and the slope of the line joining P to the origin is the secant modulus. The value of the secant modulus depends on the stress and rate of application of the load. BS 1881 specifies both values to standardize determination of the secant or static modulus of elasticity.

The dynamic modulus is determined by subjecting a beam specimen to longitudinal vibration. The value obtained is unaffected by creep and is approximately equal to the initial tangent modulus shown in Fig. 2.1(b). The secant modulus can be calculated from the dynamic modulus.

BS 8110: Part 1 gives an expression for the short-term modulus of elasticity in Fig. 2.1, the short-term design stress–strain curve for concrete. A further expression for the static modulus of elasticity is given in Part 2, section 7.2. (The idealized short-term stress–strain curve is shown in Fig. 3.1.)

2.3.4 Creep

Creep in concrete is the gradual increase in strain with time in a member subjected to prolonged stress. The creep strain is much larger than the elastic strain on loading. If the specimen is unloaded there is an immediate elastic recovery and a slower recovery in the strain due to creep. Both amounts of recovery are much less than the original strains under load.

The main factors affecting creep strain are the concrete mix and strength, the type of aggregate, curing, ambient relative humidity and the magnitude and duration of sustained loading.

BS 8110: Part 2 section 7.3, adopts the recommendations of the Comité Euro-International du Béton which specifies that the creep strain ε_{cc} is calculated from the creep coefficient ϕ by the equation

$$\varepsilon_{cc} = \frac{\text{stress}}{E_t} \times \phi$$

where E_t is the modulus of elasticity of the concrete at the age of loading. The creep coefficient ϕ depends on the effective section thickness, the age of loading and the relative ambient humidity. Values of ϕ can be taken from BS 8110: Part 2, Fig. 7.1. Suitable values of relative humidity to use for indoor and outdoor exposure in the UK are indicated in the figure. The creep coefficient is used in deflection calculations (section 6.1.3).

2.3.5 Shrinkage

Shrinkage or drying shrinkage is the contraction that occurs in concrete when it dries and hardens. Drying shrinkage is irreversible but alternate wetting and drying causes expansion and contraction of concrete.

The aggregate type and content are the most important factors influencing shrinkage. The larger the size of the aggregate is, the lower is the shrinkage and the higher is the aggregate content; the lower the workability and water-to-cement ratio are, the lower is the shrinkage. Aggregates that change volume on wetting and drying, such as sandstone or basalt, give concrete with a large shrinkage strain, while non-shrinking aggregates such as granite or gravel give lower shrinkages. A decrease in the ambient relative humidity also increases shrinkage.

Drying shrinkage is discussed in BS 8110: Part 2, section 7.4. The drying shrinkage strain for normal-weight concrete may be obtained from Fig. 7.2 in the code for various values of effective section thickness and ambient relative humidity. Suitable values of humidity to use for indoor and outdoor exposure in the UK are indicated in the figure. Values of shrinkage strain are used in deflection calculations in section 6.1.3.

2.4 TESTS ON WET CONCRETE

2.4.1 Workability

The workability of a concrete mix gives a measure of the ease with which fresh concrete can be placed and compacted. The concrete should flow readily into the form and go around and cover the reinforcement, the mix should retain its consistency and the aggregates should not segregate. A mix with high workability is needed where sections are thin and/or reinforcement is complicated and congested.

The main factor affecting workability is the water content of the mix. Admixtures will increase workability but may reduce strength. The size of aggregate, its grading and shape, the ratio of coarse to fine aggregate and the aggregate-to-cement ratio also affect workability to some degree.

2.4.2 Measurement of workability

(a) Slump test

The fresh concrete is tamped into a standard cone which is lifted off after filling and the slump is measured. The slump is 25–50 mm for low workability, 50–100 mm for medium workability and 100–175 mm for high workability. Normal reinforced concrete requires fresh concrete of medium workability. The slump test is the usual workability test specified.

(b) Compacting factor test

The degree of compaction achieved by a standard amount of work is measured. The apparatus consists of two conical hoppers placed over one another and over a cylinder. The upper hopper is filled with fresh concrete which is then dropped into the second hopper and into the cylinder which is struck off flush. The compacting factor is the ratio of the weight of concrete in the cylinder to the weight of an equal volume of fully compacted concrete. The compacting factor for concrete of medium workability is about 0.9.

(c) Other tests

Other tests are specified for stiff mixes and superplasticized mixes. Reference should be made to specialist books on concrete.

2.5 TESTS ON HARDENED CONCRETE

2.5.1 Normal tests

The main destructive tests on hardened concrete are as follows.

(a) Cube test

Refer to section 2.3.1 above.

(b) Tensile splitting test

Refer to section 2.3.2 above.

(c) Flexure test

A plain concrete specimen is tested to failure in bending. The theoretical maximum tensile stress at the bottom face at failure is calculated. This is termed the modulus of rupture. It is about 1.5 times the tensile stress determined by the splitting test.

(d) Test cores

Cylindrical cores are cut from the finished structure with a rotary cutting tool. The core is soaked, capped and tested in compression to give a measure of the concrete strength in the actual structure. The ratio of core height to diameter and the location where the core is taken affect the strength. The strength is lowest at the top surface and increases with depth through the element. A ratio of core height-to-diameter of 2 gives a standard cylinder test.

2.5.2 Non-destructive tests

The main non-destructive tests for strength on hardened concrete are as follows.

(a) Rebound hardness test

The Schmidt hammer is used in the rebound hardness test in which a metal hammer held against the concrete is struck by another spring-driven metal mass and rebounds. The amount of rebound is recorded on a scale and this gives an indication of the concrete strength. The larger the rebound number is, the higher is the concrete strength.

(b) Ultrasonic pulse velocity test

In the ultrasonic pulse velocity test the velocity of ultrasonic pulses that pass through a concrete section from a transmitter to a receiver is measured. The pulse velocity is correlated against strength. The higher the velocity is, the stronger is the concrete.

(c) Other non-destructive tests

Equipment has been developed to measure

1. crack widths and depths
2. water permeability and the surface dampness of concrete
3. depth of cover and the location of reinforcing bars
4. the electrochemical potential of reinforcing bars and hence the presence of corrosion

2.5.3 Chemical tests

A complete range of chemical tests is available to measure

1. depth of carbonation
2. the cement content of the original mix
3. the content of salts such as chlorides and sulphates that may react and cause the concrete to disintegrate or cause corrosion of the reinforcement

The reader should consult specialist literature.

2.6 REINFORCEMENT

Reinforcing bars are produced in two grades: hot rolled mild steel bars have a yield strength f_y of $250 \, N/mm^2$; hot rolled or cold worked high yield steel bars have a yield strength f_y of $460 \, N/mm^2$. Steel fabric is made from cold drawn steel wires welded to form a mesh; it has a yield strength f_y of $460 \, N/mm^2$.

The stress–strain curves for reinforcing bars are shown in Fig. 2.2. The hot rolled bars have a definite yield point. A defined proof stress is recorded for the cold worked bars. The value of Young's modulus E is $200 \, kN/mm^2$. The idealized design stress–strain curve for all reinforcing bars is shown in BS 8110: Part 1 (see Fig. 3.1(b)). The behaviour in tension and compression is taken to be the same.

Mild steel bars are produced as smooth round bars. High yield bars are produced as deformed bars in two types defined in the code to increase bond stress:

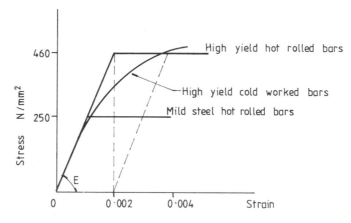

Fig. 2.2 Stress–strain curves for reinforcing bars.

Type 1   Square twisted cold worked bars
Type 2   Hot rolled bars with transverse ribs

Type 1 bars are obsolete.

2.7 FAILURES IN CONCRETE STRUCTURES

2.7.1 Factors affecting failure

Failures in concrete structures can be due to any of the following factors:

1. incorrect selection of materials
2. errors in design calculations and detailing
3. poor construction methods and inadequate quality control and supervision
4. chemical attack
5. external physical and/or mechanical factors including alterations made to the structure

The above items are discussed in more detail below.

2.7.2 Incorrect selection of materials

The concrete mix required should be selected to meet the environmental or soil conditions where the concrete is to be placed. The minimum grade that should be used for reinforced concrete is grade 30. Higher grades should be used for some foundations and for structures near the sea or in an aggressive industrial environment. If sulphates are present in the soil or groundwater, sulphate-resisting Portland cement should be used. Where freezing and thawing occurs air entrainment should be adopted. Further aspects of materials selection are discussed below.

2.7.3 Errors in design calculations and detailing

An independent check should be made of all design calculations to ensure that the section sizes, slab thickness etc. and reinforcement sizes and spacing specified are adequate to carry the worst combination of design loads. The check should include overall stability, robustness and serviceability and foundation design.

Incorrect detailing is one of the commonest causes of failure and cracking in concrete structures. First the overall arrangement of the structure should be correct, efficient and robust. Movement joints should be provided where required to reduce or eliminate cracking. The overall detail should be such as to shed water.

Internal or element detailing must comply with the code requirements. The provisions specify the cover to reinforcement, minimum thicknesses for fire resistance, maximum and minimum steel areas, bar spacing limits and reinforcement to control cracking, lap lengths, anchorage of bars etc.

2.7.4 Poor construction methods

The main items that come under the heading of poor construction methods resulting from bad workmanship and inadequate quality control and supervision are as follows.

(a) Incorrect placement of steel

Incorrect placement of steel can result in insufficient cover, leading to corrosion of the reinforcement. If the bars are placed grossly out of position or in the wrong position, collapse can occur when the element is fully loaded.

(b) Inadequate cover to reinforcement

Inadequate cover to reinforcement permits ingress of moisture, gases and other substances and leads to corrosion of the reinforcement and cracking and spalling of the concrete.

(c) Incorrectly made construction joints

The main faults in construction joints are lack of preparation and poor compaction. The old concrete should be washed and a layer of rich concrete laid before pouring is continued. Poor joints allow ingress of moisture and staining of the concrete face.

(d) Grout leakage

Grout leakage occurs where formwork joints do not fit together properly. The result is a porous area of concrete that has little or no cement and fine aggregate. All formwork joints should be properly sealed.

(e) Poor compaction

If concrete is not properly compacted by ramming or vibration the result is a portion of porous honeycomb concrete. This part must be hacked out and recast. Complete compaction is essential to give a dense, impermeable concrete.

(f) Segregation

Segregation occurs when the mix ingredients become separated. It is the result of

1. dropping the mix through too great a height in placing (chutes or pipes should be used in such cases)
2. using a harsh mix with high coarse aggregate content
3. large aggregate sinking due to over-vibration or use of too much plasticizer

Segregation results in uneven concrete texture, or porous concrete in some cases.

(g) Poor curing

A poor curing procedure can result in loss of water through evaporation. This can cause a reduction in strength if there is not sufficient water for complete hydration of the cement. Loss of water can cause shrinkage cracking. During curing the concrete should be kept damp and covered.

(h) Too high a water content

Excess water increases workability but decreases the strength and increases the porosity and permeability of the hardened concrete, which can lead to corrosion of the reinforcement. The correct water-to-cement ratio for the mix should be strictly enforced.

2.7.5 Chemical attack

The main causes of chemical attack on concrete and reinforcement can be classified under the following headings.

(a) Chlorides

High concentrations of chloride ions cause corrosion of reinforcement and the products of corrosion can disrupt the concrete. Chlorides can be introduced into the concrete either during or after construction as follows.

(i) Before construction Chlorides can be admitted in admixtures containing calcium chloride, through using mixing water contaminated with salt water or improperly washed marine aggregates.

(ii) After construction Chlorides in salt or sea water, in airborne sea spray and from de-icing salts can attack permeable concrete causing corrosion of reinforcement.

Chlorides are discussed in BS 8110: Part 1, clause 6.2.5.2. The clause limits the total chloride content expressed as a percentage of chloride ion by mass of cement to 0.4% for concrete containing embedded metal. It was common practice in the past to add calcium chloride to concrete to increase the rate of hardening. The code now recommends that calcium chloride and chloride-based admixtures should not be added to reinforced concrete containing embedded metals.

(b) Sulphates

Sulphates are present in most cements and some aggregates. Sulphates may also be present in soils, groundwater and sea water, industrial wastes and acid rain. The products of sulphate attack on concrete occupy a larger space than the original material and this causes the concrete to disintegrate and permits corrosion of steel to begin. BS 8110: Part 1, clause 6.2.5.3, states that the total water-soluble sulphate content of the concrete mix expressed as SO_3 should not exceed 4% by mass of cement in the mix. Sulphate-resisting Portland cement should be used where sulphates are present in the soil, water or atmosphere and come into contact with the concrete. Supersulphated cement, made from blastfurnace slag, can also be used although it is not widely available. This cement can resist the highest concentrations of sulphates.

(c) Carbonation

Carbonation is the process by which carbon dioxide from the atmosphere slowly transforms calcium hydroxide into calcium carbonate in concrete. The concrete itself is not harmed and increases in strength, but the reinforcement can be seriously affected by corrosion as a result of this process.

   Normally the high pH value of the concrete prevents corrosion of the reinforcing bars by keeping them in a highly alkaline environment due to the release of calcium hydroxide by the cement during its hydration. Carbonated concrete has a pH value of 8.3 while the passivation of steel starts at a pH value of 9.5. The depth of carbonation in good dense concrete is about 3 mm at an early stage and may increase to 6–10 mm after 30–40 years. Poor concrete may have a depth of carbonation of 50 mm after say 6–8 years. The rate of carbonation depends on time, cover, concrete density, cement content, water to cement ratio and the presence of cracks.

(d) Alkali – silica reaction

A chemical reaction can take place between alkali in cement and certain forms of silica in aggregate. The reaction produces a gel which absorbs water and expands in volume, resulting in cracking and disintegration of the concrete.

BS 8110: Part 2, clause 6.2.5.4, states that the reaction only occurs when the following are present together:

1. a high moisture level in the concrete
2. cement with a high alkali content or some other source of alkali
3. aggregate containing an alkali-reactive constituent

The code recommends that the following precautions be taken if uncertainty exists:

1. Reduce the saturation of the concrete;
2. Use low alkali Portland cement and limit the alkali content of the mix to a low level;
3. Use replacement cementitious materials such as blastfurnace slag or pulverized fuel ash. Most normal aggregates behave satisfactorily.

(e) Acids

Portland cement is not acid resistant and acid attack may remove part of the set cement. Acids are formed by the dissolution in water of carbon dioxide or sulphur dioxide from the atmosphere. Acids can also come from industrial wastes. Good dense concrete with adequate cover is required and sulphate-resistant cements should be used if necessary.

2.7.6 External physical and/or mechanical factors

The main external factors causing concrete structures to fail are as follows.

(a) Restraint against movement

Restraint against movement causes cracking. Movement in concrete is due to elastic deformation and creep under constant load, shrinkage on drying and setting, temperature changes, changes in moisture content and the settlement of foundations. The design should include sufficient movement joints to prevent serious cracking. Cracking may only detract from the appearance rather than be of structural significance but cracks permit ingress of moisture and lead to corrosion of the steel. Various proprietary substances are available to seal cracks.

Movement joints are discussed in BS 8110: Part 2, section 8. The code states that the joints should be clearly indicated for both members and structure as a whole. The joints are to permit relative movement to occur without impairing structural integrity. Types of movement joints defined in the code are as follows.

1. The **contraction joint** may be a complete or partial joint with reinforcement running through the joint. There is no initial gap and only contraction of the concrete is permitted.
2. The **expansion joint** is made with a complete discontinuity and gap between the concrete portions. Both expansion and contraction can occur. The joint must be filled with sealer.
3. There is complete discontinuity in a **sliding joint** and the design is such as to permit movement in the plane of the joint.
4. The **hinged joint** is specially designed to permit relative rotation of members meeting at the joint. The Freyssinet hinge has no reinforcement passing through the joint.
5. The **settlement joint** permits adjacent members to settle or displace vertically as a result of foundation or other movements relative to each other. Entire parts of the building can be separated to permit relative settlement, in which case the joint must run through the full height of the structure.

Diagrams of some movement joints are shown in Fig. 2.3. The location of movement joints is a matter of experience. Joints should be placed where cracks would probably develop, e.g. at abrupt changes of section, corners or locations where restraints from adjoining elements occur.

(b) Abrasion

Abrasion can be due to mechanical wear, wave action etc. Abrasion reduces cover to reinforcement. Dense concrete with hard wearing aggregate and extra cover allowing for wear are required.

(c) Wetting and drying

Wetting and drying leaches lime out of concrete and makes it more porous, which increases the risk of corrosion to the reinforcement. Wetting and drying also causes movement of the concrete which can cause cracking if restraint exists. Detail should be such as to shed water and the concrete may also be protected by impermeable membranes.

(d) Freezing and thawing

Concrete nearly always contains water which expands on freezing. The freezing–thawing cycle causes loss of strength, spalling and disintegration of the concrete. Resistance to damage is improved by using an air-entraining agent.

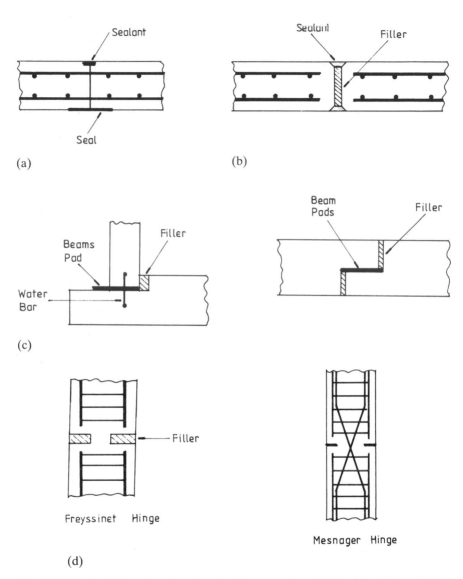

Fig. 2.3 (a) Partial contraction joint; (b) expansion joint; (c) sliding joints; (d) hinge joints.

(e) Overloading

Extreme overloading will cause cracking and eventual collapse. Factors of safety in the original design allow for possible overloads but vigilance is always required to ensure that the structure is never grossly overloaded. A change in function of the building or room can lead to overloading, e.g.

if a class room is changed to a library the imposed load can be greatly increased.

(f) Structural alterations

If major structural alterations are made to a building the members affected and the overall integrity of the building should be rechecked. Common alterations are the removal of walls or columns to give a large clear space or provide additional doors or openings. Steel beams are inserted to carry loads from above. In such cases the bearing of the new beam on the original structure should be checked and if walls are removed the overall stability may be affected.

(g) Settlement

Differential settlement of foundations can cause cracking and failure in extreme cases. The foundation design must be adequate to carry the building loads without excessive settlement. Where a building with a large plan area is located on ground where subsidence may occur, the building should be constructed in sections on independent rafts with complete settlement joints between adjacent parts.

Many other factors can cause settlement and ground movement problems. Some problems are shrinkage of clays from ground dewatering or drying out in droughts, tree roots causing disruption, ground movement from nearby excavations, etc.

(h) Fire resistance

Concrete is a porous substance bound together by water-containing crystals. The binding material can decompose if heated to too high a temperature, with consequent loss of strength. The loss of moisture causes shrinkage and the temperature rise causes the aggregates to expand, leading to cracking and spalling of the concrete. High temperature also causes reinforcement to lose strength. At 550 °C the yield stress of steel has dropped to about its normal working stress and failure occurs under service loads.

Concrete, however, is a material with very good fire resistance and protects the reinforcing steel. Fire resistance is a function of member thickness and cover. The code requirements regarding fire protection are set out below in section 2.9.2.

2.8 DURABILITY OF CONCRETE STRUCTURES

2.8.1 Code references to durability

Frequent references are made to durability in BS 8110: Part 1, section 2. The clauses referred to are as follows.

(a) Clause 2.1.3

The quality of material must be adequate for safety, serviceability and durability.

(b) Clause 2.2.1

The structure must not deteriorate unduly under the action of the environment over its design life, i.e. it must be durable.

(c) Clause 2.2.4 Durability

This states that 'integration of all aspects of design, materials and construction is required to produce a durable structure'. The main provisions in the clause are the following:

1. Environmental conditions should be defined at the design stage;
2. The design should be such as to ensure that surfaces are freely draining;
3. Cover must be adequate;
4. Concrete must be of relevant quality. Constituents that may cause durability problems should be avoided;
5. Particular types of concrete should be specified to meet special requirements;
6. Good workmanship, particularly in curing, is essential.

Detailed requirements for the durability of concrete structures are set out in section 6.2 of the code. Some extracts from this section are given below.

1. A durable concrete element protects the embedded metal from corrosion and performs satisfactorily in the working environment over its lifetime;
2. The main factor influencing durability is permeability to the ingress of water, oxygen, carbon dioxide and other deleterious substances;
3. Low permeability is achieved by having an adequate cement content and a low water-to-cement ratio and by ensuring good compaction and curing;
4. Factors influencing durability are
    (a) the shape and bulk of the concrete
    (b) the cover to the embedded steel
    (c) the environment
    (d) the type of cement
    (e) the type of aggregate
    (f) the cement content and the water-to-cement ratio
    (g) workmanship

The section gives guidance on design for durability taking account of exposure conditions, mix proportions and constituents and the placing, compacting and curing of the concrete.

2.9 CONCRETE COVER

2.9.1 Nominal cover against corrosion

The code states in section 3.3.1 that the actual cover should never be less than the nominal cover minus 5 mm. The nominal cover should protect steel against corrosion and fire. The cover to a main bar should not be less than the bar size or in the case of pairs or bundles the size of a single bar of the same cross-sectional area.

The cover depends on the exposure conditions given in Table 3.2 in the code. These are as follows.

Mild	concrete is protected against weather
Moderate	concrete is sheltered from severe rain
	concrete under water
	concrete in non-aggressive soil
Severe	concrete exposed to severe rain or to alternate wetting and drying
Very severe	concrete exposed to sea water, de-icing salts or corrosive fumes
Extreme	concrete exposed to abrasive action

Limiting values for nominal cover are given in Table 3.4 of the code and Table 2.1. Note that the water-to-cement ratio and minimum cement content are specified. Good workmanship is required to ensure that the steel is properly placed and that the specified cover is obtained.

2.9.2 Cover as fire protection

Nominal cover to all reinforcement to meet a given fire resistance period for various elements in a building is given in Table 2.2 and Table 3.5 in

Table 2.1 Nominal cover to all reinforcement including links to meet durability requirements

Conditions of exposure	Nominal cover (mm)		
Mild	25	20	20
Moderate		35	30
Severe			40
Very severe			50
Extreme	–	–	–
Maximum free water-to-cement ratio	0.65	0.6	0.55
Minimum cement content (kg/m^3)	275	300	325
Lowest grade of concrete	C30	C35	C40

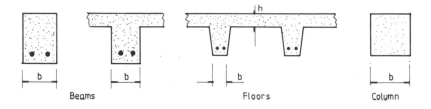

Beams   Floors   Column

Fire resistance (hour)	Min. beam b	Rib b	Min. floor thickness h	Column width full exposed b	Min. wall thickness 0·4% < p < 1%
1·0	200	125	95	200	120
1·5	200	125	110	250	140
2·0	200	125	125	300	160

Dimensions mm
p = area of steel relative to concrete

Fig. 2.4 Minimum dimensions for fire resistance.

the code. Minimum dimensions of members from Fig. 3.2 in the code are shown in Fig. 2.4. Reference should be made to the complete table and figure in the code.

Table 2.2 Nominal cover to all reinforcement including links to meet specified periods of fire resistance

Fire Resistance Hour	Nominal Cover – mm						Column
	Beams		Floors		Ribs		
	SS	C	SS	C	SS	C	
1.0	20	20	20	20	20	20	20
1.5	20	20	25	20	35	20	20
2.0	40	30	35	25	45	35	25

SS simply supported
C continuous

3

Limit state design and structural analysis

3.1 STRUCTURAL DESIGN AND LIMIT STATES

3.1.1 Aims and methods of design

Clause 2.1.1 of the code states that the aim of design is the achievement of an acceptable probability that the structure will perform satisfactorily during its life. It must carry the loads safely, not deform excessively and have adequate durability and resistance to effects of misuse and fire. The clause recognizes that no structure can be made completely safe and that it is only possible to reduce the probability of failure to an acceptably low level.

Clause 2.1.2 states that the method recommended in the code is limit state design where account is taken of theory, experiment and experience. It adds that calculations alone are not sufficient to produce a safe, serviceable and durable structure. Correct selection of materials, quality control and supervision of construction are equally important.

3.1.2 Criteria for a safe design – limit states

The criterion for a safe design is that the structure should not become unfit for use, i.e. that it should not reach a limit state during its design life. This is achieved, in particular, by designing the structure to ensure that it does not reach

1. **the ultimate limit state** – the whole structure or its elements should not collapse, overturn or buckle when subjected to the design loads
2. **serviceability limit states** – the structure should not become unfit for use due to excessive deflection, cracking or vibration

The structure must also be durable, i.e. it must not deteriorate or be damaged excessively by the action of substances coming into contact with it. The code places particular emphasis on durability (see the discussion in Chapter 2).

For reinforced concrete structures the normal practice is to design for the ultimate limit state, check for serviceability and take all necessary precautions to ensure durability.

3.1.3 Ultimate limit state

(a) Strength

The structure must be designed to carry the most severe combination of loads to which it is subjected. The sections of the elements must be capable of resisting the axial loads, shears and moments derived from the analysis.

The design is made for ultimate loads and design strengths of materials with partial safety factors applied to loads and material strengths. This permits uncertainties in the estimation of loads and in the performance of materials to be assessed separately. The section strength is determined using plastic analysis based on the short-term design stress–strain curves for concrete and reinforcing steel.

(b) Stability

Clause 2.2.2.1 of the code states that the layout should be such as to give a stable and robust structure. It stresses that the engineer responsible for overall stability should ensure compatibility of design and details of parts and components.

Overall stability of a structure is provided by shear walls, lift shafts, staircases and rigid frame action or a combination of these means. The structure should be such as to transmit all loads, dead, imposed and wind, safely to the foundations.

(c) Robustness

Clause 2.2.2.2 of the code states that the planning and design should be such that damage to a small area or failure of a single element should not cause collapse of a major part of a structure. This means that the design should be resistant to progressive collapse. The clause specifies that this type of failure can be avoided by taking the following precautions.

1. The structure should be capable of resisting notional horizontal loads applied at roof level and at each floor level. The loads are 1.5% of the characteristic dead weight of the structure between mid-height of the storey below and either mid-height of the storey above or the roof surface. The wind load is not to be taken as less than the notional horizontal load.
2. All structures are to be provided with effective horizontal ties. These are

   (a) peripheral ties
   (b) internal ties
   (c) horizontal ties to column and walls

The arrangement and design of ties is discussed in section 13.3.

3. For buildings of five or more storeys, key elements are to be identified, failure of which would cause more than a limited amount of damage. These key elements must be designed for a specially heavy ultimate load of $34 \, kN/m^2$ applied in any direction on the area supported by the member. Provisions regarding the application of this load are set out in BS 8110: Part 2, section 2.6.
4. For buildings of five or more storeys it must be possible to remove any vertical loadbearing element other than a key element without causing more than a limited amount of damage. This requirement is generally achieved by the inclusion of vertical ties in addition to the other provisions noted above.

3.1.4 Serviceability limit states

The serviceability limit states are discussed in BS 8110: Part 1, section 2.2.3. The code states that account is to be taken of temperature, creep, shrinkage, sway and settlement.

The main serviceability limit states and code provisions are as follows.

(a) Deflection

The deformation of the structure should not adversely affect its efficiency or appearance. Deflections may be calculated, but in normal cases span-to-effective depth ratios can be used to check compliance with requirements.

(b) Cracking

Cracking should be kept within reasonable limits by correct detailing. Crack widths can be calculated, but in normal cases cracking can be controlled by adhering to detailing rules with regard to bar spacing in zones where the concrete is in tension.

In analysing a section for the serviceability limit states the behaviour is assessed assuming a linear elastic relationship for steel and concrete stresses. Allowance is made for the stiffening effect of concrete in the tension zone and for creep and shrinkage.

3.2 CHARACTERISTIC AND DESIGN LOADS

The characteristic or service loads are the actual loads that the structure is designed to carry. These are normally thought of as the maximum loads which will not be exceeded during the life of the structure. In statistical terms the characteristic loads have a 95% probability of not being exceeded.

The characteristic loads used in design and defined in BS 8110: Part 1, clause 2.4.1, are as follows:

1. **The characteristic dead load** G_k is the self-weight of the structure and the weight of finishes, ceilings, services and partitions;
2. **The characteristic imposed load** Q_k is caused by people, furniture, equipment etc. on floors and snow on roofs. Imposed loads for various types of buildings are given in BS 6399: Part 1;
3. **The wind load** W_k depends on the location, shape and dimensions of the buildings. Wind loads are estimated using CP 3: Chapter V: Part 2.

The code states that nominal earth loads are to be obtained in accordance with normal practice. Reference should be made to

BS 8004: 1986: *Code of Practice for Foundations*

and textbooks on geotechnics.

The structure must also be able to resist the notional horizontal loads defined in clause 3.1.4.2 of the code. The definition for these loads was given in section 3.1.3(c) above.

design load = characteristic load × partial safety factor for loads
    $= F_k \gamma_f$

The partial safety factor γ_f takes account of

1. possible increases in load
2. inaccurate assessment of the effects of loads

Table 3.1 Load combinations

Load combination	Load type					
	Dead load		Imposed load		Earth and water pressure	Wind
	Adverse	Beneficial	Adverse	Beneficial		
1. Dead and imposed (and earth and water pressure)	1.4	1.0	1.6	0	1.4	–
2. Dead and wind (and earth and water pressure)	1.4	1.0	–	–	1.4	1.4
3. Dead, wind and imposed (and earth and water pressure)	1.2	1.2	1.2	1.2	1.2	1.2

3. unforeseen stress distributions in members
4. the importance of the limit state being considered

The code states that the values given for γ_f ensure that serviceability requirements can generally be met by simple rules. The values of γ_f to give design loads and the load combinations for the ultimate limit state are given in BS 8110: Part 1, Table 2.1 Partial safety factors are given for earth and water pressures. These factors are given in Table 3.1. The code states that the adverse partial safety factor is applied to a load producing more critical design conditions, e.g. the dead load plus a wind load acting in the same direction. The beneficial factor is applied to a load producing a less critical design condition, e.g. in the case of dead load plus wind uplift where the loads are in opposite directions.

In considering the effects of exceptional loads caused by misuse or accident γ_f can be taken as 1.05. The loads to be applied in this case are the dead load, one-third of the wind load and one-third of the imposed load except for storage and industrial buildings when the full imposed load is used.

3.3 MATERIALS – PROPERTIES AND DESIGN STRENGTHS

The characteristic strengths or grades of materials are as follows:

Concrete, f_{cu} is the 28 day cube strength in newtons per square millimetre
Reinforcement, f_y is the yield or proof stress in newtons per square millimetre

The minimum grades for reinforced concrete are given in Table 3.4 in the code. These are grades 30, 35, 40, 45 and 50 in newtons per square millimetre. The specified characteristic strengths of reinforcement given in Table 3.1 in the code are

Hot rolled mild steel $f_y = 250\,\text{N/mm}^2$
High yield steel,
    hot rolled or cold worked $f_y = 460\,\text{N/mm}^2$

Clause 3.1.7.4 of the code states that a lower value may be used to reduce deflection or control cracking.

The resistance of sections to applied stresses is based on the design strength which is defined as

$$\frac{\text{characteristic strength}}{\text{partial factor of safety for materials}} = \frac{f_k}{\gamma_m}$$

Table 3.2 Values of γ_m for the ultimate limit state

Reinforcement	1.15
Concrete in flexure or axial load	1.5
Shear strength without shear reinforcement	1.25
Bond strength	1.4
Others, e.g. bearing strength	$\geqslant 1.5$

The factor γ_m takes account of

1. uncertainties in the strength of materials in the structure
2. uncertainties in the accuracy of the method used to predict the behaviour of members
3. variations in member sizes and building dimensions

Values of γ_m from Table 2.2 in the code used for design for the ultimate limit state are given in Table 3.2. For exceptional loads γ_m is to be taken as 1.3 for concrete and 1.0 for steel.

The short-term design stress–strain curves for normal-weight concrete and reinforcement from Figs 2.1 and 2.2 in the code are shown in Figs 3.1(a) and 3.1(b) respectively. The curve for concrete in compression is an idealization of the actual compression behaviour which begins with a parabolic portion where the slope of the tangent at the origin equals the short-term value of Young's modulus. At strain ε_0, which depends on the concrete grade, the stress remains constant with increasing load until a strain of 0.0035 is reached when the concrete fails. Expressions for E_c and ε_0 are given in the figure. The maximum design stress in the concrete is given as $0.67 f_{cu}/\gamma_m$. The coefficient 0.67 takes account of the relation between the cube strength and the bending strength in a flexural member. It is not a partial factor of safety.

The stress–strain curve for reinforcement shown in Fig. 3.1(b) is bilinear with one yield point. The behaviour and strength of reinforcement are taken to be the same in tension and compression. In previous codes a reduced strength was specified for compression reinforcement.

3.4 STRUCTURAL ANALYSIS

3.4.1 General provisions

The general provisions relating to analysis of the structure set out in BS 8110: Part 1, section 2.5, are discussed briefly. The methods of frame analysis outlined in section 3.2 are set out. Examples using these methods are given later in the book.

The object of analysis of the structure is to determine the axial forces, shears and moments throughout the structure. The code states that it is

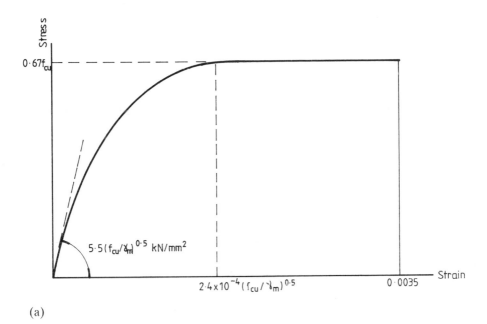

(a)

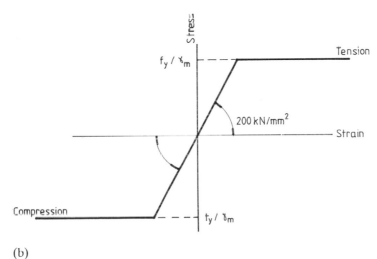

(b)

Fig. 3.1 Short-term design stress–strain curve for (a) normal-weight concrete and (b) reinforcement.

generally satisfactory to obtain maximum design values from moment and shear envelopes constructed from linear elastic analysis and to allow for moment redistribution if desired and for buckling effects in frames with slender columns. The code also states that plastic methods such as yield line analysis may also be used.

The member stiffness to be used in linear elastic analysis can be based on

1. the gross concrete section ignoring reinforcement
2. the gross concrete section including reinforcement on the basis of the modular ratio
3. the transformed section (the compression area of concrete and the transformed area of reinforcement in tension and compression based on the modular ratio are used)

The code states that a modular ratio of 15 may be assumed. It adds that a consistent approach should be used for all elements of the structure.

3.4.2 Methods of frame analysis

The complete structure may be analysed using rigorous manual elastic analysis or a matrix computer program adopting the basis set out above. It is normal practice to model beam elements using only the rectangular section of T-beam elements in the frame analysis (Fig. 1.3). The T-beam section is taken into account in the element design.

Approximate methods of analysis are set out in the code as an alter-

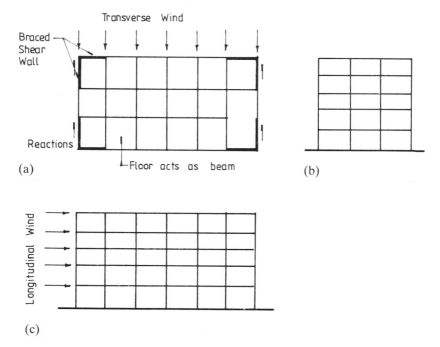

Fig. 3.2 Braced multistorey building: (a) plan; (b) rigid transverse frame; (c) side elevation.

native to a rigorous analysis of the whole frame. These methods are discussed below.

3.4.3 Monolithic braced frame

Shear walls, lifts and staircases provide stability and resistance to horizontal loads. A braced frame is shown in Fig. 3.2. The approximate methods of analysis and the critical load arrangements are as follows.

(a) Division into subframes

The structural frame is divided into subframes consisting of the beams at one level and the columns above and below that level with ends taken as fixed. The moments and shears are derived from an elastic analysis (Figs 3.3(a) and 3.3(b)).

(b) Critical load arrangement

The critical arrangements of vertical load are

1. all spans loaded with the maximum design ultimate load of $1.4G_k + 1.6Q_k$
2. alternate spans loaded with the maximum design ultimate load of $1.4G_k + 1.6Q_k$ and all other spans loaded with the minimum design ultimate load of $1.0G_k$

where G_k is the total dead load on the span and Q_k is the imposed load on the span. The load arrangements are shown in Fig. 3.3(b).

(c) Simplification for individual beams and columns

The simplified subframe consists of the beam to be designed, the columns at the ends of the beam and the beams on either side if any. The column and beam ends remote from the beam are taken as fixed and the stiffness of the beams on either side should be taken as one-half of their actual value (Fig. 3.3(c)).

The moments for design of an individual column may be found from the same subframe analysis provided that its central beam is the longer of the two beams framing into the column.

(d) Continuous-beam simplification

The beam at the floor considered may be taken as a continuous beam over supports providing no restraint to rotation. This gives a more conservative design than the procedures set out above. Pattern loading as set out in (b) is applied to determine the critical moments and shear for design (Fig. 3.3(d)).

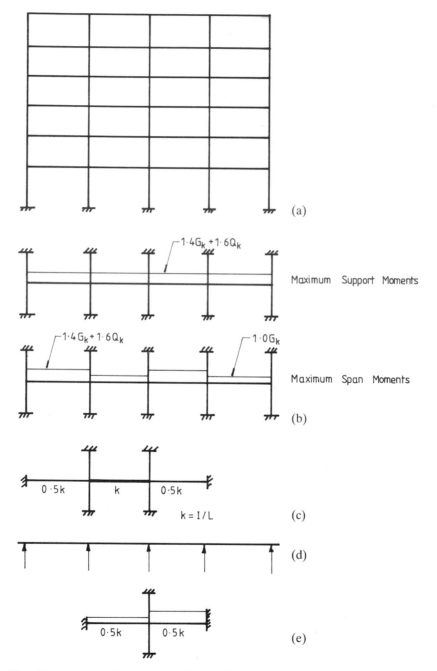

Fig. 3.3 Analysis for vertical load: (a) frame elevation; (b) subframes; (c) simplified subframe; (d) continuous-beam simplification; (e) column moments analysis for (d).

(e) Asymmetrically loaded column

The asymmetrically loaded column method is to be used where the beam has been analysed on the basis of the continuous-beam simplification set out in (d) above. The column moments can be calculated on the assumption that the column and beam ends remote from the junction under consideration are fixed and that the beams have one-half their actual stiffnesses. The imposed load is to be arranged to cause maximum moment in the column (Fig. 3.3(e)).

3.4.4 Rigid frames providing lateral stability

Where the rigid frame provides lateral stability it must be analysed for horizontal and vertical loads. Clause 3.1.4.2 of the code states that all buildings must be capable of resisting a notional horizontal load equal to 1.5% of the characteristic dead weight of the structure applied at roof level and at each floor.

The complete structure may be analysed for vertical and horizontal loads using a computer analysis program. As an alternative the code gives the following method for sway frames of three or more approximately equal bays (the design is to be based on the more severe of the conditions):

1. elastic analysis for vertical loads only with maximum design load $1.4G_k + 1.6Q_k$ (refer to sections 3.4.3(a) and 3.4.3(b) above)
2. or the sum of the moments obtained from

    (a) elastic analysis of subframes as defined in section 3.4.3(a) with all beams loaded with $1.2G_k + 1.2Q_k$ (horizontal loads are ignored)
    (b) elastic analysis of the complete frame assuming points of contra-flexure at the centres of all beams and columns for wind load $1.2W_k$ only

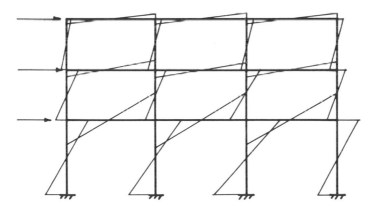

Fig. 3.4 Horizontal loads.

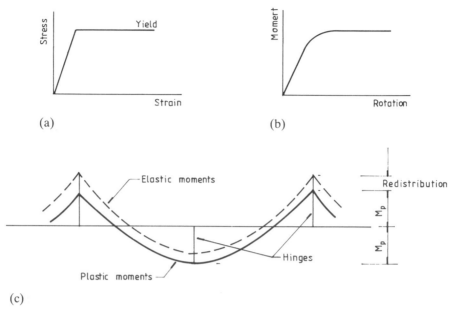

Fig. 3.5 (a) Stress–strain curve; (b) moment–rotation curve; (c) elastic and plastic moment distributions.

The column bases may be considered as pinned if this assumption gives more realistic analyses. A sway frame subjected to horizontal load is shown in Fig. 3.4.

The methods of analysis for horizontal load, the portal and cantilever methods, are discussed in Chapters 13 and 14. Examples in the use of these methods are also given.

3.4.5 Redistribution of moments

Plastic analysis based on the stress–strain curve shown in Fig. 3.5(a), which gives the moment–rotation curve in Fig. 3.5(b), has been developed for steel structures. At ultimate loads plastic hinges form at the points of maximum moment and the moment distribution changes from elastic to plastic. This redistribution is shown in Fig. 3.5(c) for the internal span of a continuous beam. For the steel beam at collapse the hogging and sagging moments are the same. The amount of redistribution is the reduction in the peak elastic moment over the support, as shown in the figure.

An under-reinforced concrete section has a similar moment–rotation curve to that shown for steel in Fig. 3.5(b). Thus it is possible to carry out a full plastic analysis on the same basis as for steel structures. However, serious cracking could occur at the hinges in reinforced concrete frames and because of this the code adopts a method that gives the designer control over the amount of redistribution and hence of rotation that is permitted to take place. In clause 3.2.2 the code allows a reduction of up to 30% of the peak elastic moment to be made whilst keeping internal and external forces in equilibrium. The conditions under which this can carried out are set out later in sections 4.7 and 7.2.5.

4

Section design
for moment

4.1 TYPES OF BEAM SECTION

The three common types of reinforced concrete beam section are

1. rectangular section with tension steel only (this generally occurs as a beam section in a slab)
2. rectangular section with tension and compression steel
3. flanged sections of either T or L shape with tension steel and with or without compression steel

Beam sections are shown in Fig. 4.1. It will be established later that all beams of structural importance must have steel top and bottom to carry links to resist shear.

4.2 REINFORCEMENT AND BAR SPACING

Before beginning section design, reinforcement data and code requirements with regard to minimum and maximum areas of bars in beams and bar spacings are set out. This is to enable practical sections to be designed. Requirements for cover were discussed in section 2.9.

4.2.1 Reinforcement data

In accordance with BS 8110: Part 1, clause 3.12.4.1, bars may be placed singly or in pairs or in bundles of three or four bars in contact. For design purposes the pair or bundle is treated as a single bar of equivalent area. Bars are available with diameters of 6, 8, 10, 12, 16, 20, 25, 32 and 40 mm and in two grades with characteristic strengths f_y:

Hot rolled mild steel $f_y = 250 \, \text{N/mm}^2$
High yield steel $f_y = 460 \, \text{N/mm}^2$

For convenience in design, areas of groups of bars are given in Table 4.1.

In the *Standard Method of Detailing Reinforced Concrete* [4] bar types are specified by letters:

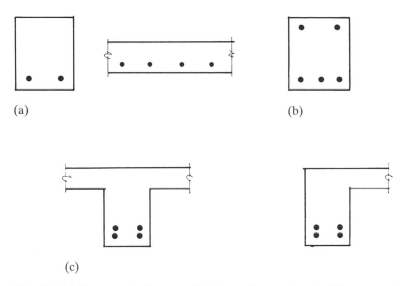

(a)   (b)

(c)

Fig. 4.1 (a) Rectangular beam and slab, tension steel only; (b) rectangular beam, tension and compression steel; (c) flanged beams.

R   mild steel bars
T   high yield bars

Bars are designated on drawings as, for example, 4T25, i.e. four 25 mm diameter bars of grade 460. This system will be used to specify bars in figures.

4.2.2 Minimum and maximum areas of reinforcement in beams

The minimum areas of reinforcement in a beam section to control cracking as well as resist tension or compression due to bending in different types of beam section are given in BS 8110: Part 1, clause 3.12.5.3 and Table 3.2.7. Some commonly used values are shown in Fig. 4.2. Other values will be discussed in appropriate parts of the book, e.g. in section 6.2 where crack control is discussed.

The maximum area of both tension and compression reinforcement in beams is specified in BS 8110: Part 1, clause 3.12.6.1. Neither should exceed 4% of the gross cross-sectional area of the concrete.

4.2.3 Minimum spacing of bars

The minimum spacing of bars is given in BS 8110: Part 1, clause 3.12.11.1. This clause states the following:

Table 4.1 Areas of groups of bars

Diamenter (mm)	Number of bars in groups							
	1	2	3	4	5	6	7	8
6	28	56	84	113	141	169	197	226
8	50	100	150	201	251	301	351	402
10	78	157	235	314	392	471	549	628
12	113	226	339	452	565	678	791	904
16	201	402	603	804	1005	1206	1407	1608
20	314	628	942	1256	1570	1884	2199	2513
25	490	981	1472	1963	2454	2945	3436	3927
32	804	1608	2412	3216	4021	4825	5629	6433

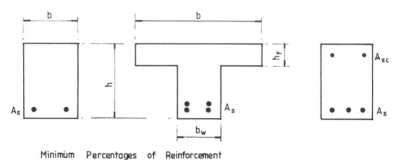

Minimum Percentages of Reinforcement

	Percentage	Minimum f_y 250 N/mm^2	Percentage f_y 460 N/mm^2
Tension Reinforcement			
Rectangular beam	100 A_s / A_c	0·24	0·13
Flanged beam – web in tension			
b_w / b < 0·4	100 A_s / b_wh	0·32	0·18
b_w / b ⩾ 0·4	100 A_s / b_wh	0·24	0·13
Compression Reinforcement			
Rectangular beam	100 A_{sc} / A_c	0·2	0·2
Flanged beam – flange in compression	100 A_{sc} / $b_w h_f$	0·2	0·2

A_c = total area of concrete
A_s = minimum area of reinforcement
A_{sc} = area of steel in compression
b, b_w, h, h_f – beam dimensions

Fig. 4.2

1. The horizontal distance between bars should not be less than h_{agg} + 5 mm;
2. Where there are two or more rows

   (a) the gap between corresponding bars in each row should be vertically in line and
   (b) the vertical distance between bars should not be less than $2h_{agg}/3$

   where h_{agg} is the maximum size of coarse aggregate. The clause also states that if the bar size exceeds h_{agg} + 5 mm the spacing should not be less than the bar size.

Note that pairs or bundles are treated as a single bar of equivalent area.

The above spacings ensure that the concrete can be properly compacted around the reinforcement. Spacing of top bars of beams should also permit the insertion of a vibrator. The information is summarized in Fig. 4.3.

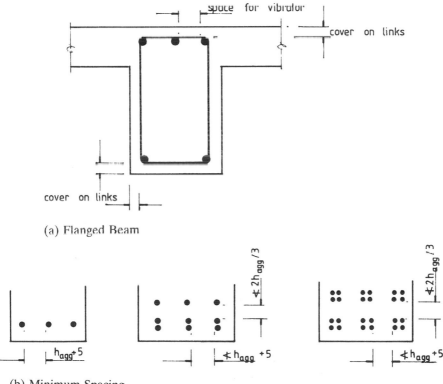

(a) Flanged Beam

(b) Minimum Spacing

Fig. 4.3 (a) Flanged beam; (b) minimum spacing.

4.3 BEHAVIOUR OF BEAMS IN BENDING

Concrete is strong in compression but weak and unreliable in tension. Reinforcement is required to resist tension due to moment. A beam with loads at the third points where the central third is subjected to moment only is shown in Fig. 4.4(a). Tension cracks at collapse due to moment are shown.

The load–deflection curve is given in Fig. 4.4(b). Initially the concrete in the uncracked section will resist tension, but it soon cracks. The behaviour of the cracked section is elastic at low loads and changes to plastic at higher loads.

The effective section resisting moment at a cracked position is shown in Fig. 4.4(c). The concrete at the top of the section resists compression and the steel resists tension. At low loads the concrete stress in compression and the steel stress in tension are in the elastic range. At collapse the stresses are at ultimate values.

Originally the design of concrete sections was to elastic theory with linearly varying compressive stress in the concrete, as shown in Fig. 4.4(c). Design now is based on the strength of the section calculated from the stress distribution at collapse which has been determined from tests.

Beam section design for the ultimate limit state is given first. The elastic section analysis is then set out because this is required in calculations for checking the serviceability limit states.

4.4 SINGLY REINFORCED RECTANGULAR BEAMS

4.4.1 Assumptions and stress–strain diagrams

The ultimate moment of resistance of a section is based on the assumptions set out in BS 8110: Part 1, clause 3.4.4.1. These are as follows:

1. The strains in the concrete and reinforcement are derived assuming that plane sections remain plane;
2. The stresses in the concrete in compression are derived using either

   (a) the design stress–strain curve given in Fig. 4.5(a) with $\gamma_m = 1.5$ (Fig. 4.6(c)) or
   (b) the simplified stress block shown in Fig. 4.6(d) where the depth of the stress block is 0.9 of the depth to the neutral axis

   Note that in both cases the strain in the concrete at failure is 0.0035;
3. The tensile strength of the concrete is ignored;
4. The stresses in the reinforcement are derived from the stress–strain curve shown in Fig. 4.5(b) where $\gamma_m = 1.15$;
5. Where the section is designed to resist flexure only, the lever arm should not be assumed to be greater than 0.95 of the effective depth.

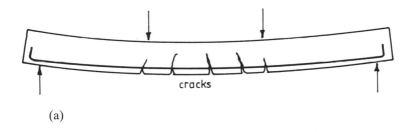

(a)

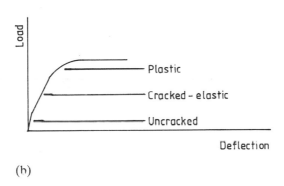

(b)

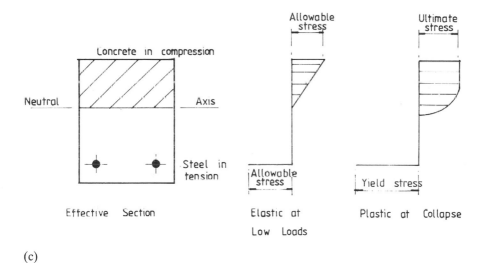

(c)

Fig. 4.4 (a) Flexural cracks at collapse; (b) load–deflection curve; (c) effective section and stress distributions.

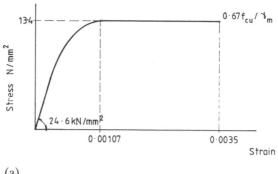

(a)

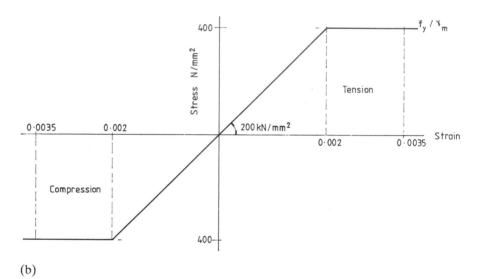

(b)

Fig. 4.5 (a) Concrete, $f_{cu} = 30$ N/mm², (b) high yield steel, $f_y = 460$ N/mm².

On the basis of these assumptions the strain and stress diagrams for the two alternative stress distributions for the concrete in compression are as shown in Fig. 4.6, where the following symbols are used:

h overall depth of the section
d effective depth
     depth to the centreline of the steel
b breadth of the section
x depth to the neutral axis
A_s area of tension reinforcement
ε_c strain in the concrete (0.0035)
ε_s strain in the steel

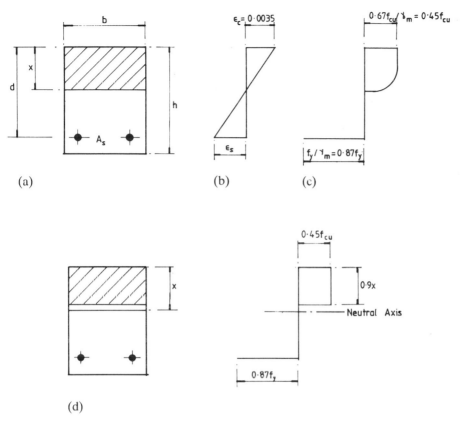

Fig. 4.6 (a) Section; (b) strain; (c) rectangular parabolic stress diagram; (d) simplified stress diagram.

The alternative stress distributions for the compressive stress in the concrete, the rectangular parabolic stress diagram and the simplified stress block, are shown in Figs 4.6(c) and 4.6(d) respectively. The maximum strain in the concrete is 0.0035 and the strain ε_s in the steel depends on the depth of the neutral axis.

Stress–strain curves for grade 30 concrete and for high yield steel are shown in Figs 4.5(a) and 4.5(b) respectively.

4.4.2 Moment of resistance – simplified stress block

The method of calculating the moment of resistance of a concrete section is given first using the simplified stress block. The calculation is made for the case where the depth x to the neutral axis is $d/2$. This is the maximum depth to the neutral axis permitted in clause 3.4.4.4 of the code (section 4.4.4

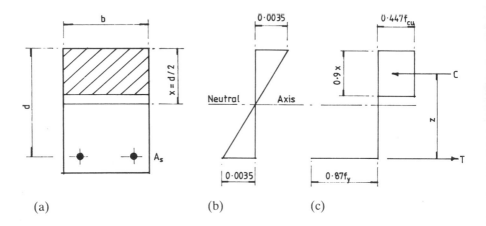

Fig. 4.7 (a) Section; (b) strain diagram; (c) stress diagram.

below). The beam section and the strain and stress diagrams are shown in Fig. 4.7. The concrete stress is

$$\frac{0.67f_{cu}}{\gamma_m} = \frac{0.67f_{cu}}{1.5} = 0.447f_{cu}$$

which is generally rounded off to $0.45f_{cu}$. The strain is 0.0035 as shown in Fig. 4.5(a). Referring to Fig. 4.5(b) for high yield bars, the steel stress is

$$f_y/1.15 = 0.87f_y$$

From the stress diagram in Fig. 4.7(c) the internal forces are

C = force in the concrete in compression
    = $0.447f_{cu} \times 0.9b \times 0.5d$
    = $0.201f_{cu}bd$

T = force in the steel in tension
    = $0.87f_yA_s$

For the internal forces to be in equilibrium $C = T$.

z = lever arm
    = $d - 0.5 \times 0.9 \times 0.5d$
    = $0.775d$

M_{RC} = moment of resistance with respect to the concrete
    = Cz
    = $0.201f_{cu}bd \times 0.775d$

$$= 0.156 f_{cu} b d^2$$
$$= K b d^2$$

where the constant $K = 0.156 f_{cu}$.

M_{RS} = moment of resistance with respect to the steel
$$= Tz$$
$$= 0.87 f_y A_s \times 0.775 d$$
$$= 0.674 f_y A_s d$$

The area of steel $A_s = M_{RS}/0.674 f_y d$. Because the internal forces are equal the moments of resistance with respect to the steel and concrete are equal, i.e. $M_{RS} = M_{RC}$. Then the percentage p of steel in the section is defined as

$$p = \frac{100 A_s}{bd}$$
$$= \frac{100 \times 0.156 f_{cu} b d^2}{0.674 \times f_y d \times bd}$$
$$= 23.15 f_{cu}/f_y$$

For grade 30 concrete and high yield reinforcement where $f_y = 460\,\text{N/mm}^2$, the design constants are

$$K = 0.156 \times 30 = 4.68$$
$$p = 23.1 \times 30/460 = 1.51$$

4.4.3 Moment of resistance – rectangular parabolic stress block

The moment of resistance of the section using the rectangular parabolic stress block is calculated for the same case as above where the depth to the neutral axis is equal to $d/2$. The beam section, strain diagram and stress diagram with internal forces are shown in Fig. 4.8. The stresses are

$$0.67 f_{cu}/\gamma_m = 0.67 f_{cu}/1.5 = 0.45 f_{cu}$$

for concrete. For steel, refer to Fig. 4.5(b). For a strain of 0.0035

$$\text{stress} = f_y/\gamma_m = f_y/1.15 = 0.87 f_y$$

Expressions for the value and location of the compressive force C in the concrete are given in BS 8110: Part 3, Appendix A. For a depth to the neutral axis of x these are

$$C = k_1 b x$$

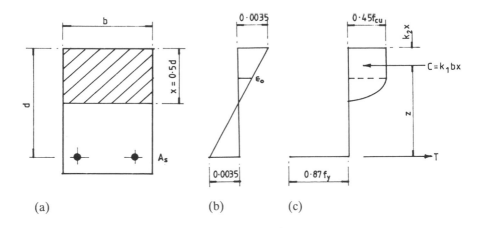

Fig. 4.8 (a) Section; (b) strain diagram; (c) stress diagram.

where

$$k_1 = \frac{0.45 f_{cu}}{0.0035}\left(0.0035 - \frac{\varepsilon_0}{3}\right)$$

The force C acts at $k_2 x$ from the edge of the beam in compression where

$$k_2 = \frac{(2 - \varepsilon_0/0.0035)^2 + 2}{4(3 - \varepsilon_0/0.0035)}$$

ε_0 is the strain at the end of the parabolic part of the stress diagram, i.e.

$$\varepsilon_0 = 2.4 \times 10^{-4}(f_{cu}/\gamma_m)^{1/2}$$

The expressions for k_1 and k_2 are readily derived from the dimensions of the stress block using the geometrical properties of the parabola and rectangle.

The design constants can be calculated for the case where $x = d/2$. Calculations are given for grade 30 concrete and high yield reinforcement where $f_y = 460\,\text{N/mm}^2$:

$$\varepsilon_0 = 2.4 \times 10^{-4}(30/1.5)^{1/2} = 0.00107$$

$$C = \frac{0.45 \times 30bx}{0.0035}\left(0.0035 - \frac{0.00107}{3}\right)$$

$$= 12.12bx$$

$$k_2 x = \frac{(2 - 0.00107/0.0035)^2 + 2}{4(3 - 0.00107/0.0035)}x = 0.452x$$

For $x = 0.5d$,

$$C = 6.06bd$$
$$z = d - 0.226d = 0.774d$$
$$M_{RC} = Cz = 6.06bd \times 0.774d = 4.69bd^2$$
$$T = 0.87f_yA_s = C = 6.06bd$$
$$p = \frac{100A_s}{bd} = \frac{100 \times 6.06bd}{0.87 \times 460 \times bd} = 1.51$$

The values for $K = 4.69$ and $p = 1.51$ are the same as those obtained above using the simplified stress block.

In design, the problem is to determine the beam section and steel area to resist a given moment M. If the breadth b is assumed, then

$$\text{effective depth } d = (M/Kb)^{1/2}$$
$$\text{steel area } A_s = pbd/100$$

☐ Example 4.1 Singly reinforced rectangular beam – balanced design

A simply supported rectangular beam of 8 m span carries a uniformly distributed dead load which includes an allowance for self-weight of 7 kN/m and an imposed load of 5 kN/m. The breadth of the beam is 250 mm. Find the depth and steel area when the depth to the neutral axis is one-half the effective depth. Use grade 30 concrete and high yield steel reinforcement.

The design load is calculated using the values of partial factors of safety given in BS 8110: Part 1, Table 2.1 (see Table 3.1).

$$\text{design load} = (1.4 \times 7) + (1.6 \times 5) = 17.8\,\text{kN/m}$$
$$\text{ultimate moment} = 17.8 \times 8^2/8 = 142.4\,\text{kN m}$$

Use the design constants $K = 4.69$ and $p = 1.51$ derived above to obtain

$$d = \left(\frac{142.4 \times 10^6}{250 \times 4.69}\right)^{1/2} = 348.5\,\text{mm}$$
$$A_s = 1.51 \times 250 \times 348.5/100 = 1315.6\,\text{mm}^2$$

Refer to Table 4.1. Provide three 25 mm diameter bars to give a steel area of 1472 mm^2.

From BS 8110: Part 1, Table 3.4, the cover on the links is 25 mm for mild exposure. Referring to Table 3.5 of the code, this cover also gives a fire resistance of 1.5 h. If the link diameter is 10 mm the overall depth of the beam on rounding the effective depth up to 350 mm and placing the bars in vertical pairs is

$$h = 350 + 12.5 + 10 + 25 = 397.5\,\text{mm}$$

The beam section is shown in Fig. 4.9.   ■

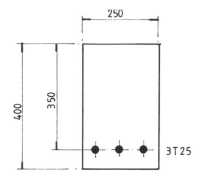

Fig. 4.9

4.4.4 Types of failure and beam section classification

Referring to the stress–strain diagrams for concrete and grade 460 steel in Fig. 4.5 three failure situations can occur depending on the amount of reinforcement provided. These are as follows.

1. The concrete fails and the steel yields simultaneously at ultimate load (Fig. 4.10(a)). The concrete strain is 0.0035 and the steel strain 0.002. From the strain diagram

$$\frac{x}{0.0035} = \frac{d - x}{0.002}$$

   or

$$x = 0.64d$$

   The amount of steel to give this situation can be determined by equating the internal forces C and T in the concrete. This is the theoretical balanced design case.
2. If less steel is provided than in case 1 the steel has reached yield and continues yielding before the concrete fails at ultimate load (Fig. 4.10(b)). This is termed an under-reinforced beam. Cracks appear, giving a warning of failure.
3. If more steel than in case 1 is provided, the concrete fails suddenly without warning before the steel reaches yield. This is termed an over-reinforced beam (Fig. 4.10(c)).

For a singly reinforced beam the code in clause 3.4.4.4 limits the depth to the neutral axis to $0.5d$ to ensure that the design is for the under-reinforced case where failure is gradual, as noted above.

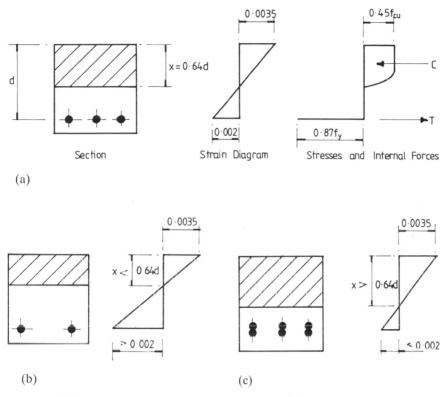

Fig. 4.10 (a) Theoretical balanced design case; (b) under-reinforced beam; (c) over-reinforced beam.

4.4.5 General design of under-reinforced beams

In the design procedures in sections 4.4.2 and 4.4.3 above the effective depth and amount of reinforcement were determined to make the depth to the neutral axis one-half the effective depth. This gives the minimum permitted depth for the beam. In most design cases the beam dimensions are fixed with the effective depth greater than in the case above and the depth to the neutral axis less than one-half the effective depth. The problem is to determine the steel area required. This is the general case of design for under-reinforced beams. It is normal design.

The analytical solution given in BS 8110: Part 1, clause 3.4.4.4, is derived first. This is based on the simplified stress block for the case where moment redistribution does not exceed 10%. Moment redistribution is discussed in section 4.7. A second method of solution where a design chart is constructed using the rectangular parabolic stress block is then given.

4.4.6 Under-reinforced beam – analytical solution

A beam section subjected to a moment M is shown in Fig. 4.11(a) and the internal stresses and forces are shown in Fig. 4.11(b).

$$
\begin{aligned}
C &= \text{force in the concrete in compression} \\
&= 0.447 f_{cu} b \times 0.9x \\
&= 0.402 f_{cu} bx \\
z &= \text{lever arm} \\
&= d - 0.45x \\
M &= \text{applied moment} \\
&= Cz \\
&= 0.402 f_{cu} bx(d - 0.45x) \\
&= 0.402 f_{cu} bdx - 0.181 f_{cu} bx^2 \\
& x^2 - 2.221dx + 5.488M/f_{cu}b = 0
\end{aligned}
$$

Solve the quadratic equation to give

$$
\begin{aligned}
x &= 1.11d + (1.233d^2 - 5.488M/f_{cu}b)^{1/2} \\
z &= d - 0.45x \\
&= d[0.5 + (0.25 - K/0.9)^{1/2}]
\end{aligned}
$$

where $K = M/f_{cu}bd^2$. This is the expression given in the code. The lever arm z is not to exceed $0.95d$.

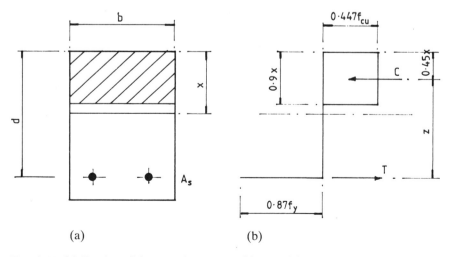

Fig. 4.11 (a) Section; (b) stress diagram and internal forces.

$$A_s = \text{area of tension steel}$$
$$= M/(0.87f_y z)$$

□ Example 4.2 Singly reinforced rectangular beam – under-reinforced design

A simply supported rectangular beam of 8 m span carries a design load of 17.8 kN/m. The beam dimensions are breadth 250 mm and effective depth 400 mm. Find the steel area required. The concrete is grade 30 and the steel grade 460.

$$\text{ultimate moment } M = 17.8 \times 8^2/8 = 142.4 \,\text{kN m}$$

$$\text{factor } K = \frac{M}{f_{cu}bd^2} = \frac{142.4 \times 10^6}{30 \times 250 \times 400^2} = 0.119$$

$$\text{lever arm } z = 400[0.5 + (0.25 - 0.119/0.9)^{1/2}]$$
$$= 337.3 \,\text{mm} \not> 0.95d = 380 \,\text{mm}$$

$$\text{steel area } A_s = \frac{142.4 \times 10^6}{0.87 \times 460 \times 337.3} = 1079.7 \,\text{mm}^2$$

Provide four 20 mm diameter bars; $A_s = 1260 \,\text{mm}^2$. The beam section is shown in Fig. 4.12.

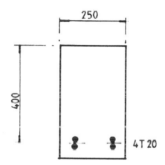

Fig. 4.12

4.4.7 Design chart

The design chart is constructed for grade 30 concrete and high yield reinforcement. Values of $K = M/bd^2$ and $p = 100A_s/bd$ are calculated for values of x less than $0.5d$. The rectangular parabolic stress block is used for the concrete stress. The value of the steel stress is $0.87f_y$ in all cases. Refer to the calculations for K and p in section 4.4.3 above. Values of K and p for various depths to the neutral axis are given in Table 4.2.

Note that the code stipulates in clause 3.4.4.4 that the lever arm z must not be more than $0.95d$ in order to give a reasonable concrete area in

Table 4.2 Values for constructing design charts

x	$C = 12.12bx$	$k_2x = 0.452x$	$z = d - k_2x$	$Cz = Kbd^2$	$p = \dfrac{100C}{0.87f_ybd}$	$\dfrac{Cz}{bd^2f_{cu}}$
$0.5d$	$6.06bd$	$0.226d$	$0.774d$	$4.69bd^2$	1.51	0.156
$0.4d$	$4.85bd$	$0.181d$	$0.819d$	$3.97bd^2$	1.21	0.132
$0.3d$	$3.64bd$	$0.136d$	$0.864d$	$3.14bd^2$	0.91	0.105
$0.2d$	$2.42bd$	$0.09d$	$0.91d$	$2.2bd^2$	0.60	0.073
$0.11d$	$1.34bd$	$0.05d$	$0.95d$	$1.27bd^2$	0.33	0.042

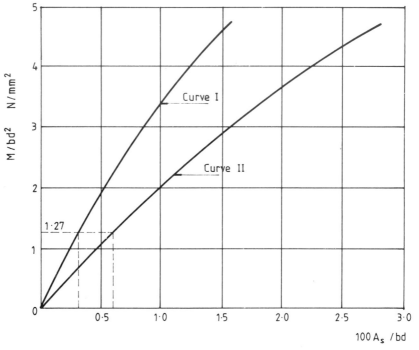

Curve I　f_{cu} = 30 N/mm²
　　　　　f_y = 460 N/mm²

Curve II　f_{cu} = 30 N/mm²
　　　　　f_y = 250 N/mm²

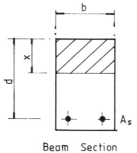

Beam Section

Fig. 4.13

compression. At this value $M/bd^2 = 1.27$. The design chart is shown in Fig. 4.13. A series of design charts is given in BS 8110: Part 3.

For design, the moment M and the beam dimensions b and d are given, M/bd^2 is calculated and $100A_s/bd$ is read from the chart. The steel area A_s can then be determined. Note that when M/bd^2 is less than 1.27 the steel area should be calculated using $z = 0.95d$.

The lever arm ratio z/d can also be plotted against Cz/bd^2f_{cu}, i.e. M/bd^2f_{cu}. Values of Cz/bd^2f_{cu} are shown in Table 4.2. Note that the ratio z/d varies between 0.774 when $x/d = 0.5$ and 0.95, the maximum value permitted in the code. The chart is shown in Fig. 4.14. The advantage of this chart is that it can be used for all grades of concrete. This can be checked by calculating z/d and Cz/bd^2f_{cu} for other grades of concrete. The curves for the different concrete grades coincide closely.

For design, M/bd^2f_{cu} is calculated and the ratio z/d is read off the chart in Fig. 4.14. The steel area is given by

$$A_s = M/0.87f_y z$$

□ Example 4.3 Singly reinforced rectangular beam – design chart

A simply supported rectangular beam of 8 m span carries a design load of 17.8 kN/m. The beam dimensions are breadth 250 mm and effective depth 400 mm. Find the steel area required. The concrete is grade 30 and steel grade 460.

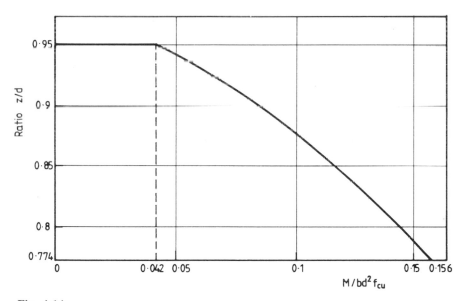

Fig. 4.14

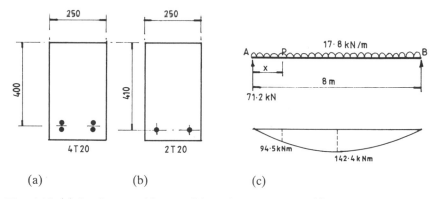

Fig. 4.15 (a) Section at mid-span; (b) section at support; (c) loading and bending moment diagram.

$$\text{ultimate moment } M = 142.4\,\text{kN m} \qquad (\text{section } 4.4.5)$$

$$\text{factor } \frac{M}{bd^2} = \frac{142.4 \times 10^6}{250 \times 400^2} = 3.56$$

From Fig. 4.13, $100A_s/bd = 1.05$. Therefore

$$A_s = 1.05 \times 250 \times 400/100 = 1050\,\text{mm}^2$$

Provide four 20 mm diameter bars; $A_s = 1256\,\text{mm}^2$.
    Recheck the design using the chart in Fig. 4.14:

$$\frac{M}{bd^2 f_{cu}} = \frac{142.4 \times 10^6}{250 \times 400^2 \times 30} = 0.119$$

$$z = 0.838d$$

$$A_s = \frac{142.4 \times 10^6}{0.87 \times 460 \times 0.838 \times 400} = 1061.5\,\text{mm}^2$$

The beam section is shown in Fig. 4.15(a). ∎

□ Example 4.4 Singly reinforced rectangular beam – reinforcement cut-off

Determine the position along the beam where theoretically two 20 mm diameter bars may be cut off in the above example.

The section at cut-off has two 20 mm diameter bars: $A_s = 628\,\text{mm}^2$. The effective depth here is 410 mm (Fig. 4.15(b)).

$$\frac{100A_s}{bd} = \frac{100 \times 628}{250 \times 410} = 0.61$$

$$M/bd^2 = 2.25 \qquad \text{from Fig. 4.13}$$

$$M = 2.25 \times 250 \times 410^2/10^6 = 94.5 \, \text{kN m}$$

Determine the position of P along the beam such that $M_P = 94.5 \, \text{kN m}$ (Fig. 4.15(c)), i.e.

$$94.5 = 71.2x - 0.5 \times 17.8x^2$$

The solutions of this equation are

$$x = 1.67 \, \text{m and} \, x = 6.33 \, \text{m from end A} \qquad \blacksquare$$

□ Example 4.5 Singly reinforced one-way slab section

A slab section 1 m wide and 130 mm deep with an effective depth of 100 mm is subjected to a moment of 10.5 kN m. Find the area of reinforcement required. The concrete is grade 30 and the reinforcement grade 460.

$$\frac{M}{bd^2} = \frac{10.5 \times 10^6}{1000 \times 100^2} = 1.05 < 1.27$$

The steel area is calculated using

$$z = 0.95d$$

$$A_s = \frac{10.5 \times 10^6}{0.87 \times 460 \times 0.95 \times 100} = 276.2 \, \text{mm}^2$$

Using 8 mm bars with an area of 50 mm^2 per bar, the spacing is

$$\frac{1000 \times 50}{276.2} = 181 \, \text{mm}$$

Provide 8 mm diameter bars at 180 mm centres. The reinforcement for the slab is shown in Fig. 4.16.

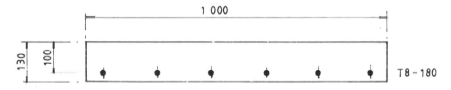

Fig. 4.16

$\blacksquare$

4.5 DOUBLY REINFORCED BEAMS

4.5.1 Design formulae using the simplified stress block

If the concrete alone cannot resist the applied moment in compression, reinforcement can be provided in the compression zone. The design formulae for a doubly reinforced beam are derived using the simplified stress block. These are based on

1. a depth $x = d/2$ to the neutral axis and a depth $0.9x$ of the stress block
2. a stress of $0.45f_{cu}$ in the concrete in compression
3. a stress of $0.87f_y$ in the reinforcement in tension and compression

The beam section, strain diagram and stress diagram with internal forces are shown in Fig. 4.17, where the symbols are as follows:

$$
\begin{aligned}
&d' &&\text{inset of the compression steel} \\
&A_s' &&\text{area of compression steel} \\
&\varepsilon_{sc} &&\text{strain in the compression steel} \\
&C_c &&\text{force in the concrete in compression} \\
&C_s &&\text{force in the compression steel}
\end{aligned}
$$

Referring to Fig. 4.5(b), the stress in the compression steel will reach $0.87f_y$ if the strain ε_{sc} is not less than 0.002, i.e.

$$\varepsilon_{sc} = 0.0035 \frac{d/2 - d'}{d/2} = 0.002$$

or

$$d' \not> 0.214d \not> 0.43x$$

If d' exceeds this limit the stress in the compression steel must be taken from Fig. 4.5(b).

The moment of resistance of the concrete was calculated in section 4.4.2 above and is

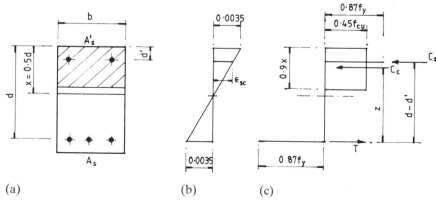

Fig. 4.17 (a) Section; (b) strain diagram; (c) stress diagram and internal forces.

$$M_{RC} = 0.156 f_{cu} bd^2$$

If this is less than the applied moment M, the compression steel resists a moment $M - M_{RC}$. The force in the compression steel is then

$$C_s = \frac{M - M_{RC}}{d - d'}$$

The area of compression steel is

$$A_s' = C_s/0.87 f_y$$

For internal equilibrium

$$
\begin{aligned}
T &= C_c + C_s \\
&= 0.45 f_{cu} \times 0.9 \times 0.5 bd + 0.87 f_y A_s' \\
&= 0.203 f_{cu} bd + 0.87 f_y A_s'
\end{aligned}
$$

The area of tension steel is

$$A_s = T/0.87 f_y$$

□ Example 4.6 Doubly reinforced rectangular beam

A rectangular beam is simply supported over a span of 6 m and carries a dead load including self-weight of 12.7 kN/m and an imposed load of 6.0 kN/m. The beam is 200 mm wide by 300 mm effective depth and the inset of the compression steel is 40 mm. Design the steel for mid-span of the beam for grade 30 concrete and grade 460 reinforcement.

$$\text{design load} = (12.7 \times 1.4) + (6 \times 1.6) = 27.4 \, kN/m$$
$$\text{ultimate moment} = 27.4 \times 6^2/8 = 123.3 \, kN \, m$$
$$M_{RC} = 0.156 \times 30 \times 200 \times 300^2/10^6 = 84.24 \, kN \, m$$
$$d'/x = 40/150 = 0.27 < 0.43$$

The stress in the compression steel is $0.87 f_y$. Therefore

$$A_s' = \frac{(123.3 - 84.24)10^6}{(300 - 40) \times 0.87 \times 460} = 374.4 \, mm^2$$
$$
\begin{aligned}
C_c + C_s &= (0.203 \times 30 \times 200 \times 300) + (374.4 \times 0.87 \times 460) \\
&= 365.4 \times 10^3 + 149.8 \times 10^3 \\
&= 515.2 \times 10^3 \, N
\end{aligned}
$$
$$A_s = \frac{515.2 \times 10^3}{0.87 \times 460} = 1287.4 \, mm^2$$

For the compression steel two 16 mm diameter bars give $A_s' = 402 \, mm^2$. For the tension steel two 25 mm diameter plus two 16 mm diameter bars give $A_s = 1383 \, mm^2$. The beam section and reinforcement steel are shown in Fig. 4.18.

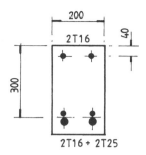

Fig. 4.18

4.5.2 Design chart using rectangular parabolic stress block

Design charts are very useful for the solution of doubly reinforced beam problems and a complete range of charts is given in BS 8110: Part 3. The construction of a chart from grade 30 concrete and grade 460 reinforcement is set out.

The beam section, strain diagram and stress diagram with internal forces are shown in Figs 4.19(a), 4.19(b) and 4.19(c) respectively. The stress–strain diagram for reinforcement in tension and compression is also shown. A value of $0.15d$ is used for the inset d' of the compression steel. Separate charts are required for different values of d'. The steps in the construction of the chart are given below.

1. Construct the chart for a beam section with tension steel only as set out in section 4.4.7. Values of $K_1 = M_{RC}/bd^2$ and $p_1 = 100A_s/bd$ are calculated for values of x ranging from $0.15d$ to $0.5d$.
2. Take a range of values for the compression steel $p_2 = 100A_s'/bd$ of 0.5, 1.0, 1.5 and 2.0. For a given value of p_2, $A_s' = p_2bd/100$. The strain in the compression steel from Fig. 4.19(b) is

$$\varepsilon_{sc} = 0.0035(x - 0.15d)/x$$

The stress f_{sc} in the compression steel is taken from the stress–strain diagram in Fig. 4.19(d). The moment of resistance of the compression steel is

$$A_s'f_{sc}(d - d') = 0.0085p_2f_{sc}bd^2$$
$$= K_2bd^2$$

where $K_2 = 0.0085p_2f_{sc}$.
3. The strain in the tension steel is

$$\varepsilon_{st} = 0.0035(d - x)/x$$

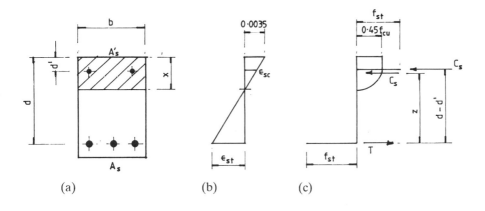

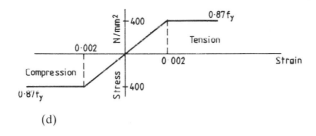

Fig. 4.19 (a) Section; (b) strain diagram; (c) stress diagram and internal forces; (d) stress–strain diagram for steel in tension and compression.

The stress f_{st} in the tension steel is taken from the stress–strain diagram in Fig. 4.19(d). This is always $0.87f_y$. The additional tension steel to balance the compression steel p_2 is

$$p_3 = p_2 f_{sc}/f_{st}$$

The total tension steel $p = p_1 + p_3$.
4. The total moment factor $K = K_1 + K_2$.

A sample calculation is given for $x = 0.3d$, $p_2 = 0.5$. From Table 4.2 $K_1 = 3.14$, $p_1 = 0.91$ for tension steel only.

$$\varepsilon_{sc} = 0.0035(0.3 - 0.15)/0.3 = 0.00175$$
$$f_{sc} = 0.0017 \times 0.87f_y/0.002 = 0.76f_y \quad \text{(Fig. 4.19(d))}$$
$$K_2 = 0.0085 \times 0.5 \times 0.76f_y = 1.49$$

ε_{st} is greater than 0.0035.

$$f_{st} = 0.87f_y$$

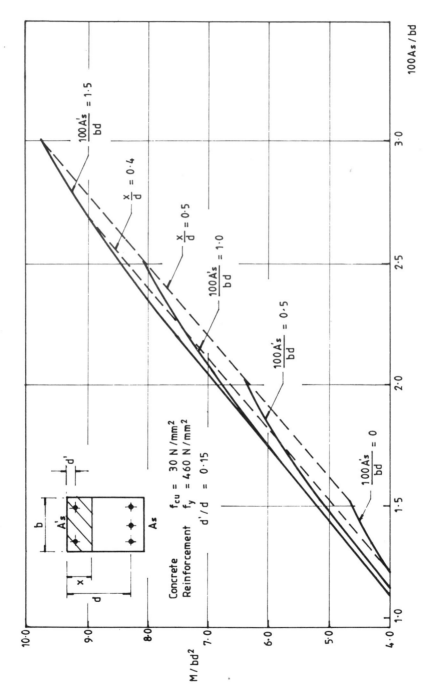

Fig. 4.20

$$p_3 = 0.5 \times 0.76/0.87 = 0.44$$
$$K = 3.14 + 1.49 = 4.63$$
$$p = 0.91 + 0.44 = 1.35$$

Further points can be calculated for other values of x and the process can be repeated for other values of p_2. The chart is formed by plotting K against p with a separate branch of the curve for each value of p_2. A portion of the chart is shown in Fig. 4.20. No allowance has been made for the area occupied by the compression steel.

□ Example 4.7 Doubly reinforced rectangular beam – design chart

A rectangular beam section 200 mm wide by 300 mm effective depth is subjected to an ultimate moment of 123.3 kN m. The inset of the compression steel is 40 mm. The materials are grade 30 concrete and grade 460 reinforcement. Use the design chart in Fig. 4.20 to determine the steel areas required in tension and compression for $x = 0.5d$.

$$K = \frac{M}{bd^2} = \frac{123.3 \times 10^6}{200 \times 300^2} = 6.85$$

From Fig. 4.20

$$100A_s/bd = 2.14$$
$$100A_s'/bd = 0.625$$

Tension steel $A_s = 2.14 \times 200 \times 300/100 = 1284 \text{ mm}^2$

Compression steel $A_s' = 0.625 \times 200 \times 300/100 = 375 \text{ mm}^2$

These results can be compared with the results for Example 4.6 in section 4.5.1 above (Fig. 4.18). The chart is difficult to read accurately, particularly for values of $100A_s'/bd$. ■

4.6 CHECKING EXISTING SECTIONS

A check on an existing section can be carried out by calculating the ultimate moment of resistance of the section and comparing this with the applied ultimate moment. It is convenient to use the simplified stress block for manual calculations. Alternatively the design charts can be used. The method is illustrated in the following examples.

□ Example 4.8 Singly reinforced rectangular beam – moment of resistance

Calculate the moment of resistance of the singly reinforced beam section shown in Fig. 4.21(a). The materials are grade 30 concrete and grade 460 reinforcement.

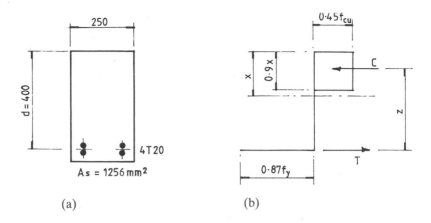

Fig. 4.21 (a) Section; (b) stress diagram and internal forces.

The stress distribution and internal forces are shown in Fig. 4.21(b). The problem may be solved by considering the equilibrium of the internal forces.

$$T = 0.87f_y A_s = 0.87 \times 460 \times 1256 = 5.03 \times 10^5 \, \text{N}$$
$$C = 0.45f_{cu} \times 0.9xb = 0.45 \times 30 \times 0.9x \times 250$$
$$= 3037.5x \, \text{N}$$

Equate T and C and solve for x:

$$x = \frac{5.03 \times 10^5}{3037.5} = 165.6 \, \text{mm}$$
$$z = d - 0.5 \times 0.9x$$
$$= 400 - 0.5 \times 0.9 \times 165.6 = 325.5 \, \text{mm}$$
$$M_R = T_z = 5.03 \times 10^5 \times 325.5/10^6 = 163.7 \, \text{kN m}$$ ■

□ Example 4.9 Singly reinforced rectangular beam – moment of resistance using design chart

Use the design chart in Fig. 4.13 to solve the above problem.

$$\frac{100A_s}{bd} = \frac{100 \times 1256}{250 \times 400} = 1.256$$
$$M/bd^2 = 4.05$$
$$M = 4.05 \times 250 \times 400^2/10^6 = 162 \, \text{kN m}$$ ■

□ Example 4.10 Doubly reinforced rectangular beam – moment of resistance

Calculate the moment of resistance of the beam section shown in Fig. 4.22. The materials are grade 30 concrete and grade 460 reinforcement.

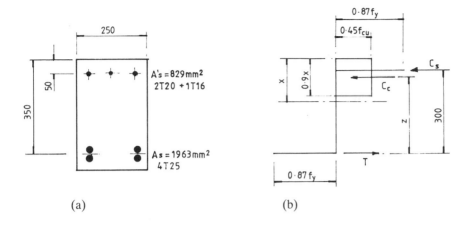

Fig. 4.22 (a) Section; (b) stress diagram and internal forces.

$$d' = 50d/350 = 0.143d \not> 0.214d$$

The stress in the compression steel is $0.87f_y$.

$$T = 0.87f_yA_s - 0.87 \times 460 \times 1963 = 7.86 \times 10^5\,\text{N}$$
$$C_s = 0.87f_yA_s' = 0.87 \times 460 \times 829 = 3.32 \times 10^5\,\text{N}$$
$$C_c = T - C_s = (7.86 - 3.32) \times 10^2 = 4.54 \times 10^5\,\text{N}$$
$$= 0.45f_{cu} \times 0.9xb$$
$$x = \frac{4.54 \times 10^5}{0.45 \times 30 \times 0.9 \times 250} = 149.5\,\text{mm}$$
$$z = d - 0.5 \times 0.9x$$
$$= 350 - 0.5 \times 0.9 \times 149.5 = 282.7\,\text{mm}$$
$$M_R = [(4.54 \times 282.7) + (3.32 \times 300)]10^3/10^6$$
$$= 227.9\,\text{kN}\,\text{m}$$ ■

☐ Example 4.11 Doubly reinforced rectangular beam – moment of resistance using design chart

Use the design chart in Fig. 4.20 to solve the above problem.

$$\frac{100A_s}{bd} = \frac{100 \times 1963}{250 \times 350} = 2.24$$

$$\frac{100A_s'}{bd} = \frac{100 \times 829}{250 \times 350} = 0.95$$

From the chart $M/bd^2 = 7.4$. Therefore

$$M_R = 7.4 \times 250 \times 350^2/10^6 = 226.6\,\text{kN}\,\text{m}$$ ■

4.7 MOMENT REDISTRIBUTION AND SECTION MOMENT RESISTANCE

Under clause 3.2.2 the code permits the redistribution of moments in continuous beams and rigid frames obtained from a rigorous elastic analysis. This allows plastic behaviour to occur and permits design with comparable values for sagging and hogging moments. This is discussed further in section 7.2.5.

One of the conditions that must be met is that the neutral axis depth x must be given by

$$x \not> (\beta_b - 0.4)d$$

where

$$\beta_b = \frac{\text{moment at the section after redistribution}}{\text{moment at the section before redistribution}} \leqslant 1$$

The resistance moment must be at least 70% of the moment from the elastic analysis. The limitation on x ensures that the section has sufficient rotation capacity for the redistribution to occur. No reduction in x need be made if redistribution does not exceed 10%.

A rectangular section with compression reinforcement is analysed for the case where redistribution exceeds 10%. The simplified stress block is used. The section and stress diagram are shown in Fig. 4.23.

$$x = (\beta_b - 0.4)d$$
$$z = d - 1/2 \times 0.9(\beta_b - 0.4)d$$

The moment of resistance of concrete is

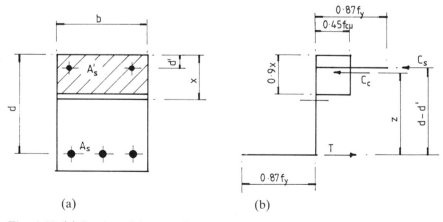

Fig. 4.23 (a) Section; (b) stress diagram.

$$M_{RC} = C_c z$$
$$= 0.45 f_{cu} b \times 0.9(\beta_b - 0.4)d[d - 0.45(\beta_b - 0.4)d]$$
$$\frac{M_{RC}}{bd^2 f_{cu}} = 0.405(\beta_b - 0.4)[1 - 0.45(\beta_b - 0.4)]$$
$$= 0.405(\beta_b - 0.4) - 0.18(\beta_b - 0.4)^2$$
$$= K'$$

This is the expression given in the code.

If the applied moment M exceeds M_{RC} compression reinforcement is required. The area of compression steel is

$$A_s' = \frac{M - M_{RC}}{(d - d')0.87f_y}$$

Note that for $d'/x > 0.43$ the stress in the compression steel must be taken from the stress–strain diagram for reinforcement (Fig. 4.5).

$$T = C_c + C_s$$
$$= 0.405 f_{cu} bd(\beta_b - 0.4) + 0.87 f_y A_s'$$
$$A_s = T/0.87f_y$$

☐ Example 4.12 Doubly reinforced rectangular beam – design after moment redistribution

The beam section shown in Fig. 4.24 is subjected to an ultimate moment of 111.3 kN m which results after a redistribution of 20%. Determine the reinforcement required. The concrete is grade 30 and the reinforcement grade 460.

$$\beta_b = 0.8$$
$$x = (0.8 - 0.4)d = 0.4d = 120 \, mm$$

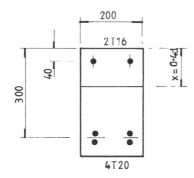

Fig. 4.24

$$M_{RC} = \frac{200 \times 300^2 \times 30}{10^6} (0.405 \times 0.4 - 0.18 \times 0.4^2)$$

$$= 71.9 \, \text{kN} \, \text{m}$$

$$\frac{d'}{x} = \frac{40}{120} = 0.33 < 0.43$$

The stress in the compression steel is $0.87f_y$.

$$A_s' = \frac{(111.3 - 71.9) \times 10^6}{260 \times 0.87 \times 460} = 378.6 \, \text{k} \, \text{mm}^2$$

$$C_c + C_s = (0.405 \times 30 \times 200 \times 300 \times 0.4) + (0.87 \times 460 \times 378.6)$$

$$= (2.92 + 1.52)10^5$$

$$= 4.44 \times 10^5 \, \text{N}$$

$$A_s = \frac{4.44 \times 10^5}{0.87 \times 460} = 1109.4 \, \text{mm}^2$$

For compression steel, two 16 mm diameter bars give $A_s' = 402 \, \text{mm}^2$. For tension steel four 20 mm diameter bars give $A_s = 1256 \, \text{mm}^2$.

Redesign the section using the chart in Fig. 4.20.

$$x/d = 0.4$$

$$\frac{M}{bd^2} = \frac{111.3 \times 10^6}{200 \times 300^2} = 6.18$$

From the chart $100A_s'/bd = 0.65$. Therefore

$$A_s' = 0.65 \times 200 \times 300/100 = 390 \, \text{mm}^2$$

$$100A_s/bd = 1.86$$

$$A_s = 1.86 \times 200 \times 300/100 = 1118 \, \text{mm}^2$$

The point where the horizontal line through $M/bd^2 = 6.18$ cuts the $x/d = 0.4$ line gives the values for $100A_s'/bd$ and $100A_s/bd$. The chart cannot be read accurately. ∎

4.8 FLANGED BEAMS

4.8.1 General considerations

Flanged beams occur where beams are cast integral with and support a continuous floor slab. Part of the slab adjacent to the beam is counted as acting in compression to form T- and L-beams as shown in Fig. 4.25 where b is the effective breadth of the compression flange, b_w is the breadth of the web of the beam and h_f is the thickness of the flange.

The effective breadth b of flanged beams is given in BS 8110: Part 1, clause 3.4.1.5:

1. T-beams – web width $b_w + l_z/5$ or the actual flange width if less
2. L-beams – web width $b_w + l_z/10$ or the actual flange width if less

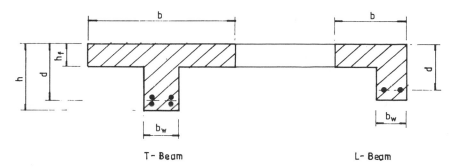

Fig. 4.25

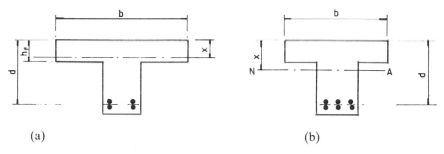

(a)   (b)

Fig. 4.26 (a) Neutral axis in flange; (b) neutral axis in web.

where l_z is the distance between points of zero moment in the beam. In continuous beams l_z may be taken as 0.7 times the effective span.

The design procedure depends on where the neutral axis lies. The neutral axis may lie in the flange or in the web, as shown in Fig. 4.26.

4.8.2 Neutral axis in flange

The beam may be treated as a rectangular beam of breadth b and the methods set out in sections 4.4.6 and 4.4.7 above apply. When the simplified stress block is used the actual neutral axis may be in the web provided that $0.9x$ does not exceed the flange depth h_f. The moment of resistance of the section for the case when $0.9x = h_f$ is

$$M_R = 0.45 f_{cu} b h_f (d - h_f/2)$$

The design curves in Fig. 4.13 can also be used for values of $0.9x$ not exceeding h_f. If the applied moment M is greater than M_R the neutral axis lies in the web.

4.8.3 Neutral axis in web

The case of the neutral axis in the web can be analysed using the assumptions for moment of resistance given in BS 8110: Part 1, clause 3.4.4.1. As an alternative, a conservative formula for calculating the steel area is given in clause 3.4.4.5 of the code.

The equation in the code is derived using the simplified stress block with $x = 0.5d$ (Fig. 4.27).

$$\text{depth of stress block} = 0.9x = 0.45d$$

The concrete forces in compression are

$$C_1 = 0.45f_{cu}h_f(b - b_w)$$
$$C_2 = 0.45f_{cu} \times 0.45db_w$$
$$= 0.2f_{cu}b_wd$$

The steel force in tension is

$$T = 0.87f_yA_s$$

The values of the lever arms are

$$z_1 = d - 0.5h_f$$
$$z_2 = d - 0.5 \times 0.4d = 0.77d$$

The moment of resistance of the section is found by taking moments about force C_1:

$$M = Tz_1 - C_2(z_1 - z_2)$$
$$= 0.87f_yA_s(d - 0.5h_f) - 0.2f_{cu}b_wd(0.225d - 0.5h_f)$$

from which

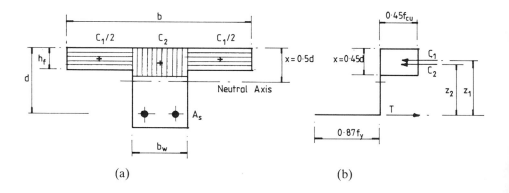

(a)   (b)

Fig. 4.27 (a) Section; (b) stresses and internal forces.

$$A_s = \frac{M + 0.1f_{cu}b_wd(0.45d - h_f)}{0.87f_y(d - 0.5h_f)}$$

This is the expression given in the code. It gives conservative results for cases where x is less than $0.5d$. The equation only applies when h_f is less than $0.45d$.

For a section with tension reinforcement only, the applied moment must not exceed the moment of resistance of the concrete given by

$$M = C_1z_1 + C_2z_2$$
$$= 0.45f_{cu}h_f(b - b_w)(d - 0.5h_f) + 0.155f_{cu}b_wd^2$$

Thus

$$\frac{M}{f_{cu}bd^2} = 0.45\frac{h_f}{d}\left(1 - \frac{b_w}{b}\right)\left(1 - \frac{h_f}{2d}\right) + 0.155\frac{b_w}{b}$$

or

$$M = \beta_ff_{cu}bd^2$$

where β_f is the expression immediately above. Thus the equation for the steel area A_s only applies when the ultimate moment M is less than $\beta_ff_{cu}bd^2$. This is the expression given in the code. A further stipulation is that not more than 10% redistribution has been carried out.

Sections can be designed using the basic assumptions for the following cases:

1. when the applied moment exceeds $\beta_1f_{cu}bd^2$ and compression reinforcement is required
2. where redistribution exceeds 10% and the depth to the neutral axis must be limited

☐ Example 4.13 Flanged beam – neutral axis in flange

A continuous slab 100 mm thick is carried on T-beams at 2 m centres. The overall depth of the beam is 350 mm and the breadth of the web is 250 mm. The beams are 6 m span and are simply supported. The dead load including self-weight and finishes is 7.4 kN/m² and the imposed load is 5 kN/m². Design the beam using the simplified stress block. The materials are grade 30 concrete and grade 460 reinforcement.

$$\text{design load} = (7.4 \times 2 \times 1.4) + (5 \times 2 \times 1.6) = 36.7\,\text{kN/m}$$
$$\text{ultimate moment} = 36.7 \times 6^2/8 = 165\,\text{kN m}$$
$$\text{breadth of flange } b = 250 + 6000/5 = 1450\,\text{mm}$$

The beam section is shown in Fig. 4.28. From BS 8110: Part 1, Table 3.4, the nominal cover on the links is 25 mm for grade 30 concrete. If the links are 8 mm in diameter and the main bars are 25 mm in diameter, then $d = 350 - 25 - 8 - 12.5 =$

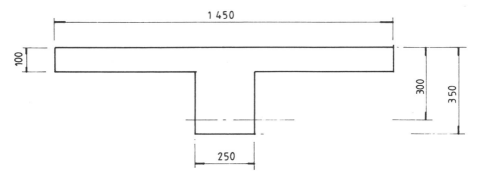

Fig. 4.28

304.5 mm, say 300 mm. The moment of resistance of the section when the slab depth $h_f = 100$ mm is equal to 0.9 of the depth x to the neutral axis is

$$M_R = 0.45 \times 30 \times 1450 \times 100(300 - 0.5 \times 100)/10^6$$
$$= 489.3 \text{ kN m}$$

The neutral axis lies in the flange. Using the code expressions in clause 3.4.4.4

$$K = \frac{165 \times 10^6}{30 \times 1450 \times 300^2} = 0.042$$

$$z = 300[0.5 + (0.25 - 0.042/0.9)^{1/2}]$$
$$= 285.1 \text{ mm} > 0.95d = 285 \text{ mm}$$

$$A_s = \frac{165 \times 10^6}{0.87 \times 460 \times 285} = 1447 \text{ mm}^2$$

Provide three 25 mm diameter bars; $A_s = 1472$ mm^2.
Redesign the beam using the chart in Fig. 4.13.

$$\frac{M}{bd^2} = \frac{165 \times 10^6}{1450 \times 300^2} = 1.26$$

This is less than 1.27. Calculate the steel area using $z = 0.95d$ as above.   ■

□ Example 4.14 Flanged beam – neutral axis in web

Determine the area of reinforcement required for the T-beam section shown in Fig. 4.29 which is subjected to an ultimate moment of 260 kN m. The materials are grade 30 concrete and grade 460 reinforcement.

Check the location of the neutral axis. If 0.9 multiplied by the neutral axis depth is equal to h_f, the moment of resistance of the concrete is

$$M_R = 0.45 f_{cu} b d h_f (d - 0.5 h_f)$$
$$= 0.45 \times 30 \times 600 \times 100 \times 290/10^6 = 234.9 \text{ kN m}$$
$$< \text{applied moment}$$

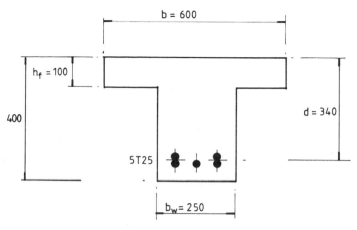

Fig. 4.29

The neutral axis lies in the web. The steel area is calculated using the expression from clause 3.4.4.5 of the code (see above).

$$A_s = \frac{260 \times 10^6 + 0.1 \times 30 \times 250 \times 340(0.45 \times 340 - 100)}{0.87 \times 460(340 - 0.5 \times 100)}$$

$$= 2357 \, mm^2$$

Provide five 25 mm diameter bars; $A_s = 2454 \, mm^2$.

Check the moment of resistance of the concrete.

$$\beta_f = \frac{0.45 \times 100}{340} \left(1 - \frac{250}{600}\right)\left(1 - \frac{100}{2 \times 340}\right) + \frac{0.155 \times 250}{600}$$

$$= 0.129$$

$$M_R = 0.129 \times 30 \times 600 \times 340^2/10^6 = 269.6 \, kN \, m$$

This is greater than the applied moment. The section is satisfactory with tension reinforcement only. ∎

4.9 ELASTIC THEORY

4.9.1 Assumptions and terms used

Reinforced concrete beams are designed for the ultimate limit state using plastic analysis. Elastic analysis is required to check the serviceability limit states in the calculation of deflections and crack widths.

The assumptions made in analysing a reinforced concrete section are as follows:

1. Plane sections before bending remain plane after bending;
2. Concrete is elastic, i.e. the concrete stress varies from zero at the neutral axis to a maximum at the extreme fibre;

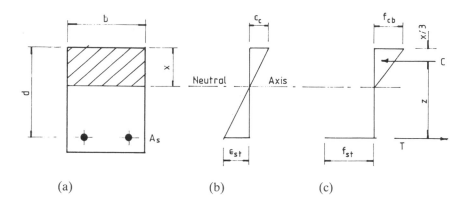

Fig. 4.30 (a) Section; (b) strain diagram; (c) stress diagram and internal forces.

3. The concrete is ineffective in tension and the reinforcing steel resists all the tension due to bending.

The beam section, strain diagram and stress diagram with internal forces are shown in Fig. 4.30, where the following terms and elastic relationships apply:

E_c Young's modulus for concrete
E_s Young's modulus for steel
α_e modular ratio E_s/E_c (this is specified as 15 in elastic design)
f_{cb} compressive stress due to bending in the concrete
f_{st} tensile stress due to bending in the steel
ε_c strain in the concrete, f_{cb}/E_c
ε_{st} strain in the steel, $f_{st}/E_s = f_{st}/\alpha_e E_c$
C force in the concrete in compression, $0.5 f_{cb} bx$
T force in the steel in tension, $f_{st} A_s$
z lever arm, $d - x/3$

4.9.2 Section analysis

The problem is to determine the maximum stress in the concrete and the steel stress in a given section subjected to a moment M, i.e. given $b, d, A_s,$ M and α_e, determine f_{cb} and f_{st}.
   Referring to Fig. 4.30(b)

$$\frac{x}{d - x} = \frac{\varepsilon_c}{\varepsilon_{st}} = \frac{f_{cb}}{E_c} \frac{\alpha_e E_c}{f_{st}} = \frac{f_{cb} \alpha_e}{f_{st}}$$

Solve the equation to give

$$x = \frac{\alpha_e f_{cb}}{\alpha_e f_{cb} + f_{st}} d$$

For equilibrium the internal forces C and T are equal:

$$0.5 f_{cb} b x = f_{st} A_s$$

or

$$f_{st} = 0.5 f_{cb} b x / A_s$$

Substituting for f_{st} in the expression for x gives

$$x = \frac{\alpha_e f_{cb}}{\alpha_e f_{cb} + 0.5 f_{cb} b x / A_s}$$

Rearrange to give the quadratic equation

$$x^2 + \frac{2 A_s \alpha_e}{b} x - \frac{2 A_s \alpha_e d}{b} = 0$$

Solve for x.

The moment of resistance of the concrete is

$$M = Cz = 0.5 f_{cb} b x (d - x/3)$$

The concrete stress is

$$f_{cb} = \frac{2M}{b x (d - x/3)}$$

The steel stress is

$$f_{st} = 0.5 f_{cb} b x / A_s$$

The method can be applied to doubly reinforced and flanged beams.

4.9.3 Transformed area method – singly reinforced beam

The transformed area method where the reinforcement is replaced by an equivalent area of concrete is a more convenient method to use for section analysis than that set out above.

The beam section shown in Fig. 4.31(a) is subjected to a moment M. The problem is to determine the maximum stress f_{cb} in the concrete and the stress f_{st} in the steel. The strain and stress diagrams are shown in Figs 4.31(b) and 4.31(c) respectively.

The strain in the tension steel is $f_{st}/\alpha_e E_c$. If the steel were replaced by concrete the stress in that concrete would be f_{st}/α_e. The force in the steel is

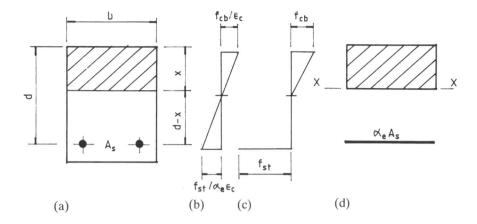

Fig. 4.31 (a) Section; (b) strain diagram; (c) stress diagram; (d) transformed section.

$f_{st}A_s$ and the equivalent concrete must carry the same force. Hence the equivalent area of concrete is $\alpha_e A_s$. To form the transformed section, the steel is replaced by an area of concrete equal to α_e times the area of steel (Fig. 4.31(d)).

Moments are taken about the neutral axis to find the depth to the neutral axis. This gives the quadratic equation

$$0.5bx^2 = \alpha_e A_s(d - x)$$

The positive root gives the depth to the neutral axis. The moment of inertia about the neutral axis is

$$I_x = bx^3/3 + \alpha_e A_s(d - x)^2$$

The stresses in the concrete and steel are given by

$$\text{Concrete} \quad f_{cb} = M_x/I_x$$
$$\text{Steel} \qquad f_{st} = \alpha_e M(d - x)/I_x$$

Note that to obtain the stress in the steel the stress in the equivalent concrete is multipled by the modular ratio α_e.

☐ Example 4.15 Elastic theory – stresses in singly reinforced rectangular beam

The dimensions of a rectangular beam section and the reinforcing steel provided are shown in Fig. 4.32(a). The section is subjected to a moment of 40 kN m. Determine the maximum stress in the concrete and the stress in the steel. The modular ratio $\alpha_e = 15$. Using the equation from section 4.9.2

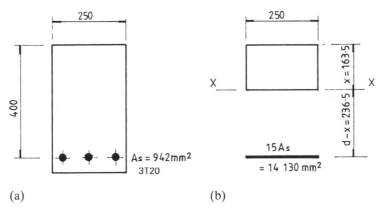

Fig. 4.32 (a) Section; (b) transformed section.

The coefficients are

$$\frac{2A_s\alpha_e}{b} = \frac{2 \times 15 \times 942}{250} = 113.04$$

$$2A_s\alpha_e d/b = 45216$$

The equation is

$$x^2 + 113.04x - 45216 = 0$$

and $x = 163.5$ mm. The concrete stress is

$$f_{cb} = \frac{2 \times 40 \times 10^6}{250 \times 163.5(400 - 163.5/3)} = 5.67\,\text{N/mm}^2$$

The steel stress is

$$f_{st} = 0.5 \times 5.67 \times 250 \times 163.5/942 = 123\,\text{N/mm}^2$$

■

□ Example 4.16 Elastic theory – stresses in singly reinforced rectangular beam using the transformed area method

The transformed area is $\alpha_e A_s = 15 \times 942 = 14130\,\text{mm}^2$. The transformed section is shown in Fig. 4.32(b). Take moments about the neutral axis.

$$0.5 \times 250 \times x^2 = 14130(400 - x)$$

$$x^2 + 113.04x - 45216 = 0$$

$$x = 163.5\,\text{mm}$$

$$I_x = 250 \times 163.5^3/3 + 14130 \times 236.5^2$$

$$= 1.154 \times 10^9\,\text{mm}^4$$

$$\text{concrete stress } f_{cb} = \frac{40 \times 10^6 \times 163.5}{1.154 \times 10^9} = 5.67 \text{ N/mm}^2$$

$$\text{steel stress } f_{st} = \frac{40 \times 10^6 \times 236.5 \times 15}{1.154 \times 10^9} = 123 \text{ N/mm}^2$$

■

4.9.4 Doubly reinforced beam

A doubly reinforced beam section is shown in Fig. 4.33(a). The transformed section is shown in Fig. 4.33(b). For the compression steel $\alpha_e - 1$ times the area is added to the gross concrete area in compression.

The position of the neutral axis is found by taking moments of area about the neutral axis. This gives the equation

$$0.5bx^2 + (\alpha_e - 1)A_s'(x - d') = \alpha_e(d - x)A_s$$

which can be solved for x. The moment of inertia about the neutral axis is given by

$$I_x = \tfrac{1}{3}bx^2 + (\alpha_e - 1)A_s'(x - d')^2 + \alpha_e A_s(d - x)^2$$

The stresses are given by the following expressions.

$$\text{Concrete} \qquad f_{cb} = \frac{Mx}{I_x}$$

$$\text{Compression steel} \quad f_{sc} = \frac{\alpha_e M(x - d')}{I_x}$$

$$\text{Tension steel} \qquad f_{st} = \frac{\alpha_e M(d - x)}{I_x}$$

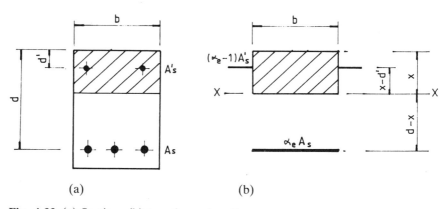

Fig. 4.33 (a) Section; (b) transformed section.

□ Example 4.17 Elastic theory – stresses in doubly reinforced rectangular beam using transformed area method

The dimensions of a rectangular beam section and the reinforcing steel provided are shown in Fig. 4.34(a). The section is subjected to a moment of 47 kN m. Determine the maximum stress in the concrete and the stresses in the reinforcement. Take the modular ratio α_e to be 15.

Compression steel $\qquad A_s' = 402\,\text{mm}^2$

$\qquad\qquad\qquad$ transformed area $= 14 \times 402 = 5628\,\text{mm}^2$

Tension steel $\qquad\qquad A_s = 1472\,\text{mm}^2$

$\qquad\qquad\qquad$ transformed area $= 15 \times 1472 = 22080\,\text{mm}^2$

The transformed section is shown in Fig. 4.34(b).
Take moments about the neutral axis:

$$0.5 \times 250 \times x^2 + 5628(x - 45) = 22080(300 - x)$$

Solve the equation to give $x = 148.3\,\text{mm}$.

$$I_x = 250 \times 148.3^3/3 + 5628 \times 103.3^2 + 22080 \times 151.7^2$$
$$= 839.9 \times 10^6\,\text{mm}^4$$

This concrete stress is

$$f_{cb} = \frac{47 \times 10^6 \times 148.3}{839.9 \times 10^6}$$
$$= 8.3\,\text{N/mm}^2$$

The compression steel stress is

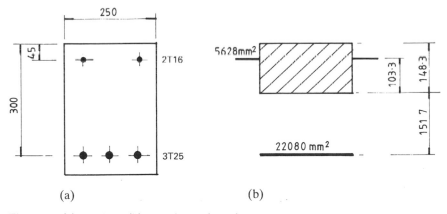

(a) $\qquad\qquad\qquad\qquad\qquad\qquad$ (b)

Fig. 4.34 (a) Section; (b) transformed section.

$$f_{sc} = \frac{15 \times 47 \times 10^6 \times 103.3}{839.9 \times 10^6}$$

$$= 86.7 \, \text{N/mm}^2$$

The tension steel stress is

$$f_{st} = \frac{15 \times 47 \times 10^6 \times 151.7}{839.9 \times 10^6}$$

$$= 127.3 \, \text{N/mm}^2$$

∎

5

Shear, bond and torsion

5.1 SHEAR

Shear forces accompany a change in bending moment in beams and give rise to diagonal tension in the concrete and bond stresses between the reinforcement and the concrete.

5.1.1 Shear in a homogeneous beam

In a homogeneous elastic beam a vertical shear force causes complimentary shear stresses and diagonal tensile and compressive stresses of the same magnitude. This is shown in Figs 5.1(a) and 5.1(b) where the stresses are shown on the small element Λ near the neutral axis. The beam section is shown in 5.1(c) and the parabolic shear stress distribution in 5.1(d). The maximum shear stress at the neutral axis of the section is given by

$$v_{max} = 1.5V/bd$$

5.1.2 Shear in a reinforced concrete beam without shear reinforcement

(a) Shear failure

Shear in a reinforced concrete beam without shear reinforcement causes cracks on inclined planes near the support as shown in Fig. 5.2. The cracks are caused by the diagonal tensile stress mentioned above. The shear failure mechanism is complex and depends on the shear span ratio a_v/d. When this ratio is large the failure is as shown in Fig. 5.2.

The following three actions form the mechanism resisting shear in the beam:

1. shear stresses in the compression zone with a parabolic distribution as set out above
2. aggregate interlock along the cracks
3. dowel action in the bars where the concrete between the cracks transmits shear forces to the bars

(b) Shear capacity

An accurate analysis for shear strength is not possible. The problem is solved by establishing first the strength of concrete in shear by test. The

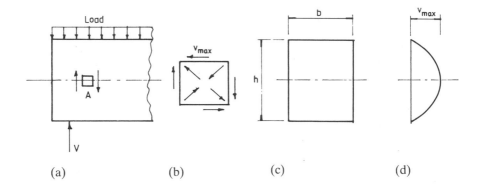

(a)	(b)	(c)	(d)

Fig. 5.1 (a) Beam; (b) enlarged element A; (c) section; (d) shear stress.

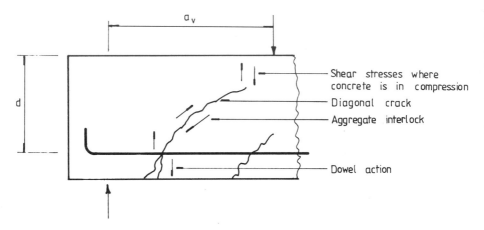

Fig. 5.2

shear capacity is represented by the simple formula to calculate the nominal shear stress given in BS 8110: Part 1, clause 3.4.5.2:

$$v = V/b_v d$$

where b_v is the breadth of the section; for a flanged beam this is taken as the width of the rib below the flange. V is the design shear force due to ultimate loads and d is the effective depth. The code gives in Table 3.9 the design concrete shear stress v_c which is used to determine the shear capacity of the concrete alone. Values of v_c depend on the percentage of steel in the member, the depth and the concrete grade. An increase in the amount of tension steel as well as an increase in the dowel action component increases the aggregate interlock value by restricting the width of

Table 5.1 Design concrete shear strength v_c

$\dfrac{100A_s}{b_v d}$	Design concrete shear strength v_c (N/mm^2)					
	$d = 125$	150	200	250	300	$\geqslant 400$
$\leqslant 0.15$	0.47	0.45	0.42	0.41	0.38	0.36
0.5	0.71	0.68	0.64	0.59	0.57	0.53
1.0	0.89	0.86	0.79	0.75	0.72	0.67
1.5	1.03	0.97	0.91	0.86	0.83	0.76

Effective depth d is in millimetres.

the shear cracks. Finally, it is found that deeper beams have a lower shear capacity than shallower beams.

The design concrete shear stress is given by the following formula from Table 3.9 in the code:

$$v_c = \frac{0.79(100A_s/(b_v d))^{1/3}(400/d)^{1/4}}{\gamma_m}$$

where $100A_s/(b_v d)$ should not be greater than 3.0 and $400/d$ should not be less than unity. The code notes (clause 3.4.5.4) that for tension steel to be counted in calculating A_s it must continue for a distance d past the section being considered. Anchorage requirements must be satisfied at supports (section 3.12.9.4 in the code).

This formula gives values of v_c for concrete grade 25. For higher grades of concrete values should be multiplied by $(f_{cu}/25)^{1/3}$. The value of f_{cu} should not be greater than 40. Some values of v_c for grade 30 concrete are given in Table 5.1. The value of γ_m is 1.25.

(c) Enhanced shear capacity near supports

The code states (clause 3.4.5.8) that shear failure in beam sections without shear reinforcement normally occurs at about 30° to the horizontal. If the angle is steeper due to the load causing shear or because the section where the shear is to be checked is close to the support (Fig. 5.3), the shear capacity is increased. The increase is because the concrete in diagonal compression resists shear. The shear span ratio a_v/d is small in this case.

The design concrete shear can be increased from v_c as determined above to $2v_c d/a_v$ where a_v is the length of that part of a member traversed by a shear plane.

(d) Maximum shear stress

BS 8110: Part 1, clauses 3.4.52 and 3.4.58, states that the nominal shear stress $v = V/b_v d$ must in no case exceed $0.8f_{cu}^{1/2}$ or $5\,\text{N/mm}^2$ even if the

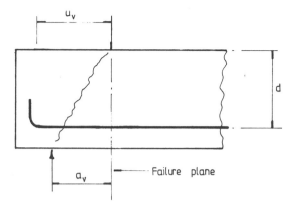

Fig. 5.3

beam is reinforced to resist shear. This upper limit prevents failure of the concrete in diagonal compression. If v is exceeded the beam must be made larger.

5.1.3 Shear reinforcement in beams

(a) Action of shear reinforcement

As stated in section 5.1.1 the complementary shear stresses give rise to diagonal tensile and compressive stresses as shown in Fig. 5.1. Taking a simplified view, concrete is weak in tension, and so shear failure is caused by a failure in diagonal tension with cracks running at 45° to the beam axis. Shear reinforcement is provided by bars which cross the cracks, and theoretically either vertical links or inclined bars will serve this purpose, as shown in Fig. 5.4. In practice either vertical links or a combination of links and bent-up bars are provided.

(b) Vertical links

The formula for the spacing of vertical links given in BS 8110: Part 1, Table 3.8, is derived. The following terms are defined:

$$V_c = v_c b_v d \text{ is the shear resistance of the concrete}$$
$$V = v b_v d \text{ is the ultimate applied shear which exceeds } V_c$$
$$V - V_c = (v - v_c) b_v d \text{ is the shear resisted by the reinforcement}$$

A length of beam near the support is shown in Fig. 5.5(a) with a 45° crack crossing links spaced s_v apart. The formula is derived for the two-leg link shown in Fig. 5.5(b) where the cross-sectional area of the two legs is A_{sv}. In cases of heavy shear forces double links may be required.

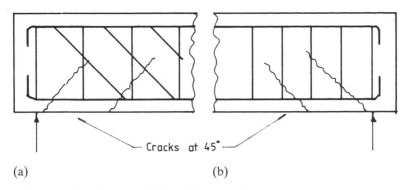

Fig. 5.4 (a) Inclined bars and links; (b) vertical links.

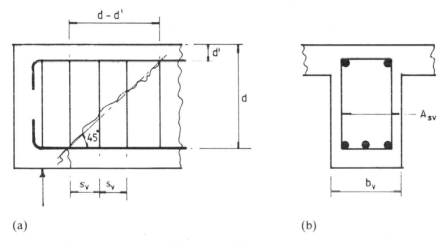

(a)   (b)

Fig. 5.5 (a) Beam elevation; (b) two-leg links

$d - d' \approx d$ horizontal length of the crack
d/s_v number of links crossing the crack
f_{yv} characteristic strength of the links

The shear force to be taken by the links is equated to the strength of the links, i.e.

$$(v - v_c)b_v d = 0.87 f_{yv} A_{sv} d/s_v$$

or

$$A_{sv} = \frac{b_v s_v (v - v_c)}{0.87 f_{yv}}$$

This is the formula given in the code. If the bar characteristic strength and diameter are chosen the spacing s_v can be calculated.

The spacing of links should be such that every potential crack is crossed by at least one link. To ensure this the code (clause 3.4.5.5) limits the spacing to $0.75d$ in the direction of the span. The spacing of links at right angles to the span is to be such that no tension bar is more than 150 mm from a vertical leg. The spacing of legs should not exceed d in any case.

The code states in Table 3.8 that the minimum area of link is to be

$$A_{sv} = 0.4b_v s_v / 0.87 f_{yv}$$

The minimum links provide a design shear resistance of $0.4\,N/mm^2$.

Also in Table 3.8 the code notes that all beams of structural importance should be provided with minimum links throughout their length. In minor beams such as lintels, links may be omitted provided that v is less than $0.5v_c$. Note that where compression reinforcement is required in a beam clause 3.12.7.1 states that the size of the link should not be less than one-quarter of the size of the largest bar in compression or 6 mm and the spacing should not exceed 12 times the size of the smallest compression bar.

(c) Bent-up bars

BS 8110: Part 1, clause 3.4.5.6, states that the design shear resistance of a system of bent-up bars may be calculated by assuming that the bent-up bars form the tension members of one or more single systems of trusses in which the concrete forms the compression members. A single truss system is shown in Fig. 5.6(a). The truss is to be arranged so that the angles α and β are greater than or equal to $45°$.

A number of bars inclined at an angle α crossing a cracked section where the crack is inclined at an angle β is shown in Fig. 5.6(b). This represents a multiple truss system. The following terms are defined:

s_b spacing of the bent-up bars
A_{sb} cross-sectional area of a pair of bars
f_{yv} characteristic strength of the bent-up bars

$T = 0.87 f_{yv} A_{sb}$ is the ultimate force in a pair of bars, and $(d - d') \times (\cot\beta + \cot\alpha)$ is the horizontal length over which bent-up bars cross the crack. The number of bars crossing the crack is $(d - d')(\cot\beta + \cot\alpha)/s_b$. The design shear strength of the bent-up bars is then

V_b = vertical component of the sum of the forces in the bars
$= 0.87 f_{yv} A_{sb} \sin\alpha (d - d')(\cot\beta + \cot\alpha)/s_b$
$= 0.87 f_{yv} A_{sb}(\cos\alpha + \sin\alpha \cot\beta)(d - d')/s_b$

This is the expression given in the code in clause 3.4.5.6. The formula for

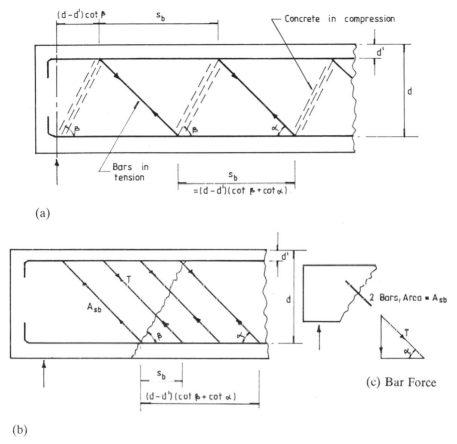

(a)

(b)

(c) Bar Force

Fig. 5.6 (a) Equivalent single-truss system; (b) inclined bars crossing crack.

vertical links discussed in section 5.1.3(b) above is a special case of the general expression.

Bent-up bars alone are not satisfactory as shear reinforcement. The code states that links must also be provided and that they must make up at least 50% of the shear reinforcement.

(d) Shear reinforcement close to support

Clause 3.4.5.9 of the code deals with shear reinforcement for sections close to the support. The total area specified is

$$\Sigma A_{sv} = \frac{a_v b_v (v - 2dv_c/a_v)}{0.87 f_{yv}}$$
$$\geq \frac{0.4 b_v a_v}{0.87 f_{yv}}$$

Refer to Fig. 5.3 where a_v is the distance from the support traversed by the failure plane. The term $2dv_c/a_v$ is the enhanced shear stress. The second expression ensures that minimum links are provided. This reinforcement should be provided within the middle three-quarters of a_v.

The code (clause 3.4.5.10) also gives a simplified approach for design taking enhanced shear strength into account. This applies to beams carrying uniform load or where the principal load is applied more than $2d$ from the face of the support. The procedure given is as follows:

1. Calculate the shear stress at d from the face of the support;
2. Determine v_c and the amount of shear reinforcement in the form of vertical links using Table 3.8 (section 5.1.3(d));
3. Provide this shear reinforcement between the section at d and the support. No further checks for shear reinforcement are required;
4. Check for maximum shear stress at the face of the support.

□ Example 5.1 Design of shear reinforcement for T-beam

A simply supported T-beam of 6 m clear span (Fig. 5.7) carries an ultimate load of 38 kN/m. The beam section dimensions, support particulars and tension reinforcement are shown in the figure. Design the shear reinforcement for the beam. The concrete is grade 25 and the shear reinforcement grade 250.

The load and shear force diagrams are shown in Fig. 5.7(d). The shear is calculated at the face of the support and at d and $2d$ from the face of the support. The steps in design are as follows.

(a) Determine the length in the centre of the beam over which nominal links are required

The shear resistance of concrete where five 20 mm diameter bars form tension reinforcement is to be determined.

$$A_s = 1570 \, \text{mm}^2$$
$$d = 400 - 20 \approx 380 \, \text{mm}$$
$$\frac{100A_s}{bd} = \frac{100 \times 1570}{250 \times 380} = 1.65$$

The design shear strength is

$$v_c = 0.79 \times 1.65^{1/3} \times (400/380)^{1/4}/1.25$$
$$= 0.755 \, \text{N/mm}^2$$

The shear resistance of the concrete is

$$V_c = 0.755 \times 380 \times 250/1000 = 71.7 \, \text{kN}$$

The distance from the support is found from the equation

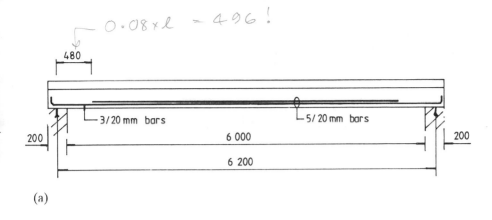

0.08 × ℓ = 496!

480

3/20 mm bars

5/20 mm bars

200

6 000

200

6 200

(a)

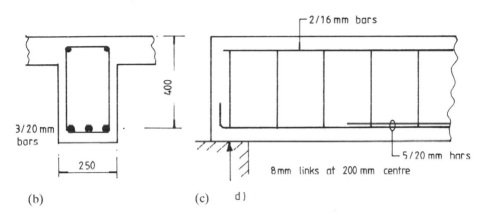

2/16 mm bars

400

3/20 mm bars

250

5/20 mm bars

8 mm links at 200 mm centre

(b)

(c)   d)

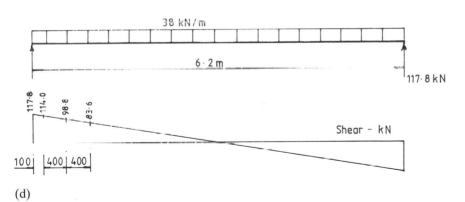

38 kN/m

6·2 m

117·8 kN

117·8
114·0
98·8
83·6

Shear - kN

100   400   400

(d)

Fig. 5.7 (a) Side elevation; (b) section at support; (c) shear reinforcement; (d) load and shear force diagram.

$$71.7 = 117.8 - 38x$$
$$x = 1.21\,\text{m}$$

Adopt 8 mm diameter links where the area of two legs is 100 mm². The spacing of the links is given by

$$s_v = \frac{0.87 f_{yv} A_{sv}}{0.4 b_v} = \frac{0.87 \times 250 \times 100}{0.4 \times 250} = 217.5\,\text{mm}$$

$$\not> 0.75d = 0.75 \times 380 = 285\,\text{mm}$$

Provide 8 mm diameter links at 200 mm centres over the centre 3.8 m length of beam, i.e. at 1.1 m from the face of the support.

(b) Check the maximum shear stress at the face of the support

At the face of the support $d = 400$ mm.

$$v = \frac{114 \times 10^3}{250 \times 400} = 1.14\,\text{N/mm}^2$$

This is not greater than $0.8 f_{cu}^{1/2} = 4.8\,\text{N/mm}^2$ or $5\,\text{N/mm}^2$.

(c) Section between $2d = 800$ mm and $2d = 1100$ mm from the face of the support

Check at 800 mm from the support.

maximum shear = 83.6 kN

For tension reinforcement to be counted it must continue a distance d beyond the section where shear is checked. In this case the two curtailed bars stop 320 mm past the section and so are not considered.
The tension steel area $A_s = 942$ mm² and $d = 400$ mm.

$$\frac{100 A_s}{bd} = \frac{100 \times 942}{250 \times 400} = 0.94$$

$$v_c = 0.79 \times 0.94^{1/3}/1.25 = 0.619\,\text{N/mm}^2$$

The shear at $2d$ from the face of the support is 83.6 kN.

$$v = \frac{83.6 \times 1000}{250 \times 400} = 0.836\,\text{N/mm}^2$$

For the spacing of the 8 mm diameter links,

$$s_v = \frac{0.87 f_{yv} A_s}{bv(v - v_c)}$$

$$= \frac{0.87 \times 250 \times 100}{250(0.836 - 0.619)} = 400.9\,\text{mm}$$

Provide minimum links at 200 mm centres.

(d) Section between the face of the support and $2d$ from the face

Design using the simplified approach. The shear at d from the face of the support is 98.8 kN.

$$v = \frac{98.8 \times 1000}{250 \times 400} = 0.988\,\text{N/mm}^2$$

The design shear strength v_c was calculated above to be $0.619\,\text{N/mm}^2$. For the spacing of the 8 mm diameter links,

$$s_v = \frac{0.87 \times 250 \times 100}{250(0.988 - 0.619)} = 235.7\,\text{mm}$$

Provide minimum links at 200 mm centres.

(e) Check the section in (d) using enhanced design shear stress

The enhanced shear stress at $a_v = d$ from the support is

$$\frac{2dv_c}{a_v} = 2 \times 0.619 = 1.238\,\text{N/mm}^2$$

This exceeds the applied shear stress $v = 0.988\,\text{N/mm}^2$ and so minimum links only are required in this case. Note that the shear stress in this part of the beam does not exceed either the enhanced design shear stress or the maximum shear stress.

(f) Shear reinforcement

The shear reinforcement is shown in Fig. 5.7(c). Two 16 mm diameter bars are provided at the top of the beam to carry the links. Note that the top bars are not designed as compression steel. Thus the requirements of clause 3.12.7.1 set out in section 5.1.3(b) do not apply. ∎

□ Example 5.2 Design of shear reinforcement for rectangular beam

Design the shear reinforcement for a rectangular beam with the dimensions, loads and moment steel shown in Fig. 5.8. The concrete is grade 30 and the shear reinforcement grade 250.

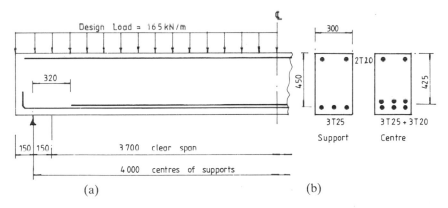

Fig. 5.8 (a) Side elevation; (b) section and moment steel.

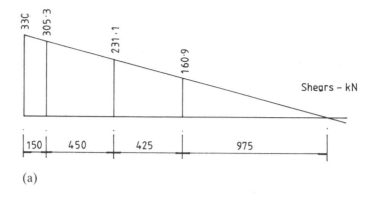

(a)

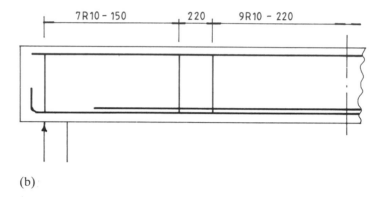

(b)

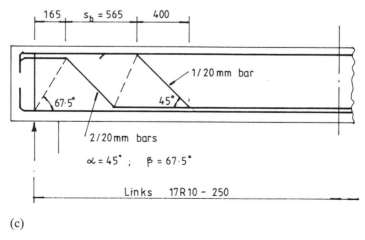

(c)

Fig. 5.9 (a) Shear force diagram; (b) shear reinforcement, vertical links; (c) shear reinforcement, bent-up bars and vertical links.

The shear at critical points is calculated and the results are shown in Fig. 5.9.

(a) Minimum links

At the centre of the beam $A_s = 2414\,mm^2$.

$$\frac{100A_s}{bd} = \frac{100 \times 2414}{300 \times 425} = 1.89$$

$$v_c = 0.79 \times 1.89^{1/3} \times (30/25)^{1/3}/1.25 = 0.83\,N/mm^2$$
$$V_c = 0.83 \times 300 \times 425/10^3 = 105.8\,kN$$

The distance from the support where the shear is equal to 105.8 kN is found from

$$105.8 = 330 - 165x$$
$$x = 1.36\,m$$

Adopt 10 mm diameter links; $A_{sv} = 157\,mm^2$.

$$s_v = \frac{0.87 \times 250 \times 157}{0.4 \times 300} = 284.6\,mm$$

$$\not> 0.75 \times 425 = 318.8$$

Top bars are designed as compression steel:

$$s_v \not> 12 \times 20 = 240\,mm$$

Provide 10 mm links at 220 mm centres in the centre 1.25 m length of the beam, i.e. at 1.225 m from the face of the support (Fig. 5.9(b)).

(b) Maximum shear at the face of the support

$$v = \frac{305.3 \times 10^3}{300 \times 450} = 2.26\,N/mm^2$$

$$\not> 0.8 f_{cu}^{1/2} = 4.38\,N/mm^2$$

This is satisfactory.

(c) Section between $2d = 875\,mm$ and $2d = 1225\,mm$ from the face of the support

The maximum shear is 160.9 kN.

$$v = \frac{160.9 \times 10^3}{300 \times 425} = 1.26\,N/mm^2$$

$$v_c = 0.83\,N/mm^2 \qquad \text{(see (a) above)}$$

Two rows of bars continue 705 mm past the section.

$$s_v = \frac{0.87 \times 250 \times 157}{300(1.26 - 0.83)} = 264.7\,mm$$

Provide links at 250 mm centres.

(d) Section between the face of the support and $2d = 875\,mm$ from the face

Consider first the accurate approach given in clause 3.4.5.9. Take the section at $d = 450\,mm$ from support. The curtailed bars do not extend d past the section, and so $A_s = 1472\,mm^2$.

$$\frac{100A_s}{bd} = \frac{100 \times 1472}{300 \times 450} = 1.09$$

$$v_c = 0.79(1.09)^{1/3}(30/25)^{1/3}/1.25 = 0.69 \, \text{N/mm}^2$$

$$a_v = d = 450 \, \text{mm}$$

At the section $V = 231.1 \, \text{kN}$:

$$v = \frac{231.1 \times 10^3}{300 \times 450} = 1.71 \, \text{N/mm}^2$$

The area of shear steel required is

$$\Sigma A_{sv} = \frac{450 \times 300(1.71 - 2 \times 0.69)}{0.87 \times 250} = 204.8 \, \text{mm}^2$$

Provide two 10 mm diameter links where $\Sigma A_{sv} = 314 \, \text{mm}^2$; space at 150 mm centres. Continue the same spacing to 900 mm from the support and then change to minimum links at 250 mm centres.

(e) Redesign the links in (d) using the simplified approach

The spacing for the 10 mm diameter links is given by

$$s_v = \frac{0.87 \times 250 \times 157}{300(1.71 - 0.69)} = 111.5 \, \text{mm}$$

Provide links at 100 mm centres between $2d$ and the face of the support.

(f) Shear reinforcement

This is shown in Fig. 5.9(b).   ∎

☐ Example 5.3 Design of shear reinforcement using bent up bars

Redesign the shear reinforcement in Example 5.2 using bent-up bars.

The arrangement for the bent-up bars is shown in Fig. 5.9(c) where the bars are bent up at 45°. The shear resistance of one 25 mm diameter grade 460 bar, where $A_{sb} = 490 \, \text{mm}^2$, is

$$V_b = 490 \times 0.87 \times 460(\cos 45° + \sin 45° \cot 67.5°) \frac{400}{565 \times 10^3}$$

$$= 138 \, \text{kN}$$

The shear at section XX 730 mm from the centre of the support is

$$V = 209.6 \, \text{kN}$$

Links must be provided to resist one-half the shear, i.e. 104.8 kN.
     At 165 mm from the centre of the support

$$V = 302.8 \, \text{kN}$$

For two 20 mm bent-up bars the shear resistance is

$$V_b = 276 \text{ kN}$$

Links must be provided to resist 151.4 kN.

Calculate the shear resistance of the section with minimum links, 10 mm links at 250 mm centres. The design shear strength of the concrete is

$$v_c = 0.69 \text{ N/mm}^2 \qquad \text{(Example 5.2(d))}$$

for the section with three 25 mm diameter tension bars. The nominal shear stress is

$$v = 0.69 + \frac{157 \times 0.87 \times 250}{250 \times 300} = 1.14 \text{ N/mm}^2$$

The shear resistance is

$$V = 1.14 \times 300 \times 450/10^3 = 154.6 \text{ kN}$$

The minimum links are satisfactory. The shear reinforcement is shown in Fig. 5.9(c).
■

5.1.4 Shear resistance of solid slabs

Slab design is treated in Chapter 8. One-way and two-way solid slabs are designed on the basis of a strip of unit width. The shear resistance of solid slabs is set out in BS 8110: Part 1, section 3.5.5.

The design shear stress is given by

$$v = V/bd$$

where b is the breadth of slab considered, generally 1 m.

The form and area of shear reinforcement is given in Table 3.17 of the code. When v is less than the design concrete shear stress v_c given in Table 3.9, no shear reinforcement is required. In Table 3.9 v_c increases with decrease in effective depth. This reflects the findings from tests that the shear resistance of members increses with decrease in depth.

Slabs carrying moderate loads such as floor slabs in office buildings and apartments do not normally require shear reinforcement. It is not desirable to have shear reinforcement in slabs with an effective depth of less than 200 mm. Where shear reinforcement is required, reference should be made to Table 3.17 of the code. The equations are similar to those for rectangular beams discussed earlier in the chapter.

5.1.5 Shear due to concentrated loads on slabs

Shear in slabs under concentrated loads is set out in BS 8110: Part 1, section 3.7.7. A concentrated load causes punching failure which occurs on inclined faces of a truncated cone or pyramid depending on the shape of the loaded area. The clause states that it is satisfactory to consider rectangular failure perimeters. The main rules for design for punching are as follows (Fig. 5.10).

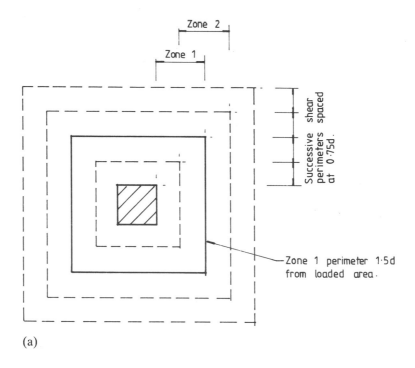

Zone 2

Zone 1

Successive shear perimeters spaced at 0·75d.

Zone 1 perimeter 1·5d from loaded area.

(a)

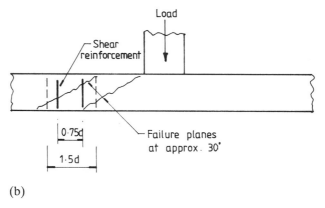

Load

Shear reinforcement

0·75d

1·5d

Failure planes at approx. 30°

(b)

Fig. 5.10 (a) Plan; (b) section.

(a) Maximum design shear capacity

The maximum design shear stress is

$$v_{\max} = \frac{V}{u_0 d}$$

where u_0 is the effective length of the perimeter which touches a loaded area. This is the perimeter of the column in Fig. 5.10. The shear stress v_{max} is not to exceed $0.8f_{cu}^{1/2}$ or $5\,N/mm^2$.

(b) Design shear stress for a failure zone

The nominal shear stress in a failure zone is given by

$$v = V/ud$$

where u is the effective length of the perimeter of the failure zone.

If v is less than v_c (Table 3.9 of the code) no shear reinforcement is required. The code also states that enhancement of v_c may not be applied to the shear strength of a perimeter at a distance of $1.5d$ or more from the face of the loaded area. For a perimeter less than $1.5d$, v_c can be enhanced by the factor $1.5d/a_v$ where a_v is the distance from the face of the loaded area to the perimeter considered.

The code (Fig. 3.17) shows the location of successive shear perimeters on which shear stresses are checked and the division of the slab into shear zones for design of shear reinforcement. Shear perimeters and zones are shown in Fig. 5.10. The design procedure is set out in clause 3.7.7.6 of the code. Zone 1, which has its perimeter at $1.5d$ from the loaded area, is checked first. The clause states that if this zone does not require reinforcement, i.e. the shear stress v is less than v_c, then no further checks are required.

Design of shear reinforcement is set out in clause 3.7.7.5 of the code for slabs over 200 mm thick. The reader is referred to the code for further information.

5.2 BOND, LAPS AND BEARING STRESSES IN BENDS

Bond is the grip due to adhesion or mechanical interlock and bearing in deformed bars between the reinforcement and the concrete. A distinction is made between two types of bond:

anchorage bond
local bond

5.2.1 Anchorage bond

Anchorage is the embedment of a bar in concrete so that it can carry load through bond between the steel and concrete. A pull-out test on a bar is shown in Fig. 5.11(a). If the anchorage length is sufficient the full strength of the bar can be developed by bond. Anchorages for bars in a beam to external column joints and in a column base are shown in 5.11(b) and 5.11(c) respectively. Clause 3.12.8.1 of the code states that the embedment

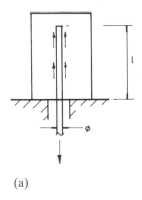

(a)

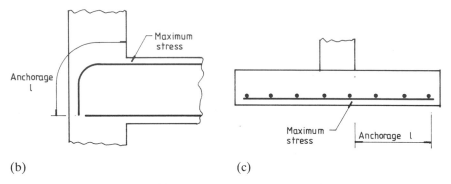

(b)   (c)

Fig. 5.11 (a) Pull-out test; (b) beam to external column; (c) column base.

length in the concrete is to be sufficient to develop the force in the bar.

Clause 3.12.8.3 of the code states that the design anchorage bond stress is assumed to be constant over the anchorage length. It is given by

$$f_b = \frac{F_s}{\pi \phi_e l}$$

where F_s is the force in the bar or group of bars, l is the anchorage length and ϕ_e is the nominal diameter for a single bar or the diameter of a bar of equal total area for a group of bars. The anchorage length l should be such that the bond stress does not exceed the design ultimate anchorage bond stress given by

$$f_{bu} = \beta f_{cu}^{1/2}$$

β is a coefficient that depends on the bar type. Values of β are given in Table 3.28 of the code from which the following is extracted:

Plain bars   tension $\beta = 0.28$
                          compression $\beta = 0.35$
Type 2 deformed bars   tension $\beta = 0.5$
                          compression $\beta = 0.63$

Type 2 bars are rolled with transverse ribs. The values of β apply in slabs and beams with minimum links. End bearing is taken into account in bars in compression and this gives a higher ultimate bond stress. The values include a partial safety factor $\gamma_m = 1.4$.

☐ Example 5.4 Calculation of anchorage lengths

Calculate the anchorage lengths in tension and compression for a grade 460 type 2 deformed bar of diameter ϕ in grade 30 concrete.

(a) Tension anchorage

The ultimate anchorage bond stress is

$$f_{bu} = 0.5 \times 30^{1/2} = 2.74 \, \text{N/mm}^2$$

Equate the anchorage bond resistance to the ultimate strength of the bar (Fig. 5.11(a)):

$$f_{bu}\pi\phi l = 0.87 f_y \pi \phi^2 / 4$$
$$l = \frac{0.87 \times 460 \times \pi\phi^2}{4 \times \pi\phi \times 2.74} = 37\psi$$

(b) Compression anchorage

$$f_{bu} = 0.63 \times 30^{1/2} = 3.74 \, \text{N/mm}^2$$
$$l = 29\phi$$

Ultimate anchorage bond lengths are given in BS 8110: Part 1, Table 3.29. ■

5.2.2 Local bond

For a reinforced concrete beam to act as designed there must be no slip between the concrete and the reinforcement. Local bond stresses are set up in sections of elements subjected to shear where the change in force in the tension steel is transmitted to the concrete in bond.

The theoretical expression for the local bond stress can be derived by reference to Fig. 5.12. The bar tension $T = M/z$. The change in tension on the short length of bar shown in Fig. 5.12(c) is

$$\delta T = \delta M / z$$

The change in bending moment is

$$\delta M = V \delta x$$

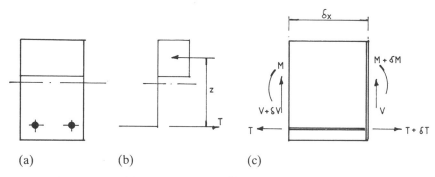

Fig. 5.12 (a) Section; (b) internal forces; (c) short length of beam.

The force δT is transmitted by bond to the concrete. If the local bond stress is f and the sum of the bar perimeters is U, then

$$fU\,\delta x = V\,\delta x/z$$
$$f = V/Uz$$

Clause 3.12.8.1 of the code states that if the required embedment length is provided on either side of any cross-section the local bond stress may be ignored. Thus no check for local bond stress is required.

5.2.3 Hooks and bends

Hooks and bends are used to shorten the length required for anchorage. Clause 3.12.8.23 of the code states that the effective length of a hook or bend is the length of the straight bar which has the same anchorage value as that part of the bar between the start of the bend and a point four bar diameters past the end of the bend.

The effective anchorage lengths given in the code are as follows.

1. 180° hook: whichever is the greater of
    (a) 8 times the internal radius of the hook but not greater than 24 times the bar diameter or
    (b) the actual length of the hook including the straight portion
2. 90° bend: whichever is the greater of
    (a) 4 times the internal radius of the bend but not greater than 12 times the bar diameter or
    (b) the actual length of the bar

For the 90° bend any length past four bar diameters at the end of the bend may also be included in the anchorage.

The radius of bend should not be less than twice the radius of the bend guaranteed by the manufacturer. A radius of two bar diameters is generally

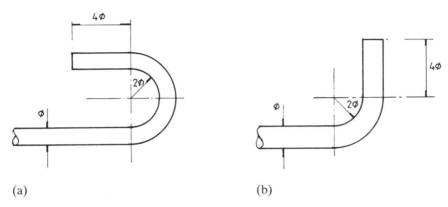

Fig. 5.13 (a) 180° hook; (b) 90° bend.

used for mild steel and three bar diameters for high yield steel. The hook and bend are shown in Fig. 5.13.

5.2.4 Laps and joints

Lengths of reinforcing bars are joined by lapping, by mechanical couplers or by butt or lap welded joints. Only lapping is discussed here.

The minimum lap length specified in clause 3.12.8.11 is not to be less than 15 × the bar diameter or 300 mm. From clause 3.12.8.13 the requirements for tension laps are the following:

1. The lap length is not to be less than the tension anchorage length;
2. If the lap is at the top of the section and the cover is less than two bar diameters the lap length is to be increased by 1.4;
3. If the lap is at the corner of a section and the cover is less than two bar diameters the lap length is to be increased by 1.4;
4. If conditions 2 and 3 both apply the lap length is to be doubled.

The length of compression laps should be 1.25 times the length of compression anchorage.

Note that all lap lengths are based on the smaller bar diameter. The code gives values for lap lengths in Table 3.29. It also sets out requirements for mechanical couplers in clause 3.12.8.16.2 and for the welding of reinforcing bars in clauses 3.12.8.17 and 3.12.8.18.

5.2.5 Bearing stresses inside bends

It is often necessary to anchor a bar by extending it around a bend in a stressed state, as shown in Fig. 5.14(a). It may also be necessary to take a stressed bar through a bend as shown in Fig. 5.14(b).

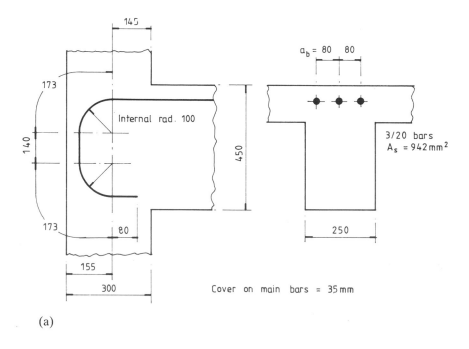

(a)

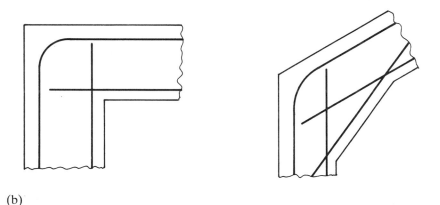

(b)

Fig. 5.14 (a) Anchorage at end of beam; (b) stressed bars carried around bends.

In BS 8110: Part 1, clause 3.12.8.25.1, it is stated that if the bar does not extend or is not assumed to be stressed beyond a point four times the bar diameter past the end of the bend no check need be made. If it is assumed to be stressed beyond this point, the bearing stress inside the bend must be checked using the equation

$$\text{bearing stress} = \frac{F_{bt}}{r\phi}$$

The bearing stress is not to exceed

$$\frac{2f_{cu}}{1 + 2(\phi/a_b)}$$

where F_{bt} is the tensile force due to ultimate loads in the bar or group of bars, r is the internal radius of the bend, ϕ is the bar diameter or, for a group, the size of bar of equivalent area and a_b, for a bar or group of bars in contact, is the centre-to-centre distance between the bars or groups perpendicular to the bend; for a bar or group of bars adjacent to the face of a member a_b is taken as the cover plus ϕ.

□ Example 5.5 Design of anchorage at beam support

Referring to Fig. 5.14(a), three 20 mm diameter grade 460 deformed type 2 bars are to be anchored past the face of the column. The concrete is grade 30. From Table 3.4 of the code the nominal cover to 10 mm diameter links for mild exposure is 25 mm. The area of tension reinforcement required in the design is 810 mm². Design the anchorage required for the bars.

The ultimate anchorage bond stres is

$$f_{cu} = 0.5 \times 30^{1/2} = 2.74 \, \text{N/mm}^2$$

The anchorage length (see section 5.2.1) is

$$l = \frac{0.87 \times 460 \times 810\phi}{4 \times 2.74 \times 942} = 31.4\phi = 628 \, \text{mm}$$

The full anchorage length is $37\phi - 740$ mm. The internal radius of the bends is taken to be 100 mm and the cover on the main bars is 35 mm. The arrangement for the anchorage is shown in Fig. 5.14(a).

Referring to section 5.2.3 the anchorage length for the lower 90° bend is the greater of

1. 4 × internal radius = 400 but not greater than 12 × bar diameter = 240 or
2. the actual length of the bar, i.e. 173 + 80 = 253

Thus the total anchorage provided past the face of the column is

$$145 + 173 + 140 + 253 = 711 \, \text{mm}$$

From the figure the bars are at 80 mm centres. The ultimate bearing stress is

$$\frac{2 \times 30}{1 + 2(20/80)} = 40 \, \text{N/mm}^2$$

The tensile force due to ultimate loads at the centre of the top bend in one bar is

$$F_{bt} = \frac{711 - 231.5}{711} \frac{0.87 \times 460 \times 810 \times 314}{942 \times 10^3} = 72.9\,kN$$

$$\text{bearing stress} = \frac{72.9 \times 10^3}{100 \times 20} = 36.5\,N/mm^2$$

The arrangement is satisfactory. Full anchorage could be provided by increasing the length past the lower bend from 80 to 110 mm. ∎

5.3 TORSION

5.3.1 Occurrence and analysis

BS 8110: Part 1, clause 3.4.5.13, states that in normal slab and beam or framed construction specific calculations for torsion are not usually necessary. Shear reinforcement will control cracking due to torsion adequately. However, when the design relies on torsional resistance, specific design for torsion is required. Such a case is the overhanging slab shown in Fig. 5.15(a).

5.3.2 Structural analysis including torsion

Rigid frame buildings, although three dimensional, are generally analysed as a series of plane frames. This is a valid simplification because the torsional stiffness is much less than the bending stiffness. Figure 5.16(a)

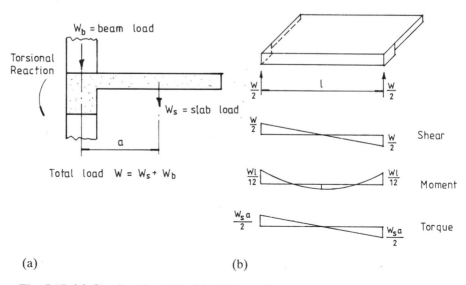

(a)   (b)

Fig. 5.15 (a) Overhanging slab; (b) design actions

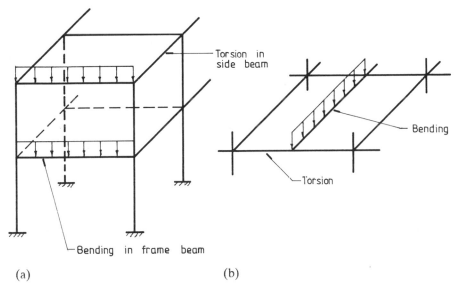

Fig. 5.16 (a) Three-dimensional frame; (b) floor system.

shows where bending in the beams in the transverse frames causes torsion in the longitudinal side beams, where only the end frame beams are loaded. In Fig. 5.16(b) the loading on the intermediate floor beam causes torsion in the support beams. Analysis of the building as a space frame for various arrangements of loading would be necessary to determine maximum design conditions including torsion for all members.

It torsion is to be taken into account in structural analysis BS 8110: Part 2, clause 2.4.3, specifies that

$$\text{torsional rigidity} = GC$$

where $G = 0.42E_c$ is the shear modulus, E_c is the modulus of elasticity of the concrete and C is the torsional constant and is equal to one-half of the St Venant value for the plain concrete section.

The code states that the St Venant torsional stiffness may be calculated from the equation

$$C = \beta h_{min}^{3} h_{max}$$

where β depends on the ratio h/b of the overall depth divided by the breadth. Values of β are given in Table 2.2 in the code. If the section is square $\beta = 1.4$. Also, h_{max} is the larger dimension of a rectangular section and h_{min} is the smaller dimension. The code also gives a procedure for dealing with non-rectangular sections.

5.3.3 Torsional shear stress in a concrete section

In an elastic material the maximum shear stress due to pure torsion occurs in the middle of the longer side of a rectangular section $b \times h$ (Fig. 5.17(a)). The torsional shear stress is given by

$$f_v = T/Kb^2h$$

where T is the applied torque and K is a constant that depends on the ratio h/b. For a square section $K = 0.2$. See *Theory of Elasticity* [14].

In elastic theory the torsional shear stress is found by solving a partial differential equation. An analogous problem involving the same equation occurs if the end of a thin wall tube of the same shape as the section is covered with a membrane and subjected to pressure, as shown in Fig. 5.17(b). It is found that the slope of the membrane at any point is proportional to the shear stress at that point and the volume enclosed by the

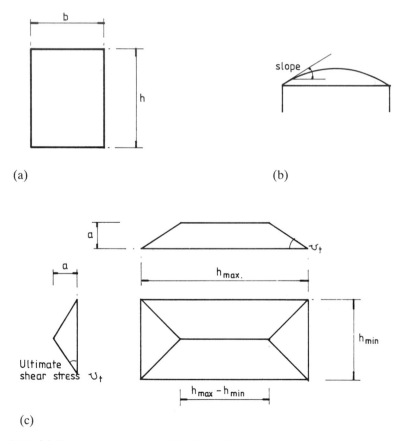

(a)   (b)

(c)

Fig. 5.17 (a) Rectangular section; (b) elastic film; (c) ultimate limit state.

membrane is proportional to the applied torque. This is the membrane analogy and is used as an experimental method for determining torsional shear stresses.

If the analogy is extended to the plastic state, the stresses reach the yield value, the slope of the membrane is constant and the shear stress is now at its ultimate value v_t. This is called the sand heap analogy. The heap is conical for a circular section, pyramid shaped for a square and pitched-roof-shaped for the rectangular section shown in Fig. 5.17(c). The expression for the torsional shear stress and ultimate torque given in BS 8110: Part 2, clause 2.4.4, can be derived for the sand heap shape as follows, where h_{max}, h_{min} are section dimensions, a is the height of the sand heap, the torsional shear stress v_t is equal to the slope of the sand heap, i.e. $v_t = 2a/h_{min}$, and the ultimate torque T is twice the volume of the sand heap, i.e.

$$T = 2[\tfrac{1}{3}h_{min}{}^2 a + \tfrac{1}{2}h_{min}a(h_{max} - h_{min})]$$

Substitute $a = \tfrac{1}{2}v_t h_{min}$. Then

$$T = 0.5 v_t h_{min}{}^2(h_{max} - h_{min}/3)$$

and

$$v_t = \frac{2T}{h_{min}{}^2(h_{max} - h_{min}/3)}$$

The code states that T- and L-sections are to be treated by dividing them into component rectangles. The division is to be such as to maximize the function $\Sigma(h_{min}{}^3 h_{max})$. This will be achieved if the widest rectangle is made as long as possible. The torque resisted by each component rectangle is to be taken as

$$T\frac{h_{min}{}^3 h_{max}}{\Sigma(h_{min}{}^3 h_{max})}$$

If the torsional shear stress v_t exceeds the value of $v_{t,min}$ given in BS 8110: Part 2, Table 2.3, reinforcement must be provided.

The sum $v + v_t$ of the shear stresses from direct shear and torsion must not exceed the value of v_{tu} given in Table 2.4 of the code. In addition, for small sections where $y_1 < 550$ mm, v_t should not exceed $v_{tu}y_1/550$, where y_1 is the larger dimension of the link. This restriction is to prevent concrete breaking away at the corners of small sections. Values of shear stresses in design for torsion are given by

$$v_{t,min} = 0.067 f_{cu}{}^{1/2} \qquad \text{but } v_{t,min} \not> 0.4\,\text{N/mm}^2$$
$$v_{tu} = 0.8 f_{cu}{}^{1/2} \qquad \text{but } v_{tu} \not> 5.0\,\text{N/mm}^2$$

5.3.4 Torsional reinforcement

A concrete beam subjected to torsion fails in diagonal tension on each face to form cracks running in a spiral around the beam, as shown in Fig. 5.18(a). The torque may be replaced by the shear forces V on each face. The action on each face is similar to vertical shear in a beam. Reinforcement to resist torsion is provided in the form of closed links and longitudinal bars. This steel together with diagonal bands of concrete in compression form a space truss which resists torsion. This is illustrated in Fig. 5.18(b).

Refer to Fig. 5.18(c) which shows the torsional reinforcement. Define the terms as follows.

x_1 smaller dimension of the link
y_1 larger dimension of the link
A_{sv} area of two legs of the link
f_{yv} characteristic strength of the link

Assuming cracks at 45° the number of links crossing the cracks is y_1/s_v on the sides and x_1/s_v on the top and bottom faces. The force in one link due to torsion is $0.87f_{yv}A_{sv}/2$. The torsional resistance of all links crossing the cracks is

$$\frac{0.87f_{yv}A_{sv}}{2}\left(\frac{x_1y_1}{s_v} + \frac{y_1x_1}{s_v}\right)$$

Thus the torque is

$$T = 0.87f_{yv}A_{sv}x_1y_1/s_v$$

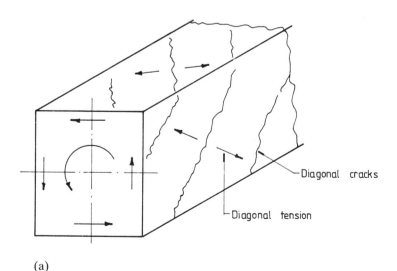

Diagonal cracks

Diagonal tension

(a)

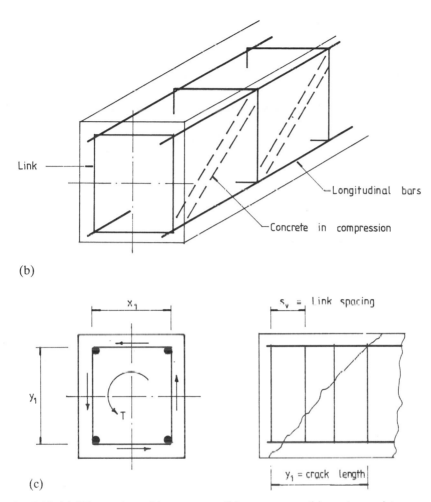

(b)

(c)

Fig. 5.18 (a) Diagonal cracking pattern; (b) space truss; (c) torsion resistance.

The expression given in the BS 8110: Part 2, clause 2.4.7, is

$$\frac{A_{sv}}{s_v} > \frac{T}{0.8x_1y_1(0.87f_{yv})}$$

A safety factor of 1/0.8 has been introduced.

The links and longitudinal bars should fail together. This is achieved by making the steel volume multiplied by the characteristic strength the same for each set of bars. This gives

$$A_{sv}(x_1 + y_1)f_{yv} = A_s s_v f_y$$

01

$$A_s = \frac{A_{sv}f_{yv}(x_1 + y_1)}{s_v f_y}$$

where A_s is the area of longitudinal reinforcement and f_y is the characteristic strength of the longitudinal reinforcement. This is the expression given in the code.

The code also states that the spacing of the links is not to exceed x_1, $y_1/2$ or 200 mm. The links are to be of the closed type to shape code 74 in BS 4466 (1981), as shown in Fig. 5.19(a). The longitudinal reinforcement is to be distributed evenly around the inside perimeter of the links. The clear distance between these bars should not exceed 300 mm and at least four bars, one in each corner, are required.

The torsion reinforcement is in addition to that required for moment and shear. In design, the longitudinal steel areas for moment and torsion and the link size and spacing for shear and torsion are calculated separately and combined.

BS 8110: Part 2, clause 2.4.10, states that the link cages should interlock in T- and L-sections and tie the component rectangles together as shown in Fig. 5.19(b). If the torsional shear stress in a minor component rectangle does not exceed $v_{t,min}$ then no torsional shear reinforcement need be provided in that rectangle.

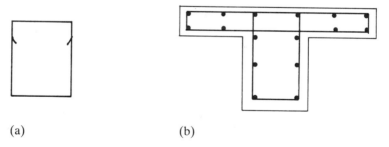

(a)   (b)

Fig. 5.19 (a) Closed link; (b) torque reinforcement for a T-beam.

☐ Example 5.6 Design of torsion steel for rectangular beam

A rectangular beam section has an overall depth of 500 mm and a breadth of 300 mm. It is subjected to an ultimate vertical hogging moment of 387.6 kN m, an ultimate vertical shear of 205 kN and a torque of 13 kN m. Design the longitudinal steel and links required at the section. The materials are grade 30 concrete, grade 460 reinforcement for the main bars and grade 250 for the links.

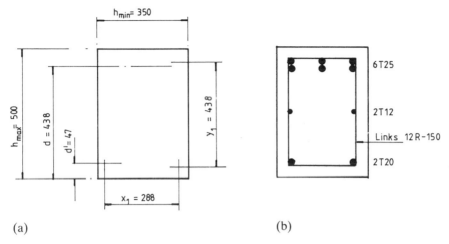

Fig. 5.20 (a) Section and design dimensions; (b) reinforcement.

The section is shown in Fig. 5.20(a) with the internal dimensions for locations of longitudinal bars and links taken for design. These dimensions are based on 25 mm cover, 12 mm diameter links and 25 mm diameter main bars at the top in vertical pairs and 20 mm bars at the bottom.

(a) Vertical bending moment (section 4.5.1)

$$M_{RC} = 0.156 \times 30 \times 350 \times 438^2/10^6 = 314.2 \, \text{kN m}$$

$$A_s' = \frac{(387.6 - 346.6)10^6}{(438 - 47) \times 0.87 \times 460} = 469.1 \, \text{mm}^2$$

$$A_s = \frac{(0.203 \times 30 \times 350 \times 438) + (0.87 \times 460 \times 469.1)}{0.87 \times 460}$$

$$= 2801.9 \, \text{mm}^2$$

(b) Vertical shear reinforcement (sections 5.1.2 and 5.1.3)

$$\frac{100 A_s}{bd} = \frac{100 \times 2801.9}{350 \times 460} = 1.74$$

$$v_c = 0.79 \times 1.74^{1/3} \times (30/25)^{1/3}/1.75$$

$$= 0.81 \, \text{N/mm}^2$$

$$v = \frac{205 \times 10^3}{438 \times 350} = 1.34 \, \text{N/mm}^2$$

Assuming a spacing for the links of 150 mm,

$$A_{sv} = \frac{350 \times 150(1.34 - 0.81)}{0.87 \times 250} = 127.9 \, \text{mm}^2$$

This exceeds the minimum area of the links:

$$A_{sv} = 0.4b_v s_v / 0.87 f_{yv}$$

The spacing selected is less than $0.75d$. The steel area will be added to that required for torsion below.

(c) Torsion reinforcement

$$v_t = \frac{2 \times 13 \times 10^6}{350^2(500 + 350/3)} = 0.55 \, \text{N/mm}^2$$

From BS 8110: Part 2, Table 2.3,

$$v_{t,min} = 0.37 \, \text{N/mm}^2$$

$$v + v_t = 1.334 + 0.55 = 1.89 \, \text{N/mm}^2$$

This is less than $v_{tu} = 4.38 \, \text{N/mm}^2$ from Table 2.3. The value of v_t is also less than

$$\frac{v_{tu} y_1}{550} = \frac{4.38 \times 438}{550} = 3.49 \, \text{N/mm}^2$$

For 150 mm spacing of links the area of links to resist torsional shear is

$$A_{sv} = \frac{150 \times 13 \times 10^6}{0.8 \times 288 \times 438 \times 0.87 \times 250} = 88.8 \, \text{mm}^2$$

The total area of one leg of a link is

$$(88.8 + 127.9)/2 = 108.4 \, \text{mm}^2$$

Links 12 mm in diameter with an area of 113 mm^2 are required.

The spacing must not exceed $x_1 = 288$ mm, $y_1/2 = 438/2 = 219$ or 200 mm. The spacing of 150 mm is satisfactory.

The area of longitudinal reinforcement

$$A_s = \frac{88.8 \times 250(288 + 438)}{150 \times 460} = 233.6 \, \text{mm}^2$$

This area is to be distributed equally around the perimeter.

(d) Arrangement of reinforcement

The clear distance between longitudinal bars required to resist torsion is not to exceed 300 mm. Six bars with a theoretical area of $233.6/6 = 38.9 \, \text{mm}^2$ per bar are required. For the bottom steel

$$A_s' = 469.1 + 2 \times 38.9 = 546.9 \, \text{mm}^2$$

Provide two 20 mm diameter bars, of area 628 mm^2. For the top steel

$$A_s = 2801.9 + 2 \times 38.9 = 2879.7 \, \text{mm}^2$$

Provide six 25 mm diameter bars in vertical pairs, of area 2945 mm^2. for the centre bars provide two 12 mm diameter bars of area 113 mm^2 per bar. The reinforcement is shown in Fig. 5.20(b). ∎

☐ Example 5.7 Design of torsion steel for T-beam

The T-beam shown in Fig. 5.21(a) spans 8 m. The ends of the beam are simply supported for vertical load and restrained against torsion. The beam carries an ultimate distributed verical load of 24 kN/m. A column is supported on one flange at the centre of the beam and transmits an ultimate load of 50 kN to the beam as shown. Design the reinforcement at the centre of the beam for the T-beam section only. A transverse strengthening beam would be provided at the centre of the beam but design for this is not part of the problem. The materials are grade 30 concrete, grade 460 for the longitudinal reinforcement and grade 280 for the links.

The ultimate beam actions are calculated. The maximum vertical shear is

$$V_A = (0.5 \times 24 \times 8) + (0.5 \times 50) = 121 \, \text{kN}$$

The maximum vertical moment is

$$M_c = 24 \times 8^2/8 + 50 \times 8/4 = 292 \, \text{kN m}$$

The torque is

$$T = 50 \times 0.7 \times 0.5 = 17.5 \, \text{kN m}$$

The load, shear force, bending moment and torque diagrams are shown in Fig. 5.21(c).

The T-section is split into component rectangles such that $\Sigma (h_{min}{}^3 h_{max})$ is a maximum. Check:

1. flange (1600 × 150) + rib (350 × 300) gives

$$(150^3 \times 1600) + (300^2 \times 350) = 5.4 \times 10^9 + 9.45 \times 10^9$$
$$= 14.85 \times 10^9$$

2. rib (500 × 300) + two flanges (650 × 150) gives

$$(300^3 \times 500) + (2 \times 150^3 \times 650) = 13.5 \times 10^9 + 4.39 \times 10^9$$
$$= 17.89 \times 10^9$$

Arrangement 2 is adopted where the widest rectangle has been made as long as possible. The dimensions adopted for design are shown in Fig. 5.21(b). Cover has been taken as 25 mm, the links are 12 mm in diameter and the main bars 25 mm diameter.

(a) Vertical moment

Refer to sections 4.8.2 and 4.4.6. For the case where $0.9x = h_f = 150$ mm

$$M_R = 0.45 \times 30 \times 1600 \times 150(438 - 0.5 \times 100)/10^6$$
$$= 1257.1 \, \text{kN m}$$
$$> 292 \, \text{kN m}$$

The neutral axis lies in the flange.

$$K = \frac{292 \times 10^6}{30 \times 1600 \times 438^2} = 0.032$$

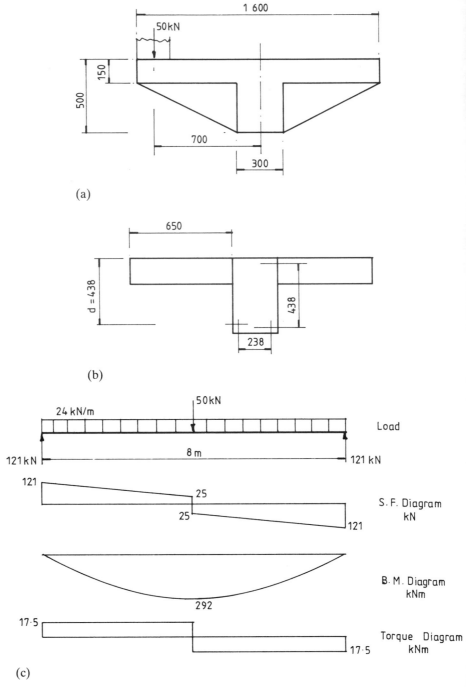

Fig. 5.21 (a) Section; (b) dimensions for design; (c) beam design actions.

$$z = 438[0.5 + (0.25 - 0.032/0.9)^{0.5}]$$
$$= 421.8 \, \text{mm}$$
$$> 0.95d = 416.1 \, \text{mm}$$
$$A_s = \frac{292 \times 10^6}{0.87 \times 460 \times 416.1} = 1753.3 \, \text{mm}^2$$

(b) Vertical shear at the centre of the beam

$$\frac{100A_s}{bd} = \frac{100 \times 1753.5}{300 \times 438} = 1.33$$
$$v_c = 0.79[1.33^{1/3} \times (30/25)^{1/3}]/1.25$$
$$= 0.738 \, \text{N/mm}^2$$
$$v = \frac{25 \times 10^3}{300 \times 438} = 0.19 \, \text{N/mm}^2$$

Nominal links only are required. If a spacing of 175 mm is adopted the minimum area of two legs is

$$A_{sv} = \frac{0.4 \times 300 \times 175}{0.87 \times 250} = 96.6 \, \text{mm}^2$$

(c) Torsion stress and reinforcement

The torsion taken by the two flange sections is

$$\frac{4.39 \times 10^9 \times 17.5}{17.89 \times 10^9} = 4.29 \, \text{kN m}$$

The torque taken by the rib is

$$17.5 - 4.29 = 13.21 \, \text{kN m}$$

Flange $$v_t = \frac{2 \times 4.298 \times 10^6}{2 \times 150^2(650 - 150/3)} = 0.32 \, \text{N/mm}^2$$

Rib $$v_t = \frac{2 \times 13.21 \times 10^6}{300^2(500 - 300/3)} = 0.734 \, \text{N/mm}^2$$

From BS 8110: Part 2, Table 2.3,

$$v_{t,\text{min}} = 0.37 \, \text{N/mm}^2$$

For the rib

$$v + v_t = 0.19 + 0.734 = 0.924 \, \text{N/mm}^2$$
$$v_{tu} = 4.38 \, \text{N/mm}^2 \qquad \text{(Table 2.3)}$$
$$v_{tu} \times 438/550 = 3.49 \, \text{N/mm}^2$$

The stresses are satisfactory with regard to maximum values.
The torsion steel is designed for the rib taking a spacing for the links of 175 mm:

$$A_{sv} = \frac{175 \times 13.21 \times 10^6}{0.8 \times 238 \times 438 \times 0.87 \times 250} = 127.5 \, \text{mm}^2$$

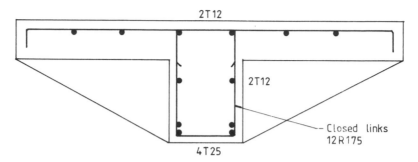

Fig. 5.22 Reinforcement in centre rib.

The total area for two legs is $96.6 + 127.5 = 224.1 \, \text{mm}^2$. Provide 12 mm diameter links, with the area of two legs equal to $226 \, \text{mm}^2$. The link spacing must not be greater than $x_1 = 238 \, \text{mm}$, $y_1/2 = 438/2 = 219$ or 200 mm. The spacing of 175 mm is satisfactory.

The area of longitudinal steel required is

$$A_s = \frac{109.3 \times 250(238 + 438)}{175 \times 460} = 229.5 \, \text{mm}^2$$

Six bars with a theoretical area of $38.2 \, \text{mm}^2$ per bar are required.

For the flange portions, v_t is less than $v_{t,\text{min}}$ and torsional reinforcement is not required.

(d) Reinforcement arrangement

For the bottom steel

$$A_s = 1753.5 + 2 \times 38.2 = 1829.9 \, \text{mm}^2$$

Provide four 25 mm diameter bars, of area $1963 \, \text{mm}^2$. For the top and centre of the rib, provide two 12 mm diameter bars at each location. The distance between the longitudinal bars is not to exceed 300 mm. Reinforcement would have to be provided to support the load on the flange. The moment shear and torsion reinforcement for the rib is shown in Fig. 5.22. ■

6

Deflection and cracking

6.1 DEFLECTION

6.1.1 Deflection limits and checks

Limits for the serviceability limit state of deflection are set out in BS 8110: Part 2, clause 3.2.1. It is stated in this clause that the deflection is noticeable if it exceeds $L/250$ where L is the span of a beam or length of a cantilever. Deflection due to dead load can be offset by precambering.

The code also states that damage to partitions, cladding and finishes will generally occur if the deflection exceeds

1. $L/500$ or 20 mm whichever is the lesser for brittle finishes
2. $L/350$ or 20 mm whichever is the lesser for non-brittle finishes

Design can be made such as to accommodate the deflection of structural members without causing damage to partitions or finishes.

Two methods are given in BS 8110: Part 1 for checking that deflection is not excessive:

1. limiting the span-to-effective depth ratio using the procedure set out in clause 3.4.6 – this method should be used in all normal cases
2. calculation of deflection from curvatures set out in BS 8110: Part 2, sections 3.6 and 3.7

6.1.2 Span to effective depth ratio

In a homogeneous elastic beam of span L, if the maximum stress is limited to an allowable value p and the deflection is limited to span/q, then for a given load a unique value of span-to-depth ratio L/d can be determined to limit stress and deflection to their allowable values simultaneously. Thus for the simply supported beam with a uniform load shown in Fig. 6.1

$$\text{maximum stress } p = \frac{WL}{8} \frac{d}{2I}$$

where I is the moment of inertia of the beam section, d is the depth of the beam and L is the span. The allowable deflection is

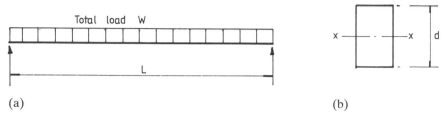

Fig. 6.1 (a) Beam load; (b) section.

$$\frac{L}{q} = \frac{5WL^3}{384EI}$$

$$= \frac{WLd}{16I}\frac{5L^2}{24Ed}$$

Thus

$$\frac{\text{span}}{\text{depth}} = \frac{L}{d} = \frac{4.8E}{pq}$$

where E is Young's modulus.

Similar reasoning may be used to establish span-to-effective depth ratios for reinforced concrete beams to control deflection. The method in the code is based on calculation and confirmed by tests. The main factors affecting the deflection of the beam are taken into account. The allowable value for the span-to-effective depth ratio calculated using the procedure given in clause 3.4.6 of the code for normal cases depends on

1. the basic span-to-effective depth ratio for rectangular or flanged beams and the support conditions
2. the amount of tension steel and its stress
3. the amount of compression steel

These considerations are discussed briefly below.

(a) Basic span-to-effective depth ratios

The code states that the basic span-to-effective depth ratios given in Table 3.10 for rectangular and flanged beams are so determined as to limit the total deflection to span/250. This ensures that deflection occurring after construction is limited to span/350 or 20 mm whichever is the less. The support conditions are also taken into account.

The values given for rectangular beams are modified when a flanged beam is checked. Thus:

1. If the web width b_w is less than or equal to 0.3 of the effective flange width b, the reduction is 0.8;

Table 6.1 Basic span-to-effective depth ratios

Support conditions	Span-to-effective depth ratio	
	Rectangular beam	*Flanged beams, $b_w/b \leqslant 0.3$*
Cantilever	7	5.6
Simply supported	20	16.0
Continuous	26	20.8

2. If the web width b_w is greater than 0.3 of the effective flange width b, reduction is to vary linearly between 0.8 at $b_w/b = 0.3$ to 1.0 at $b_w/b = 1$.

The reduction is made because in the flanged beam there is not as much concrete in the tension zone and the stiffness of the beam is reduced (see calculation of deflection below).

The basic span-to-effective depth ratios from Table 3.10 of the code are given in Table 6.1. The values in the table apply to beams with spans up to 10 m. Refer to clause 3.4.6.4 of the code for beams of longer span.

(b) Tension reinforcement (clause 3.4.6.5 of the code)

The deflection is influenced by the amount of tension reinforcement and the value of the stress at service loads at the centre of the span for beams or at the support for cantilevers. The basic span-to-effective depth ratio from Table 3.10 of the code is multiplied by the modification factor from Table 3.11. The modification factor is given by the formula in the code:

$$\text{modification factor} = 0.55 + \frac{477 - f_s}{120(0.9 + M/bd^2)} \leqslant 2.0$$

Note that the amount of tension reinforcement present is measured by the term M/bd^2, (section 4.4.7).

The service stress is estimated from the equation

$$f_s = \frac{5f_y A_{s,req}}{8A_{s,prov}} \frac{1}{\beta_b}$$

where $A_{s,req}$ is the area of tension steel required at mid-span to support ultimate loads (at the support for a cantilever), $A_{s,prov}$ is the area of tension steel provided at mid-span (at the support for a cantilever) and

$$\beta_b = \frac{\text{moment after redistribution}}{\text{moment before redistribution}}$$

(moments are from the maximum moment diagrams). The following comments are made concerning the expression for service stress:

1. The stress due to service loads is given by $\frac{5}{8}f_y$. This takes account of partial factors of safety for loads and materials used in design for the ultimate limit state;
2. If more steel is provided than required the service stress is reduced by the ratio $A_{s,req}/A_{s,prov}$;
3. If the service stress has been modified by redistribution, it is corrected by the amount adopted.

It is stated in Table 3.11 of the code that for a continuous beam if the amount of redistribution is not known f_s may be taken as $\frac{5}{8}f_y$.

It can be noted from Table 3.11 in the code that for a given section with the reinforcement at a given service stress the allowable span/d ratio is lower when the section contains a larger amount of steel. This is because when the steel stress, measured by M/bd^2, is increased

1. the depth to the neutral axis is increased and therefore the curvature for a given steel stress increases (see calculation of deflections below)
2. there is a larger area of concrete in compression which leads to larger deflections due to creep
3. the smaller portion of concrete in the tension zone reduces the stiffness of the beam

Providing more steel than required reduces the service stress and this increases the allowable span/d ratio for the beam.

(c) Compression reinforcement

All reinforcement in the compression zone reduces shrinkage and creep and therefore the curvature. This effect decreases the deflection. The modification factors for compression reinforcement are given in BS 8110: Part 1, Table 3.12. The modification factor is given by the formula

$$1 + \frac{100A'_{s,prov}}{bd} \bigg/ \left(3 + \frac{100A'_{s,prov}}{bd}\right) \leqslant 1.5$$

where $A'_{s,prov}$ is the area of compression reinforcement.

(d) Deflection check

The allowable span-to-effective depth ratio is the basic ratio multiplied by the modification factor for tension reinforcement multiplied by the modification factor for compression reinforcement. This value should be greater than the actual span/d ratio for the beam to be satisfactory with respect to deflection.

(e) Deflection checks for slabs

The deflection checks applied to slabs are discussed under design of the various types of slab in Chapter 8.

□ Example 6.1 Deflection check for T-beam

The section at mid-span designed for a simply supported T-beam of 6 m span is shown in Fig. 6.2. The design moment is 165 kN m. The calculated area of tension reinforcement was 1447 mm^2 and three 25 mm diameter bars of area 1472 mm^2 were provided. To carry the links, two 12 mm diameter bars have been provided in the top of the beam. Using the rules set out above, check whether the beam is satisfactory for deflection. Refer to section 4.8.2 for design of the tension steel. The materials used are concrete grade 30 and reinforcement grade 460.

From BS 8110: Part 1, Table 3.10,

$$\frac{\text{web width}}{\text{effective flange width}} = \frac{b_w}{b} = \frac{250}{1450} < 0.3$$

The basic span-to-effective depth ratio is 16.

$$\frac{M}{bd^2} = \frac{165 \times 10^6}{1450 \times 300^2} = 1.26$$

The service stress is

$$f_s = \frac{5 \times 460 \times 1447}{8 \times 1472} = 282.6 \text{ N mm}^2$$

The beam is simply supported and $\beta_b = 1$. The modification factor for tension reinforcement using the formula given in Table 3.10 in the code is

$$0.55 + \frac{477 - 282.6}{120(0.9 + 1.26)} - 1.3 < 2.0$$

For the modification factor for compression reinforcement, with $A'_{s,prov} = 226$ mm^2,

$$\frac{100 A'_{s,prov}}{bd} = \frac{100 \times 226}{1450 \times 300} = 0.052$$

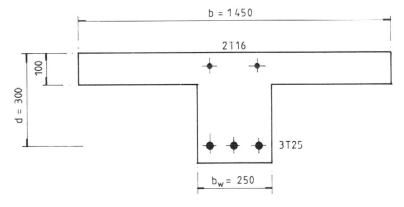

Fig. 6.2

and the modification factor is

$$1 + [0.052/(3 + 0.052)] = 1.017$$
$$\text{allowable span}/d = 16 \times 1.3 \times 1.017 = 21.1$$
$$\text{actual span}/d = 6000/300 = 20$$

The beam is satisfactory with respect to deflection.   ■

6.1.3 Deflection calculation

(a) Loads on the structure

The design loads for the serviceability limit state are set out in BS 8110: Part 2, clause 3.3. The code distinguishes between calculations

1. to produce a best estimate of likely behaviour
2. to comply with serviceability limit state requirements – this may entail taking special restrictions into account

In choosing the loads to be used the code again distinguishes between characteristic and expected values. For best estimate calculations, expected values are to be used. The code states that

1. for dead loads characteristic and expected values are the same
2. for imposed loads the expected values are to be used in best estimate calculations and the characteristic loads in serviceability limit state requirements (in apartments and office buildings 25% of the imposed load is taken as permanently applied)

Characteristic loads are used in deflection calculations.

(b) Analysis of the structure

An elastic analysis based on the gross concrete section may be used to obain moments for calculating deflections. The loads are as set out in 6.1.3(a) above.

(c) Method for calculating deflection

The method for calculating deflection is set out in BS 8110: Part 2, section 3.7. The code states that a number of factors which are difficult to assess can seriously affect results. Factors mentioned are

1. inaccurate assumptions regarding support restraints
2. that the actual loading and the amount that is of long-term duration which causes creep cannot be precisely estimated
3. whether the member has or has not cracked
4. the difficulty in assessing the effects of finishes and partitions

The method given is to assess curvatures of sections due to moment and to use these values to calculate deflections.

(d) Calculation of curvatures

The curvature at a section can be calculated using assumptions set out for a cracked or uncracked section. The larger value is used in the deflection calculations. Elastic theory is used for the section analysis.

(i) Cracked section The assumptions used in the analysis are as follows:

1. Strains are calculated on the basis that plane sections remain plane;
2. The reinforcement is elastic with a modulus of elasticity of 200 kN/mm^2;
3. The concrete in compression is elastic;
4. The modulus of elasticity of the concrete to be used is the mean value given in BS 8110: Part 2, Table 7.2;
5. The effect of creep due to long-term loads is taken into account by using an effective modulus of elasticity with a value of $1/(1 + \phi)$ times the short-term modulus from Table 7.2 of the code, where ϕ is the creep coefficient;
6. The stiffening effect of the concrete in the tension zone is taken into account by assuming that the concrete develops some stress in tension. The value of this stress is taken as varying linearly from zero at the neutral axis to 1 N/mm^2 at the centroid of the tension steel for short-term loads and reducing to 0.55 N/mm^2 for long-term loads.

To show the application of the method for calculating curvature, consider the doubly reinforced beam section shown in Fig. 6.3(a). The strain dia-

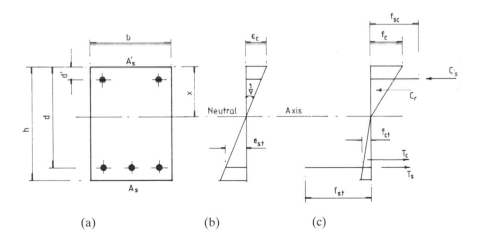

(a) (b) (c)

Fig. 6.3 (a) Section; (b) strain diagram; (c) stresses and forces in section.

gram and stresses and internal forces in the section are shown in 6.3(b) and 6.3(c) respectively. The terms used in the figure are defined as follows:

f_c stress in the concrete in compression
f_{sc} stress in the compression steel
f_{st} stress in the tension steel
f_{ct} stress in the concrete in tension at the level of the tension steel
      1 N/mm² for short-term loads; (0.55 N/mm² for long-term loads)
A_s area of steel in tension
A_s' area of steel in compression
x depth to the neutral axis
h depth of the beam
d effective depth
d' inset of the compression steel
C_c force in the concrete in compression
C_s force in the steel in compression
T_c force in the concrete in tension
T_s force in the steel in tension

The following further definitions are required:

E_c modulus of elasticity of the concrete
E_s modulus of elasticity of the steel
α_e modular ratio, E_s/E_c

Note that for long-term loads the effective value of E_c is used. The section analysis is outlined below.

The stresses in the reinforcement can be expressed in terms of the concrete stress in compression f_c and modular ratio α_e as follows:

$$f_{sc} = \alpha_e f_c (x - d')/x$$
$$f_{st} = \alpha_e f_c (d - x)/x$$

The concrete stress in tension of the bottom face is

$$f_{ct}(h - x)/(d - x)$$

The internal forces are given by

$$C_c = 0.5 f_c b x$$
$$C_s = \alpha_e f_c A_s'(x - d')/x$$
$$T_s = \alpha_e f_c A_s(d - x)/x$$
$$T_c = 0.5 f_{ct} b(h - x)^2/(d - x)$$

The sum of the internal forces is zero:

$$C_c + C_s - T_s - T_c = 0$$

The sum of the moments of the internal forces about the neutral axis is equal to the external moment M:

$$M = 0.67C_c x + C_s(x - d') + T_s(d - x) + 0.67T_c(h - x)$$

These two equations can be solved by successive trials to obtain the values of f and x. Note that the area of concrete occupied by the reinforcement has not been deducted in the expressions given above. The curvature is determined as set out below.

The problem is simplified with little sacrifice in accuracy if the neutral axis depth is determined for the cracked section only using the transformed area method set out in section 4.9.3. The transformed section is shown in Fig. 6.4(b).

The depth to the neutral axis is found by taking moments about the XX axis to give the equation

$$0.5bx^2 + \alpha_e A_s'(x - d') = \alpha_e A_s(d - x)$$

This is solved to give x. The moment of inertia of the transformed section about the XX axis is given by

$$I_x = 0.34bx^3 + \alpha_e A_s'(x - d')^2 + \alpha_e A_s(d - x)^2$$

The stiffening effect of the concrete in the tension zone is taken into account by calculating its moment of resistance about the XX axis. Referring to Fig. 6.4(c) the tensile stress at the outer fibre in the concrete is $f_{ct}(h - x)/(d - x)$. The force in concrete in tension is

$$T_c = 0.5f_{ct}(h - x)^2/(d - x)$$

The moment of resistance of the concrete in tension is

$$M_c - 2T_c(h - x)/3$$

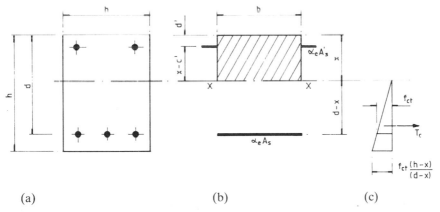

(a)   (b)   (c)

Fig. 6.4 (a) Section; (b) transformed section; (c) tension in concrete.

This moment is subtracted from the applied moment M to give a reduced moment

$$M_R = M - M_c$$

The compressive stress in the concrete is given by

$$f_c = M_R x / I_x$$

The compressive strain in the concrete is given by

$$\varepsilon_c = f_c / E_c$$

where the modulus E_c depends on whether the loads are of short- or long-term duration. Referring to the strain diagram in Fig. 6.3(b) the curvature is

$$\frac{1}{r} = \frac{\varepsilon_c}{x} = \frac{M_R}{EI_x}$$

Solutions are required for both short- and long-term loads.

(ii) Uncracked Section   For an uncracked section the concrete and steel are both considered to act elastically in tension and compression. An uncracked section is shown in Fig. 6.5(a), the strain diagram is given in 6.5(b) and the transformed section in 6.5(c). The section analysis to derive the depth to the neutral axis, the stresses and curvature is given below.

Referring to the transformed section in Figure. 6.5(c) the equivalent area is

$$A_e = bh + \alpha_e(A_s' + A_s)$$

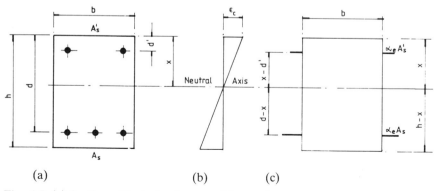

(a)   (b)   (c)

Fig. 6.5 (a) Section; (b) strain diagram; (c) transformed section.

The location of the centroid is found by taking moments of all areas about the top face and dividing by A_e:

$$x = \frac{bh^2/2 + \alpha_e(A_s'd' + A_sd)}{A_e}$$

The moment of inertia I_x about the XX axis is

$$I_x = \frac{bh^3}{12} + bh\left(\frac{h}{2} - x\right)^2 + \alpha_e A_s(d - x)^2 + \alpha_e A_s'(x - d')^2$$

The curvature is

$$\frac{1}{r} = \frac{M}{E_c I_x}$$

(e) Long-term loads – creep

The effect of creep must be considered for long-term loads. Load on concrete causes an immediate elastic strain and a long-term time-dependent strain known as creep. The strain due to creep may be much larger than that due to elastic deformation. On removal of the load, most of the strain due to creep is not recovered.

Creep is discussed in BS 8110: Part 2, section 7.3. The creep coefficient ϕ is used to evaluate the effect of creep. Values of ϕ depend on the age of loading, effective section thickness and ambient relative humidity. The code recommends suitable values for indoor and outdoor exposure in the UK and defines the effective section thickness for uniform sections as twice the cross-sectional area divided by the exposed perimeter.

In deflection calculations, creep is taken into account by using a reduced or effective value for the modulus of elasticity of the concrete equal to

$$E_{eff} = E_c/(1 + \phi)$$

for calculating the curvature due to the long-term loads. E_c is the short-term modulus for the concrete, values of which at 28 days are given in BS 8110: Part 2, Table 7.2.

(f) Shrinkage curvature

Concrete shrinks as it dries and hardens. This is termed drying shrinkage and is discussed in of BS 8110: Part 2, section 7.4. The code states that shrinkage is mainly dependent on the ambient relative humidity, the surface area from which moisture can be lost relative to the volume of concrete, and the mix proportions. It is noted that certain aggregates produce concrete with a higher initial drying shrinkage than normal.

Values of drying shrinkage strain ε_{cs} for plain concrete which depend on the effective thickness and ambient relative humidity may be taken from

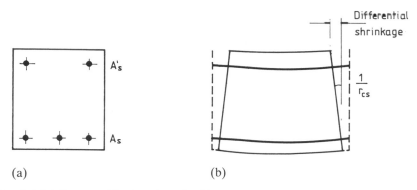

Fig. 6.6 (a) Section; (b) short length of beam.

BS 8110: Part 2, Fig. 7.2. A plain concrete member shrinks uniformly and does not deflect laterally. Reinforcement prevents some of the shrinkage through bond with the concrete and if it is asymmetrical as in a singly reinforced beam this causes the member to curve and deflect. BS 8110: Part 2, Clause 3.7, gives the following equation for calculating the shrinkage curvature:

$$\frac{1}{r_{cs}} = \frac{\varepsilon_{cs}\alpha_e S_s}{I}$$

where $\alpha_e = E_s/E_{eff}$ is the modular ratio, ε_{cs} is the free shrinkage strain, $E_{eff} = E_c/(1 + \phi)$ is the effective modulus of elasticity (see 6.1.3(e) above) and I is the moment of inertia of the cracked or gross section depending on which value is used to calculate the curvature due to the applied loads; the modular ratio α_e is used to find the transformed area of steel. S_s is the first moment of area of the reinforcement about the centroid of the cracked or gross section.

The curvature caused by shrinkage is illustrated by reference to Fig. 6.6. More shrinkage occurs at the top of the doubly reinforced beam because the steel area is less at the top than at the bottom.

(g) Total long-term curvature

BS 8110: Part 2, section 3.6, gives the followng four-step procedure for assessing the total long-term curvatures of a section:

1. Calculate the instantaneous curvatures under the total load and under the permanent load;
2. Calculate the long-term curvature under the permanent load;
3. Add to the long-term curvature under the permanent load the differ-

ence between the instantaneous curvatures under the total and the permanent load;

4. Add the shrinkage curvature.

(h) Deflection calculation

The deflection is calculated from the curvatures using the method given in BS 8110: Part 2, clause 3.7.2, where it is stated that the deflected shape is related to the curvatures by the equation

$$\frac{1}{r_x} = \frac{d^2a}{dx^2}$$

where $1/r_x$ is the curvature at x and a is the deflection at x.

Deflection can be calculated directly by calculating curvatures at sections along the member and using a numerical integration technique. The code gives the following simplified method as an alternative: the deflection a is calculated from

$$a = Kl^2 \frac{1}{r_b}$$

where l is the effective span of the member, $1/r_b$ is the curvature at mid-span of the beam or at the support for a cantilever and K is a constant that depends on the shape of the bending moment diagram. Values of K for various cases are given in BS 8110: Part 2, Table 3.1 (see 6.1.3(i) below).

(i) Evaluation of constant K

The curvature at any section along a beam a distance x from the support is

$$\frac{1}{r} = \frac{d^2a}{dx^2} = \frac{M}{EI}$$

where a is the deflection at the section, M is the moment at the section, E is Young's modulus and I is the moment of inertia of the section.

Figure 6.7 shows a uniform beam loaded with the M/EI diagram and the deflected shape of the beam. The moment area theorems are as follows:

1. The change in slope ϕ between any two points such as C and B is equal to the area A of the M/EI diagram between those two points;
2. The vertical deflection of B away from the tangent at C is equal to the moment of the area under the M/EI curve between C and B taken about B, i.e. $A\bar{x}$.

Useful geometrical properties for a parabola are shown in Fig. 6.7(c).

Values of the constant K are calculated for four common load cases.

(i) Simply supported beam with uniform load   Refer to Fig. 6.8. The centre deflection is

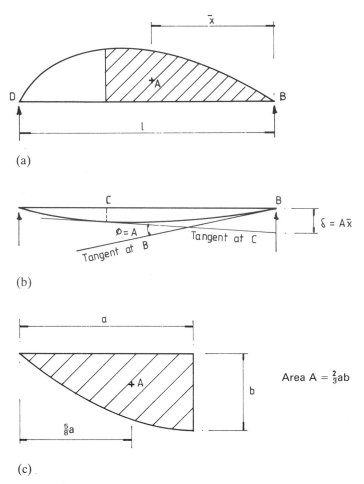

Fig. 6.7 (a) Beam load with M/EI diagram; (b) deflected shape of beam; (c) properties of parabola.

$$\delta = \frac{2}{3}\frac{M}{EI}\frac{l}{2}\frac{5}{8}\frac{l}{2}$$

$$= \frac{5}{48}l^2\frac{M}{EI}$$

$$= Kl^2\frac{1}{r_b}$$

$$K = 5/48 = 0.104 \qquad \text{(BS 8110: Part 2, Table 3.1)}$$

(ii) Moment at one end of a simply supported beam   Refer to Fig. 6.9. The deflection of A away from the tangent at C is

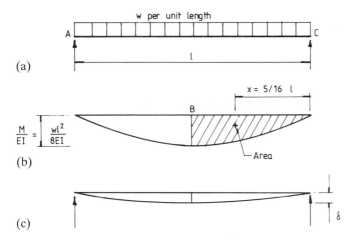

(a)

(b)

(c)

Fig. 6.8 (a) Load; (b) M/EI diagram; (c) deflected shape.

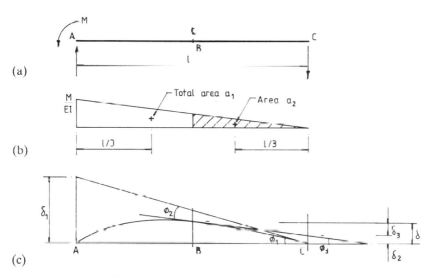

(a)

(b)

(c)

Fig. 6.9 (a) Load; (b) M/EI diagram; (c) deflected shape.

$$\delta_1 = \frac{1}{2}\frac{Ml}{EI}\frac{l}{3} = \frac{Ml^2}{6EI}$$

The slope ϕ_1 at C is $Ml/6EI$ and the change of slope ϕ_2 between the tangents at C and B is

$$\text{area } a_2 = \frac{1}{2}\frac{M}{2EI}\frac{l}{2} = \frac{Ml}{8EI}$$

The slope ϕ_3 at C is

$$\phi_3 = \phi_1 - \phi_2$$
$$= \frac{Ml}{EI}\left(\frac{1}{6} - \frac{1}{8}\right) = \frac{Ml}{24EI}$$

The deflection δ_2 of C away from the tangent at B is

$$\delta_2 = \frac{a_2 l}{3} = \frac{Ml}{8EI}\frac{l}{3} = \frac{Ml^2}{24EI}$$

The deflection δ_3 at C due to the slope at B is

$$\delta_3 = \frac{\phi_3 l}{2} = \frac{Ml}{24EI}\frac{l}{2} = \frac{Ml^2}{48EI}$$

Thus the total deflection δ at B is

$$\delta = \delta_2 + \delta_3$$
$$= \left(\frac{1}{24} + \frac{1}{48}\right)l^2\frac{M}{EI} = \frac{1}{16}l^2\frac{1}{r_b}$$
$$K = 1/16 = 0.0625 \qquad \text{(BS 8110: Part 2, Table 3.1)}$$

(iii) Intermediate span with uniform load and end moments   The solution in (ii) is used in this case. Refer to Fig. 6.10.
The deflection δ_A at B due to M_A/EI loading is

$$\delta_A = -\frac{1}{16}l^2\frac{M_A}{EI}$$

The deflection δ_B at C due to M_B/EI loading is

$$\delta_B = -\frac{1}{16}l^2\frac{M_B}{EI}$$

The deflection δ_M at C due to M/EI loading is

$$\delta_M = \frac{5}{48}l^2\frac{M}{EI}$$

and the resultant deflection δ_C at C is thus

$$\delta_C = \delta_M - (\delta_A + \delta_B)$$
$$= \frac{5}{48}l^2\frac{M}{EI} - \frac{1}{16}l^2\left(\frac{M_A}{EI} + \frac{M_B}{EI}\right)$$
$$= \frac{5}{48}l^2\frac{M_C}{EI} - \frac{1}{96}l^2\left(\frac{M_A}{EI} + \frac{M_B}{EI}\right)$$

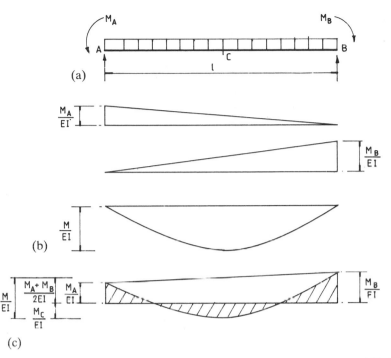

Fig. 6.10 (a) Load; (b) individual M/EI diagrams; (c) combined M/EI diagram.

Equate this expression to $Kl^2 M_C/EI)$, i.e.

$$Kl^2 \frac{M_C}{EI} = \left(\frac{5}{48} - \frac{M_A + M_B}{96 M_C} \right) l^2 \frac{1}{r_C}$$

and

$$K = \frac{5}{48} - \frac{M_A + M_B}{96 M_C}$$

$$= 0.104(1 - \beta/10)$$

where

$$\beta = \frac{M_A + M_B}{M_C}$$

This is the expression given in BS 8110: Part 2, Table 3.1.

□ Example 6.2 Deflection calculation for T-beam

A simply supported T-beam of 6 m span carries a dead load including self-weight of 14.8 kN/m and an imposed load of 10 kN/m. The T-beam section with the tension reinforcement designed for the ultimate limit state and the bars in the top to support the links is shown in Fig. 6.11. Calculate the deflection of the beam at mid-span.

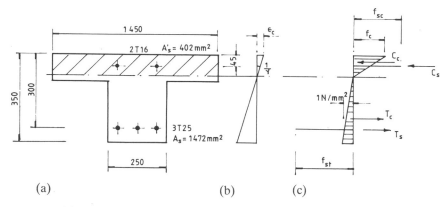

Fig. 6.11 (a) Section; (b) strain diagram; (c) stresses and forces.

The materials are grade 30 concrete and grade 460 reinforcement. Refer to Example 4.13 for the design of the tension steel and to section 6.1.2 for the application of the rules for checking deflection for the beam.

(a) Moments

The deflection calculation will be made for characteristic dead and imposed loads to comply with serviceability limit state requirements. The permanent load is taken as the dead load plus 25% of the imposed load as recommended in BS 8110: Part 2, clause 3.3.

$$\text{total load} = 14.8 + 10 = 24.8 \, \text{kN/m}$$
$$\text{permanent load} = 14.8 + 0.25 \times 10 = 17.3 \, \text{kN/m}$$

The moments at mid-span are

Total load $M_T = 24.8 \times 6^2/8 = 111.6 \, \text{kN m}$
Permanent load $M_P = 17.3 \times 6^2/8 = 77.85 \, \text{kN m}$

(b) Instantaneous curvatures for the cracked section – accurate analysis

The instantaneous curvatures for the total and permanent loads are calculated first. The static modulus of elasticity from BS 8110: Part 2, Table 7.2, is $E_c = 26 \, \text{kN/mm}^2$ for grade 30 concrete. For steel $E_s = 200 \, \text{kN/mm}^2$ from BS 8110: Part 1, Fig. 2.2. The modular ratio $\alpha_e = 200/26 = 7.69$.

The stress and internal forces in the section are shown in Fig. 6.11(c). The stress in the concrete in tension at the level of the tension steel is $1.0 \, \text{N/mm}^2$. The neutral axis is assumed to be in the flange. This is checked on completion of the analysis. The stresses in the steel in terms of the concrete stress f_c in compression are

$$f_{sc} = 7.69 f_c (x - 45)/x$$
$$f_{st} = 7.69 f_c (300 - x)/x$$

Table 6.2 Forces and moments due to internal forces

	Force	Lever Arm	Moment
C_c	$725xf_c$	$2x/3$	$483x^2f_c$
C_s	$3091f_c(x-45)/x$	$(x-45)$	$309f_c(x-45)^2/x$
T_s	$1131f_c(300-x)/x$	$(300-x)$	$11319f_c(300-x)^2/x$
T_c	$125(350-x)^2/(300-x)$	$2(350-x)/3$	$83.3(350-x)^3/(300-x)$
	$600(100-x)^2/(300-x)$	$2(100-x)/3$	$400(100-x)^3/(300-x)$
Σ	0		$111.6 \times 10^6\,\mathrm{N\,mm}$

The internal forces in the section, the lever arms of the forces about the neutral axis and the moments of the forces about the neutral axis are shown in Table 6.2. The two equations are solved for f_c and x by successive trials. The solution is

$$x = 63.9\,\mathrm{mm}$$
$$f_c = 8.7\,\mathrm{N/mm^2}$$

The neutral axis lies in the flange as assumed.
  The compressive strain in the concrete is

$$\varepsilon_c = f_c/E_c$$

The curvature for the total loads is

$$\frac{1}{r} = \frac{\varepsilon_c}{x} = \frac{8.7}{26 \times 10^3 \times 63.9}$$
$$= 5.24 \times 10^{-6}$$

(c) Instantaneous curvature for permanent loads

For the instantaneous curvature for permanent loads the sum of the moments in Table 6.2 is 77.85 kN m. The solution of the equations is

$$x = 65.3\,\mathrm{mm^2}$$
$$f_c = 6.05\,\mathrm{N/mm^2}$$
$$\frac{1}{r} = \frac{6.05}{26 \times 10^3 \times 65.3} = 3.56 \times 10^{-6}$$

(d) Long-term curvature under permanent loads

The creep coefficient ϕ is estimated using data given in BS 8110: Part 2, section 7.3.

$$\text{effective area } A_c = 2[(250 \times 350) + (1200 \times 100)]$$
$$= 4.15 \times 10^5\,\mathrm{mm^2}$$
$$\text{exposed perimeter} = 1450 + 1200 + (2 \times 250) + 250$$
$$= 3400$$
$$\text{effective section thickness} = \frac{4.15 \times 10^5}{3400} = 122\,\mathrm{mm}$$

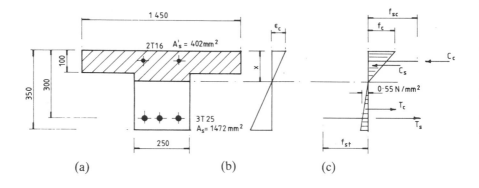

(a)   (b)   (c)

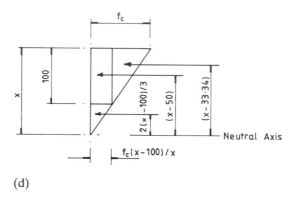

(d)

Fig. 6.12 (a) Section; (b) strain diagram; (c) stresses and forces; (d) forces in concrete in compression.

The relative humidity for indoor exposure is 45%. If the age of loading is 14 days, say, when the soffit form and props are removed, the creep coefficient ϕ from Fig. 7.1 is 3.5. The effective modulus of elasticity is

$$E_{\text{eff}} = \frac{E_c}{1 + \phi} = \frac{26}{1 + 3.5} = 5.78 \text{ kN/mm}^2$$

The modular ratio $\alpha_e = 200/5.78 = 34.6$.

The stresses and internal forces in the section are shown in Fig. 6.12. The tensile stress in the concrete at the level of the tension steel is taken to be 0.55 N/mm². The neutral axis is assumed to be in the beam web in this case.

The internal forces, the lever arms and the moments of forces about the neutral axis are shown in Table 6.3. Note that the force in compression in the concrete is divided into three forces for ease of calculation, as shown in Fig. 6.12(d). The solution of the equation is

Table 6.3 Forces and moments due to internal forces

	Force	Lever Arm	Moment
	$1450f_c(x - 100)/x$	$(x - 50)$	$1450f_c(x - 100)(x - 50)/x$
C_c	$7.25 \times 10^6 f_c/x$	$(x - 33.34)$	$7.25 \times 10^6 f_c(x - 33.34)/x$
	$125f_c(x - 100)^2/x$	$2(x - 100)/3$	$83.3f_c(x - 100)^3/x$
C_s	$13909f_c(x - 45)/x$	$(x - 45)$	$13909f_c(x - 45)^2/x$
T_s	$50931f_c(300 - x)/x$	$(300 - x)$	$50931f_c(300 - x)^2/x$
T_c	$68.75(350 - x)^2/(300 - x)$	$2(350 - x)/3$	$45.83(350 - x)^3/(300 - x)$
Σ	0		$77.86 \times 10^6\,\text{N mm}$

$$x = 110\,\text{mm}$$
$$f_c = 4.66\,\text{N/mm}^2$$

The curvature for the permanent loads is

$$\frac{1}{r} = \frac{4.66}{5.78 \times 10^3 \times 110} = 5.08 \times 10^{-6}$$

(e) Curvature due to shrinkage

The value of drying shrinkage for plain concrete is evaluated from of BS 8110: Part 2, Fig. 7.2, for an effective thickness of 122 mm and a relative humidity of 45%. The 30 year shrinkage value is

$$\varepsilon_{cs} = 420 \times 10^{-6}$$

The moment of inertia of the cracked section is calculated using the depth to the neutral axis determined in (c) above. The effective modulus for an age of loading of 14 days is

$$E_{eff} = 5.78\,\text{kN/mm}^2$$
$$\alpha_e = 34.6$$

The transformed section is shown in Fig. 6.13.

$$I_x = 1450 \times 100 \times 60^2 + 1450 \times 100^3/12 + 250 \times 10^3/3 + 13909 \times 65^2$$
$$+ 50931 \times 190^2$$
$$= 2.541 \times 10^9\,\text{mm}^4$$

The first moment of area of the reinforcement about the centroid of the cracked sections is

$$S_s = (402 \times 65) + (1472 \times 190) = 3.058 \times 10^5\,\text{mm}^3$$

The shrinkage curvature is

$$\frac{1}{r_{cs}} = \frac{420 \times 34.6 \times 3.058 \times 10^5}{10^6 \times 2.541 \times 10^9} = 1.75 \times 10^{-6}$$

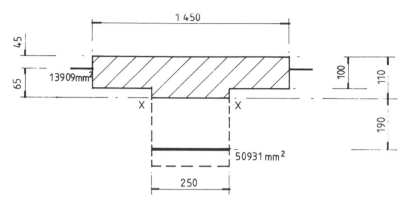

Fig. 6.13

(f) Final curvature

The final curvature $1/r_b$ is the instantaneous curvature under the total load minus the instantaneous curvature under the permanent load plus the long-term curvature under the permanent load plus shrinkage curvature:

$$\frac{1}{r_b} = (5.24 - 3.56 + 5.08 + 1.75)10^{-6}$$
$$= 8.51 \times 10^{-6}$$

(g) Beam deflection

For a simply supported beam carrying a uniform load, $K = 5/48$.

$$\text{deflection } a = \frac{5 \times 6000^2 \times 8.51}{48 \times 10^6} = 31.9 \text{ mm}$$

$$\text{permissible deflection} = 6000/250 = 24 \text{ mm}$$
$$\text{or } 20 \text{ mm}$$

The beam does not meet deflection requirements for the creep and shrinkage conditions selected. The beam is satisfactory when checked by span/d ratio rules.

(h) Curvatures for the uncracked section

The instantaneous curvature for the total load is calculated where $\alpha_e = 7.69$. The transformed section is shown in Fig. 6.14. The calculations for the section properties are given in Table 6.4.

$$y = \frac{52.82 \times 10^6}{221.98 \times 10^3} = 237.9 \text{ mm}$$
$$I_x = (14.34 + 0.45)10^9 - 221.98 \times 10^3 \times 237.9^2$$
$$= 2.22 \times 10^9$$

The instantaneous curvature for the total load is

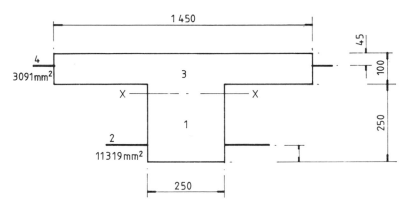

Fig. 6.14

$$\frac{1}{r} = \frac{111.6 \times 10^6}{26 \times 10^3 \times 2.22 \times 10^9}$$

$$= 1.933 \times 10^{-6}$$

This is much less than the value of 5.24×10^{-6} calculated in (b) for the cracked section. Deflection calculations based on the cracked section should be used.

(i) Approximate method for curvature

Recalculate the curvatures using the approximate method outlined earlier. The instantaneous curvature for the total load is calculated and the value is compared with that obtained by the accurate method used above. The transformed section with the neutral axis in the flange is shown in Fig. 6.15(a).

Locate the neutral axis by solving the equation

$$725x^2 + 3091(x - 45) = 11319(300 - x)$$

This gives $x = 60.6$ mm.

$$I_x = 1450 \times 60.6^3/3 + 3091 \times 15.6^2 + 11319 \times 239.4^2$$

$$= 757 \times 10^6 \, \text{mm}^4$$

Table 6.4 Properties of transformed section

No.	Area	y	Ay	Ay^2	i_c
1	6.25×10^3	125	0.781×10^6	$.097 \times 10^9$	0.33×10^9
2	11.39×10^3	50	0.57×10^6	0.03×10^9	$-$
3	145.0×10^3	300	43.5×10^6	13.05×10^9	0.12×10^9
4	3.09×10^3	305	0.94×10^6	0.29×10^9	
	221.98×10^3		52.82×10^6	14.34×10^9	0.45×10^9

i_c, moment of mertia of section about its own centroidal axis

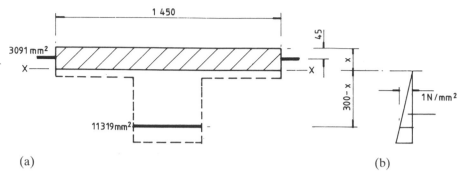

Fig. 6.15 (a) Transformed section; (b) tension in concrete.

Calculate the moment of resistance due to the concrete in tension where the tensile stress is 1 N/mm^2 for short-term loads at the centre of the reinforcement (Fig. 6.15(b)). The stress at the bottom face is

$$1 \times 289.4/239.4 = 1.21 \text{ N/mm}^2$$

The stress at the bottom of the flange is

$$1 \times 39.4/239.4 = 0.16 \text{ N/mm}^2$$

$$\begin{aligned} M_R &= 0.5 \times 1.21 \times 250 \times 289.4^2 \times 2/(3 \times 10^6) \\ &+ 0.5 \times 0.16 \times 1200 \times 39.4^2 \times 2/(3 \times 10^6) \\ &= 8.53 \text{ kN m} \end{aligned}$$

$$\text{net moment} = 111.6 - 8.53 = 103.07 \text{ kN m}$$

The curvature for the total load is

$$\frac{1}{r} = \frac{103.07 \times 10^6}{26 \times 10^3 \times 757 \times 10^6}$$
$$= 5.24 \times 10^{-6}$$

This gives the same result as that obtained with the exact method. ∎

6.2 CRACKING

6.2.1 Cracking limits and controls

Any prominent crack in reinforced concrete greatly detracts from the appearance. Excessive cracking and wide deep cracks affect durability and can lead to corrosion of reinforcement although strength may not be affected. BS 8110: Part 1, clause 2.2.3.4.1, states that for reinforced concrete cracking should be kept within reasonable bounds. The clause specifies two methods for crack control:

1. in normal cases a set of rules for limiting the maximum bar spacing in the tension zone of members
2. in special cases use of a formula given in BS 8110: Part 2, section 3.8, for assessing the design crack width

6.2.2 Bar spacing controls

Cracking is controlled by specifying the maximum distance between bars in tension. The spacing limits are specified in clause 3.12.11.2. The clause indicates that in normal conditions of internal or external exposure the bar spacings given will limit crack widths to 0.3 mm. Calculations of crack widths can be made to justify larger spacings. The rules are as follows.

1. Bars of diameter less than 0.45 of the largest bar in the section should be ignored except when considering bars in the side faces of beams.
2. The clear horizontal distance S_1 between bars or groups near the tension face of a beam should not be greater than the values given in Table 3.30 of the code which are given by the expression (Fig. 6.16)

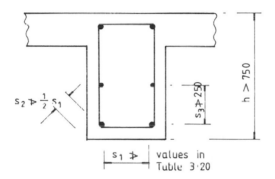

Fig. 6.16

$$\text{clear spacings} \geqslant \frac{75000\beta_b}{f_y} \leqslant 300$$

where

$$\beta_b = \frac{\text{moment after redistribution}}{\text{moment before redistribution}}$$

The moments are taken from the maximum moments diagram.

The maximum clear distance depends on the grade of reinforcement and a smaller spacing is required with high yield bars to control cracking because stresses and strains are higher than with mild steel bars.

For zero redistribution the maximum clear distance between bars is

Reinforcement grade 250   300 mm
Reinforcement grade 460   160 mm

3. As an alternative the clear spacing between bars can be found from the expression

$$\text{clear spacing} \geq \frac{47000}{f_s} \leq 300$$

where f_s is the service stress estimated from equation 8 in BS 8110: Part 1, Table 3.11 (section 6.1.2(b) above).

4. The clear distance s_2 from the corner of a beam to the surface of the nearest horizontal bar should not exceed one-half of the values given in BS 8110: Part 1, Table 3.20.

5. If the overall depth of the beam exceeds 750 mm, longitudinal bars should be provided at a spacing not exceeding 250 mm over a distance of two-thirds of the overall depth from the tension face. The size of bar should not be less than (see BS 8110: Part 1, clause 3.12.5.4) $s_b^{1/2}b/f_y$ where s_b is the bar spacing and b is the breadth of the beam.

The maximum clear spacing between bars in slabs is given in BS 8110: Part 1, clause 3.12.11.7. This clause states that the clear distance between bars should not exceed three times the effective depth or 750 mm. It also states that no further checks are required if

(a) grade 250 steel is used and the slab depth does not exceed 250 mm
(b) grade 460 steel is used and the slab depth does not exceed 200 mm
(c) the reinforcement percentage $100A_s/bd$ is less than 0.3% where A_s is the minimum recommended area, b is the breadth of the slab considered and d is the effective depth

Refer to clauses 3.12.11.7 and 3.12.11.8 for other requirements regarding crack control in slabs.

6.2.3 Calculation of crack widths

(a) Cracking in reinforced concrete beams

A reinforced concrete beam is subject to moment cracks on the tension face when the tensile strength of the concrete is exceeded. Primary cracks form first and with increase in moment secondary cracks form as shown in Fig. 6.17(a). Cracking has been extensively studied both experimentally and theoretically. The crack width at a point on the surface of a reinforced concrete beam has been found to be affected by two factors:

1. the surface strain found by analysing the sections and assuming that plane sections remain plane and
2. the distance of the point from a point of zero crack width. Points of zero

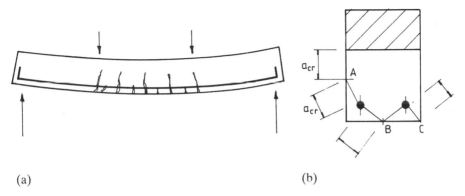

Fig. 6.17 (a) Cracking in a beam; (b) crack locations.

crack width are the neutral axis and the surface of longitudinal reinforcing bars. The larger this distance is, the larger the crack width will be.

Referring to Fig. 6.17(b) the critical locations for cracking on the beam
surface are

1. at A equidistant between the neutral axis and the bar surface
2. at B equidistant between the bars
3. at C on the corner of the beam

(b) Crack width equation

The calculation of crack widths is covered in BS 8110: Part 2, section 3.8.
The code notes that the width of a flexural crack depends on the factors
listed above. It also states that cracking is a semi-random phenomenon and
that it is not possible to predict an absolute maximum crack width.

The following expression is given in BS 8110: Part 2, clause 3.8.3, to
determine the design surface crack width:

$$\text{design crack width} = \frac{3a_{cr}\varepsilon_m}{1 + 2(a_{cr} - c_{min})/(h - x)}$$

The code states that this formula can be used provided that the strain in the
tension reinforcement does not exceed $0.8f_y/E_s$. The terms in the expression are defined as follows:

a_{cr} distance of the point considered to the surface of the
         nearest longitudinal bar

ε_m average strain at the level where the cracking is being
         considered (this is discussed below)

c_{min} minimum cover to the tension steel

h overall depth of the member

x depth of the neutral axis

The average strain ε_m can be calculated using the method set out for determining the curvature in BS 8110: Part 2, section 3.6, and section 6.1.3 above. The code gives an alternative approximation in which

1. the strain ε_1 at the level considered is calculated ignoring the stiffening effect of the concrete in the tension zone (the transformed area method is used in this calculation)
2. the strain ε_1 is reduced by an amount equal to the tensile force due to the stiffening effect of the concrete in the tension zone acting over the tension zone divided by the steel area
3. ε_m for a rectangular tension zone is given by

$$\varepsilon_m = \varepsilon_1 - \frac{b_t(h - x)(a' - x)}{3E_s A_s(d - x)}$$

where b_t is the width of the section at the centroid of the tension steel and a' is the distance from the compression face to the point at which the crack width is required

The code adds the following comments and requirements regarding use of the crack width formula:

1. A negative value of ε_m indicates that the section is not cracked;
2. The modulus of elasticity of the concrete is to be taken as one-half the instantaneous value to calculate strains;
3. If the drying shrinkage is very high, i.e. greater than 0.0006, ε_m should be increased by adding 50% of the shrinkage strain. In normal cases shrinkage may be neglected.

□ Example 6.3 Crack width calculation for T-beam

The section and reinforcement at mid-span of a simply supported T-beam are shown in Fig. 6.18(a). The total moment at the section due to service loads is 111.6 kN m. The materials are grade 30 concrete and grade 460 reinforcement. Determine the crack widths at the corner A, at the centre of the tension face B and at C on the side face midway between the neutral axis and the surface of the tension reinforcement.

The alternative approximate method set out above is used in the calculation. The properties of the transformed section are computed first. The values for the moduli of elasticity are as follows:

$$\begin{array}{lll} \text{Reinforcement} & E_s = 200\,\text{kN/mm}^2 \\ \text{Concrete} & E_c = \tfrac{1}{2} \times 26 = 13\,\text{kN/mm}^2 \\ \text{Modular ratio} & \alpha_e = 200/13 = 15.4 \end{array}$$

The transformed section is shown in Fig. 6.18(b). The neutral axis is located first:

$$725x^2 + 6191(x - 45) = 22669(300 - x)$$

Solve to give $x = 80.9\,\text{mm}$.

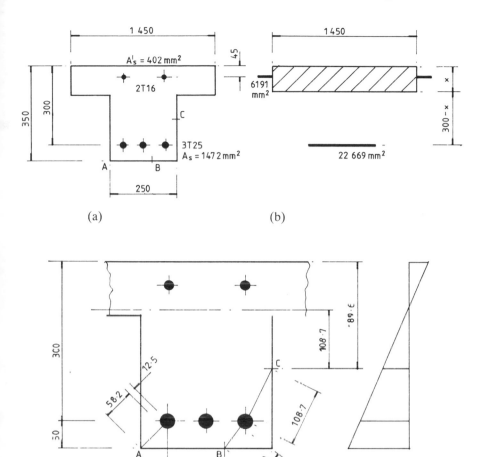

Fig. 6.18 (a) Section; (b) transformed section; (c) crack locations and dimensions a_{cr}; (d) stress diagram.

The moment of inertia about the neutral axis is

$$I_x = 1450 \times 80.9^3/3 + 6191 \times 35.9^2 + 22669 \times 219.1^2$$
$$= 13.22 \times 10^8\,mm^4$$

The stress in the tension steel is

$$f_t = \frac{111.6 \times 10^6 \times 219.1 \times 15.4}{13.22 \times 10^8}$$
$$= 284.8\,N/mm^2$$

The strain in the tension steel is

$$\frac{284.8}{200 \times 10^3} = 1.44 \times 10^{-3}$$

Neglect the stiffening effect of the concrete in tension in the flange of the T-beam.

(a) Crack width at A (Fig. 6.18(c))

The strain in the concrete at A is

$$\varepsilon_1 = \frac{1.424 \times 10^{-3} \times (350 - 80.9)}{300 - 80.9}$$

$$= 1.749 \times 10^{-3}$$

The strain reduction due to the stiffening effect of the concrete in the tension zone, where $a' = h = 350\,\text{mm}$, is

$$\frac{250(350 - 80.9)^2}{3 \times 200 \times 10^3 \times 1472(300 - x)} = 9.35 \times 10^{-5}$$

The average strain at the crack location is therefore

$$\varepsilon_m = (1.749 - 0.094)10^{-3} = 1.635 \times 10^{-3}$$

The design surface crack width at A where $a_{cr} = 58.2\,\text{mm}$ and $c_{min} = 37.5\,\text{mm}$ is

$$\frac{3 \times 58.2 \times 1.655 \times 10^{-3}}{1 + 2(58.2 - 37.5)/(350 - 80.9)} = 0.25\,\text{mm}$$

(b) Crack width at B (Fig. 6.18(c))

The dimension $a_{cr} = 50\,\text{mm}$ and the average strain $\varepsilon_m = 1.655 \times 10^{-3}$. Therefore

$$\text{crack width} = 0.23\,\text{mm}$$

(c) Crack width at C

C is midway between the neutral axis and the surface of the reinforcement (Fig. 6.18(c)). The location of C is found by successive trials. If C is 108.7 mm from the neutral axis, it is also 108.7 mm from the surface of the bar and $a' = 189.6\,\text{mm}$.
The strain in the concrete at C is

$$\varepsilon_1 = \frac{1.424 \times 10^{-3} \times 108.7}{300 - 80.9}$$

$$= 0.706 \times 10^{-3}$$

The strain reduction due to the stiffening effect of the concrete is

$$\frac{250(350 - 80.9)^2(189.6 - 80.9)}{3 \times 200 \times 10^3 \times 1472(300 - 80.9)} = 3.78 \times 10^{-5}$$

The average strain at the crack location is

$$(0.706 - 0.038)10^{-3} = 0.668 \times 10^{-3}$$

The design surface crack width at C, where $a_{cr} = 108.7$ mm, is

$$\frac{3 \times 108.7 \times 0.668 \times 10^{-3}}{1 + 2(108.7 - 37.5)/(350 - 80.9)} = 0.14 \text{ mm}$$

All crack widths are less than 0.3 mm and are satisfactory.   ■

7

Simply supported and continuous beams

The aim in this chapter is to put together the design procedures developed in Chapters 4, 5 and 6 to make a complete design of a reinforced concrete beam. Beams carry lateral loads in roofs, floors etc. and resist the loading in bending, shear and bond. The design must comply with the ultimate and serviceability limit states.

Further problems in beam design are treated in the chapter as they arise. These include arrangement of loads for maximum moments and shear forces, analysis of continuous beams, redistribution of moments, maximum moment and shear envelopes, curtailment of reinforcement and end anchorage.

7.1 SIMPLY SUPPORTED BEAMS

Simply supported beams do not occur as frequently as continuous beams in *in situ* concrete construction. They are an important element in precast concrete construction.

The effective span of a simply supported beam is defined in BS 8110: Part 1, clause 3.4.1.2. This should be taken as the smaller of

1. the distance between centres of bearings or
2. the clear distance between supports plus the effective depth

7.1.1 Steps in beam design

The steps in beam design are as follows.

(a) Preliminary size of beam

The size of beam required depends on the moment and shear that the beam carries. The reinforcement provided must be within the limits set out in BS 8110: Part 1, clause 3.12.6.1 and Table 3.2, for maximum and minimum percentage respectively. A general guide to the size of beam required is

$$\text{overall depth} = \text{span}/15$$
$$\text{breadth} = 0.6 \times \text{depth}$$

The breadth may have to be very much greater in some cases. The size is generally chosen from experience.

(b) Estimation of loads

The loads include an allowance for self-weight which will be based on experience or calculated from the assumed dimensions for the beam. The original estimate may require checking after the final design is complete. The estimation of loads should also include the weight of screed, finish, partitions, ceiling and services if applicable. The imposed loading depending on the type of occupancy is taken from BS 6399: Part 1.

(c) Analysis

The design loads are calculated using appropriate partial factors of safety from BS 8110: Part 1, Table 2.1. The reactions, shears and moments are determined and the shear force and bending moment diagrams are drawn.

(d) Design of moment reinforcement

The reinforcement is designed at the point of maximum moment, usually the centre of the beam. Refer to BS 8110: Part 1, section 3.4.4, and Chapter 4.

(e) Curtailment and end anchorage

A sketch of the beam in elevation is made and the cut-off point for part of the tension reinforcement is determined. The end anchorage for bars continuing to the end of the beam is set out to comply with code requirements.

(f) Design for shear

Shear stresses are checked and shear reinforcement is designed using the procedures set out in BS 8110: Part 1, section 3.4.5, and discussed in Chapter 5, section 5.1. Note that except for minor beams such as lintels all beams must be provided with links as shear reinforcement. Small diameter bars are required in the top of the beam to carry and anchor the links.

(g) Deflection

Deflection is checked using the rules from BS 8110: Part 1, section 3.4.6.9, which are given in Chapter 6, section 6.1.2.

(h) Cracking

The maximum clear distance between bars on the tension face is checked against the limits given in BS 8110: Part 1, clause 3.12.11 and Table 3.30. See Chapter 6, section 6.2.1.

(i) Design sketch

Design sketches of the beam with elevation and sections are completed to show all information for the draughtsman.

7.1.2 Curtailment and anchorage of bars

General and simplified rules for curtailment of bars in beams are set out in BS 8110: Part 1, section 3.12.9. The same section also sets out requirements for anchorage of bars at a simply supported end of a beam. These provisions are set out below.

(a) General rules for curtailment of bars

Clause 3.12.9.1 of the code states that except at end supports every bar should extend beyond the point at which it is no longer required to resist moment by a distance equal to the greater of

1. the effective depth of the beam
2. twelve times the bar size

In addition, where a bar is stopped off in the tension zone, one of the following conditions must be satisfied:

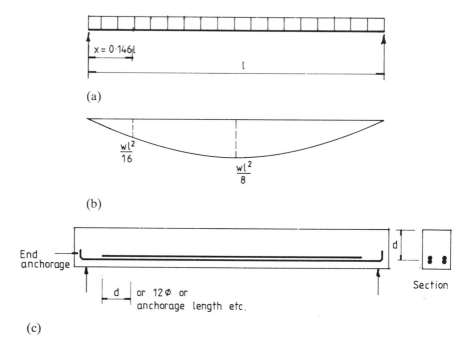

(a)

(b)

(c)

Fig. 7.1 (a) Load; (b) bending moment diagram; (c) beam and moment reinforcement.

1. The bar must extend an anchorage length past the theoretical cut-off point;
2. The bar must extend to the point where the shear capacity is twice the design shear force;
3. The bars continuing past the actual cut-off point provide double the area to resist moment at that point.

These requirements are set out in Fig. 7.1 for the case of a simply supported beam with uniform load. The section at the centre has four bars of equal area.

The theoretical cut-off point or the point at which two of the bars are no longer required is found from the equation

$$\frac{wl^2}{16} = \frac{wlx}{2} - \frac{wx^2}{2}$$

which gives $x = 0.146l$.

In a particular case calculations can be made to check that one only of the three conditions above is satisfied. Extending a bar a full anchorage length beyond the point at which it is no longer required is the easiest way of complying with the requirements.

(b) Anchorage of bars at a simply supported end of a beam

BS 8110: Part 1, clause 3.12.9.4, states that at the ends of simply supported beams the tension bars should have an anchorage equal to one of the following lengths:

1. Twelve bar diameters beyond the centre of the support; no hook or bend should begin before the centre of the support.
2. Twelve bar diameters plus one-half the effective depth ($d/2$) from the face of the support; no hook or bend should begin before $d/2$ from the face of the support.

(c) Simplified rules for curtailment of bars in beams

The simplified rules for curtailment of bars in simply supported beams and cantileveres are given in clause 3.12.10.2 and Fig. 3.24(b) of the code. The clause states that the beams are to be designed for predominantly uniformly distributed loads. The rules for beams and cantilevers are shown in Fig. 7.2.

□ Example 7.1 Design of a simply supported L-beam in footbridge

(a) Specification

The section through a simply supported reinforced concrete footbridge of 7 m span is shown in Fig. 7.3(a). The imposed load is $5\,kN/m^2$ and the materials to be used

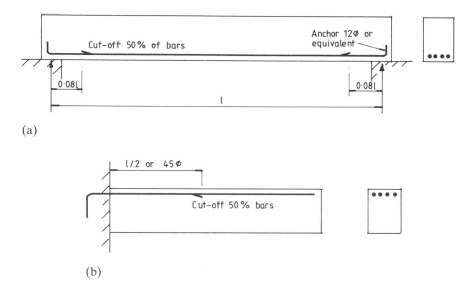

(a)

(b)

Fig. 7.2 (a) Simply supported beam; (b) cantilever.

are grade 30 concrete and grade 460 reinforcement. Design the L-beams that support the bridge. Concrete weighs $2400\,kg/m^3$, i.e. $23.5\,kN/m^3$, and the weight of the hand rails are $16\,kg/m$ per side.

(b) Loads, shear force and bending moment diagram

The dead load carried by one L-beam is

$$[(0.15 \times 0.8) + (0.2 \times 0.28)]23.5 + 16 \times 9.81/10^3 = 4.3\,kN/m$$

The imposed load carried by one L-beam is $0.8 \times 5 = 4\,kN/m$. The design load is

$$(1.4 \times 4.3) + (1.6 \times 4) = 12.42\,kN/m$$

The ultimate moment at the centre of the beam is

$$12.42 \times 7^2/8 = 76.1\,kN\,m$$

The load, shear force and bending moment diagrams are shown in Figs 7.3(b), 7.3(c) and 7.3(d) respectively.

(c) Design of moment reinforcement

The effective width of the flange of the L-beam is given by the lesser of

1. the actual width, 800 mm, or
2. $b = 200 + 8000/10 = 1000\,mm$

From BS 8110: Part 1, Table 3.4, the cover for moderate exposure is 35 mm. The effective depth

$$d = 400 - 35 - 8 - 12.5 = 344.5\,mm,\ \text{say } 340\,mm$$

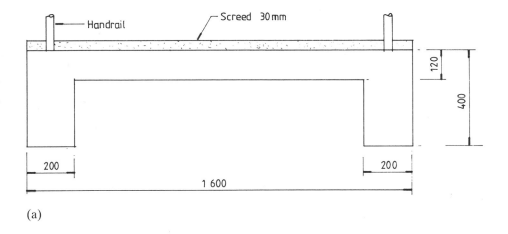

(a)

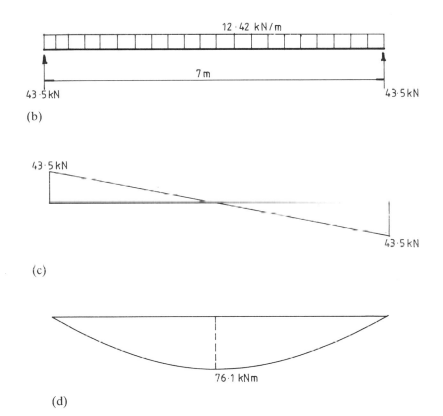

(b)

(c)

(d)

Fig. 7.3 (a) Section through footbridge; (b) design load; (c) shear force diagram; (d) bending moment diagram.

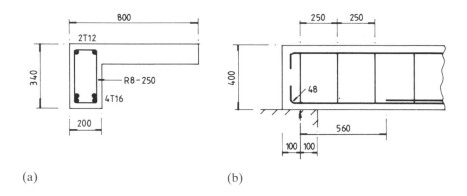

(a)   (b)

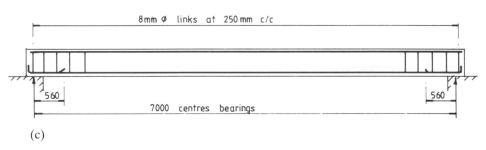

(c)

Fig. 7.4 (a) Beam section; (b) beam support; (c) beam elevation.

The L-beam is shown in Fig. 7.4(a).

The moment of resistance of the section when 0.9 of the depth to the neutral axis is equal to the slab depth $h_f = 120$ mm is

$$M_R = 0.45 \times 30 \times 800 \times 120(340 - 0.5 \times 120)/10^6$$
$$= 362.9 \text{ kN m}$$

The neutral axis lies in the flange. Using the code expressions in clause 3.4.4.4,

$$K = \frac{76.1 \times 10^6}{30 \times 800 \times 340^2} = 0.027$$

$$z = 340[0.5 + (0.25 - 0.027/0.9)^{0.5}]$$
$$= 329.5 \text{ mm}$$
$$> 0.95d = 0.95 \times 340 = 323 \text{ mm}$$

$$A_s = \frac{76.1 \times 10^6}{0.87 \times 460 \times 323} = 589 \text{ mm}^2$$

Provide four 16 mm diameter bars, area 804 mm². Using the simplified rules for curtailment of bars (Fig. 7.2(a)) two bars are cut off as shown in Fig. 7.4(c) at 0.08 of the span from each end.

(d) Design of shear reinforcement

The enhancement of shear strength near the support using the simplified approach given in clause 3.4.5.10 is taken into account in the design for shear. The maximum shear stress at the support is

$$v = \frac{43.5 \times 10^3}{200 \times 340} = 0.64 \, \text{N/mm}^2$$

This is less than $0.8 \times 30^{1/2} = 4.38 \, \text{N/mm}^2$ or $5 \, \text{N/mm}^2$. The shear at $d = 340 \, \text{mm}$ from the support is

$$V = 43.5 - 0.34 \times 12.43 = 38.8 \, \text{kN}$$
$$\text{shear stress } v = \frac{38.8 \times 10^3}{200 \times 340} = 0.57 \, \text{N/mm}^2$$

The effective area of steel at d from the support is two 16 mm diameter bars of area $402 \, \text{mm}^2$:

$$\frac{100 A_s}{bd} = \frac{100 \times 402}{200 \times 340} = 0.59$$

The design concrete shear strength from the formula in BS 8110: Part 1, Table 3.9, is

$$v_c = 0.79(0.59)^{1/3}(400/340)^{1/4}(30/25)^{1/3}/1.25$$
$$= 0.586 \, \text{N/mm}^2$$

Provide 8 mm diameter two-leg vertical links, $A_{sv} = 100 \, \text{mm}^2$, in grade 250 reinforcement. The spacing required is determined using Table 3.8 of the code.

$$v < v_c$$

The spacing for minimum links is

$$s_v = \frac{0.87 \times 250 \times 100}{0.4 \times 200} = 271.9 \, \text{mm}$$
$$\not> 0.75 \times 340 = 255 \, \text{mm}$$

The links will be spaced at 250 mm throughout the beam. Two 12 mm diameter bars are provided to carry the links at the top of the beam. The shear reinforcement is shown in Figs 7.4(b) and 7.4(c).

(e) End anchorage

The anchorage of the bars at the supports must comply with BS 8110: Part 1, clause 3.12.9.4. The bars are to be anchored 12 bar diameters past the centre of the support. This will be provided by a 90° bend with an internal radius of three bar diameters. From clause 3.12.8.23, the anchorage length is the greater of

1. $4 \times$ internal radius $= 4 \times 48 = 192 \, \text{mm}$ but not greater than $12 \times 16 = 192 \, \text{mm}$
2. the actual length of the bar $(4 \times 16) + 56 \times 2\pi/4 = 151.9 \, \text{mm}$

The anchorage is 12 bar diameters.

(f) Deflection check

The deflection of the beam is checked using the rules given in BS 8110: Part 1, clause 3.4.6. Referring to Table 3.10 of the code,

$$\frac{\text{web width}}{\text{effective flange width}} = \frac{b_w}{b} = \frac{200}{800} = 0.25 < 0.3$$

The basic span-to-effective depth ratio is 16.

$$\frac{M}{bd^2} = \frac{76.1 \times 10^6}{800 \times 340^2} = 0.82$$

The service stress is

$$f_s = \frac{5 \times 460 \times 589}{8 \times 804} = 210.6 \, \text{N/mm}^2$$

The modification factor for tension reinforcement using the formula in Table 3.11 in the code is

$$0.55 + \frac{477 - 210.6}{120(0.9 + 0.82)} = 1.84 < 2.0$$

For the modification factor for compression reinforcement, with $A'_{s,prov} = 226 \, \text{mm}^2$,

$$\frac{100A'_{s,prov}}{bd} = \frac{100 \times 226}{800 \times 340} = 0.083$$

The modification factor from the formula in Table 3.12 is

$$1 + [0.083/(3 + 0.083)] = 1.027$$
$$\text{allowable span}/d = 16 \times 1.84 \times 1.027 = 30.23$$
$$\text{actual span}/d = 7000/340 = 20.5$$

The beam is satisfactory with respect to deflection.

(g) Check for cracking

The clear distance between bars on the tension face does not exceed 160 mm. The distance from the corner of the beam to the nearest longitudinal bar with cover 35 mm and 8 mm diameter links is 72 mm and this is satisfactory because it is not greater than 80 mm (BS 8110: Part 1, section 3.12.11). The beam is satisfactory with regard to cracking.

(h) End bearing

No particular design is required in this case for the end bearing. With the arrangement shown in Fig. 7.4(b) the average bearing stress is 1.09 N/mm². The ultimate bearing capacity of concrete is $0.35f_{cu} = 10.5 \, \text{N/mm}^2$.

(i) Beam reinforcement

The reinforcement for each L-beam is shown in Fig. 7.4. Note that the slab reinforcement also provides reinforcement across the flange of the L-beam. ∎

☐ Example 7.2 Design of simply supported doubly reinforced rectangular beam

(a) Specification

A rectangular beam is 300 mm wide by 450 mm effective depth with inset to the compression steel of 55 mm. The beam is simply supported and spans 8 m. The dead load including an allowance for self-weight is 20 kN/m and the imposed load is 11 kN/m. The materials to be used are grade 30 concrete and grade 460 reinforcement. Design the beam.

(b) Loads and shear force and bending moment diagrams

$$\text{design load} = (1.4 \times 20) + (1.6 \times 11) = 45.6 \, \text{kN/m}$$
$$\text{ultimate moment} = 45.6 \times 8^2/8 = 364.8 \, \text{kN m}$$

The loads and shear force and bending moment diagrams are shown in Fig. 7.5.

(c) Design of the moment reinforcement (section 4.5.1)

When the depth x to the neutral is $0.5d$, the moment of resistance of the concrete only is $M_{RC} = 0.156 \times 30 \times 300 \times 450^2/10^6 = 284 \, \text{kN m}$. Compression reinforcement is required.

$$\frac{d'}{x} = \frac{55}{225} = 0.24 < 0.43$$

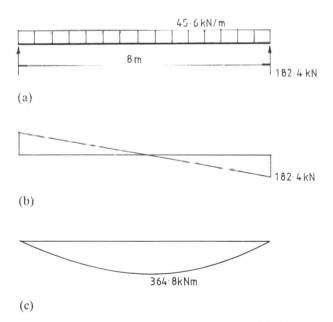

(a)

(b)

(c)

Fig. 7.5 (a) Design loading; (b) ultimate shear force diagram; (c) ultimate bending moment diagram.

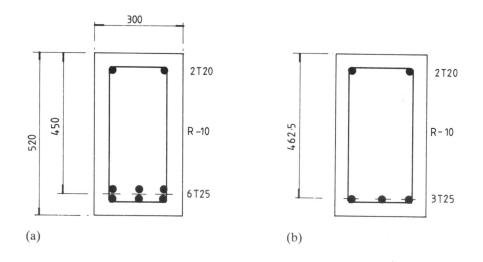

(a)   (b)

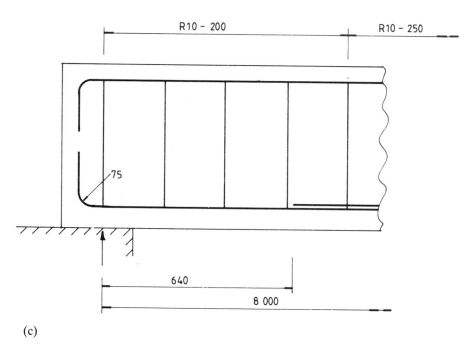

(c)

Fig. 7.6 (a) Section at centre; (b) end section; (c) part side elevation.

The stress in the compression reinforcement is $0.87f_y$. The area of compression steel is

$$A_s' = \frac{(364.8 - 284)10^6}{(450 - 55) \times 0.87 \times 460} = 508\,\text{mm}^2$$

Provide two 20 mm diameter bars, $A_s' = 628\,\text{mm}^2$.

$$A_s = \frac{(0.203 \times 30 \times 300 \times 450) + (0.87 \times 460 \times 508)}{0.87 \times 460}$$

$$= 2562\,\text{mm}^2$$

Provide six 25 mm diameter bars, $A_s = 2945\,\text{mm}^2$. The reinforcement is shown in Fig. 7.6(a). In accordance with the simplified rules for curtailment, three 25 mm diameter tension bars will be cut off at 0.08 of the span from each support. The compression bars will be carried through to the ends of the beam to anchor the links. The end section of the beam is shown in Fig. 7.6(b) and the side elevation in 7.6(c). The cover to the reinforcement is taken as 35 mm for moderate exposure.

(d) Design of shear reinforcement

The design for shear is made using the simplified approach in clause 3.4.5.10 of the code to take account of the enhancement of shear strength near the support. The maximum shear stress at the support is

$$v = \frac{182.4 \times 10^3}{300 \times 462.5} = 1.31\,\text{N/mm}^2$$

This is less than $0.8 \times 30^{1/2} = 4.38\,\text{N/mm}^2$ or $5\,\text{N/mm}^2$. The shear at d = 462.5 mm from the support is

$$V = 182.4 - 0.46 \times 45.6 = 161.4\,\text{N/mm}^2$$

$$v = \frac{161.4 \times 10^3}{300 \times 462.5} = 1.16\,\text{N/mm}^2$$

The area of steel at the section is $1472\,\text{mm}^2$.

$$\frac{100A_s}{bd} = \frac{100 \times 1472}{300 \times 462.5} = 1.06$$

The design shear strength from the formula in BS 8110: Part 1, Table 3.9, is

$$v_c = 0.79(1.06)^{1/3}(30/25)^{1/3}/1.25$$

$$= 0.68\,\text{N/mm}^2$$

Provide 10 mm diameter two-leg vertical links, $A_{sv} = 157\,\text{mm}^2$, in grade 250 steel. The spacing required is determined using Table 3.8 of the code:

$$s_v = \frac{157 \times 0.87 \times 250}{300(1.16 - 0.68)} = 237.1\,\text{mm}$$

For minimum links the spacing is

$$s_v = \frac{157 \times 0.87 \times 250}{300 \times 0.4} = 284.6\,\text{mm}$$

The spacing is not to exceed $0.75d = 346.8$ mm. This distance x from the support where minimum links only are required is determined. In this case $v = v_c$. The design shear strength where $A_s = 2945$ mm^2 and $d = 450$ mm is

$$100A_s/bd = 2.18$$
$$v_c = 0.87\,\text{N/mm}^2$$

Referring to Fig. 7.5 the distance x is found by solving the equation

$$0.87 \times 300 \times 450/10^3 = 182.4 - 45.6x$$
$$x = 1.42\,\text{m}$$

Space links at 200 mm centres for 2 m from each support and then at 250 mm centres over the centre 4 m. Note that the top layer of three 25 mm diameter bars continues for 780 mm greater than d past the section when $v = v_c$.

(e) End anchorage

The tension bars are anchored 12 bar diameters past the centre of the support. The end anchorage is shown in Fig. 7.6(c) where a 90° bend with an internal radius of three bar diameters is provided.

(f) Deflection check

The deflection of the beam is checked using the rules given in BS 8110: Part 1, clause 3.4.6. The basic span/d ratio from Table 3.10 of the code is 20 for a simply supported rectangular beam.

$$\frac{M}{bd^2} = \frac{364.8 \times 10^6}{300 \times 450^2} = 6.0$$

The service stress is

$$f_s = \frac{5 \times 460 \times 2631.2}{8 \times 2945} = 256.9\,\text{N/mm}^2$$

The modification factor for tension reinforcement using the formula in Table 3.11 of the code is

$$0.55 + \frac{477 - 256.9}{120(0.9 + 6.0)} = 0.816$$

The modification factor for compression reinforcement, with $A'_{s.prov} = 628$ mm^2, is

$$\frac{100A'_{s.prov}}{bd} = \frac{100 \times 628}{300 \times 450} = 0.46$$

The modification factor from the formula in Table 3.12 is

$$1 + [0.4/(3 + 0.46)] = 1.13$$
$$\text{allowable span}/d = 20 \times 0.816 \times 1.13 = 18.4$$
$$\text{actual span}/d = 8000/450 = 17.8$$

The beam is just satisfactory with respect to deflection.

(g) Check for cracking

The clear distance between bars on the tension face does not exceed 160 mm and the clear distance from the corner of the beam to the nearest longitudinal bar does not exceed 80 mm. The beam is satisfactory with regard to cracking (BS 8110: Part 1, section 3.12.11).

(h) Beam reinforcement

The beam reinforcement is shown in Fig. 7.6.   ■

7.2 CONTINUOUS BEAMS

7.2.1 Continuous beams in *in situ* concrete floors

Continuous beams are a common element in cast-*in-situ* construction. A reinforced concrete floor in a multistorey building is shown in Fig. 7.7. The floor action to support the loads is as follows:

1. The one-way slab carried on the edge frame, intermediate T-beams and centre frame spans transversely across the building;
2. Intermediate T-beams on line AA span between the transverse end and interior frames to support the floor slab;
3. Transverse end frames DD and interior frames EE span across the building and carry loads from intermediate T-beams and longitudinal frames;
4. Longitudinal edge frames CC and interior frame BB support the floor slab.

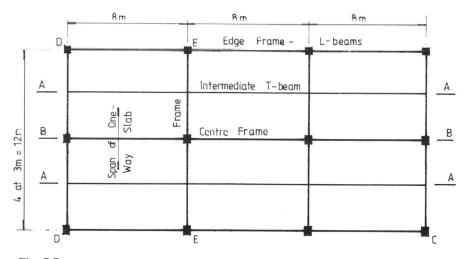

Fig. 7.7

The horizontal members of the rigid frames may be analysed as part of the rigid frame. This is discussed in of BS 8110: Part 1, section 3.2.1, and in Chapter 13. The code gives a continuous beam simplification in clause 3.2.1.2.4 where moments and shears may be obtained by taking the members as continuous beams over supports with the columns providing no restraint to rotation (Chapter 3, section 3.4.2).

The steps in design of continuous beams are the same as those set out in section 7.1.1 for simple beams.

7.2.2 Loading on continuous beams

(a) Arrangement of loads to give maximum moments

The loading is to be applied to the continuous beam to give the most adverse conditions at any section along the beam. To achieve this the following critical loading arrangements are set out in BS 8110: Part 1, clause 3.2.1.2.2 (G_k is the characteristic dead load and Q_k is the characteristic imposed load):

1. All spans are loaded with the maximum design ultimate load $1.4G_k + 1.6Q_k$;
2. Alternate spans are loaded with the maximum design ultimate load $1.4G_k + 1.6Q_k$ and all other spans are loaded with the minimum design ultimate load $1.0G_k$.

(b) Example of critical loading arrangements

The total dead load on the floor in Fig. 7.7 including an allowance for the ribs of the T-beams, screed, finishes, partitions, ceiling and services is $6.6\,\text{kN/m}^2$ and the imposed load is $3\,\text{kN/m}^2$. Calculate the design load and set out the load arrangements to comply with BS 8110: Part 1, clause 3.2.1.2.2, for the continuous T-beam on lines AA and BB.

The characteristic dead load is

$$G_k = 3 \times 6.6 = 19.8\,\text{kN/m}$$

The characteristic imposed load is

$$Q_k = 3 \times 3 = 9\,\text{kN/m}$$

The maximum design ultimate load is

$$(1.4 \times 19.8) + (1.6 \times 9) = 42.12\,\text{kN/m}$$

The loading arrangements are shown in Fig. 7.8. Case 1 gives maximum hogging moment at B and maximum shear on either side of B. Case 2 gives the maximum sagging moment at Q, and case 3 gives maximum sagging moment at P, maximum hogging moment or minimum sagging moment at Q and maximum shear at A.

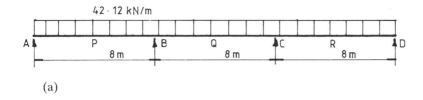

(a)

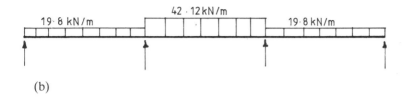

(b)

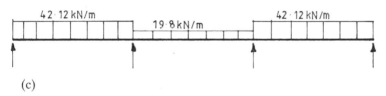

(c)

Fig. 7.8 (a) Case 1, all spans loaded with $1.4G_k + 1.6Q_k$; (b) case 2, alternate spans loaded with $1.4G_k + 1.6Q$k; (c) case 3, alternate spans loaded with $1.4G_k + 1.6Q_k$.

(c) Loading from one-way slabs

Continuous beams supporting slabs designed as spanning one way can be considered to be uniformly loaded. The slab is assumed to consist of a serious of beams as shown in Fig. 7.9. This is the application of the load discussed in section 7.2.1(a) above. Note that some two-way action occurs at the ends of one-way slabs.

(d) Loading from two-way slabs

If the beam is designed as spanning two ways, the four edge beams assist in carrying the loading. The load distribution normally assumed for analyses of the edge beams is shown in Fig. 7.10 where lines at 45° are drawn from the corners of the slab. This distribution gives triangular and trapezoidal loads on the edge beams as shown in the figure.

Exact analytical methods can be used for calculating fixed end and span moments. Handbooks [6] also list moments for these cases. If a computer program is used for the analysis uniformly varying loads can be entered directly in the data.

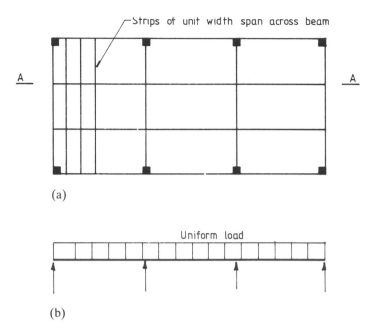

(a)

(b)

Fig. 7.9 (a) Floor plan; (b) beam AA.

The fixed end moments for the two load cases shown in Figs 7.10(b) and 7.10(c) are as follows.

(i) Trapezoidal load   The load is broken down into a uniform central portion

$$\frac{l_y - l_x}{l_y - 0.5l_x} W_1$$

and two triangular end portions each

$$\frac{0.25l_x}{l_y - 0.5l_x} W_1$$

where W_1 is the total load on one span of the beam, l_x is the short span of the slab and l_y is the long span of the slab. The fixed end moments for the two spans in the beam on AA are

$$M_1 = \frac{l_y - l_x}{l_y - 0.5l_x} \frac{W}{24l_y} [3l_y{}^2 - (l_y - l_x)^2]$$
$$+ \frac{Wl_x{}^2}{48l_y} \frac{4l_y - 1.5l_x}{l_y - 0.5l_x}$$

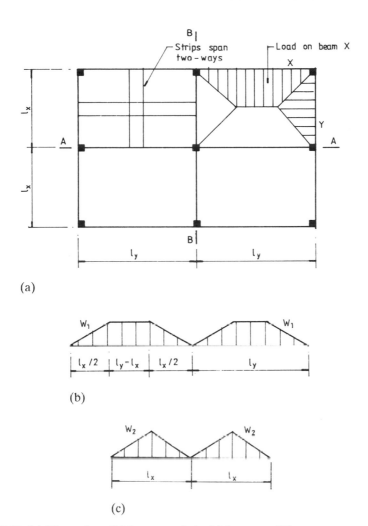

(a)

(b)

(c)

Fig. 7.10 (a) Floor plan; (b) beam on AA; (c) beam on BB.

(ii) Triangular load The fixed end moments for the two spans in the beam on line BB in Fig. 7.10(a) are

$$M_2 = 5W_2l_x/48$$

where W_2 is the total load on one span of the beam.

(e) Alternative distribution of loads from two-way slabs

BS 8110: Part 1, Fig. 3.10, gives the distribution of load on a beam supporting a two-way spanning slab. This distribution is shown in Fig. 7.11(a). The design loads on the supporting beams are as follows:

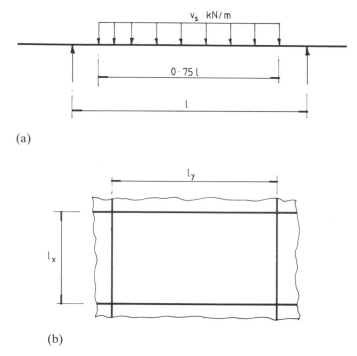

Fig. 7.11 (a) Load distribution; (b) two-way slab.

$$\text{Long span } v_{sy} = \beta_{vy} n l_x \text{ kN/m}$$
$$\text{Short span } v_{sx} = \beta_{vx} n l_x \text{ kN/m}$$

where n is the design load per unit area. Values of the coefficients β_{vx} and β_{vy} are given in Table 3.16 of the code. The β_{vx} values depend on the ratio l_y/l_x of the lengths of the sides. The total ultimate load carried by the slab is n kN/m^2.

For a square slab of side l

$$\beta_{vx} = \beta_{vy} = 0.33$$

and the total load on the edge beams is $0.99nl^2$.

7.2.3 Analysis for shear and moment envelopes

The following methods of analysis can be used to find the shear forces and bending moments for design:

1. manual elastic analysis using the method of moment distribution
2. computer analyses using a program based on the matrix stiffness method
3. using coefficients for moments and shear from BS 8110: Part 1, Table 3.6

Table 7.1 Design ultimate bending moments and shear forces for continuous beams

	At outer support	Near middle of end span	At first interior support	At middle of interior span	At interior supports
Moment	0	0.09Fl	−0.11Fl	0.07Fl	−0.08Fl
Shear	0.45F	–	0.6F	–	0.55F

L, effective span; F, total design ultimate load on a span, equal to $1.4G_k + 1.6Q_k$.

In using method 1, the beam is analysed for the various load cases, the shear force and bending moment diagrams are drawn for these cases and the maximum shear and moment envelopes are constructed. Precise values are then available for moments and shear at every point in the beam. This method must be used for two span beams and beams with concentrated loads not covered by Table 3.6 of the code. It is also necessary to use rigorous elastic analysis if moment redistribution is to be made, as set out in section 7.2.4 below.

Computer programs are available to analyse and design continuous reinforced concrete beams. These carry out all the steps including analysis, moment redistribution, design for moment and shear reinforcement, check for deflection and cracking and output of a detail drawing of the beam.

BS 8110: Part 1, clause 3.4.3, gives moments and shear forces in continuous beams with uniform loading. The design ultimate moments and shear forces are given in Table 3.6 in the code which is reproduced as Table 7.1 here. The use of the table is subject to the following conditions:

1. The characteristic imposed load Q_k may not exceed the characteristic dead load G_k;
2. The loads should be substantially uniformly distributed over three or more spans;
3. Variations in span length should not exceed 15% of the longest span.

The code also states that no redistribution of moments calculated using this table should be made.

□ Example 7.3 Elastic analysis of a continuous beam

(a) Specification

Analyse the continuous beam for the three load cases shown in Fig. 7.8 and draw the separate shear force and bending moment diagrams. Construct the maximum shear force and bending moment envelopes. Calculate the moments and shears using the coefficients from BS 8110: Part 1, Table 3.6.

A	B		C		D
AB	BA	BC	CB	CD	DC
	0·43	0·57	0·57	0·43	
00	336·96	− 224·64	+ 224·64	− 224·64	+ 224·64
	− 48·3	− 64·02			
	0 0	+ 32·01	Beam		
	− 13·76	− 18·25	is		
	0 0	+ 9·13	symmetrically		
	− 3·93	− 5·2			
	0 0	+ 2·6	loaded		
	− 1·12	− 1·48			
00	+ 269·85	− 269·85			

(a)

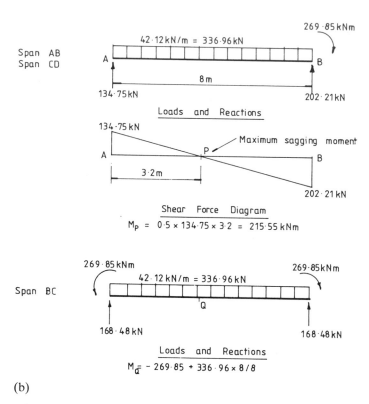

(b)

Fig. 7.12 (a) Moment distribution; (b) shears and span moments.

(b) Analysis by moment distribution

The full analysis for case 1 in Fig. 7.8 is given and the results only for cases 2 and 3.
The fixed end moments are

$$\text{Span AB} \quad M = 42.12 \times 8^2/8 \; = 336.96 \, \text{kN m}$$
$$\text{Span BC} \quad M = 42.12 \times 8^2/12 = 224.64 \, \text{kN m}$$

The distribution factors for joint B are

$$\text{BA:BC} = \frac{0.75:1.0}{1.75} = 0.43:0.57$$

The moment distribution is shown in Fig. 7.12(a) and calculations for shears and span moments are given in Fig. 7.12(b). The loads, shear force and bending moment diagrams for the three load cases are shown in Fig. 7.13. The shear force and bending moment envelopes for the elastic analysis carried out above are shown in Fig. 7.14.

(c) Analysis using BS 8110: Part 1, Table 3.6

The values of the maximum shear forces and bending moments at appropriate points along the beam are calculated using coefficients from BS 8110: Part 1, Table 3.6.

$$F - \text{total design ultimate load per span}$$
$$= 42.12 \times 8 = 336.96 \, \text{kN}$$

The values of moments and shears are tabulated in Table 7.2. Corresponding values from the elastic analysis are shown for comparison. Note that, if the beam had been analysed for a load of $1.4G_k + 1.6Q_k$ on spans AB and BC and $1.0G_k$ on span CD, the maximum hogging moment at support B would be 292.5 kN m, which agrees with the values from Table 3.6 of the code.

Table 7.2 Moments and shears in continuous beam

	Position	Table 3.6 value	Elastic analysis
Shear forces (kN)	A	$0.45 \times 336.96 = 151.63$	154.99
	BA	$0.6 \times 336.96 = 202.18$	202.21
	BC	$0.55 \times 336.96 = 185.33$	168.48
Bending moments (kN m)	P	$0.09 \times 336.96 \times 8 = 242.61$	284.4
	B	$-0.11 \times 336.96 \times 8 = -296.52$	−269.85
	Q	$0.07 \times 336.96 \times 8 = 188.69$	138.45

7.2.4 Moment redistribution

In an under-reinforced beam with tension steel only or a doubly reinforced beam the tension steel yields before failure if the load is increased. A hinge forms at the point of maximum elastic moment, i.e. at the hogging moment

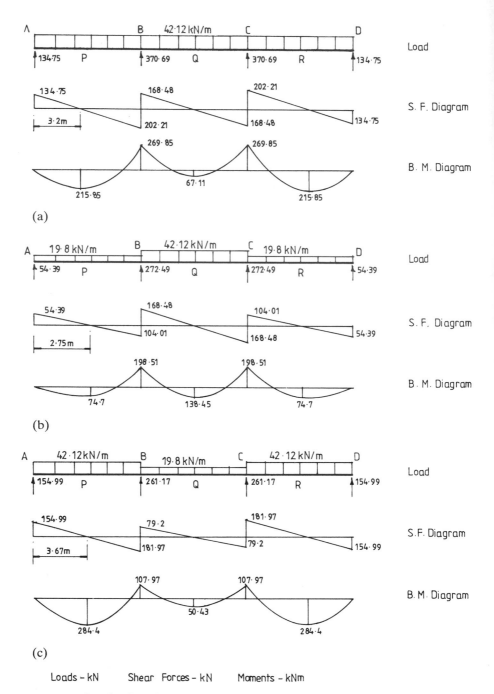

Fig. 7.13 Loads, shear force and bending moment diagrams: (a) case 1; (b) case 2; (c) case 3.

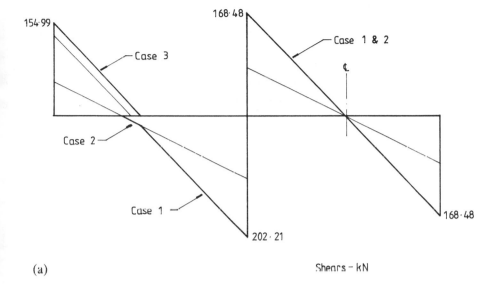

154·99

168·48

Case 3

Case 1 & 2

₵

Case 2

Case 1

202·21

168·48

(a)

Shears – kN

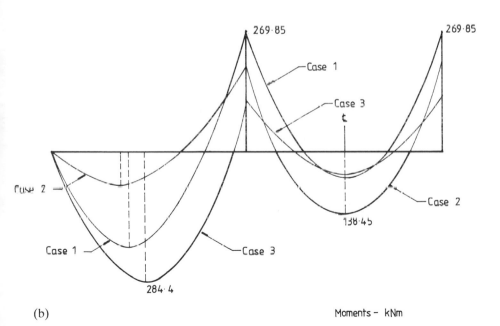

269·85

269·85

Case 1

Case 3

₵

Case 2

Case 2

138·45

Case 1

Case 3

284·4

(b)

Moments – kNm

Fig. 7.14 (a) Shear force envelope; (b) bending moment envelope.

over the support in a continuous beam. As the hinge rotates a redistribution of moments takes place in the beam where the hogging moment reduces and the sagging moment increases.

A beam section can be reinforced to yield at a given ultimate moment. Theoretically the moment of resistance at the support can be made to any value desired and the span moment can be calculated to be in equilibrium with the support moment and external loads.

A full plastic analysis such as has been developed for structural steel could be applied to reinforced concrete beam design. However, it is necessary to ensure that, while there is adequate rotation capacity at the hinge, serious cracking does not occur.

To take account of the plastic behaviour described above the code sets out the procedure for moment redistribution in section 3.2.2. This section states that a redistribution of moments obtained by a rigorous elastic analysis or by other simplified methods set out in the code may be carried out provided that the following hold:

1. Equilibrium between internal and external forces is maintained under all appropriate combinations of design ultimate load;
2. Where the design ultimate resistance moment at a section is reduced by redistribution from the largest moment within that region, the neutral axis depth x should not be greater than

$$x = (\beta_b - 0.4)d$$

where

$$\beta_b = \frac{\text{moment after redistribution}}{\text{moment before redistribution}}$$
$$\leqslant 1$$

The moments before and after redistribution are to be taken from the respective maximum moment diagrams. This provision ensures that there is adequate rotation capacity at the section for redistribution to take place;
3. The ultimate resistance moment provided at any section should be at least 70% of the moment obtained from the elastic maximum moment diagram covering all appropriate load combinations.

The third condition implies that the maximum redistribution permitted is 30%, i.e. the largest moment given in the elastic maximum moments diagram may be reduced by up to 30%.

This third condition is also necessary because when the hogging moment at the support is reduced and the sagging moment in the span is increased to maintain equilibrium the points of contraflexure move nearer the supports. Figure 7.15 shows an internal span in a continuous beam where the

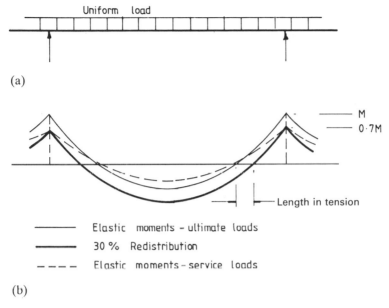

(a)

(b)

Fig. 7.15 (a) Load; (b) moment diagrams.

peak elastic moment at the supports is reduced by 30% and the sagging moment is increased. At service loads the moments are about $1/1.5 = 0.7$ of the elastic moments at ultimate loads where 1.5 is the average of the partial safety factors for dead and imposed loads. The elastic moment diagram for service loads, also given, shows a length of beam in tension which would be in compression under the redistributed moments. The limitation prevents this possibility occurring. There is generally sufficient reinforcement in the top of the beam to resist the small moment in this area.

Redistribution gives a more even arrangement for the reinforcement, relieving congestion at supports. It also leads to a saving in the amount of reinforcement required.

☐ Example 7.4 Moment redistribution for a continuous beam

(a) Specification

Referring to the three-span continuous beam analysed in Example 7.3 above redistribute the moments after making a 20% reduction in the maximum hogging moment at the interior support. Draw the envelopes for maximum shear force and bending moment.

(b) Moment redistribution

Consider case 1 from Fig. 7.13. The hogging moments at supports B and C are reduced by 20% to a value of 215.88 kN m. The shears and internal moments for the three spans AB, BC and CD are recalculated and the redistributed moment diagram is drawn. The calculations and diagrams are shown in Fig. 7.16. Note the length in tension due to hogging moment from the redistribution.

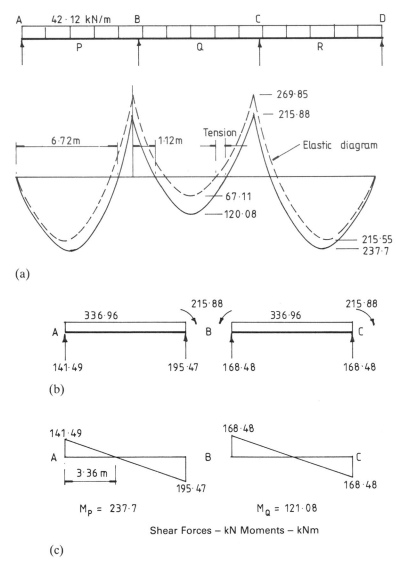

Fig. 7.16 (a) Bending moment diagram; (b) span loads; (c) shear forces and span moments.

Using the reduced value for moments at interior supports B and C the redistribution of moments is carried out for cases 2 and 3 in Fig. 7.13. The shear force and bending moment diagrams for these cases are shown in Figs 7.17(a) and 7.17(b) respectively.

The shear force and bending moment envelopes are then constructed. These are shown in Figs 7.18(a) and 7.18(b) respectively. The maximum elastic sagging moment diagrams are drawn for the two spans. These show that the redistributed moment does not meet the code requirement that the ultimate resistance moment must not be less than 70% of the elastic maximum moment near the internal supports. The redistributed moment diagram must then be modified as shown in Fig. 7.18(b). This situation has occurred because the support moment has been increased from the values obtained by elastic analysis shown for cases 2 and 3 in Fig. 7.13.

When Figs 7.14 and 7.18 are compared, it is noted that the maximum hogging and sagging moments from the elastic bending moment envelope have both been reduced by the moment redistribution. The redistribution gives a saving in the amount of reinforcement required.

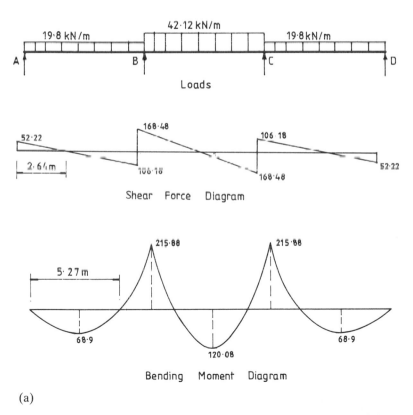

(a)

Fig. 7.17 Shear force diagram and bending moment diagram: (a) case 2; (b) case 3.

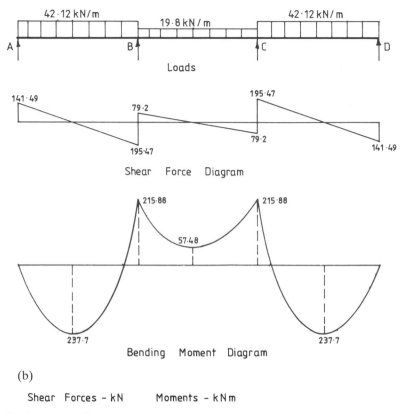

Fig. 7.17 (b) case 3.

7.2.5 Curtailment of bars

The curtailment of bars may be carried out in accordance with the detailed provisions set out in BS 8110: Part 1, clause 3.12.9.1. These were discussed in section 7.1.2. The anchorage of tension bars at the simply supported ends is dealt with in clause 3.12.9.4 of the code.

Simplified rules for curtailment of bars in continuous beams are given in clause 3.12.10.2 and Fig. 3.24(a) of the code. The clause states that these rules may be used when the following provisions are satisfied:

1. The beams are designed for predominantly uniformly distributed loads;
2. The spans are approximately equal in the case of continuous beams.

The simplified rules for curtailment of bars in continuous beams are shown in Fig. 7.19.

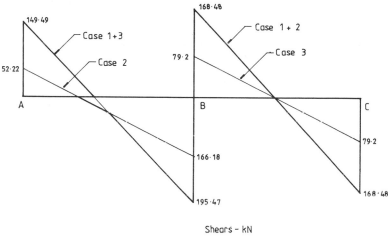

Shears – kN

(a)

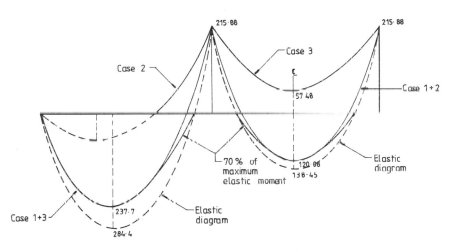

Moments – kNm

(b)

Fig. 7.18 (a) Shear force envelope; (b) bending moment envelope. The envelopes are symmetrical about the centreline of the beam.

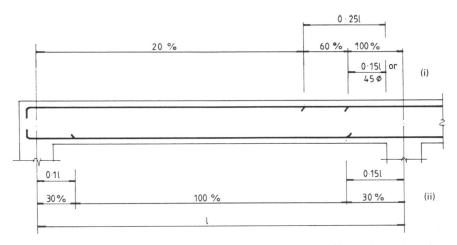

Fig. 7.19 Reinforcement as percentage of that required for (i) maximum hogging moment over support and (ii) maximum sagging moment in span.

□ Example 7.5 Design for the end span of a continuous beam

(a) Specification

Design the end span of the continuous beam analysed in Example 7.3. The design is to be made for the shear forces and moments obtained after a 20% redistribution from the elastic analysis has been made. The shear force and moment envelopes are shown in Fig. 7.18. The materials are grade 30 concrete and grade 460 reinforcement.

(b) Design of moment steel

The assumed beam sections for mid-span and over the interior support are shown in Figs 7.20(a) and 7.20(b) respectively. The cover for mild exposure from Table 3.4 in the code is 25 mm. The cover for a fire resistance period of 2 h from Table 3.5 is 30 mm for continuous beams. Cover of 30 mm is provided to the links.

(i) Section near the centre of the span   The beam acts as a T-beam at this section. The design moment is 237.7 kN m (Fig. 7.17(b)).

$$\text{breadth of flange} = (0.7 \times 8000/5) + 250$$
$$= 1370 \, \text{mm}$$

The cover on 10 mm links is 30 mm and if 25 mm main bars in vertical pairs are required

$$\text{effective depth } d = 450 - 30 - 10 - 25 = 385 \, \text{mm}$$

The moment of resistance of the section when 0.9 multiplied by the depth x to the neutral axis is equal to the slab depth $h_f = 125 \, \text{mm}$ is

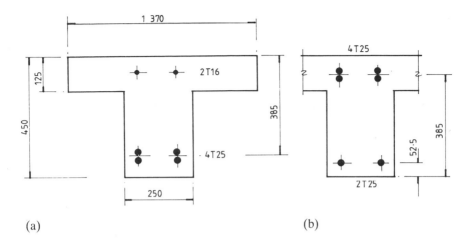

Fig. 7.20 (a) T-beam at mid-span; (b) rectangular beam over support.

$$M_R = 0.45 \times 30 \times 1370 \times 125(385 - 0.5 \times 125)/10^6$$
$$= 745.6 \, \text{kN m}$$

The neutral axis lies in the flange.

Using the code expression in clause 3.4.4.4

$$K = \frac{237.7 \times 10^6}{30 \times 1370 \times 385^2} = 0.039$$
$$z = 385[0.5 + (0.25 - 0.039/0.9)^{0.5}]$$
$$= 367.5 \, \text{mm}$$
$$> 0.95 \times 383 = 365.7 \, \text{mm}$$
$$A_s = \frac{237.7 \times 10^6}{0.87 \times 460 \times 365.7} = 1624.1 \, \text{mm}^2$$

Provide four 25 mm diameter bars; $A_s = 1963 \, \text{mm}^2$.

Note that in this case the amount of redistribution from the elastic moment of 284.4 kN m is 16.4% i.e. $\beta_b = 0.84$, and the depth x to the neutral axis must not exceed $0.44d$. The actual value of x is much less.

The moment of resistance after cutting off two 25 mm diameter bars where $d = 397.5$ mm, $z = 0.95d$ and $A_s = 981 \, \text{mm}^2$ is calculated. Note that $z = 0.95d$ when the moment is 237.7 kN m and so the beam will have the same limiting value at a section where the moment is less.

$$M_R = 0.87 \times 460 \times 0.95 \times 397.5 \times 981/10^6$$
$$= 148.3 \, \text{kN m}$$

Referring to case 3 in Fig. 7.17(b) the theoretical cut-off points for two 25 mm diameter bars on the redistributed moment diagram can be determined by solving the equation

$$141.9x - 21.06x^2 = 148.3$$

which gives $x = 1.29$ m and $x = 5.45$ m from end A. Referring to the maximum elastic bending moment for sagging moment, case 3 in Fig. 7.13, the distance from end A of the beam where the moment of resistance equals 0.7 of the elastic moment can be determined from the equation

$$0.7(154.99x - 21.06x^2) = 148.3$$

Solve to give $x = 5.54$ m. This over-riding condition gives the theoretical cut-off point for the bars.

The anchorage length for type 2 deformed bars is calculated. Refer to clause 3.12.8.3 and Table 3.29 in the code and section 5.2.1 here where the anchorage length is given as

$$l = 37\phi = 925 \text{ mm}$$

To comply with the detailed provisions for curtailment of bars given in clause 3.12.9.1 of the code the two 25 mm diameter bars will be stopped off at 925 mm beyond the theoretical cut-off points. This also satisfies the condition that bars extend a distance equal to the greater of the effective depth or 12 bar diameters beyond the theoretical cut-off points. Other provisions in the clause need not be examined. At the support the tension bars must be anchored 12 bar diameters past the centreline of the support. The cut-off points are shown in Fig. 7.21. These are at 350 mm from the end support and 1600 mm from the interior support.

(ii) Section at the interior support The beam acts as a rectangular beam at the support. The section is shown in Fig. 7.20(b). The redistribution of 20% has been carried out and so the depth to the neutral axis should not exceed

$$x = (\beta_b - 0.4)d = 0.4d$$

where $\beta_b = 0.8$. The design moment is 215.88 kN m.

The moment of resistance with respect to the concrete is calculated from the expressions given in clause 3.4.4.4 of the code. Refer to section 4.7.

$$M_{RC} = [(0.405 \times 0.4) - 0.18 \times 0.4^2] \times 250 \times 385^2 \times 30/10^6$$
$$= 148.1 \text{ kN m}$$

Compression reinforcement is required.

$$\frac{d'}{x} = \frac{52.5}{0.4 \times 385} = 0.34 < 0.43$$

The stress in the compression steel is $0.87f_y$.

$$A_s' = \frac{(215.88 - 148.1)10^6}{(385 - 52.5)0.87 \times 460}$$
$$= 509.4 \text{ mm}^2$$

The tension reinforcement area is

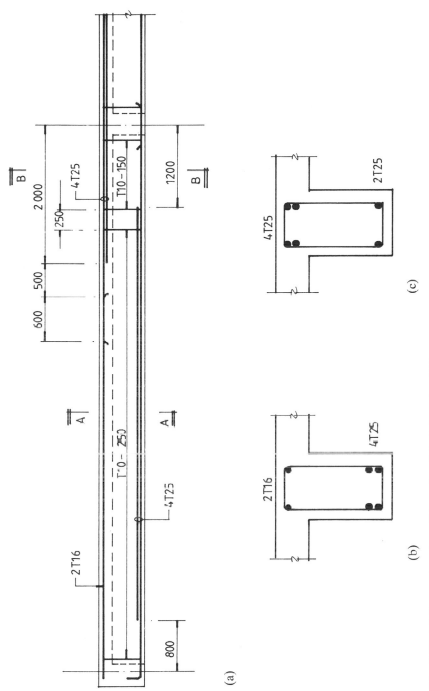

Fig. 7.21 (a) Beam elevation; (b) section AA; (c) section BB.

(a)

(b)

(c)

2T16

4T25

2 000

4T25

T10 – 150

250

600

500

1200

800

T10 – 250

A

A

B

B

4T25

2T25

2T16

4T25

$$T = \frac{0.405 \times 30 \times 250 \times 385 \times 0.4}{0.87 \times 460} + 509.4$$

$$= 1678.3 \, \text{mm}^2$$

The compression reinforcement will be provided by carrying two 25 mm diameter mid-span bars through the support. For tension reinforcement, provide four 25 mm diameter bars with area 1963 mm².

The theoretical and actual cut-off points for two of the four top bars are determined. The moment of resistance of the section with two 25 mm diameter bars and an effective depth $d = 397.5$ mm is calculated. Refer to section 4.6.

$$T = 0.87 \times 460 \times 981 = 3.926 \times 10^5 \, \text{N}$$

$$C = 0.45 \times 30 \times 0.9x \times 250 = 3038x \, \text{N}$$

$$x = 3.926 \times 10^5/3038 = 129.2 \, \text{mm}$$

$$z = 397.5 - 0.5 \times 0.9 \times 129.2 = 339.4 \, \text{mm}$$

$$< 0.95d \qquad\qquad = 377.6 \, \text{mm}$$

The moment of resistance is

$$M_R = 3.926 \times 10^5 \times 339.4/10^6 = 133.2 \, \text{kN m}$$

Referring to case 2 in Fig. 7.17(a), the theoretical cut-off point can be found by solving the equation

$$-52.22x + 9.9x^2 = 133.2$$

This gives $x = 7.15$ m from support A.

The actual cut-off point after continuing the bars from an anchorage length is $8000 - 7150 + 925 = 1775$ mm from support B. The bar cut-off is shown in Fig. 7.21. The 25 mm diameter bars will be cut off and two 20 mm diameter bars lapped on to provide top reinforcement through the span and carry the links.

(c) Design of shear reinforcement

The design will take account of enhancement of shear strength near the support (BS 8110: Part 1, clause 3.4.5.10).

(i) Simply supported end The maximum shear is 141.49 kN (Fig. 7.18(a)).

$$v = \frac{141.49 \times 10^3}{280 \times 397.5} = 1.42 \, \text{N/mm}^2$$

$$< 0.8 \times 30^{1/2} = 4.38 \, \text{N/mm}^2 \text{ or } 5 \, \text{N/mm}^2$$

The shear at $d = 397.5$ mm from the support is

$$141.49 - 42.12 \times 0.39 = 125.1 \, \text{N/mm}^2$$

$$v = \frac{125.1 \times 10^3}{250 \times 397.5} = 1.25 \, \text{N/mm}^2$$

$$\frac{100A_s}{bd} = \frac{100 \times 981}{250 \times 391.5} = 0.987$$

$$v_c = 0.79(0.987)^{1/3}(400/3975)^{1/4} \times (30/25)^{1/3}/1.25$$
$$= 0.67 \, \text{N/mm}^2$$

Provide 10 mm diameter grade 460 links. $A_{sv} = 157 \, \text{mm}^2$ for two-legs. Spacing

$$s_v = \frac{0.87 \times 460 \times 157}{297.5(1.25 - 0.67)} = 267.9 \, \text{mm}$$

$$\not> 0.75d \qquad\qquad = 298.1 \, \text{mm}$$

Minimum links are required when $v = v_c$. For the section with four 25 mm diameter bars, $d = 385$ mm.

$$100A_s/bd = 2.04$$
$$v_c = 0.86 \, \text{N/mm}^2$$
$$V = 0.86 \times 250 \times 385/10^3$$
$$= 82.8 \, \text{kN}$$

Referring to Fig. 7.18(a), the distance x along the beam is given by solving the equation

$$82.8 = 141.49 - 42.12x$$
$$x = 1.39 \, \text{m}$$

For minimum links the spacing is

$$s_v = \frac{157 \times 0.7 \times 460}{385 \times 0.4} = 407 \, \text{mm}$$

$$\not> 0.75 \times 385 = 288.7$$

Rationalize the results from the above calculations and space links at 250 mm centres.

(ii) Near the internal support   The maximum shear is 195.47 kN (Fig. 7.18(a)).

$$v = \frac{195.47 \times 10^3}{385 \times 250} = 2.03 \, \text{N/mm}^3$$

$$< 4.38 \, \text{N/mm}^2$$

The shear at $d = 385$ mm from the support is

$$V = 179.5 \, \text{kN}$$
$$v = 1.86 \, \text{N/mm}^2$$
$$v_c = 0.86$$
$$s_v = \frac{0.87 \times 460 \times 157}{385(1.96 - 0.86)} = 163.2 \, \text{mm}$$

The distance from the support where links at 250 mm centres are required is determined. Rearrange the link spacing equation:

$$v - 0.86 = \frac{0.87 \times 460 \times 157}{385 \times 250} = 0.65$$

$$v = 1.51 \, \text{N/mm}^2$$
$$V = 1.51 \times 250 \times 385/10^3 = 145.3 \, \text{kN}$$
$$x = (195.47 - 145.3)/42.12 = 1.19 \, \text{m}$$

Note that the cut-off point for the two top bars is 1.775 m from the support. Thus four bars are effective in resisting shear at the section.

Space links at 150 mm centres from the internal support for a distance of 1200 mm and then at 250 mm centres over the remainder of the span. A more elaborate spacing system could be adopted. The arrangement of links is shown in Fig. 7.21.

(d) Deflection

$$\frac{\text{web width}}{\text{effective flange width}} = \frac{b_w}{b} = \frac{250}{1370} = 0.18 < 0.3$$

The basic span-to-effective depth ratio is 20.8 (BS 8110: Part 1, Table 3.10).

$$\frac{M}{bd^2} = \frac{237.7 \times 10^6}{1370 \times 385} = 1.17$$

$$f_s = \frac{5 \times 460 \times 1624.1 \times 0.8}{8 \times 1963} = 190.3 \, \text{N/mm}^2$$

The modification factor for tension reinforcement from Table 3.11 of the code is

$$0.55 + \frac{477 - 190.3}{120(0.9 + 1.17)} = 1.7 < 2.0$$

Two 20 mm diameter bars, $A_s' = 625 \, \text{mm}^2$, are provided in the top of the beam.

$$\frac{100A_s'}{bd} = \frac{100 \times 625}{1370 \times 385} = 0.12$$

The modification factor is

$$1 + 0.12/(3 + 0.12) = 1.04$$

allowable span/d ration $20.8 \times 1.7 \times 1.04 = 36.8$
actual span/d ratio $8000/385 = 20.8$

The beam is satisfactory with respect to deflection.

(e) Cracking

From Fig. 7.21 the clear distance between bars on the tension faces at mid-span and over the support is 120 mm. This does not exceed the 130 mm permitted in Table 3.30 of the code for 20% redistribution. The distance from the corner to the nearest longitudinal bar is 61.7 mm which should not exceed 65 mm. The beam is satisfactory with respect to crack control.

(f) Sketch of beam

A sketch of the beam with the moment and shear reinforcement and curtailment of bars is shown in Fig. 7.21.   ∎

8

Slabs

8.1 TYPES OF SLAB AND DESIGN METHODS

Slabs are plate elements forming floors and roofs in buildings which normally carry uniformly distributed loads. Slabs may be simply supported or continuous over one or more supports and are classified according to the method of support as follows:

1. spanning one way between beams or walls
2. spanning two ways between the support beams or walls
3. flat slabs carried on columns and edge beams or walls with no interior beams

Slabs may be solid of uniform thickness or ribbed with ribs running in one or two directions. Slabs with varying depth are generally not used. Stairs with various support conditions form a special case of sloping slabs.

Slabs may be analysed using the following methods.

1. **Elastic analysis** covers three techniques:
   (a) idealization into strips or beams spanning one way or a grid with the strips spanning two ways
   (b) elastic plate analysis
   (c) finite element analysis – the best method for irregularly shaped slabs or slabs with non-uniform loads
2. For the method of **design coefficients** use is made of the moment and shear coefficients given in the code, which have been obtained from yield line analysis.
3. The **yield line and Hillerborg strip methods** are limit design or collapse loads methods. Simple applications of the yield line method are discussed in the book.

8.2 ONE-WAY SPANNING SOLID SLABS

8.2.1 Idealization for Design

(a) Uniformly loaded slabs

One-way slabs carrying predominantly uniform load are designed on the assumption that they consist of a series of rectangular beams 1 m wide spanning between supporting beams or walls. The sections through a simply

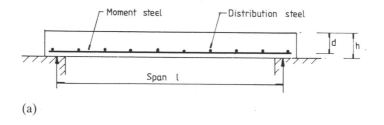

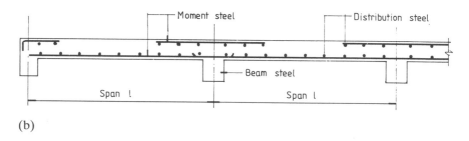

Fig. 8.1 (a) Simply supported slab; (b) continuous one-way slab.

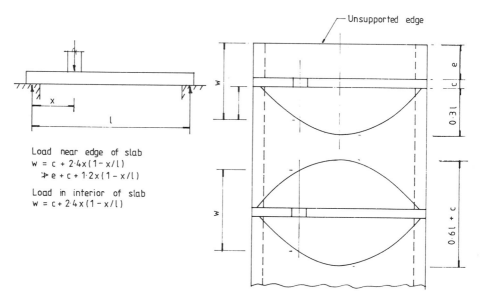

Load near edge of slab
$w = c + 2.4x(1 - x/l)$
$\not> e + c + 1.2x(1 - x/l)$

Load in interior of slab
$w = c + 2.4x(1 - x/l)$

Fig. 8.2

supported slab and a continuous slab are shown in Figs 8.1(a) and 8.1(b) respectively.

(b) Concentrated loads on a solid slab

BS 8110: Part 1 specifies in clause 3.5.2.2 that, for a slab simply supported on two edges carrying a concentrated load, the effective width of slab resisting the load may be taken as

$$w = \text{width of load} + 2.4x(1 - x/l)$$

where x is the distance of the load from the nearer support and l is the span of the slab. If the load is near an unsupported edge the effective width should not exceed

1. w as defined above or
2. $0.5w$ + distance of the centre of the load from the unsupported edge

The effective widths of slab supporting a load in the interior of the slab and near an unsupported edge are shown in Figs 8.2(a) and 8.2(b) respectively.
    Refer to the code for provisions regarding other types of slabs.

8.2.2 Effective span, loading and analysis

(a) Effective span

The effective span for one-way slabs is the same as that set out for beams in section 7.1. Refer to BS 8110: Part 1, clauses 3.4.1.2 and 3.4.1.3. The effective spans are

Simply supported slabs	the smaller of the centres of bearings or the clear span + d
Continuous slabs	centres of supports

(b) Arrangement of loads

The code states in clause 3.5.2.3 that in principle the slab should be designed to resist the most unfavourable arrangement of loads. However, normally it is only necessary to design for the single-load case of maximum design load on all spans or panels. This is permitted subject to the following conditions:

1. The area of each bay, i.e. the building width × column spacing, exceeds $30\,m^2$;
2. The ratio of characteristic imposed load to characteristic dead load does not exceed 1.25;
3. The characteristic imposed load does not exceed $5\,kN/m^2$ excluding partitions.

(c) Analysis and redistribution of moments

A complete analysis can be carried out using moment distribution in a similar way to that performed for the continuous beam in Example 7.3. Moment redistribution can also be made in accordance with clause 3.2.2.1 which was discussed in section 7.2.4.

Clause 3.5.2.3 referred to above states that if the analysis is carried out for the single-load case of all spans loaded, the support moments except at supports of cantilevers should be reduced by 20%. This gives an increase in the span moments. The moment envelope should satisfy all the provisions of clause 3.2.2.1 in the code regarding redistribution of moments. No further redistribution is to be carried out.

The case of a slab with cantilever overhang is also discussed in clause 3.5.2.3 of the code. In this case if the cantilever length exceeds one-third of the span the load case of $1.4G_k + 1.6Q_k$ on the cantilever and $1.0G_k$ on the span should be considered (G_k is the characteristic dead load and Q_k is the characteristic imposed load).

(d) Analysis using moment coefficients

The code states in clause 3.5.2.4 that where the spans of the slab are approximately equal and conditions set out in clause 3.5.2.3 discussed above are met the moments and shears for design may be taken from Table 3.13. This table allows for 20% redistribution and is reproduced as Table 8.1.

Table 8.1 Ultimate moments and shears in one-way spanning slabs

	At outer support	Near middle of end span	At first interior support	At middle of interim support	At interior supports
Moment	0	0.086Fl	−0.086Fl	0.063Fl	−0.063Fl
Shear	0.4F	–	0.6F	–	0.5F

F, total design load; l, span.

8.2.3 Section design and slab reinforcement curtailment and cover

(a) Main moment steel

The main moment steel spans between supports and over the interior supports of continuous slabs as shown in Fig. 8.1. The slab sections are designed as rectangular beam sections 1 m wide and the charts given in section 4.4.7 for singly reinforced beams can be used.

The minimum area of main reinforcement is given in Table 3.27 of the code. For rectangular sections and solid slabs this is

Mild steel $f_y = 250\,\text{N/mm}^2$, $100A_s/A_c = 0.24$
High yield steel $f_y = 460\,\text{N/mm}^2$, $100A_s/A_c = 0.13$

where A_s is the minimum area of reinforcement and A_c is the total area of concrete.

(b) Distribution steel

The distribution or secondary steel runs at right angles to the main moment steel and serves the purpose of tying the slab together and distributing non-uniform loads through the slab. The area of secondary reinforcement is the same as the minimum area for main reinforcement set out in (a) above. Note that distribution steel is required at the top parallel to the supports of continuous slabs. The main steel is placed nearest to the surface to give the greatest effective depth.

(c) Slab reinforcement

Slab reinforcement is a mesh and may be formed from two sets of bars placed at right angles. Table 8.2 gives bar spacing data in the form of areas of steel per metre width for various bar diameters and spacings. Alternatively cross-welded wire fabric to BS 4483 can be used. This is produced from cold reduced steel wire with a characteristic strength of $460\,\text{N/mm}^2$. The particulars of fabric used are given in Table 8.3, taken from BS 4483, Table 1.

(d) Curtailment of bars in slabs

The general recommendations given in clause 3.12.9.1 for curtailment of bars apply. These were discussed in connection with beams in section 7.1.2. The code sets out simplified rules for slabs in clause 3.12.10.3 and Fig. 3.25 in the code. These rules may be used subject to the following provisions:

1. The slabs are designed for predominantly uniformly distributed loads;
2. In continuous slabs the design has been made for the single load case of maximum design load on all spans.

The simplified rules for simply supported, cantilever and continuous slabs are as shown in Figs 8.3(a), 8.3(b) and 8.3(c) respectively.

The code states in clause 3.12.10.3.2 that while the supports of simply supported slabs or the end support of a continuous slab cast integral with an L-beam have been taken as simple supports for analysis, negative moments may arise and cause cracking. To control this, bars are to be provided in the top of the slab of area equal to one-half of the steel at mid-span but not less than the minimum area specified in Table 3.27 in the

Table 8.2 Bar spacing data

Diameter (mm)	Area (mm²) for spacing mm												
	s = 80	100	120	140	150	160	180	200	220	240	260	280	300
6	350	282	235	201	188	176	157	141	128	117	113	100	94
8	628	502	418	359	335	314	279	251	228	209	201	179	167
10	981	785	654	560	523	490	436	392	356	327	314	280	261
12	1413	1130	942	807	753	706	628	565	514	471	452	403	376
16	2513	2010	1675	1436	1340	1256	1117	1005	913	837	804	718	670

Spacing s in millimetres.

Table 8.3 Fabric types

Fabric reference	Longitudinal wire			Cross wire		
	Wire size (mm)	Pitch (mm)	Area (mm²/m)	Wire size (mm)	Pitch (mm)	Area (mm²/m)
Square mesh						
A393	10	200	393	Same as for longitudinal		
A252	8	200	252	wires		
A193	7	200	193			
A142	6	200	142			
A98	5	200	98			
Structural mesh						
B1131	12	100	1131	8	200	252
B785	10	100	785	8	200	252
B503	8	100	503	8	200	252
B385	7	100	385	7	200	193
B285	6	100	283	7	200	193
B196	5	100	196	7	200	193
Long mesh						
C785	10	100	785	6	400	70.8
C636	9	100	663	6	400	70.8
C503	8	100	503	5	400	49
C385	7	100	385	5	400	49
C283	6	100	503	5	400	49
Wrapping mesh						
D98	5	200	98	Same as for longitudinal		
D49	2.5	100	49	wires		

code. The bars are to extend not less than $0.15l$ or 45 bar diameters into the span. These requirements are shown in Figs 8.3(a) and 8.3(c).

Bottom bars at a simply supported end are generally anchored 12 bar diameters past the centreline of the support as shown in Fig. 8.3(a). However, these bars may be stopped at the line of the effective support where the slab is cast integral with the edge beam as shown in 8.3(a) and 8.3(b) (see design for shear below).

Note that where a one-way slab ends in edge beams or is continuous across beams parallel to the span some two-way action with negative moments occurs at the top of the slab. Reinforcement in the top of the slab of the same area as that provided in the direction of the span at the dis-

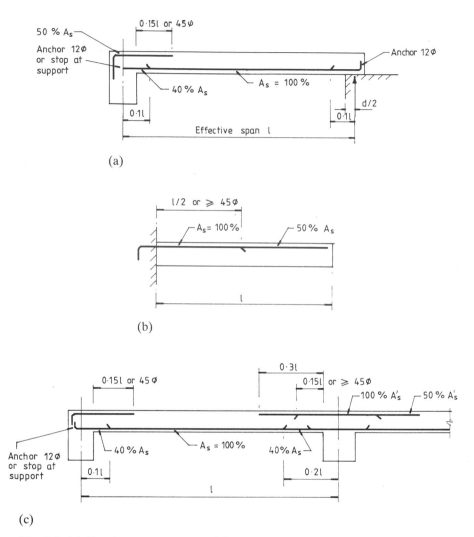

Fig. 8.3 (a) Simply supported span; (b) cantilever; (c) continuous beam.

continuous edge should be provided to control cracking. This is shown in Fig. 8.4(c).

(e) Cover

The amount of cover required for durability and fire protection is taken from Tables 3.4 and 3.5 of the code. For grade 30 concrete the cover is 25 mm for mild exposure and this will give 2 h of fire protection in a continuous slab.

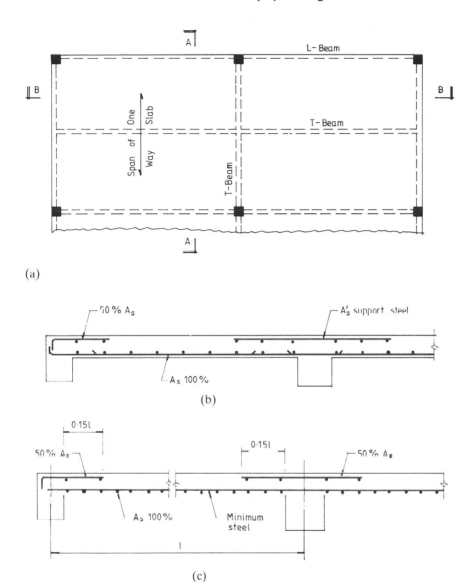

Fig. 8.4 (a) Part floor plan; (b) section AA; (c) section BB.

8.2.4 Shear

Under normal loads shear stresses are not critical and shear reinforcement is not required. Shear reinforcement is provided in heavily loaded thick slabs but should not be used in slabs less than 200 mm thick. The shear resistance is checked in accordance with BS 8110: Part 1, section 3.5.5.

The shear stress is given by

$$v = V/bd$$

where V is the shear force due to ultimate loads. If v is less than the value of v_c given in Table 3.9 in the code no shear reinforcement is required. Enhancement in design shear strength close to supports can be taken into account. This was discussed in section 5.1.2. The form and area of shear reinforcement in solid slabs is set out in Table 3.17 in the code. The design is similar to that set out for beams in section 5.1.3.

The shear resistance at the end support which is integral with the edge beam where the slab has been taken as simply supported in the analysis depends on the detailing. The following procedures are specified in clause 3.12.10.3 of the code:

1. If the tension bars are anchored 12 diameters past the centreline of the support the shear resistance is based on the bottom bars;
2. If the tension bars are stopped at the line of effective support, the shear resistance is based on the top bars.

Note that top bars of area one-half the mid-span steel are required to control cracking.

8.2.5 Deflection

The check for deflection is a very important consideration in slab design and usually controls the slab depth. The deflection of slabs is discussed in BS 8110: Part 1, section 3.5.7.

In normal cases a strip of slab 1 m wide is checked against span-to-effective depth ratios including the modification for tension reinforcement set out in section 3.4.6 of the code. Only the tension steel at the centre of the span is taken into account.

8.2.6 Crack control

To control cracking in slabs, maximum values for clear spacing between bars are set out in BS 8110: Part 1, clause 3.12.11.2.7. The clause states that in no case should the clear spacing exceed the lesser of three times the effective depth or 750 mm. No further check is needed for slabs in normal cases

1. if grade 250 steel is used and the slab depth is not greater than 250 mm or
2. if grade 460 is used and the slab depth is not greater than 200 mm or
3. if the amount of steel, $100A_s/bd$, is less than 0.3%

☐ Example 8.1 Continuous one-way slab

(a) Specification

A continuous one-way slab has three equal spans of 3.5 m each. The slab depth is assumed to be 140 mm. The loading is as follows:

Dead loads – self-weight, screed, finish, partitions, ceiling   5.2 kN/m²
Imposed load   3.0 kN/m²

The construction materials are grade 30 concrete and grade 460 reinforcement. The condition of exposure is mild and the cover required is 25 mm. Design the slab and show the reinforcement on a sketch of the cross-section.

(b) Design loads

Consider a strip 1 m wide.

$$\text{design load} = (1.4 \times 5.2) + (1.6 \times 3) = 12.08 \text{ kN/m}$$
$$\text{design load per span} = 12.08 \times 3.5 = 42.28 \text{ kN}$$

The single load case of maximum design loads on all spans is shown in Fig. 8.5 where the critical points for shear and moment are also indicated.

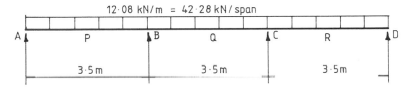

Fig. 8.5

(c) Shear forces and bending moments in the slab

The shear forces and moments in the slab are calculated using BS 8110: Part 1, Table 3.13. The values are shown in Table 8.4. The redistribution is 20%.

Table 8.4 Design ultimate shears and moments

Position	Shear (kN)	Moment (kN m)
A	$0.4 \times 42.28 = 16.91$	
P		$+0.086 \times 42.28 \times 3.5 = \quad 12.73$
B	$0.6 \times 42.28 = 25.37$	$-0.086 \times 42.28 \times 3.5 = -12.73$
Q		$+0.063 \times 42.28 \times 3.5 = \quad 9.32$

(d) Design of moment steel

Assume 10 mm diameter bars with 25 mm cover. The effective depth is

$$d = 140 - 25 - 5 = 110\,\text{mm}$$

The calculations for steel areas are set out below. Reference is made to clause 3.4.4.4 in the code for the section design.

(i) Section at support B, M = 12.73 kNm   Redistribution is 20%; when Table 3.13 is used, with $\beta_b = 0.8$,

$$K' = 0.402 \times 0.4 - 0.18 \times 0.4^2 = 0.132$$
$$K = \frac{12.73 \times 10^6}{1000 \times 110^2 \times 30} = 0.035 < K'$$
$$z = 110[0.5 + (0.25 - 0.035/0.9)^{1/2}]$$
$$= 105.5\,\text{mm}$$
$$> 0.95d = 104.5\,\text{mm}$$
$$A_s = \frac{12.73 \times 10^6}{0.87 \times 460 \times 0.95 \times 110}$$
$$= 304.4\,\text{mm}^2/\text{m}$$

Provide 8 mm bars at 160 mm centres to give an area of 314 mm²/m. Provide the same reinforcement at section P.

(ii) Section Q, M = 9.32 kNm/m

$$z = 0.95d$$
$$A_s = 222.9\,\text{mm}^2/\text{m}$$

Provide 8 mm bars at 220 mm centres to give an area of 228 mm²/m. The minimum area of reinforcement is

$$0.13 \times 1000 \times 140/1000 = 182\,\text{mm}^2/\text{m}$$

The above areas exceed this value.

The moment reinforcement is shown in Fig. 8.6. Curtailment of bars has not been made because one-half of the calculated steel areas would fall below the minimum area of steel permitted.

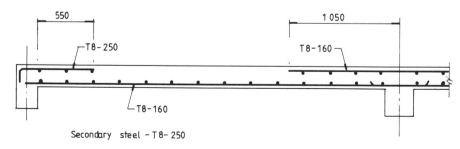

Secondary steel – T8– 250

Fig. 8.6

At the end support A, top steel equal in area to one-half the mid-span steel, i.e. 152.2 mm²/m, but not less than the minimum area of 182 mm²/m has to be provided. The clear spacing between bars is not to exceed $3d = 330$ mm. Provide 8 mm bars at 250 mm centres to give 201 mm²/m. The tension bars in the bottom of the slab at support A are stopped off at the line of support.

(e) Distribution steel

The minimum area of reinforcement (182 mm²/m) has to be provided. The spacing is not to exceed $3d = 330$ mm. Provide 8 mm bars at 250 mm centres to give an area of 201 mm²/m.

(f) Shear resistance

Enhancement in design strength close to the support has not been taken into account.

(i) End support   The shear resistance is based on the top bars, 8 mm diameter bars at 250 mm centres with area 7201 mm²/m.

$$\frac{100A_s}{bd} = \frac{100 \times 201}{1000 \times 110} = 0.183$$

$$v_c = 0.79(0.183)^{1/3}(400/110)^{1/4}(30/25)^{1/3}/1.25 = 0.53 \, \text{N/mm}^2$$

$$v = \frac{16.91 \times 10^3}{1000 \times 110} = 0.15 \, \text{N/mm}^2$$

No shear reinforcement is required.

(ii) Interior Support

$$\frac{100A_s}{bd} = \frac{100 \times 314}{1000 \times 110} = 0.285$$

$$v_c = 0.61 \, \text{N/mm}^2$$

$$v = \frac{25.37 \times 10^3}{10^3 \times 110} = 0.23 \, \text{N/mm}^2$$

No shear reinforcement is required.

(g) Deflection

The slab is checked for deflection using the rules from section 3.4.6 of the code. The end span is checked. The basic span-to-effective depth ratio is 26 for the continuous slab.

$$M/bd^2 = 1.05$$

$$f_s = \frac{5 \times 460 \times 304.4}{8 \times 314} = 278.7 \, \text{N/mm}^2$$

The modification factor is

$$0.55 + \frac{477 - 278.7}{120(0.9 + 1.05)} = 1.39$$

allowable span/d ratio – $1.39 \times 26 – 36.1$
actual span/d ratio = $3500/110 = 31.8$

The slab is satisfactory with respect to deflection.

(h) Crack control

Because the steel grade is 460, the slab depth is less than 200 mm and the clear spacing does not exceed $3d = 330$ mm, the slab is satisfactory with respect to cracking. Refer to BS 8110: Part 1, clause 3.12.11.2.7.

(i) Sketch of cross-section of slab

A sketch of the cross-section of the slab with reinforcement is shown in Fig. 8.6.

■

8.3 ONE-WAY SPANNING RIBBED SLABS

8.3.1 Design considerations

Ribbed slabs are more economical than solid slabs for long spans with relatively light loads. They may be constructed in a variety of ways as discussed in BS 8110: Part 1, section 3.6. Two principal methods of construction are

1. ribbed slabs without permanent blocks
2. ribbed slabs with permanent hollow or solid blocks

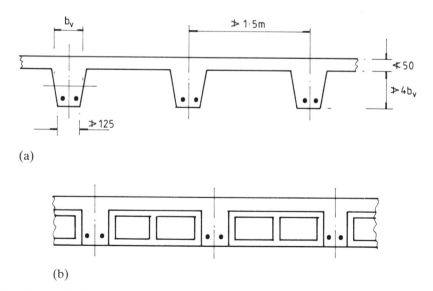

(a)

(b)

Fig. 8.7 (a) Ribbed slab; (b) ribbed slab with hollow blocks.

These two types are shown in Fig. 8.7.

The topping or concrete floor panels between ribs may or may not be considered to contribute to the strength of the slab. The hollow or solid blocks may also be counted in assessing the strength using rules given in the code. The design of slabs with topping taken into account but without permanent blocks is discussed.

8.3.2 Ribbed slab proportions

Proportions for ribbed slabs without permanent blocks are set out in section 3.6 of the code. The main requirements are as follows:

1. The centres of ribs should not exceed 1.5 m;
2. The depth of ribs excluding topping should not exceed four times their average width;
3. The minimum rib width should be determined by consideration of cover, bar spacing and fire resistance. Referring to Fig. 3.2 in the code, the minimum rib width is 125 mm;
4. The thickness of structural topping or flange should not be less than 50 mm or one-tenth of the clear distance between ribs (Table 3.18 in the code).

Note that, to meet a specified fire resistance period, non-combustible finish, e.g. screed on top or sprayed protection, can be included to give the minimum thickness for slabs set out in Fig. 3.2 in the code. See also Part 2, section 4.2, of the code. For example, a slab thickness of 110 mm is required to give a fire resistance period of 2 h.

The requirements are shown in Fig. 8.7(a).

8.3.3 Design procedure and reinforcement

(a) Shear forces and moments

Shear forces and moments for continuous slabs can be obtained by analysis as set out for solid slabs in section 8.1 or by using Table 3.13 in the code.

(b) Design for moment and moment reinforcement

The mid-span section is designed as a T-beam with flange width equal to the distance between ribs. The support section is designed as a rectangular beam. The slab may be made solid near the support to increase shear resistance.

Moment reinforcement consisting of one or more bars is provided in the top and bottom of the ribs. If appropriate, bars can be curtailed in a similar way to bars in solid slabs (section 8.2.3(d)).

(c) Shear resistance and shear reinforcement

The design shear stress is given in clause 3.6.4.2 by

$$v = V/b_v d$$

where V is the ultimate shear force on a width of slab equal to the distance between ribs, b_v is the average width of a rib and d is the effective depth. In no case should the maximum shear stress v exceed $0.8f_{cu}^{1/2}$ or $5\,\text{N/mm}^2$. No shear reinforcement is required when v is less than the value of v_c given in Table 3.9 of the code. Shear reinforcement is required when v exceeds v_c. This design is set out in section 5.1.3.

Clause 3.6.1.3 states that if the rib contains two or more bars links must be provided for $v > v_c/2$. Nominal links are designed as set out in Table 3.8 in the code (section 5.1.3). The spacing should not exceed $0.75d$. Links are not required in ribs containing one bar.

(d) Reinforcement in the topping

The code states in clause 3.6.6.2 that fabric with a cross-sectional area of not less than 0.12% of the area of the topping in each direction should be provided. The spacing of wires should not exceed one-half the centre-to-centre distance of the ribs. The mesh is placed in the centre of the topping and requirements for cover given in section 3.3.7 of the code should be satisfied. If the ribs are widely spaced the topping may need to be designed for moment and shear as a continuous one-way slab between ribs.

8.3.4 Deflection

The deflection can be checked using the span-to-effective depth rules given in section 3.4.6 of the code.

□ Example 8.2 One-way ribbed slab

(c) Specification

A ribbed slab is continuous over four equal spans of 6 m each. The dead loading including self-weight, finishes, partitions etc. is $4.5\,\text{kN/m}^2$ and the imposed load is $2.5\,\text{kN/m}^2$. The construction materials are grade 30 concrete and grade 460 reinforcement. Design the end span of the slab.

(b) Trial section

A cross-section through the floor and a trial section for the slab are shown in Fig. 8.8. The thickness of topping is made 60 mm and the minimum width of a rib is 125 mm. The deflection check will show whether the depth selected is satisfactory. The cover for mild exposure is 25 mm. For 12 mm diameter bar

$$\text{effective depth} = 275 - 25 - 6 = 244, \text{ say } 240\,\text{mm}$$

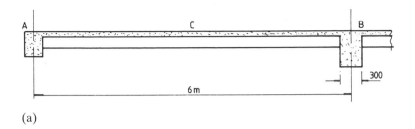

(a)

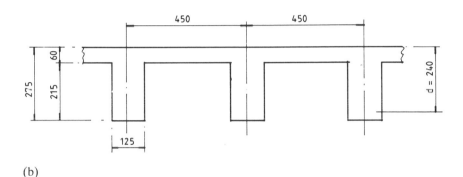

(b)

Fig. 8.8 (a) Section through floor; (b) section through slab.

(c) Shear and moments in the rib

Consider 0.45 m width of floor. The design load per span is

$$0.45[(1.4 \times 4.7) + (1.6 \times 2.5)] = 4.76 \text{ kN/m}$$
$$= 4.76 \times 6 = 28.57 \text{ kN/span}$$

The design shears and moments taken from Table 3.13 in the code are as follows:

$$\text{shear at A} = 0.4 \times 28.57 = 11.43 \text{ kN}$$
$$\text{shear at B} = 0.6 \times 28.57 = 17.14 \text{ kN}$$
$$\text{moment at C} = +0.086 \times 28.57 \times 6 = 14.74 \text{ kN m}$$
$$\text{moment at B} = -0.086 \times 28.57 \times 6 = -14.74 \text{ kN m}$$

(d) Design of moment reinforcement

(i) Mid-span T-section See section 4.8.2. The flange breadth b is 450 mm and the moment of resistance assuming $0.9x = 60$ mm is

$$M_{RC} = 0.45 \times 30 \times 450 \times 60(240 - 0.5 \times 60)/10^6$$
$$= 76.5 > 14.74 \text{ kN m}$$

The neutral axis lies in the flange.
  Using expressions from clause 3.4.4.4 of the code

$$K = \frac{14.74 \times 10^6}{30 \times 450 \times 240^2} = 0.019$$

$$z = 240[0.5 + (0.25 - 0.019/0.9)^{1/2}]$$

$$= 234.8 \, \text{mm}$$

$$> 0.95d = 228 \, \text{mm}$$

$$A_s = \frac{14.74 \times 10^6}{0.87 \times 460 \times 228} = 161.5 \, \text{mm}^2$$

Provide two 12 diameter mm bars, area 226 mm^2.

(ii) Section at support – rectangular section 125 mm wide The redistribution is 20%, $\beta_b = 0.8$. From Clause 3.4.4.4 of the code

$$K' = 0.402 \times 0.4 - 0.18 \times 0.4^2 = 0.132$$

$$K = \frac{14.74 \times 10^6}{125 \times 240^2 \times 30} = 0.068 < K'$$

$$z = 240[0.5 + (0.25 - 0.068/0.9)^{1/2}]$$

$$= 220.2 < 0.95d$$

$$A_s = \frac{24.74 \times 10^6}{0.87 \times 460 \times 220.2} = 167.3 \, \text{mm}^2$$

Provide two 12 mm diameter bars, area 226 mm^2.

(e) Shear resistance

No account will be taken of enhancement to shear strength. At support B, $V = 17.14 \, \text{kN}$.

$$v = \frac{17.14 \times 10^3}{125 \times 240} = 0.57 \, \text{N/mm}^2$$

$$\frac{100A_s}{bd} = \frac{100 \times 226}{125 \times 240} = 0.75$$

$$v_c = 0.79(0.75)^{1/3}(400/240)^{1/4}(30/25)^{1/3}/1.25$$

$$= 0.69 \, \text{N/mm}^2$$

The shear exceeds $v_c/2$ and two bars are placed in the rib. Nominal links must be provided although shear reinforcement is not required.

Provide 6 mm diameter links in grade 250 steel; $A_{sv} = 56 \, \text{mm}^2$ (section 5.1.3(b)).

$$s_v = \frac{56 \times 0.87 \times 250}{0.4 \times 125} = 243.6 \, \text{mm} > 0.75d = 180 \, \text{mm}$$

Space the links at 180 mm along the span. At the simple support A the bottom bars are to be anchored 12 diameters past the centre of the support.

(f) Deflection

$$\frac{b_w}{b} = \frac{125}{450} = 0.27 < 0.3$$

The basic span/d ratio is 20.8 (Table 3.10 of the code).

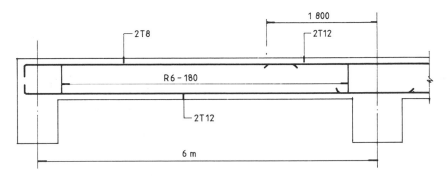

Fig. 8.9

$$\frac{M}{bd^2} = \frac{14.74 \times 10^6}{450 \times 240^2} = 0.57$$

$$f_s = \frac{5 \times 460 \times 161.5}{8 \times 226} = 205.4\,\text{N/mm}^2$$

The amount of redistribution at mid-span is not known, but the redistributed moment is greater than the elastic ultimate moment. Take β_b equal to 1.0. The modification factor is

$$0.55 + \frac{477 - 205.4}{120(0.9 + 0.57)} = 2.09 < 2.0$$

$$\text{allowable span/}d \text{ ratio} = 20.8 \times 2 = 41.6$$

$$\text{actual span/}d \text{ ratio} = 6000/240 = 25$$

The slab is satisfactory with respect to deflection.

(g) Arrangement of reinforcement in ribs

The arrangement of moment and shear reinforcement in the rib is shown in Fig. 8.9.

(h) Reinforcement in topping

The area required per metre width is

$$0.12 \times 60 \times 1000/100 = 72\,\text{mm}^2/\text{m}$$

The spacing of wires is not to be greater than one-half the centre-to-centre distance of the ribs, i.e. 225 mm. Refer to Table 8.2. Provide D98 wrapping mesh with an area of 98 mm^2/m and wire spacing 200 mm in the centre of the topping. ■

8.4 TWO-WAY SPANNING SOLID SLABS

8.4.1 Slab action, analysis and design

When floor slabs are supported on four sides two-way spanning action occurs as shown in Fig. 8.10(a). In a square slab the action is equal in each

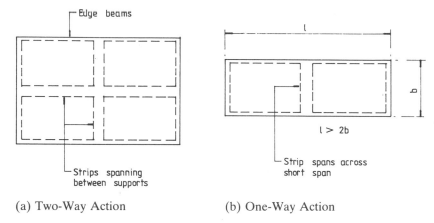

(a) Two-Way Action   (b) One-Way Action

Fig. 8.10 (a) Two-way action; (b) one-way action.

direction. In long narrow slabs where the length is greater than twice the breadth the action is effectively one way. However, the end beams always carry some slab load.

Slabs may be classified according to the edge conditions. They can be defined as follows:

1. simply supported one panel slabs where the corners can lift away from the supports
2. a one panel slab held down on four sides by integral edge beams (the stiffness of the edge beam affects the slab design)
3. slabs with all edges continuous over supports
4. a slab with one, two or three edges continuous over supports – the discontinuous edge(s) may be simply supported or held down by integral edge beams

Elastic solutions for standard cases are given in textbooks on the theory of plates. Irregularly shaped slabs, slabs with openings or slabs carrying non-uniform or concentrated loads present problems in analysis. The finite element method can be used to analyse any shape of slab subject to any loading conditions. The stiffness of edge beams and other support conditions can be taken into account.

Commonly occurring cases in slab construction in buildings are discussed. The design is based on shear and moment coefficients and the procedures and provisions set out in BS 8110: Part 1, section 3.5.3. The slabs are square or rectangular in shape and support uniformly distributed load.

8.4.2 Simply supported slabs

The design of simply supported slabs that do not have adequate provision either to resist torsion at the corners or to prevent the corners from lifting may be made in accordance with BS 8110: Part 1, clause 3.5.3.3. This clause gives the following equations for the maximum moments m_{sx} and m_{sy} at mid-span on strips of unit width for spans l_x and l_y respectively:

$$m_{sx} = \alpha_{sx} n l_x^2$$
$$m_{sy} = \alpha_{sy} n l_x^2$$

where l_x is the length of the shorter span, l_y is the length of the longer span, $n = 1.4G_k + 1.6Q_k$ is the total ultimate load per unit area and α_{sx}, α_{sy} are moment coefficients from Table 3.14 in the code.

The centre strips and locations of the maximum moments are shown in Fig. 8.11(a). A simple support for a slab on a steel beam is shown in

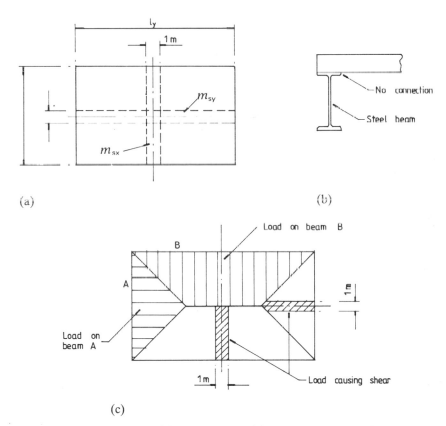

(a)   (b)

(c)

Fig. 8.11 (a) Centre strips; (b) end support; (c) loads on beams and slab shears.

8.11(b). Some values of the coefficients from BS 8110: Part 1, Table 3.14, are

$$l_y/l_x = 1.0; \quad \alpha_{sx} = 0.062, \quad \alpha_{sy} = 0.062$$
$$l_y/l_x = 1.5; \quad \alpha_{sx} = 0.104, \quad \alpha_{sy} = 0.046$$

As l_y/l_x increases, the shorter span takes an increasing share of the load.

The tension reinforcement can be designed using the formulae for rectangular beams in clause 3.4.4.4 of the code or the design chart given in section 4.4.7. The area must exceed the values for minimum reinforcement for solid slabs given in Table 3.27 of the code.

The simplified rules for curtailment given in Fig. 3.25 in the code and shown in Fig. 8.3 here apply. These rules state that 50% of the mid-span reinforcement should extend to the support and be anchored 12 bar diameters past the centre of the support. The bars are stopped off at 0.1 of the span from the support.

The generally assumed load distribution to the beams and the loads causing shear on strips 1 m wide are shown in Fig. 8.11(c). The shear forces in both strips have the same value. The shear resistance is checked using formulae given in clause 3.5.5 and Table 3.17 of the code.

The deflection of solid slabs is discussed in BS 8110: Part 1, clause 3.5.7, where it is stated that in normal cases it is sufficient to check the span-to-effective depth ratio of the unit strip spanning in the shorter direction against the requirements given in section 3.4.6 of the code. The amount of steel in the direction of the shorter span is used in the calculation (section 6.1.2).

Crack control is dealt with in clause 3.5.8 of the code which states that the bar spacing rules given in clause 3.12.11 are to be applied (section 6.2.2).

☐ Example 8.3 Simply supported two-way slab

(a) Specification

A slab in an office building measuring 5 m × 7.5 m is simply supported at the edges with no provision to resist torsion at the corners or to hold the corners down. The slab is assumed initially to be 200 mm thick. The total dead load including self-weight, screed, finishes, partitions, services etc. is 6.2 kN/m². The imposed load is 2.5 kN/m². Design the slab using grade 30 concrete and grade 250 reinforcement.

(b) Design of the moment reinforcement

Consider centre strips in each direction 1 m wide. The design load is

$$n = (1.4 \times 6.2) + (1.6 \times 2.5) = 12.68 \, \text{kN/m}^2$$
$$l_y/l_x = 7.5/5 = 1.5$$

From BS 8110: Part 1, Table 3.14, the moment coefficients are

$$\alpha_{sx} = 0.104$$
$$\alpha_{sy} = 0.046$$

For cover of 25 mm and 16 mm diameter bars the effective depths are as follows: for short-span bars in the bottom layer

$$d = 200 - 25 - 8 = 167\,\text{mm}$$

and for long-span bars in the top layer

$$d = 200 - 25 - 16 - 8 = 151\,\text{mm}$$

(i) *Short span*

$$m_{sx} = 0.104 \times 12.68 \times 5^2 = 32.97\,\text{kN/m}$$

$$\frac{m_{sx}}{bd^2} = \frac{32.97 \times 10^6}{1000 \times 167^2} = 1.18$$

Referring to Fig. 4.12, m_{sx}/bd^2 is less than 1.27 and so the lever $z = 0.95d$.

$$A_s = \frac{32.97 \times 10^6}{0.87 \times 250 \times 0.95 \times 167}$$

$$= 955.5\,\text{mm}^2/\text{m}$$

Provide 16 mm diameter bars at 200 mm centres to give an area of 1005 mm²/m.

(ii) *Long span*

$$m_{sy} = 0.046 \times 12.68 \times 5^2 = 14.58\,\text{kN m/m}$$

$$\frac{m_{sy}}{bd^2} = \frac{14.55 \times 10^6}{1000 \times 151^2} = 0.63 < 1.27$$

$$A_s = \frac{14.58 \times 10^6}{0.87 \times 250 \times 0.95 \times 151} = 467\,\text{mm}^2/\text{m}$$

Provide 12 mm diameter bars at 240 mm centres to give an area of 471 mm²/m.

(iii) *Minimum area of reinforcement*   See BS 8110: Part 1, Table 3.27.

$$A_s = 0.24 \times 167 \times 1000/100 = 400.8\,\text{mm}^2/\text{m}$$

(iv) *Curtailment*   The reinforcement will not be curtailed in either direction. If 50% of the bars in the long span were cut off the remaining area of steel would fall below the minimum allowed. All bars must be anchored 12 diameters past the centre of the support.

(c) **Shear resistance**

Referring to Fig. 8.11(c) the maximum shear at the support is given by

$$V = 12.68 \times 2.5 = 31.7\,\text{kN}$$

Check the shear stress on the long span. This will have the greatest value because d is less than on the short span. The design concrete shear stress will also be lower for the long span because the steel area is less.

$$v = \frac{31.7 \times 10^3}{10^3 \times 151} = 0.21\,\text{N/mm}^2$$

$$\frac{100A_s}{bd} = \frac{100 \times 471}{1000 \times 151} = 0.31$$

$$v_c = 0.79(0.31)^{1/3}(400/151)^{1/4}(30/25)^{1/3}/1.25$$

$$= 0.58\,\text{N/mm}^2$$

The slab is satisfactory with respect to shear.

(d) Deflection

The slab is checked for deflection across the short span. The basic span-to-effective depth ratio from Table 3.10 in the code is 20.

$$\frac{m_{sx}}{bd^2} = 1.18 \qquad \text{(see (b) above)}$$

$$f_s = \frac{5 \times 250 \times 955.5}{8 \times 1005} = 148.5\,\text{N/mm}^2$$

The modification factor for tension steel is

$$0.55 + \frac{477 - 148.5}{120(0.9 + 1.18)} = 1.87$$

$$\text{allowable span}/d \text{ ratio} = 20 \times 1.87 = 37.4$$

$$\text{actual span}/d \text{ ratio} = 5000/167 = 29.9$$

The slab is satisfactory with respect to deflections. If high yield reinforcement is used a thicker slab is needed to comply with the deflection limit.

(e) Cracking

Referring to BS 8110: Part 1, clause 3.12.11.2.7, the clear spacing is not to exceed $3d = 480\,\text{mm}$. In addition the slab depth does not exceed 250 mm for grade 250 reinforcement. No further checks are required.

(f) Slab reinforcement

The slab reinforcement is shown in Fig. 8.12.

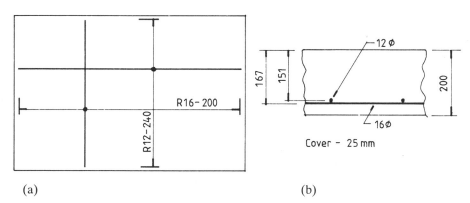

(a)   (b)

Fig. 8.12 (a) Slab steel; (b) section.

8.5 RESTRAINED SOLID SLABS

8.5.1 Design and arrangement of reinforcement

The design method for restrained slabs is given in BS 8110: Part 1, clause 3.5.3.5. In these slabs the corners are prevented from lifting and provision is made for torsion. The maximum moments at mid-span on strips of unit width for spans l_x and l_y are given by

$$m_{sx} = \beta_{sx} n l_x^2$$
$$m_{sy} = \beta_{sy} n l_y^2$$

The clause states that these equations may be used for continuous slabs when the following provisions are satisfied:

1. The characteristic dead and imposed loads are approximately the same on adjacent panels as on the panel being considered;
2. The spans of adjacent panels in the direction perpendicular to the line of the common support is approximately the same as that of the panel considered in that direction.

The moment coefficients β_{sx} and β_{sy} in the equations above are given in BS 8110. Part 1, Table 3.15. Equations are also given for deriving the coefficients. Nine slab support arrangements are covered, the first four of which are shown in Fig. 8.13(a). The locations of the moments calculated and values of some coefficients from the table are shown in 8.13(b).

The design rules for slabs are as follows.

1. The slabs are divided in each direction into middle and edge strips as shown in Fig. 8.14.
2. The maximum moments defined above apply to the middle strips. The moment reinforcement is designed using formulae in section 4.4.6 or the design charts in Fig. 4.13. The amount of reinforcement provided must not be less than the minimum area given in BS 8110: Part 1, Table 3.27. The bars are spaced uniformly across the middle strip.
3. The reinforcement is to be detailed in accordance with the simplified rules for curtailment of bars in slabs given in clause 3.12.10.3 and shown in Fig. 3.25 of the code. At the discontinuous edge, top steel of one-half the area of the bottom steel at mid-span is to be provided as specified in clause 3.12.10.3 to control cracking. Provisions are given in the same clause regarding shear resistance at the end support. This depends on the detailing of the bottom reinforcement and was discussed in section 8.2.4 above.
4. The minimum tension reinforcement given in Table 3.27 of the code is to be provided in the edge strip together with the torsion reinforcement specified in rule 5 below.

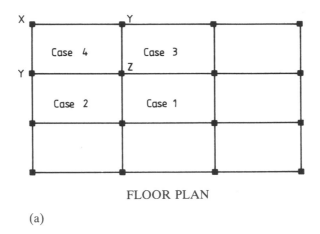

FLOOR PLAN

(a)

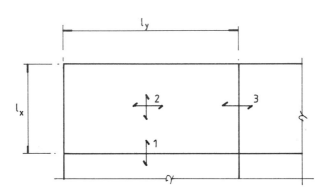

Case 4   Bending   Moment   Coefficients

Location		$l_y/l_x = 1$	$l_y/l_x = 1·5$
Short span	1	− 0·047	− 0·078
	2	0·036	0·059
Long span	3	− 0·045	− 0·045
	2	0·034	0·034

(b)

Fig. 8.13 (a) Slab arrangement, floor plan: case 1, interior panel; case 2, one short edge discontinuous; case 3, one long edge discontinuous; case 4, two adjacent edges discontinuous. (b) Moment coefficients: locations 1 and 3, negative moments at continuous edge; location 2, positive moment at mid-span.

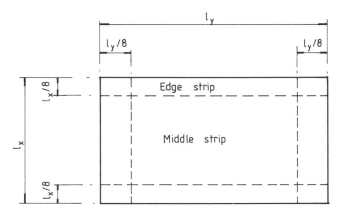

Fig. 8.14

5. Torsion reinforcement is to be provided at corners where the slab is simply supported on both edges meeting at the corners. Corners X and Y shown in Fig. 8.13(a) require torsion reinforcement. This is to consist of a top and bottom mesh with bars parallel to the sides of the slab and extending from the edges a distance of one-fifth of the shorter span. The area of bars in each of the four layers should be, at X, three-quarters of the area of bars required for the maximum mid-span moment and, at Y, one-half of the area of the bars required at corner X. Note that no torsion reinforcement is required at the internal corners Z shown in Fig. 8.13(a).

8.5.2 Adjacent panels with markedly different support moments

The moment coefficients in Table 3.15 of the code apply to slabs with similar spans and loads giving similar support moments. If the support moments for adjacent panels differ significantly, the adjustment procedure set out in clause 3.5.3.6 of the code must be used. This case is not discussed further.

8.5.3 Shear forces and shear resistance

(a) Shear forces

Shear force coefficients β_{vx} and β_{vy} for various support cases for continuous slabs are given in Table 3.16 of the code. The design loads on supporting beams per unit width are given by

$$V_{sx} = \beta_{vx}nl_x$$
$$V_{sy} = \beta_{vy}nl_x$$

Some coefficients for a slab with two adjacent edges discontinuous are shown in Fig. 8.15(a). The load distribution on a beam supporting a two-way slab, given in Fig. 3.10 in the code, is shown in Fig. 8.15(b).

(b) Shear resistance

The shear resistance for solid slabs is covered in BS 8110: Part 1, section 3.5.5, and the form and area of shear reinforcement is given in Table 3.17. Shear resistance was discussed in section 8.2.4 above.

8.5.4 Deflection

Deflection is checked in accordance with section 3.4.6 of the code by checking the span-to-effective depth ratio. Clause 3.5.7 states that the ratio

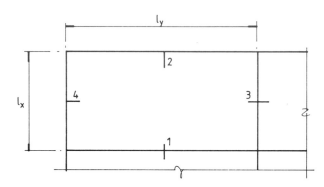

Case 4   Shear   Force   Coefficients

Location		$l_y / l_x = 1 \cdot 0$	$l_y / l_x = 1 \cdot 5$
Short span	1	0 · 4	0 · 54
	2	0 · 2	0 · 35
Long span	3	0 · 4	0 · 4
	4	0 · 26	0 · 26

(a)

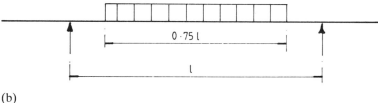

(b)

Fig. 8.15 (a) Shear force coefficients: locations 1 and 3, continuous edge; locations 2 and 4, discontinuous edge. (b) Distribution of load on support beam.

is to be based on the shorter span and its amount of tension reinforcement in that direction.

8.5.5 Cracking

Crack control is discussed in BS 8110: Part 1, clause 3.5.8. This states that the bar spacing rules given in clause 3.12.11 are the best means of controlling flexural cracking in the slabs.

□ Example 8.4 Two-way restrained solid slab

(a) Specification

The part floor plan for an office building is shown in Fig. 8.16. It consists of restrained slabs poured monolithically with the edge beams. The slab is 175 mm thick and the loading is as follows:

$$\text{total dead load} = 6.2 \, \text{kN/m}^2$$
$$\text{imposed load} = 2.5 \, \text{kN/m}^2$$

Design the corner slab using grade 35 concrete and grade 460 reinforcement. Show the reinforcement on sketches.

(b) Slab division, moments and reinforcement

The corner slab is divided into middle and edge strips as shown in Fig. 8.16(a). The moment coefficients are taken from BS 8110: Part 1, Table 3.15 for a square slab

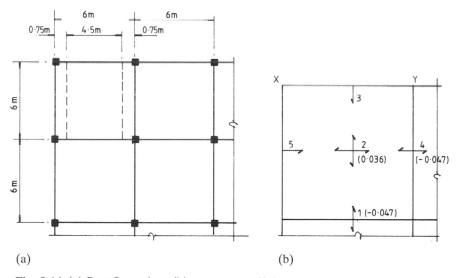

(a)   (b)

Fig. 8.16 (a) Part floor plan; (b) moment coefficients.

for the case with two adjacent edges discontinuous. The values of the coefficients and locations of moments are shown in Fig. 8.16(b).

$$\text{design load} = (1.4 \times 6.2) + (1.6 \times 2.5) = 12.68\,\text{kN/m}^2$$

Assuming 10 mm diameter bars and 20 mm cover from Table 3.4 in the code, the effective depth of the outer layer is

$$180 - 20 - 5 = 155\,\text{mm}$$

The effective depth of the inner layer is

$$180 - 20 - 5 - 10 = 145\,\text{mm}$$

The moments and steel areas for the middle strips are calculated. Because the slab is square only one direction need be considered.

(i) Positions 1 and 4, d = 155 mm

$$m_{sx} = -0.047 \times 12.68 \times 6^2 = -21.45\,\text{kN m/m}$$

$$K = \frac{21.45 \times 10^6}{35 \times 1000 \times 155^2} = 0.026 < 0.156$$

$$z = 155[0.5 + (0.25 - 0.026/0.9)^{1/2}]$$

$$= 150.4\,\text{mm}$$

$$\not> 0.95 \times 155 = 147.25\,\text{mm}$$

$$A_s = \frac{21.45 \times 10^6}{0.87 \times 460 \times 147.25} = 364\,\text{mm}^2/\text{m}$$

Provide 10 mm diameter bars at 200 mm centres to give an area of 392 mm²/m.

(ii) Position 2, d = 145 mm   Note that the smaller value of d is used.

$$m_{sx} = 0.036 \times 12.68 \times 6^2 = 16.43\,\text{kN m/m}$$

Repeat the above calculations to give

$$A_s = 293\,\text{mm}^2/\text{m}$$

Provide 8 mm diameter bars at 160 mm centres to give an area of 314 mm²/m. Check the minimum area of steel in tension from BS 8110: Part 1, Table 3.27:

$$0.13 \times 1000 \times 180/100 = 234\,\text{mm}^2/\text{m}$$

(iii) Positions 3, 5

$$A_s = 0.5 \times 293 = 149.2\,\text{mm}^2/\text{m}$$

$$\not< 234\,\text{mm}^2/\text{m} \text{ (minimum steel)}$$

Provide 8 mm diameter bars at 200 mm centres to give an area of 251 mm²/m.

In detailing, the moment steel will not be curtailed because both negative and positive steel would fall below the minimum area if 50% of the bars were cut off.

(c) Shear forces and shear resistance

(i) Positions 1, 4, d = 155 mm

$$V_{sx} = 0.4 \times 12.68 \times 6 = 30.43\,\text{kN/m}$$

$$v = \frac{30.43 \times 10^3}{10^3 \times 155} = 0.196\,\text{N/mm}^2$$

$$\frac{100A_s}{bd} = \frac{100 \times 393}{1000 \times 155} = 0.253$$

$$v_c = 0.79(0.253)^{1/3}(400/155)^{1/4}(35/25)^{1/3}/1.25$$
$$= 0.567\,\text{N/mm}^2$$

No shear reinforcement is required.

(ii) Positions 3, 5, d = 145 mm The bottom tension bars are to be stopped at the centre of the support. The shear resistance is based on the top steel with $A_s = 251\,\text{mm}^2/\text{m}$.

$$V_{sx} = 0.26 \times 12.68 \times 6 = 19.78\,\text{kN/m}$$
$$v = 0.136\,\text{N/mm}^2$$
$$v_c = 0.49\,\text{N/mm}^2$$

The shear stress is satisfactory.

(d) Torsion steel

Torsion steel of length 6/5 = 1.2 m is to be provided in the top and bottom of the slab at the three external corners marked X and Y in Fig. 8.16(b).

(i) Corner X The area of torsion steel is $0.75 \times 298.4 = 219.7\,\text{mm}^2/\text{m}$

This will be provided by the minimum steel of 8 mm diameter bars of 200 mm centres.

(ii) Corner Y The area of torsion steel is $0.5 \times 219.7 = 109.9\,\text{mm}^2/\text{m}$

Provide 8 mm diameter bars at 200 mm centres.

(e) Edge strips

Provide minimum reinforcement, 8 mm diameter bars at 200 mm centres, in the edge strips.

(f) Deflection

Check using steel at mid-span with $d = 145\,\text{mm}$.

$$\text{basic span}/d\ \text{ratio} = 26 \qquad (\text{BS 8110: Part 1, Table 3.10})$$

$$\frac{m_{sx}}{bd^2} = \frac{16.43 \times 10^6}{10^3 \times 145^2} = 0.78$$

$$f_s = \frac{5 \times 460 \times 293}{8 \times 314} = 268.3\,\text{N/mm}^2$$

The modification factor is

$$0.55 + \frac{477 - 268.3}{120(0.9 + 0.78)} = 1.59$$

$$\text{allowable span}/d\ \text{ratio} = 1.59 \times 26 = 41.34$$
$$\text{actual span}/d\ \text{ratio} = 600/145 = 41.37$$

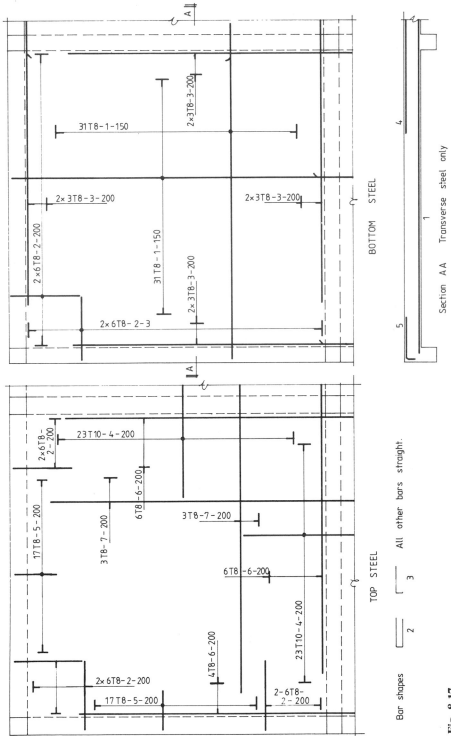

Fig. 8.17

The slab can be considered to be just satisfactory. The deflection could be based on the average value of d and the slab would be satisfactory.

(g) Cracking

The bar spacing does not exceed $3d = 3 \times 145 = 435$ mm and in addition for grade 460 steel the depth is less than 200 mm. No further checks are required as stated in clause 3.12.11.2 of the code.

(h) Sketch of slab

The arrangement of reinforcement is shown in Fig. 8.17. The top and bottom bars are shown separately for clarity. The moment steel in the bottom of the slab is stopped at the support at the outside edges and lapped with steel in the next bays at the continuous edges. Secondary steel is provided in the top of the slab at the continuous edges to tie in the moment steel. ∎

8.6 WAFFLE SLABS

8.6.1 Design procedure

Two-way spanning ribbed slabs are termed waffle slabs. The general provisions for construction and design procedure are given in BS 8110: Part 1, section 3.6. These conditions are set out in section 8.3 above dealing with one-way ribbed slabs.

Moments for design may be taken from Table 3.14 of the code for slabs simply supported on four sides or from Table 3.15 for panels supported on four sides with provision for torsion at the corners. Slabs may be made solid near supports to increase moment and shear resistance and provide flanges for support beams. In edge slabs, solid areas are required to contain the torsion steel.

☐ Example 8.5 Waffle slab

(a) Specification

Design a waffle slab for an internal panel of a floor system that is constructed on an 8 m square module. The total dead load is 6.5 kN/m^2 and the imposed load is 2.5 kN/m^2. The materials of construction are grade 30 concrete and grade 460 reinforcement.

(b) Arrangement of slab

A plan of the slab arrangement is shown in Fig. 8.18(a). The slab is made solid for 500 mm from each support. The proposed section through the slab is shown in 8.18(b). The proportions chosen for rib width, rib depth, depth of topping and rib spacing meet various requirements set out in BS 8110: Part 1, section 3.6. The rib width is the minimum specified for fire resistance given in Fig. 3.2 of the code. From Table 3.4 the cover required for mild exposure is 25 mm.

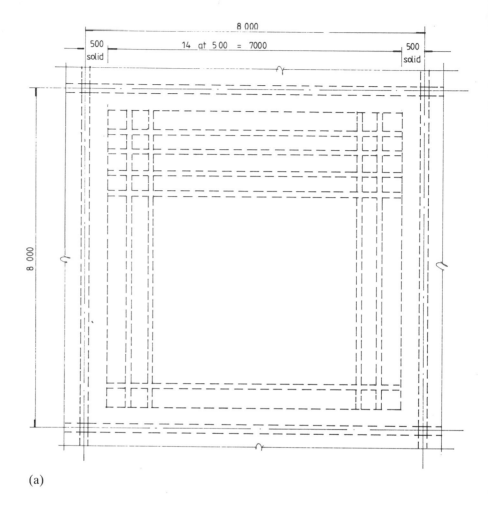

(a)

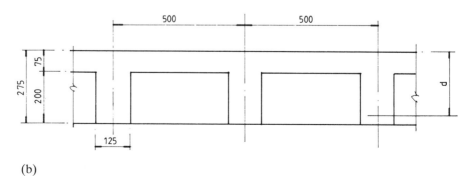

(b)

Fig. 8.18 (a) Plan of waffle slab; (b) section through slab.

(c) Reinforcement

$$\text{design load} = (1.4 \times 6.5) + (1.6 \times 2.5) = 13.1 \, \text{kN/m}^2$$

The middle strip moments for an interior panel for the slab width supported by one rib are, from Table 3.15,

$$\text{Support} \quad m_{sx} = -0.031 \times 13.1 \times 8^2/2 = -12.99 \, \text{kN m}$$
$$\text{Midspan} \quad m_{sx} = 0.024 \times 13.1 \times 8^2/2 = 10.06 \, \text{kN m}$$

The effective depths assuming 12 mm diameter main bars and 6 mm diameter links are as follows:

$$\text{Outer layer} \quad d = 275 - 25 - 6 - 6 = 238 \, \text{mm}$$
$$\text{Inner layer} \quad d = 275 - 25 - 6 - 12 - 6 = 226 \, \text{mm}$$

(i) Support – solid section 500 mm wide

$$K = \frac{M}{bd^2 f_{cu}} = \frac{12.99 \times 10^6}{500 \times 238^2 \times 30} = 0.015$$
$$z = 238[0.5 + (0.25 - 0.015/0.9)^{1/2}]$$
$$= 233.8 \, \text{mm}$$
$$\not> 0.95d = 226.1 \, \text{mm}$$
$$A_s = \frac{12.99 \times 10^6}{0.87 \times 460 \times 226.1} = 143.6 \, \text{mm}^2$$

Provide two 10 mm diameter bars to give a steel area of 157 mm².

At the end of the solid section the moment of resistance of the concrete ribs with width 125 mm is given by

$$M = 0.156 \times 30 \times 125 \times 238^2/10^6$$
$$= 33.14 \, \text{kN m}$$

This exceeds the moment at the support and so the ribs are able to resist the applied moment without compression steel. The applied moment at 500 mm from the support will be less than the support moment.

(ii) Centre of span, T-beam, d = 226 mm The flange breadth b is 500 mm. The moment of resistance of the section when 0.9x equals the depth of topping (75 mm) is

$$M_R = 0.45 \times 30 \times 500 \times 75(226 - 0.5 \times 75)/10^6$$
$$= 95.4 \, \text{kN m} > 10.06 \, \text{kN m}$$

The neutral axis lies in the flange. The steel area can be calculated in the same way as for the support steel.

$$A_s = 117.1 \, \text{mm}^2 \text{ per rib}$$

Provide two 10 mm diameter bars with area 157 mm².

(d) Shear resistance

The shear force coefficient is taken from BS 8110: Part 1, Table 3.16. The shear at the support for the width supported by one rib (Table 3.16) is

$$v_{sx} = 0.33 \times 13.1 \times 8/2 = 17.29 \, \text{kN}$$

The shear on the ribs at 500 mm from support is

$$V = 17.29 - 0.5 \times 13.1 \times 0.5 = 14.02 \, kN$$

$$v = \frac{14.02 \times 10^3}{125 \times 238} = 0.47 \, N/mm^2$$

$$\frac{100 A_s}{bd} = \frac{100 \times 157}{125 \times 238} = 0.53$$

$$v_c = 0.79(0.53)^{1/3}(400/238)^{1/4}(30/25)^{1/3}/1.25$$
$$= 0.62 \, N/mm^2$$

Shear reinforcement is not required. However, the shear stress v exceeds $v_c/2$ and two bars are provided in the rib and so links are required. Make the links 6 mm diameter in grade 250 reinforcement, $A_{sv} = 56 \, mm^2$.

$$s_v = \frac{56 \times 0.87 \times 250}{0.4 \times 125} = 243.6 \, mm \not> 0.75d = 0.75 \times 226 = 169.5 \, mm$$

Space the links at 160 mm along the rib.

(e) Deflection

$$\frac{b_w}{b} = \frac{125}{500} = 0.25 < 0.3$$

The basic span/d ratio is 20.8 (Table 3.10).

$$\frac{M}{bd^2} = \frac{10.06 \times 10^6}{500 \times 226^2} = 0.394$$

$$f_s = \frac{5 \times 460 \times 117.1}{8 \times 157} = 214.4 \, N/mm^2$$

The modification factor is

$$0.55 + \frac{477 - 214.2}{120(0.9 + 0.394)} = 2.24 < 2.0$$

$$\text{allowable span}/d \text{ ratio} = 20.8 \times 2 = 41.6$$

$$\text{actual span}/d \text{ ratio} = 8000/226 = 35.4$$

The slab is satisfactory with respect to deflection.

(f) Reinforcement in topping

The area required per metre width is

$$0.12 \times 75 \times 1000/100 = 90 \, mm^2/m$$

The spacing of the wires is not to be greater than one-half the centre-to-centre distance of the ribs, i.e. 250 mm. Refer to Table 8.2. Provide D98 wrapping mesh with area 98 mm²/m and wire spacing 200 mm in the centre of the topping.

(g) Arrangement of the reinforcement

The arrangement of the reinforcement and shear reinforcement in the rib is shown in Fig. 8.19.

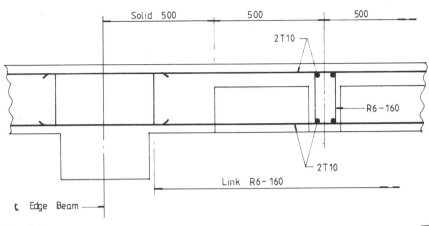

Fig. 8.19 ■

8.7 FLAT SLABS

8.7.1 Definition and construction

The flat slab is defined in BS 8110: Part 1, clause 1.2.2.1, as a slab with or without drops, supported generally without beams by columns with or without column heads. The code states that the slab may be solid or have recesses formed on the soffit to give a waffle slab. Only solid slabs will be discussed.

Flat slab construction is shown in Fig. 8.20 for a building with circular internal columns, square edge columns and drop panels. The slab is thicker than that required in T-beam floor slab construction but the omission of beams gives a smaller storey height for a given clear height and simplification in construction and formwork.

Various column supports for the slab either without or with drop panels are shown in Fig. 8.21. The effective column head is defined in the code.

8.7.2 General code provisions

The design of slabs is covered in BS 8110: Part 1, section 3.7. General requirements are given in clause 3.7.1, as follows.

1. The ratio of the longer to the shorter span should not exceed 2.
2. Design moments may be obtained by
   (a) equivalent frame method
   (b) simplified method
   (c) finite element analysis

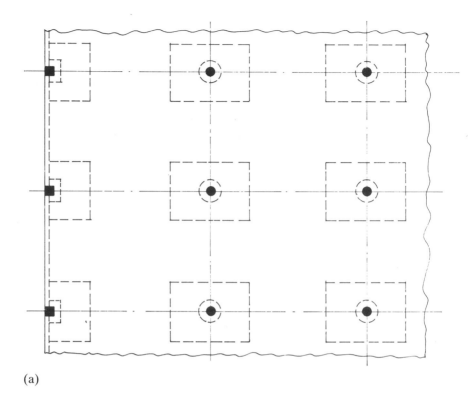

(a)

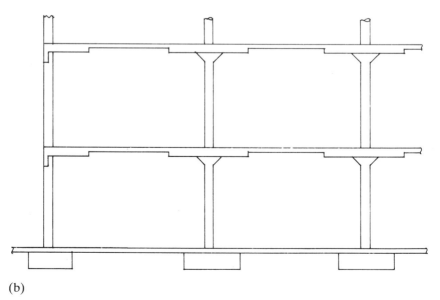

(b)

Fig. 8.20 (a) Floor plan; (b) section.

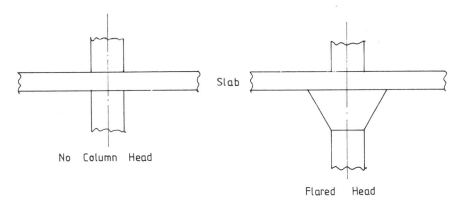

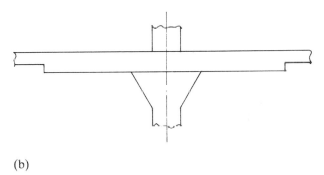

Fig. 8.21 (a) Slab without drop panel; (b) slab with drop panel and flared column head

3. The effective dimension l_h of the column head is taken as the lesser of
    (a) the actual dimension l_{hc} or
    (b) $l_{h\,max} = l_c + 2(d_h - 40)$
    where l_v is the column dimension measured in the same direction as l_h.
    For a flared head l_{hc} is measured 40 mm below the slab or drop. Column head dimensions and the effective dimension for some cases are shown in Fig. 8.22 (see also BS 8110: Part 1, Fig. 3.11).
4. The effective diameter of a column or column head is as follows:
    (a) For a column, the diameter of a circle whose area equals the area of the column
    (b) for a column head, the area of the column head based on the effective dimensions defined in requirement 3
    The effective diameter of the column or column head must not be greater than one-quarter of the shorter span framing into the column.
5. Drop panels only influence the distribution of moments if the smaller

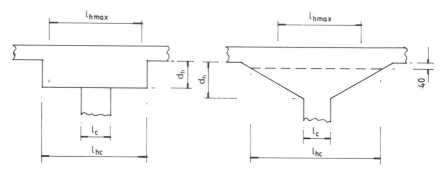

Fig. 8.22

dimension of the drop is at least equal to one-third of the smaller panel dimension. Smaller drops provide resistance to punching shear.
6. The panel thickness is generally controlled by deflection. The thickness should not be less than 125 mm.

8.7.3 Analysis

The code states that normally it is sufficient to consider only the single load case of maximum design load, 1.4 × dead load + 1.6 × imposed load on all spans. The following two methods of analysis are set out in section 3.7.2 of the code to obtain the moments and shears for design.

(a) Frame analysis method

The structure is divided longitudinally and transversely into frames consisting of columns and strips of slab. Either the entire frame or subframes can be analysed by moment distribution. This method is not considered further.

Table 8.5 Moments and shear forces for flat slabs for internal panels

	At first interior support	At centre of interior span	At interior support
Moment	−0.063Fl	+0.071Fl	−0.055Fl
Shear	0.6F		0.5F

$l = l_1 - 2h_c/3$, effective span; l_1, panel length parallel to the centre-to-centre span of the columns; h_c, effective diameter of the column or column head (section 8.7.2(d)); F, total design load on the strip of slab between adjacent columns due to 1.4 times the dead load plus 1.6 times the imposed load.

(b) Simplified method

Moments and shears may be taken from Table 3.19 of the code for structures where lateral stability does not depend on slab–column connections. The following provisions apply:

1. Design is based on the single load case mentioned above;
2. The structure has at least three rows of panels of approximately equal span in the direction considered.

The design moments and shears for internal panels from Table 3.19 of the code are given in Table 8.5. Refer to the code for the complete table.

8.7.4 Division of panels and moments

(a) Panel division

Flat slab panels are divided into column and middle strips as shown in Fig. 3.12 of the code. The division is shown in Fig. 8.23 for a slab with drop panels.

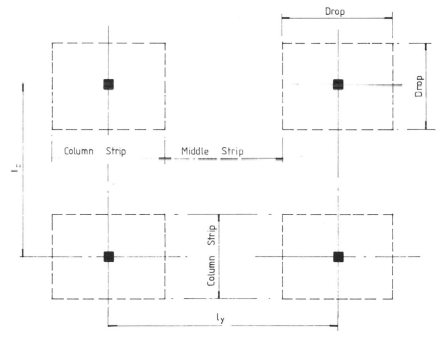

Fig. 8.23

Table 8.6 Distribution of moments in flat slabs

	Distribution between column and middle strip as percentage of total negative or positive moment	
	Column strip	Middle strip
Negative	75	25
Positive	55	45

(b) Moment division

The design moments obtained from Table 3.19 of the code are divided between column and middle strips in accordance with Table 3.20 of the code. The proportions are given in Table 8.6. Refer to the code for modifications to the table for the case where the middle strip is increased in width.

8.7.5 Design of internal panels and reinforcement details

The slab reinforcement is designed to resist moments derived from Tables 3.19 and 3.20 of the code. The code states in clause 3.7.3.1 for an internal panel that two-thirds of the amount of reinforcement required to resist negative moment in the column strip should be placed in a central zone of width one-half of the column strip.

Reinforcement can be detailed in accordance with the simplified rules given in clause 3.12.10.3.1 and Fig. 3.25 of the code (section 8.2.3(d) above).

8.7.6 Design of edge panels

Design of edge panels is not discussed. Reference should be made to the code for design requirements. The design is similar to that for an interior panel. The moments are given in Table 3.19 of the code. The column strip is much narrower than for an internal panel (Fig. 3.13 of the code). The slab must also be designed for large shear forces as shown in Fig. 3.15 of the code.

8.7.7 Shear force and shear resistance

The code states is clause 3.7.6.1 that punching shear around the column is the critical consideration in flat slabs. Rules are given for calculating the shear force and checking shear stresses.

(a) Shear forces

Equations are given in the code for calculating the design effective shear force V_{eff} at a shear perimeter in terms of the design shear V_t transferred to the column. The equations for V_{eff} include an allowance for moment transfer, i.e. the design moment transferred from the slab to the column.

The code states that in the absence of calculations it is satisfactory to take $V_{eff} = 1.15V_t$ for internal columns in braced structures with approximately equal spans. To calculate V_t all panels adjacent to the column are loaded with the maximum design load.

(b) Shear resistance

Shear due to concentrated loads on slabs is given in BS 8110: Part 1, section 3.7.7. This was discussed in section 5.1.5. The checks are as follows.

(i) Maximum shear stress at the face of the column

$$v_{max} = \frac{V}{u_0 d} \not> 0.8 f_{cu}^{1/2} \text{ or } 5\,\text{N/mm}^2$$

where u_0 is the perimeter of the column (Fig. 8.24) and V is the design ultimate value of the concentrated load.

(ii) Shear stress on a failure zone 1.5d from the face of the column

$$v = \frac{V}{ud}$$

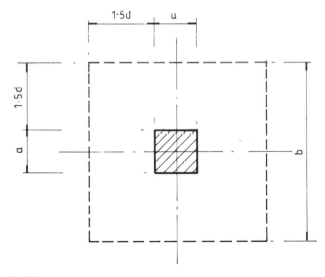

Square column
$u_0 = 4a$
$u = 4b$

Fig. 8.24

where u is the perimeter of the failure zone $1.5d$ from the face of the column (Fig. 8.24). If v is less than the design concrete shear stress given in Table 3.9 of the code, no shear reinforcement is required. If the failure zone mentioned above does not require shear reinforcement, no further checks are required. It is not desirable to have shear reinforcement in light or moderately loaded slabs.

8.7.8 Deflection

The code states in clause 3.7.8 that for slabs with drops, if the width of drop is greater than one-third of the span, the rules limiting span-to-effective depth ratios given in section 3.4.6 of the code can be applied directly. In other cases span-to-effective depth ratios are to be multiplied by 0.9. The check is to be carried out for the most critical direction, i.e. for the longest span. The modification factor for tension reinforcement is based on the total moment at mid-span of the panel and the average of column strip and middle strip tension steel.

8.7.9 Crack control

The bar spacing rules for slabs given in clause 3.12.11.2.7 of the code apply.

□ Example 8.6 Internal panel of a flat slab floor

(a) **Specification**

The floor of a building constructed of flat slabs is $30\,m \times 24\,m$. The column centres are $6\,m$ in both directions and the building is braced with shear walls. The panels are to have drops of $3\,m \times 3\,m$. The depth of the drops is $250\,mm$ and the slab depth is $200\,mm$. The internal columns are $450\,mm$ square and the column heads are $900\,mm$ square.

The loading is as follows:

$$
\begin{aligned}
\text{dead load} \quad &= \text{self-weight} + 2.5\,kN/m^2 \text{ for screed, floor finishes,} \\
&\quad \text{partitions and ceiling} \\
\text{imposed load} &= 3.5\,kN/m^2
\end{aligned}
$$

The materials are grade 30 concrete and grade 250 reinforcement.

Design an internal panel next to an edge panel on two sides and show the reinforcement on a sketch.

(b) **Slab and column details and design dimensions**

A part floor plan and column head, drop and slab details are shown in Fig. 8.25. The drop panels are made one-half of the panel dimension.

The column head dimension l_{h0}, $40\,mm$ below the soffit of the drop panel, is $870\,m$. The effective dimension l_h of the column head is the lesser of

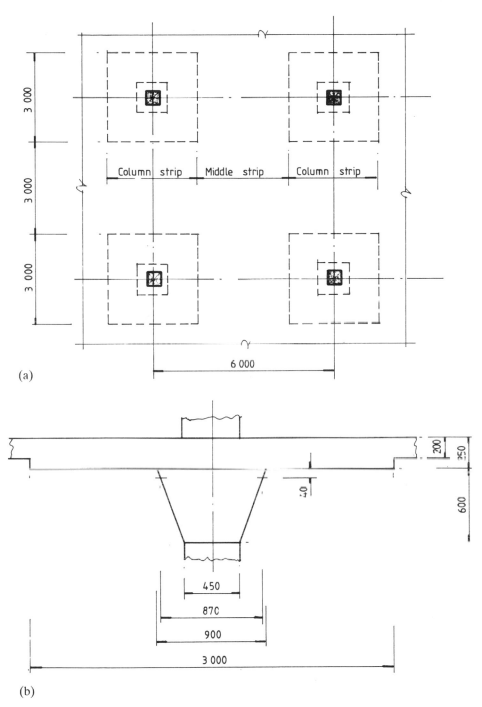

Column strip | Middle strip | Column strip

3 000

3 000

3 000

6 000

(a)

200

250

600

450

870

900

3 000

(b)

Fig. 8.25 (a) Part floor plan; (b) column head, drop and slab details.

1. $l_{h0} = 870 \, \text{mm}$ and
2. $l_{h\,\text{max}} = 450 + 2(600 - 40) = 1570 \, \text{mm}$

That is, $l_h = 870 \, \text{mm}$. The effective diameter of the column head is

$$h_c = (4 \times 870^2/\pi)^{1/2} = 981 \, \text{mm} \not> 1/4 \times 6000 = 1500 \, \text{mm}$$
$$h_c = 981 \, \text{mm}$$

The effective span is

$$l = 6000 - 2 \times 981/3 = 5346 \, \text{mm}$$

The column and middle strips are shown in Fig. 8.25(a).

(c) Design loads and moments

The average load due to the weight of the slabs and drops is

$$[(9 \times 0.25) + (27 \times 0.2)]23.6/36 = 5.02 \, \text{kN/m}^2$$

The design ultimate load is

$$n = (5.02 + 2.5)1.4 + (3.5 \times 1.6) = 16.13 \, \text{kN/m}^2$$

The total design load on the strip of slab between adjacent columns is

$$F = 16.13 \times 6^2 = 580.7 \, \text{kN}$$

The moments in the flat slab are calculated using coefficients from Table 3.19 of the code and the distribution of the design moments in the panels of the flat slab is made in accordance with Table 3.20. The moments in the flat slab are as follows. For the first interior support,

$$-0.063 \times 580.7 \times 5.35 = -195.7 \, \text{kN m}$$

For the centre of the interior span,

$$+0.071 \times 580.7 \times 5.35 = +220.6 \, \text{kN m}$$

The distribution in the panels is as follows. For the column strip

negative moment = $-0.75 \times 195.7 = -146.8 \, \text{kN m}$
positive moment = $0.55 \times 220.6 = 121.3 \, \text{kN m}$

For the middle strip

negative moment = $-0.25 \times 195.7 = -48.9 \, \text{kN m}$
positive moment = $0.45 \times 220.6 = 99.3 \, \text{kN m}$

(d) Design of moment reinforcement

The cover is 25 mm and 16 mm diameter bars in two layers are assumed. At the drop the effective depth for the inner layer is

$$250 - 25 - 16 - 8 = 201 \, \text{mm}$$

In the slab the effective depth of the inner layer is

$$200 - 25 - 16 - 8 = 151 \, \text{mm}$$

The design calculations for the reinforcement in the column and middle strip are made with width $b = 3000\,mm$.

(i) Column strip negative reinforcement

$$\frac{M}{bd^2} = \frac{146.8 \times 10^6}{3000 \times 201^2} = 1.21$$

From Fig. 4.13 this is less than 1.27 and thus

$$A_s = \frac{150.9 \times 10^6}{0.87 \times 250 \times 0.95 \times 201} = 3633.4\,mm^2$$

Provide a minimum of 19 bars 16 mm in diameter to give an area of 3819 mm². Two-thirds of the bars or 13 bars are placed in the centre half of the column strip at a spacing of 125 mm. A further four bars are placed in each of the outer strips at a spacing of 190 mm. This gives 21 bars in total.

(ii) Column strip positive reinforcement

$$\frac{M}{bd^2} = \frac{121.3 \times 10^6}{3000 \times 151^2} = 1.77$$

From Fig. 4.13 $100A_s/bd = 0.92$.

$$A_s = 0.92 \times 3000 \times 151/100 = 4167.6\,mm^2$$

Provide 21 bars 16 mm in diameter to give an area of 4221 mm² with a spacing of 150 mm.

(iii) Middle strip negative reinforcement

$$M/bd^2 = 0.71 < 1.27 \qquad \text{(Fig. 4.13)}$$

$$A_n = \frac{48.9 \times 10^6}{0.87 \times 250 \times 0.95 \times 151} = 1567.3\,mm^2$$

Provide 15 bars 12 mm in diameter to give an area of 1695 mm² with a spacing of 200 mm.

(iv) Middle strip positive reinforcement

$$M/bd' = 1.15$$
$$100A_s/bd = 0.75$$
$$A_s = 3397.5\,mm^2$$

Provide 18 bars 16 mm in diameter to give an area of 3618 mm² with a spacing of 175 mm.

(e) Shear resistance

(i) At the column face 40 mm below the soffit

$$\text{shear } V = 1.15 \times 16.13(36 - 0.87^2)$$
$$= 653.7\,kN$$

The shear stress is

$$v_{max} = \frac{653.7 \times 10^3}{4 \times 870 \times 201}$$
$$= 0.93 \, N/mm^2$$
$$< 0.8 \times 30^{1/2} = 4.38 \, N/mm^2$$

The maximum shear stress is satisfactory.

(ii) At 1.5d from the column face

$$\text{perimeter} \quad u = [(2 \times 1.5 \times 201) + 870]4$$
$$= 5892 \, mm$$
$$\text{shear} \quad V = 1.15 \times 16.13(36 - 1.473^2)$$
$$= 627.5 \, kN$$
$$\text{shear stress} \quad v = \frac{627.5 \times 10^3}{5892 \times 201} = 0.53 \, N/mm^2$$

In the centre half of the column strip 16 mm diameter bars are spaced at 125 mm centres giving an area of 160.8 mm^2/m.

$$\frac{100A_s}{bd} = \frac{1608 \times 100}{1000 \times 201} = 0.8$$

The design concrete shear stress is

$$v_c = 0.79 \times (0.8)^{1/3}(400/201)^{1/4}(30/25)^{1/3}/1.25$$
$$= 0.73 \, N/mm^2$$

The shear stress is satisfactory and no shear reinforcement is required.

(f) Deflection

The calculations are made for the middle strip using the total moment at mid-span and the average of the column and middle strip tension steel. The basic span/d ratio is 26 (Table 3.10 of the code).

$$\frac{M}{bd^2} = \frac{220.6 \times 10^6}{6000 \times 151^2} = 1.61$$
$$f_s = \frac{5 \times 250 \times 3782.5}{8 \times 3919.5} = 150.8 \, N/mm^2$$

The modification factor is

$$0.55 + \frac{477 - 150.8}{120(0.9 + 1.61)} = 1.63$$
$$\text{allowable span/}d \text{ ratio} = 1.63 \times 26 = 42.4$$
$$\text{actual span/}d \text{ ratio} = 6000/151 = 39.7$$

The slab is satisfactory with respect to deflection.

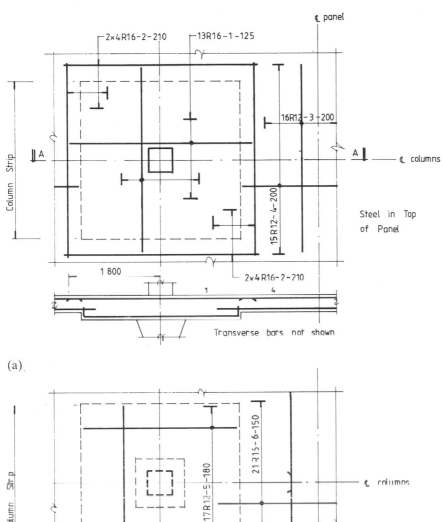

(a)

(b)

Fig. 8.26 (a) Section AA; (b) section BB.

(g) Cracking

The bar spacing does not exceed $3d$, i.e. 603 mm for the drop panel and 453 mm for the slab. In accordance with BS 8110: Part 1, clause 3.12.11.2.7, for grade 250 reinforcement the drop panel depth does not exceed 250 mm and so no further checks are required.

(h) Arrangement of reinforcement

The arrangement of the reinforcement is shown in Fig. 8.26. Secondary reinforcement is required in the drop panel and slab to tie in the moment steel. The area required is 0.24% of grade 250 steel. The areas are as follows:

Drop panel $0.24 \times 250 \times 10^3/100 = 600 \, mm^2/m$
                    12 mm diameter bars at 180 mm centres to give an area of 628 mm^2/m

Slab $0.24 \times 200 \times 10^3/100 = 480 \, mm^2/m$
                    12 mm diameter bars at 220 mm centres to give an area of 514 mm^2/m

Note that the steel spacings are rationalized in Fig. 8.26. A mat of reinforcement is placed in the bottom of the drop panel. This laps with the reinforcement in the bottom of the slab.   ■

8.8 YIELD LINE METHOD

8.8.1 Outline of theory

The yield line method is a powerful procedure for the design of slabs. It is an ultimate load method of analysis and design developed by Johansen[5] that is based on plastic yielding of an under-reinforced concrete slab section. As the load is increased the slab cracks with the reinforcement yielding at the points of high moment. As the deflection increases the cracks or yield lines propagate until the slab is broken into a number of portions at collapse.

Some yield line patterns are shown in Fig. 8.27. In the one-way continuous slab shown in Fig. 8.27(a), straight yield lines or hinges form with a sagging yield line at the bottom of the slab near mid-span and hogging yield lines over the supports. The sagging yield line forms at mid-span when the hogging moments of resistance at each support are equal. The yield line patterns for a square and a rectangular simply supported two-way slab subjected to a uniform load are shown in 8.27(b) and 8.27(c) respectively. All deformations are assumed to take place in the yield lines and the fractured slab at collapse consists of rigid portions held together by the reinforcement. The deformed shape of the square slab is a pyramid and that of the rectangular slab is roof shaped.

8.8.2 Yield line analysis

Yield line analysis is based on the following theorems from plastic theory.

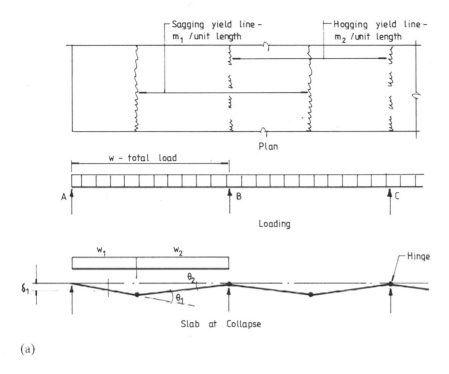

(a)

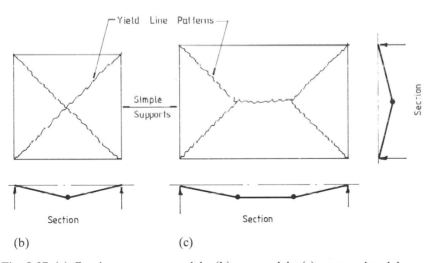

(b)   (c)

Fig. 8.27 (a) Continuous one-way slab; (b) square slab; (c) rectangular slab.

(a) Kinematic theorem

In applying the kinematic theorem the work equation is used to determine the collapse loads. The work done by the loads at collapse is equated to the work done in the yield line rotating against the moment of resistance of the reinforced concrete slab section.

Referring to Fig. 8.27(a), it is seen that at collapse the ultimate load W on the end span AB moves through a deflection δ_1 while the sagging yield line rotates θ_1 and the hogging yield line θ_2 against moments of resistance m_1 and m_2 respectively. The work equation for the end span is

$$W\delta_1 = m_1 l \theta_1 + m_2 l \theta_2$$

In general terms the equation can be written as

$$\Sigma W\delta = \Sigma m\theta l$$

where l is the length of the yield lines.

This theorem gives an upper bound solution to the true collapse load. Various yield line patterns must be examined to determine which gives the minimum collapse load.

Solutions using the work equation are given later.

(b) Static theorem

The static theorem states that if a set of internal forces can be found which are in equilibrium with the external loads and which do not cause the ultimate moment of resistance to be exceeded anywhere in the slab, then the external load is a lower bound to the collapse load.
This theorem is the basis of the Hillerborg strip method of analysis. The reader should consult references for further information regarding this method [7, 8].

8.8.3 Moment of resistance along a yield line

(a) One-way slab

In a one-way spanning slab (Fig. 8.28) the reinforcement for bending moment is placed across the span and the yield line forms at right angles to it. For a 1 m wide strip of slab of effective depth d, reinforced with steel area A_s, the ultimate moment of resistance is

$$m = Kbd^2$$

where K is taken from Fig. 4.13 for singly reinforced beams for the calculated value of $100A_s/bd$. The moment of resistance along the yield line is m per metre.

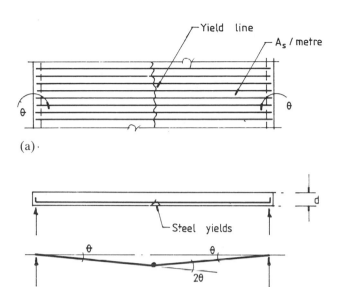

Fig. 8.28 (a) Plan; (b) section and collapse mechanism.

(b) Two-way slab

In two-way slabs reinforced with a rectangular mesh, the yield line may cut the reinforcement at any angle θ as shown in Fig. 8.29(a). The reinforcement provided in the X and Y directions in the slab shown is A_{sx} and A_{sy} per metre and the moments of resistance in the two directions are m_x and m_y respectively.

Consider the triangular element shown in Fig. 8.29(b) with length of hypotenuse 1 m. The sides perpendicular to the X and Y axes have lengths $\sin\theta$ and $\cos\theta$ respectively.

Johansen's stepped yield criterion is used where the yield line is assumed to consist of a number of steps each perpendicular to a set of bars (Fig. 8.29(b)). The moment vectors m_x and m_y are also shown. They are perpendicular to the X and Y axes to give the moments of resistance about those axes.

Resolve the moment vectors perpendicular to the N axis to give the resultant moment of resistance in the direction of the yield line:

$$m_N = m_x \sin^2\theta + m_y \cos^2\theta$$

Resolve the moment vectors perpendicular to the T axis to give the resultant twisting moment on the strip of the slab:

$$m_T = m_x \sin\theta \cos\theta - m_y \sin\theta \cos\theta$$

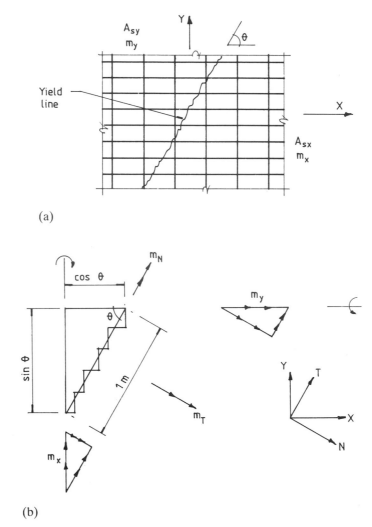

(a)

(b)

Fig. 8.29 (a) Two-way slab; (b) triangular element.

If the reinforcement is the same in the X and Y directions

$$m_x = m_y = m \qquad m_N = m \qquad m_T = 0$$

That is, the moment of resistance is the same in all directions and the twisting moment is zero. Such a slab with equal reinforcement in both directions is termed an isotropic slab. In other cases where m_x is not equal to m_y it is assumed that the twisting moment is zero. The twisting moment is considered in solutions using the equilibrium method.

8.8.4 Work done in a yield line

The work done in the yield line is $m\theta l$ where m is the moment of resistance along the yield line, θ is the rotation in the yield line and l is the length of the yield line. In the simply supported slab shown in Fig. 8.28 the yield line is parallel to the supports, the yield line rotation is 2θ and the work done in the yield line is $2m\theta l$.

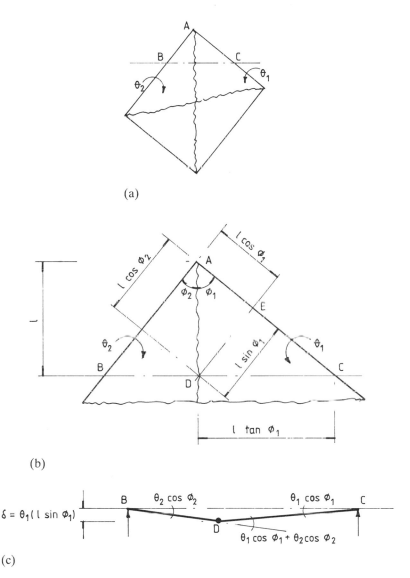

(a)

(b)

(c)

Fig. 8.30 (a) Simply supported slab; (b) part plan; (c) section BC.

In the case of a two-way slab it is necessary to derive an expression for the work done in the yield line in terms of rotations at the supports. Consider the corner ABC of the simply supported slab shown in Fig. 8.30 where the sagging yield line of length l makes angles ϕ_1 and ϕ_2 with the edges AC and AB respectively of the slab. The rigid portions of the slab rotate θ_1 and θ_2 about the edges AC and AB. Section BC is perpendicular to the yield line. In the triangle ADC, DE is perpendicular to AC. The deflection at D is

$$\delta = \text{DE } \theta_1 = (l \sin \phi_1)\theta_1$$

and the rotation at C in direction BC is

$$\frac{\delta}{\text{DC}} = \frac{(l \sin \phi_1)\theta_1}{l \tan \phi_1}$$
$$= \theta_1 \cos \phi_1$$

Similarly the rotation at B in the direction BC is $\theta_2 \cos \phi_2$. The total rotation at the yield line is

$$\theta_1 \cos \phi_1 + \theta_2 \cos \phi_2$$

If the moment of resistance of the slab along the yield line is m_N per unit length the work done in the yield line is

$$m_N l(\theta_1 \cos \phi_1 + \theta_2 \cos \phi_2)$$
$$= m_N(\theta_1 \times \text{projection of the yield line on AC} + \theta_2 \times \text{projection of the yield line on AB})$$

The expression for m_N is given in section 8.8.3, (Fig. 8.29). For an isotropic slab

$$m_N = m_x = m_y = m$$

The design method will be illustrated in the following examples.

8.8.5 Continuous one-way slab

Consider a strip of slab 1 m wide where the mid-span positive reinforcement has a moment of resistance of m per metre and the support negative reinforcement has a moment of resistance of m' per metre. The slab with ultimate load W per span is shown in Fig. 8.31(a).

(a) End span AB

The yield line forms at x from A. The rotations at A, C and B are shown in Fig. 8.31(b). The work done by the loads is $Wx\theta/2$. The work done in the yield lines is

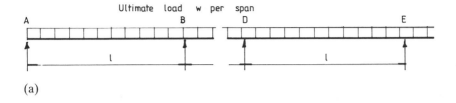

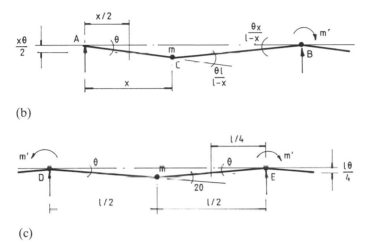

Fig. 8.31 (a) Continuous one-way slab; (b) end span; (c) internal span, fixed end beam.

$$\frac{ml\theta}{l - x} + \frac{m'x\theta}{l - x} = \frac{\theta}{l - x}(ml + m'x)$$

Equating these two expressions gives the work equation

$$W = \frac{2ml + 2m'x}{x(l - x)}$$

Locate the yield line C so that the ultimate load to cause collapse is a minimum, i.e.

$$\frac{dW}{dx} = 2m'x(l - x) - (2ml + 2m'x)(l - 2x) = 0$$

This equation can be solved for x for a given value of the ratio m'/m. Clause 3.5.2.1 of the code states that values of the ratio between support and span moments should be similar to those obtained by elastic theory. Values of m'/m should normally lie in the range 1.0–1.5. This limitation ensures that excessive cracking does not occur over the support B.

For the special case where $m = m'$ the equation $dW/dx = 0$ reduces to

$$(l + x)(l - 2x) - x(l - x) = 0$$
$$x^2 + 2lx - l^2 = 0$$

Solve to give

$$x = 0.414l$$

Substitute in the work equation to obtain the value of m:

$$m = 0.086Wl$$

The theoretical cut-off point for the top reinforcement is at $2x = 0.828l$ from the support A.

(b) Internal span DE

The hinge is at mid-span and the rotations are shown in Fig. 8.31(c). The work equation is

$$\frac{Wl\theta}{4} = 2m'\theta + 2m\theta$$

For the case where $m = m'$

$$m = Wl/16 = 0.0625Wl$$

The theoretical cut-off points for the top bars are at $0.25l$ from each support.

8.8.6 Simply supported rectangular two-way slab

The slab and yield line pattern are shown in Fig. 8.32. The ultimate loading is w per square metre and the slab is reinforced equally in each direction to give a moment of resistance of m per metre. The yield line pattern is defined by one parameter, ϕ. The standard solution is derived.

The work done by the loads can be calculated by dividing the rectangular slab into eight triangles A and two rectangles B. The rotation and deflections are shown in the figure. The work done by the loads is

$$8 \times \frac{1}{2} \times \frac{1}{2} \tan \phi \times \frac{1}{2} \times \frac{\theta b}{6} \times w + 2(a - b \tan \phi) \frac{b}{2} \times \frac{\theta b}{4} \times w$$
$$= \frac{\theta a b^2 w}{4} - \frac{\theta b^3 w \tan \phi}{12}$$

The work done in the yield line is

$$2\theta m(a - b \tan \phi) + 2\theta m b \tan \phi + 2\theta m b \cot \phi = 2\theta m a + 2\theta m b \cot \phi$$

Equate the expressions to give

$$m = \frac{wb^2}{8} \left(\frac{a - (b/3) \tan \phi}{a + b/\tan \phi} \right)$$

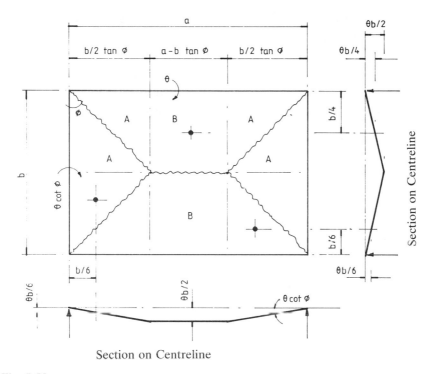

Section on Centreline

Fig. 8.32

For a given value of the ultimate load determine the value of $\tan\phi$ to make the moment of resistance a maximum. This is given by

$$\frac{dm}{d(\tan\phi)} = -\left(a + \frac{b}{\tan\phi}\right)\frac{b}{3} + \left(a - \frac{b}{3}\tan\phi\right)\frac{b}{\tan^2\phi} = 0$$

This reduces to

$$\tan^2\phi + \frac{2b}{a}\tan\phi - 3 = 0$$

and the solution is

$$\tan\phi = -\frac{b}{a} + \left(\frac{b^2}{a^2} + 3\right)^{1/2}$$

For given dimensions for a slab $\tan\phi$ can be evaluated and the design moment m can be found. For a square slab $a = b$, $\tan\phi = 1$ and $m = wa^2/24$. Note that solution can be obtained for a rectangular slab with different reinforcements is each direction.

□ Example 8.7 Yield line analysis – simply supported rectangular slab

A simply supported rectangular slab 4.5 m long by 3 m wide carries an ultimate load of $15 \, \text{kN/m}^2$. Determine the design moments for the case when the moment of resistance in the direction of the short span is 30% greater than that in the direction of the long span.

The slab and yield line pattern are shown in Fig. 8.33(a). The work done by the loads can be obtained using the expression derived above.

$$\frac{\theta \times 4.5 \times 3^2 \times 16}{4} - \frac{\theta \times 3^3 \times 16 \tan\phi}{12} = 162\theta - 36\theta \tan\phi$$

The moment of resistance in the direction of the yield line is determined using the expression derived in section 8.8.3(b) above (Fig. 8.33(b)).

$$m_N = m \sin^2\phi + 1.3m \cos^2\phi$$
$$= m(\sin^2\phi + 1.3 \cos^2\phi)$$

The work done in the yield lines is

$$2\theta \times 1.3m(4.5 - 3 \tan\phi) + 6\theta \tan\phi \times m(\sin^2\phi + 1.3 \cos^2\phi) + 6\theta \cot\phi$$
$$\times m(\sin^2\phi + 1.3 \cos^2\phi)$$

Equate the expressions to give

$$m = \frac{162 - 36 \tan\phi}{2.6(4.5 - 3 \tan\phi) + 6(\tan\phi + \cot\phi)(\sin^2\phi + 1.3 \cos^2\phi)}$$

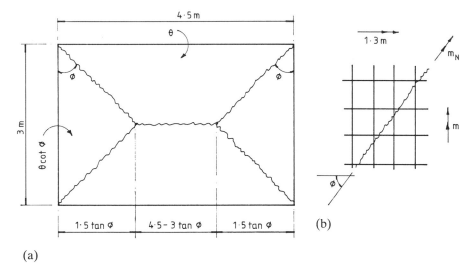

(a)

Fig. 8.33 (a) Plan and yield line pattern; (b) moment of resistance along yield line.

The equation may be solved by successive trials by assuming values for ϕ and calculating m. The value of ϕ giving the maximum value of m is the solution. This is $\phi = 56°$ when the long-span moment $m = 7.63\,\text{kN m/m}$. The short-span moment is $1.3m = 9.92\,\text{kN m/m}$ (section 8.8.8 below).   ■

8.8.7 Rectangular two-way slab continuous over supports

The solution derived in section 8.8.6 can be extended to the case of a continuous slab. The slab shown in Fig. 8.34 has a continuous hogging yield line around the supports. If the negative moment of resistance of the slab at the supports has a uniform value of m' per unit length, then the total work done in the yield lines is as follows: for the sagging yield lines

$$2\theta m(a + b \cot\phi)$$

and for the hogging yield lines

$$2\theta m'(a + b \cot\phi)$$
$$\text{total work} = 2\theta(m + m')(a + b \cot\phi)$$

Equate this to the work done by the loads to give

$$m + m' = \frac{wb^2}{8}\left(\frac{a - (b/3)\tan\phi}{a + b\tan\phi}\right)$$

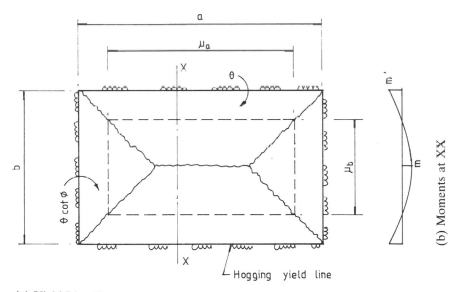

(a) Yield Line Pattern

Fig. 8.34 (a) Yield line pattern; (b) moments at XX.

The maximum value of $m + m'$ is given by the expression for $\tan \phi$ derived in section 8.8.6. The analysis can be completed by assuming a value for the ratio m'/m of between 1.0 and 1.5 as recommended in section 8.8.5 to conform to BS 8110: Part 1, clause 3.5.2.1.

The extend of the negative reinforcement required can be determined by finding the dimensions of a simply supported central region $\mu a \times \mu b$ which has a collapse moment in the yield lines of m. At the cut-off of the top bars, the hogging yield line has zero strength which simulates the simple support. The area $\mu a \times \mu b$ is shown in Fig. 8.34(a). The bars must be anchored beyond the theoretical cut-off lines.

In the bottom of the slab, reinforcement to give a moment of resistance m is required across the short span in the centre. The bending moment across the short span shown in Fig. 8.34(b) can be used to determine where one-half of the bars could be cut off. In the region of the inclined yield lines, reinforcement giving a moment of resistance m in both directions is required. Some longitudinal reinforcement could be curtailed in the central region of the slab.

8.8.8 Corner levers

In sections 8.8.6 and 8.8.7 the yield lines for both the simply supported and the continuous slabs have been taken to run directly into the corners (Figs 8.32 and 8.34). This is a simplification of the true solution in each case where it is shown that the yield line divides to form a corner lever. The correct patterns for the two cases are as follows.

1. Simply supported corner not held down – the slab lifts off the corner and the sagging yield line divides as shown in Fig. 8.35(a).
2. Continuous slab, corner held down – the sagging yield line divides and a hogging yield line forms as shown in Fig. 8.35(b).

Solutions have been obtained for these cases which show that, for a 90° corner, the corner lever mechanism decreases the overall strength of the slab by about 10%. The reinforcement should be increased accordingly

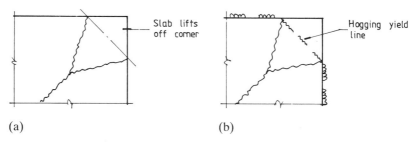

(a)   (b)

Fig. 8.35 (a) Corner not held down; (b) corner held down.

when the simplified solution is used. The top reinforcement will prevent cracking in continuous slabs on the corner lever hogging yield line.

8.8.9 Further cases

The solutions for some further common cases are discussed.

(a) Slabs with discontinuous edges

Two cases of slabs with discontinuous edges, a corner panel and an interior edge panel, are shown in Fig. 8.36. In both cases the slabs are assumed to be simply supported at the discontinuous edges on walls or beams. The bottom reinforcement has a moment of resistance m and the top reinforcement has a moment of resistance m' in each direction.

Three variables are required to define the yield line pattern for the corner slab shown in Fig. 8.36(a). The work equation can be written as

$$m + m' = f(x, y, z, a, b)w$$

This is partially differentiated with respect to x, y and z to give the simultaneous equations

$$\delta(m + m')/\delta x = 0$$
$$\delta(m + m')/\delta y = 0$$
$$\delta(m + m')/\delta z = 0$$

These can be solved to give x, y and z. In a given case a solution by successive trials can be made determining x first to give the maximum value

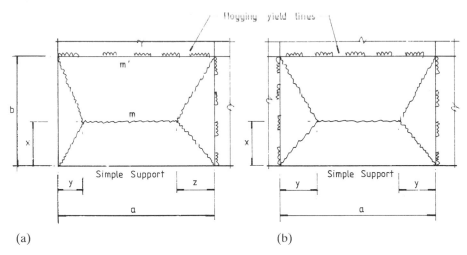

(a)   (b)

Fig. 8.36 (a) Corner panel; (b) interior edge panel.

of $m + m'$ for assumed values of y and z. Then y and z can be altered to maximize $m + m'$. A suitable ratio m'/m is selected to complete the design.

The interior edge panel shown in Fig. 8.36(b) requires two variables to define the yield line pattern. The procedure for solution is the same as for the corner panel discussed above.

(b) Slab with free edges or irregular shapes

The slabs shown in Fig. 8.37(a) have one free edge. Two possible patterns for sagging yield lines are shown. The particular pattern depends on the ratio of the side dimensions a/b. In each case one parameter only defines the yield lines. The solution can be obtained directly as discussed in section 8.8.6.

An irregular slab is shown in Fig. 8.37(b). Note that the yield lines and axes of rotation along the edge supports intersect as shown.

□ Example 8.8 Yield line analysis – corner panel of floor slab

A square corner panel of a floor slab simply supported on the outer edges on steel beams and continuous over the interior beams is shown in Fig. 8.38. The design

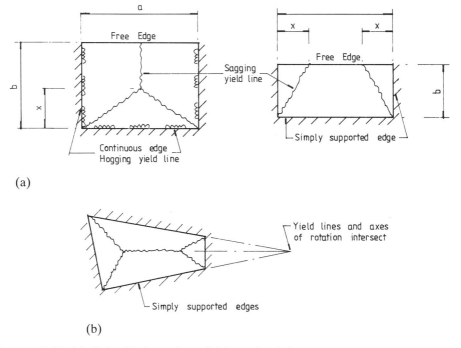

(a)

(b)

Fig. 8.37 (a) Slab with free edges; (b) irregular slab.

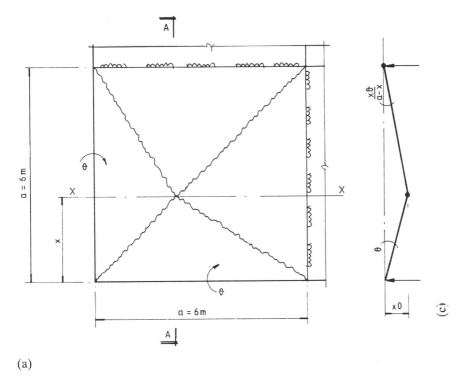

(a)

Fig. 8.38 (a) Plan; (b) section AA.

ultimate load is 12 4 kN/m² Design the slab using the yield line method. The slab is to be 175 mm thick and reinforced equally in both directions. The moment of resistance in the hogging and sagging yield lines is to be the same. The materials are grade 30 concrete and grade 250 reinforcement.

The yield line pattern, which in this case depends on one variable x, and the section showing rotations and deflections are given in Fig. 8.38. The work done by the loads is $wa^2x\theta/3$. The work done in the yield line is

$$\frac{2max\theta}{a-x} + 2ma\theta + \frac{2max\theta}{a-x} = \frac{2ma\theta(a+x)}{a-x}$$

Equate the two expressions to give

$$m = \frac{wax(a-x)}{6(a+x)}$$

The maximum value of m is given when

$$\frac{dm}{dx} = 6(a+x)wa(a-2x) - wax(a-x)6 = 0$$

This reduces to

$$x^2 + 2ax - a^2 = 0$$
$$x = 0.414a$$

Substituting in the expression for m gives

$$m = 0.0286wa^2 = 12.76 \text{ kN m/m}$$

Assume 10 mm diameter bars, 25 mm cover; the effective depth of the inner layer is

$$d = 175 - 25 - 10 - 5 = 135 \text{ mm}$$
$$\frac{m}{bd^2} = \frac{12.76 \times 10^6}{1000 \times 135^2} = 0.7$$

Referring to Fig. 4.13, m/bd^2 is less than 1.27 and so the lever arm is $0.95d$.

$$A_s = \frac{12.76 \times 10^6}{0.87 \times 250 \times 0.95 \times 135}$$
$$= 457.4 \text{ mm}^2/\text{m}$$

The steel area is increased by 10% to 505.1 mm²/m to allow for the formation of corner levers.

Provide 10 mm diameter bars at 150 mm centres to give a steel area of 523 mm²/m. The minimum area of reinforcement is

$$A_s = 0.245 \times 175 \times 1000/100 = 420 \text{ mm}^2/\text{m}$$

Using the simplified rules for curtailment of bars in slabs from Fig. 3.25 of the code the negative steel is to continue for 0.3 of the span, i.e. 1800 mm past the interior supports. The positive steel is to run into and be continuous through the supports.

The shear at the continuous edge is

$$V = 3 \times 12.4 + 12.76/6 = 39.3 \text{ kN}$$
$$\text{stress} \quad v = \frac{39.3 \times 10^3}{10^3 \times 135} = 0.29 \text{ N/mm}^2$$

The design concrete shear stress from Table 3.9 of the code is

$$v_c = 0.79 \left(\frac{100 \times 523}{1000 \times 135} \right)^{1/3} \left(\frac{400}{135} \right)^{1/4} \left(\frac{30}{25} \right)^{1/3} \Big/ 1.25$$
$$= 0.64 \text{ N/mm}^2$$

The shear stress is satisfactory.

The basic span/d ratio is 26 from Table 3.10 of the code. Referring to Table 3.11 of the code,

$$m/bd^2 = 0.7$$
$$f_s = \frac{5 \times 250 \times 503.1}{8 \times 523} = 150.3 \text{ N/mm}^2$$

The modification factor is

$$0.55 + \frac{477 - 150.3}{120(0.9 + 0.7)} = 2.25 > 2.0$$

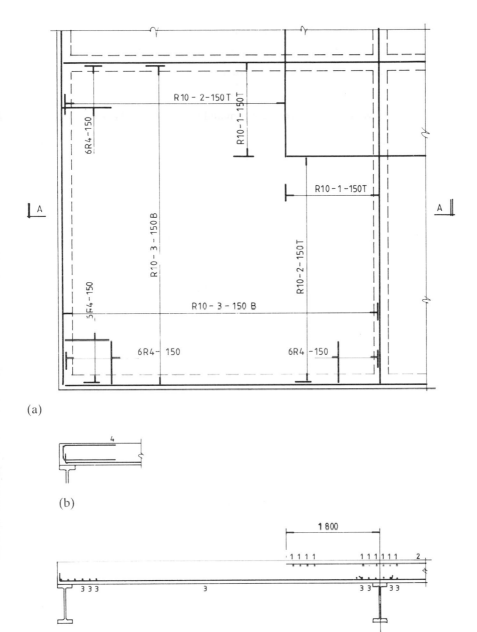

(a)

(b)

(b)

Fig. 8.39 (a) Plan; (b) corner detail; (c) section AA.

$$\text{allowable span}/d \text{ ratio} = 26 \times 2 = 52$$
$$\text{actual span}/d \text{ ratio} = 6000/135 = 44$$

The slab is satisfactory with respect to deflection. Note that a deeper slab is required if grade 460 reinforcement is used.

The minimum clear distance between bars is not to exceed $3d = 405\,\text{mm}$. The slab depth 175 mm does not exceed 250 mm and so no further checks are required.

The reinforcement is shown in Fig. 8.39. Note that U-bars are provided at the corners to anchor the bottom tension reinforcement at the sagging yield lines. This design should be compared with that in Example 8.4.

If the slab was supported on reinforced concrete L-beams on the outer edges, a value for the ultimate negative resistance moment at these edges could be assumed and used in the analysis.　　　　■

8.9 STAIR SLABS

8.9.1 Building regulations

Statutory requirements are laid down in *Building Regulations and Associated Approved Documents*, Part H [9], where private and common stairways are defined. The private stairway is for use with one dwelling and the common stairway is used for more than one dwelling. Requirements from the Building Regulations are shown in Fig. 8.40.

8.9.2 Types of stair slab

Stairways are sloping one-way spanning slabs. Two methods of construction are used.

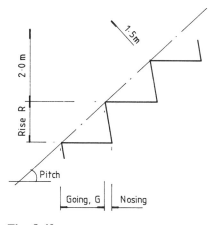

	Private	Common
Rise R	≯ 220mm	≯ 190mm
Going G	≮ 220mm	≮ 230mm
Pitch	≯ 42°	≯ 38°
No. of steps in flight	–	≯ 16

700mm > G + 2R > 550mm

Fig. 8.40

(a) Transverse spanning stair slabs

Transverse spanning stair slabs span between walls, a wall and stringer (an edge beam), or between two stringers. The stair slab may also be cantilevered from a wall. A stair slab spanning between a wall and a stringer is shown in Fig. 8.41(a).

The stair slab is designed as a series of beams consisting of one step with assumed breadth and effective depth shown in Fig. 8.41(c). The moment reinforcement is generally one bar per step. Secondary reinforcement is placed longitudinally along the flight.

(b) Longitudinal spanning stair slab

The stair slab spans between supports at the top and bottom of the flight. The supports may be beams, walls or landing slabs. A common type of staircase is shown in Fig. 8.42.

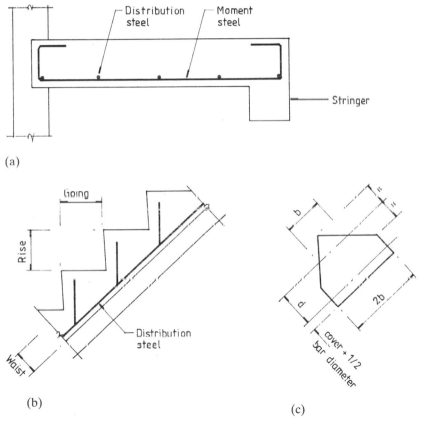

(a)

(b)

(c)

Fig. 8.41 (a) Transverse section; (b) longitudinal section; (c) assumptions for design.

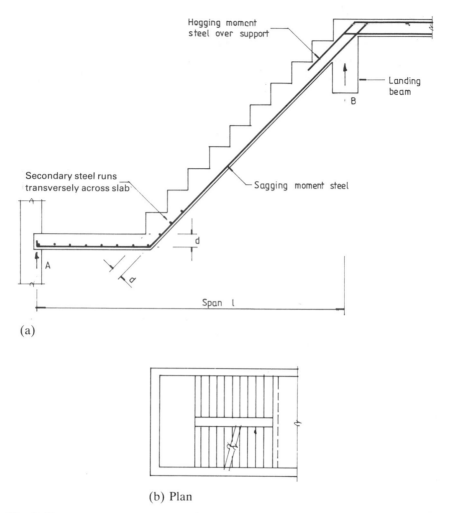

Fig. 8.42

The effective span *l* lies between the top landing beam and the centre of support in the wall. If the total design load on the stair is *W* the positive design moment at mid-span and the negative moment over top beam B are both taken as *Wl*/10. The arrangement of moment reinforcement is shown in the figure. Secondary reinforcement runs transversely across the stair.

A stair case around a lift well is shown in Fig. 8.43. The effective span *l* of the stair is defined in the code. This and other code requirements are discussed in section 8.9.3 below. The maximum moment near mid-span and over supports is taken as *Wl*/10 where *W* is the total design load on the span.

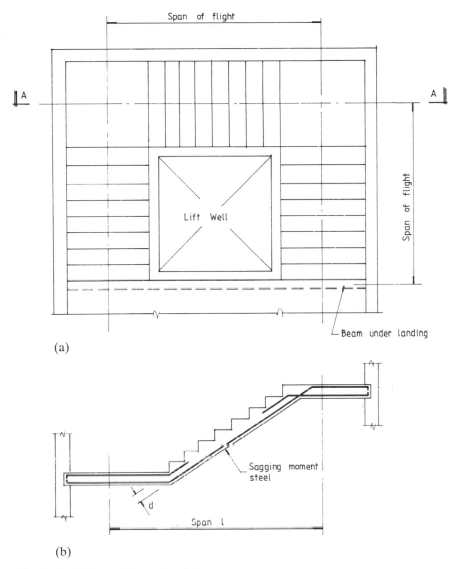

Fig. 8.43 (a) Plan; (b) section AA.

8.9.3 Code design requirements

(a) Imposed loading

The imposed loading on stairs is given in BS 6399: Part 1, Table 1. From this table the distributed loading is as follows:

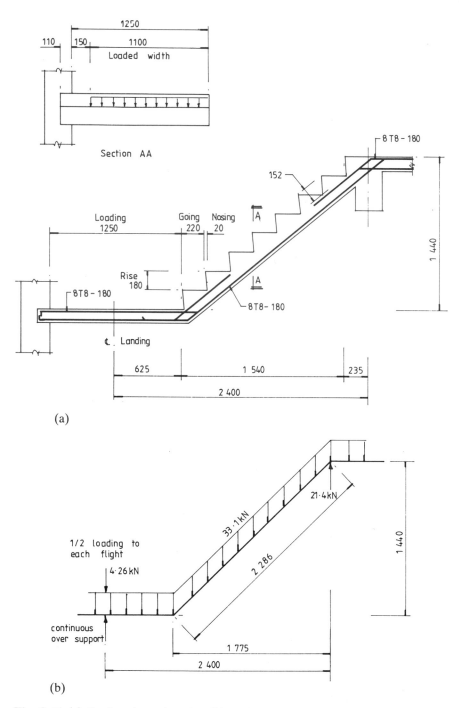

1250

110 150 1100
Loaded width

Section AA

8 T8 – 180

152

Loading
1250

Going Nosing
220 20

A

1 440

Rise
180

8T8 – 180

8T8 – 180

8T8– 180

A

₵ . Landing

625   1 540   235

2 400

(a)

21·4kN

33·1kN

1 440

1/2 loading to
each flight

4·26 kN

2·286

continuous
over support

1 775

2 400

(b)

Fig. 8.44 (a) Section through stairs; (b) loading diagram.

1. dwelling not over three storeys, $1.5\,kN/m^2$
2. all other buildings, the same as the floors to which they give access but not less than $3\,kN/m^2$ or more than $5\,kN/m^2$

(b) Design provisions

Provisions for design of staircases are set out in BS 8110: Part 1, section 3.10 and are summarized below.

1. The code states that the staircase may be taken to include a section of the landing spanning in the same direction and continuous with the stair flight;
2. The design ultimate load is to be taken as uniform over the plan area. When two spans intersect at right angles as shown in Fig. 8.43 the load on the common area can be divided equally between the two spans;
3. When a staircase or landing spans in the direction of the flight and is built into the wall at least 110 mm along part or all of the length, a strip 150 mm wide may be deducted from the loaded area (Fig. 8.44);
4. When the staircase is built monolithically at its ends into structural members spanning at right angles to its span, the effective span is given by

$$l_a + 0.5(l_{b1} + l_{b2})$$

where l_a is the clear horizontal distance between supporting members, l_{b1} is the breadth of a supporting member at one end or 1.8 m whichever is the smaller and l_{b2} is the breadth of a supporting member at the other end or 1.8 m whichever is the smaller (Fig. 8.43);
5. The effective span of simply supported staircases without stringer beams should be taken as the horizontal distance between centrelines of supports or the clear distance between faces of supports plus the effective depth whichever is the less;
6. The depth of the section is to be taken as the minimum thickness perpendicular to the soffit of the stair slab;
7. The design procedure is the same as for beams and slabs (see provision 8 below);
8. For staircases without stringer beams when the stair flight occupies at least 60% of the span the permissible span-to-effective depth ratio may be increased by 15%.

□ Example 8.9 Stair slab

(a) Specification

Design the side flight of a staircase surrounding an open stair well. A section through the stairs is shown in Fig. 8.44(a). The stair slab is supported on a beam at the top and on the landing of the flight at right angles at the bottom. The imposed loading is 5 kN/m². The stair is built 110 mm into the side wall of the stair well. The clear width of the stairs is 1.25 m and the flight consists of eight risers at 180 mm and seven goings of 220 mm with 20 mm nosing. The stair treads and landings have 15 mm granolithic finish and the underside of the stair and landing slab has 15 mm of plaster finish. The materials are grade 30 concrete and grade 460 reinforcement.

(b) Loading and moment

Assume the waist thickness of structural concrete is 100 mm, the cover is 25 mm and the bar diameter is 10 mm. The loaded width and effective breadth of the stair slab are shown in section AA in Fig. 8.44(a). The effective span of the stair slab is the clear horizontal distance (1540 mm) plus the distance of the stair to the centre of the top beam (235 mm) plus one-half of the breadth of the landing (625 mm), i.e. 2400 mm. The design ultimate loading on the stairs is calculated first.

(i) Landing slab   The overall thickness including the top and underside finish is 130 mm.

$$\text{dead load} = 0.13 \times 24 \times 1.4 = 4.4 \, \text{kN/m}^2$$

$$\text{imposed load} = 5 \times 1.6 = 8.0 \, \text{kN/m}^2$$

$$\text{total load} = 12.4 \, \text{kN/m}^2$$

$$\text{load} = 0.5 \times 12.4 \times 0.625 \times 1.1 = 4.26 \, \text{kN}$$

One-half of the load on the landing slab is included for the stair slab under consideration. The loaded width is 1.1 m.

(ii) Stair slab   The slope length is 2.29 m and the steps project 152 mm perpendicularly to the top surface of the waist. The average thickness including finishes is

$$100 + \frac{152}{2} + 30 = 206 \, \text{mm}$$

$$\text{dead load} = 0.206 \times 24 \times 2.29 \times 1.1 \times 1.4 = 17.44 \, \text{kN}$$

$$\text{imposed load} = 5 \times 1.78 \times 1.1 \times 1.6 = 15.66 \, \text{kN}$$

$$\text{total load} = 33.1 \, \text{kN}$$

The dead load is calculated using the slope length while the imposed load acts on the plan length. The loaded width is 1.1 m.

The total load on the span is

$$4.26 + 33.1 = 37.36 \, \text{kN}$$

The maximum shear at the top support is 21.44 kN. The design moment for sagging moment near mid-span and the hogging moment over the supports is

$$37.36 \times 2.4/10 = 8.97 \, \text{kN m}$$

(c) Moment reinforcement

The effective depth d is $100 - 25 - 5 = 70$ mm. The effective width will be taken as the width of the stair slab, 1250 mm.

$$\frac{M}{bd^2} = \frac{8.97 \times 10^6}{1250 \times 70^2} = 1.46$$

From Fig. 4.13

$$100A_s/bd = 0.39$$
$$A_s = 0.39 \times 70 \times 1250/100 = 341.3\,\text{mm}^2$$

Provide eight 8 mm diameter bars to give an area of 402 mm². Space the bars at 180 mm centres. The same steel is provided in the top of the slab over both supports.

The minimum area of reinforcement is

$$0.13 \times 100 \times 1000/100 = 130\,\text{mm}^2$$

Provide 8 mm diameter bars at 300 mm centres to give 167 mm²/m.

(d) Shear resistance

$$\text{shear} = 21.4\,\text{kN}$$
$$v = \frac{21.4 \times 10^3}{70 \times 1250} = 0.24\,\text{N/mm}^2$$
$$\frac{100A_s}{bd} = \frac{100 \times 402}{1250 \times 70} = 0.46$$
$$v_c = 0.79(0.46)^{1/3}(400/125)^{1/4}(30/25)^{1/3}/1.25$$
$$= 0.69\,\text{N/mm}^2$$

The slab is satisfactory with respect to shear. Note that a minimum value of d of 125 mm is used in the formula.

(e) Deflection

The slab is checked for deflection. The basic span/d ratio is 26.

$$f_s = \frac{5 \times 460 \times 341.3}{8 \times 402} = 244.1\,\text{N/mm}^2$$

The modification factor for tension reinforcement is

$$0.55 + \frac{477 - 244.1}{120(0.9 + 1.46)} = 1.37$$
$$\text{allowable span}/d = 26 \times 1.37 \times 1.15$$
$$= 41.96$$
$$\text{actual span}/d = 2400/70 = 34.3$$

Note that the stair flight with a plan length of 1540 mm occupies 64% of the span and the allowable span/d ratio can be increased by 15% (BS 8110: Part 1, clause 3.10.2.2).

(f) Cracking

For crack control the clear distance between bars is not to exceed $3d = 210\,\text{mm}$. The reinforcement spacing of 180 mm is satisfactory.

(g) Reinforcement

The reinforcement is shown in Fig. 8.44(a).   ■

9

Columns

9.1 TYPES, LOADS, CLASSIFICATION AND DESIGN CONSIDERATIONS

9.1.1 Types and loads

Columns are structural members in buildings carrying roof and floor loads to the foundations. A column stack in a multistorey building is shown in Fig. 9.1(a). Columns primarily carry axial loads, but most columns are subjected to moment as well as axial load. Referring to the part floor plan in the figure, the internal column A is designed for axial load while edge columns B and corner column C are designed for axial load and moment.

Design of axially loaded columns is treated first. Then methods are given for design of sections subjected to axial load and moment. Most columns are termed short columns and fail when the material reaches its ultimate capacity under the applied loads and moments. Slender columns buckle and the additional moments caused by deflection must be taken into account in design.

The column section is generally square or rectangular, but circular and polygonal columns are used in special cases. When the section carries mainly axial load it is symmetrically reinforced with four, six, eight or more bars held in a cage by links. Typical column reinforcement is shown in Fig. 9.1(b).

9.1.2 General code provisions

General requirements for design of columns are treated in BS 8110: Part 1, section 3.8.1. The provisions apply to columns where the greater cross-sectional dimension does not exceed four times the smaller dimension.

The minimum size of a column must meet the fire resistance requirements given in Fig. 3.2 of the code. For example, for a fire resistance period of 1.5 h a fully exposed column must have a minimum dimension of 250 mm. The covers required to meet durability and fire resistance requirements are given in Tables 3.4 and 3.5 respectively of the code.

The code classifies columns first as

1. short columns when the ratios l_{ex}/h and l_{ey}/b are both less than 15 for braced columns and less than 10 for unbraced columns and
2. slender columns when the ratios are larger than the values given above

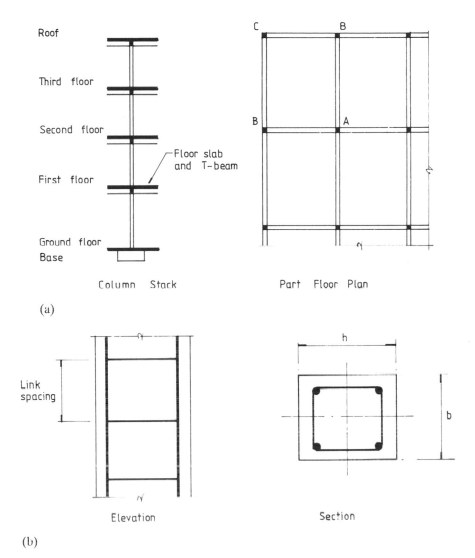

Fig. 9.1 (a) Building column; (b) column construction.

Here b is the width of the column cross-section, h is the depth of the column cross-section, l_{ex} is the effective height in respect of the major axis and l_{ey} is the effective height in respect of the minor axis.

In the second classification the code defines columns as braced or unbraced. The code states that a column may be considered to be braced in a given plane if lateral stability to the structure as a whole is provided by walls or bracing designed to resist all lateral forces in that plane. Otherwise the column should be considered as unbraced.

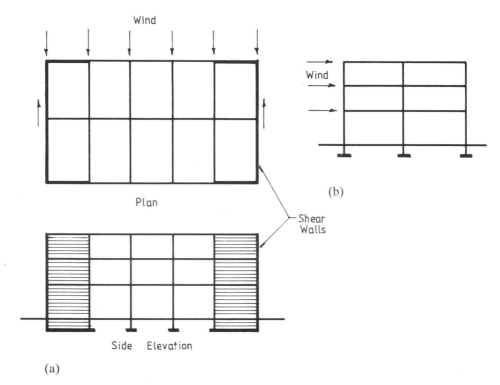

Fig. 9.2 (a) Braced frame; (b) unbraced frame.

Lateral stability in braced reinforced concrete structures is provided by shear walls, lift shafts and stair wells. In unbraced structures resistance to lateral forces is provided by bending in the columns and beams in that plane. Braced and unbraced frames are shown in Figs 9.2(a) and 9.2(b) respectively.

Clause 3.8.1.4 of the code states that if a column has a sufficiently large section to resist the ultimate loads without reinforcement, it may be designed similarly to a plane concrete wall (section 10.4).

9.1.3 Practical design provisions

The following practical considerations with regard to design of columns are extracted from BS 8110: Part 1, section 3.12. The minimum number of longitudinal bars in a column section is four. The points from the code are as follows.

(a) Minimum percentage of reinforcement

The minimum percentage of reinforcement is given in Table 3.27 of the code for both grade 250 and grade 460 reinforcement as

$$100A_{sc}/A_{cc} = 0.4$$

where A_{sc} is the area of steel in compression and A_{cc} is the area of concrete in compression.

(b) Maximum area of reinforcement

Clause 3.12.6.2 states that the maximum area of reinforcement should not exceed 6% of the gross cross-sectional area of a vertically cast column except at laps where 10% is permitted.

(c) Requirements for links

Clause 3.12.7 covers containment of compression reinforcement:

1. The diameter of links should not be less than 6 mm or one-quarter of the diameter of the largest longitudinal bar;
2. The maximum spacing is to be 12 times the diameter of the smallest longitudinal bar;
3. The links should be arranged so that every corner bar and each

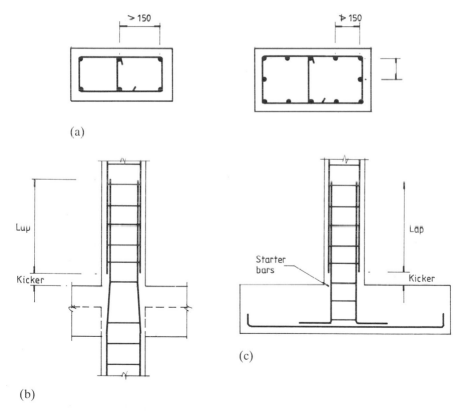

Fig. 9.3 (a) Arrangement of links; (b) column lap; (c) column base.

alternate bar in an outer layer is supported by a link passing round the bar and having an included angle of not more than 135°. No bar is to be further than 150 mm from a restrained bar. These requirements are shown in Fig. 9.3(a).

(d) Compression laps and butt joints

Clause 3.12.8.15 of the code states that the length of compression laps should be 25% greater than the compression anchorage length. Compression lap lengths are given in Table 3.29 of the code (section 5.2.1 here). Laps in columns are located above the base and floor levels as shown in Fig. 9.3(b). Clause 3.12.8.16.1 of the code also states that the load in compression bars may be transferred by end bearing of square sawn cut ends held by couplers. Welded butt joints can also be made (clause 3.12.8.17).

9.2 SHORT BRACED AXIALLY LOADED COLUMNS

9.2.1 Code design expressions

Both longitudinal steel and all the concrete assist in carrying the load. The links prevent the longitudinal bars from buckling. BS 8110: Part 1, clause 3.8.4.3, gives the following expression for the ultimate load N that a short braced axially loaded column can support.

$$N = 0.4f_{cu}A_c + 0.75A_{sc}f_y$$

where A_c is the net cross-sectional area of concrete in the column and A_{sc} is the area of vertical reinforcement. The expression allows for eccentricity due to construction tolerances but applies only to a column that cannot be subjected to significant moments. An example is column A in Fig. 9.1(a) which supports a symmetrical arrangement of floor beams. Note that for pure axial load the ultimate capacity N_{uz} of a column given in clause 3.8.3.1 of the code is

$$N_{uz} = 0.45f_{cu}A_c + 0.87f_yA_{sc}$$

Thus in the design equation for short columns the effect of the eccentricity of the load is taken into account by reducing the capacity for axial load by about 10%.

Clause 3.8.4.4 gives a further expression for short braced columns supporting an approximately symmetrical arrangement of beams. These beams must be designed for uniformly distributed imposed loads and the span must not differ by more than 15% of the longer span. The ultimate load is given by the expression

$$N = 0.35f_{cu}A_c + 0.67A_{sc}f_y$$

☐ Example 9.1 Axially loaded short column

A short braced axially loaded column 300 mm square in section is reinforced with four 25 mm diameter bars. Find the ultimate axial load that the column can carry and the pitch and diameter of the links required. The materials are grade 30 concrete and grade 460 reinforcement.

$$\text{steel area } A_{sc} = 1963 \text{ mm}^2$$
$$\text{concrete area } A_c = 300^2 - 1963 = 88037 \text{ mm}^2$$
$$N = \frac{0.4 \times 30 \times 88037}{10^3} + \frac{0.75 \times 1963 \times 460}{10^3}$$
$$= 1056 + 677 = 1733 \text{ kN}$$

The links are not to be less than 6 mm in diameter or one-quarter of the diameter of the longitudinal bars. The spacing is not to be greater than 12 times the diameter of the longitudinal bars. Provide 8 mm diameter links at 300 mm centres. The column section is shown in Fig. 9.4. From Table 3.4 of the code the cover for mild exposure is 25 mm.

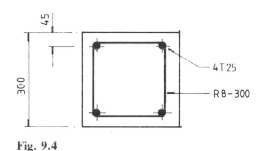

Fig. 9.4

☐ Example 9.2 Axially loaded short column

A short braced column has to carry an ultimate axial load of 1366 kN. The column size is 250 mm × 250 mm. Find the steel area required for the longitudinal reinforcement and select suitable bars. The materials are grade 30 concrete and grade 460 reinforcement.

Substitute in the expression for the ultimate load

$$1366 \times 10^3 = 0.4 \times 30(250^2 - A_{sc}) + 0.75 \times 460 A_{sc}$$
$$A_{sc} = 1850 \text{ mm}^2$$

Provide four 25 mm diameter bars to give a steel area of 1963 mm². Check:

$$\frac{100 A_{sc}}{bh} = \frac{100 \times 1963}{250^2} = 3.14$$

This is satisfactory.

9.3 SHORT COLUMNS SUBJECTED TO AXIAL LOAD AND BENDING ABOUT ONE AXIS – SYMMETRICAL REINFORCEMENT

9.3.1 Code provisions

The design of short columns resisting moment and axial load is covered in various clauses in BS 8110: Part 1, section 3.8. The main provisions are as follows

1. Clause 3.8.2.3 states that in column and beam construction in monolithic braced frames the axial force in the column can be calculated assuming the beams are simply supported. If the arrangement of beams is symmetrical, the column can be designed for axial load only as set out in section 9.2 above. The column may also be designed for axial load and a moment due to the nominal eccentricity given in provision 2 below;
2. Clause 3.8.2.4 states that in no section in a column should the design moment be taken as less than the ultimate load acting at a minimum eccentricity e_{min} equal to 0.05 times the overall dimension of the column in the plane of bending, but not more than 20 mm;
3. Clause 3.8.4.1 states that in the analysis of cross-sections to determine the ultimate resistance to moment and axial force the same assumptions should be made as when analysing a beam. These assumptions are given in Clause 3.4.4.1 of the code;
4. Clause 3.8.4.2 states that design charts for symmetrically reinforced columns are given in BS 8110: Part 3;
5. Clause 3.8.4.3 states that it is usually only necessary to design short columns for the maximum design moment about one critical axis.

The application of the assumptions to analyse the section and construction of a design chart is given below.

9.3.2 Section analysis – symmetrical reinforcement

A symmetrically reinforced column section subjected to the ultimate axial load N and ultimate moment M is shown in Fig. 9.5. The moment is equivalent to the axial load acting at an eccentricity $e = M/N$. Depending on the relative values of M and N, the following two main cases occur for analysis:

1. compression over the whole section where the neutral axis lies at the edge or outside the section as shown in Fig. 9.6(a) with both rows of steel bars in compression

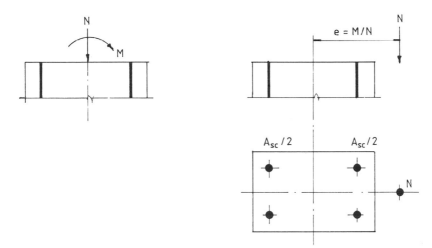

Fig. 9.5

2. compression on one side in the concrete and reinforcement and tension in the reinforcement on the other side with the neutral axis lying between the rows of reinforcement as shown in Fig. 9.6(b)

For a given location of the neutral axis, the strains and stresses in both the concrete and the steel can be determined and from these the values of the internal forces can be found. The resultant internal axial force and resistance moment can then be evaluated. For Fig. 9.6(b) the compression force C_c in the concrete is

$$C_c = k_1 bx$$

the compression force C_s in the reinforcement is

$$C_s = f_{sc}A_{sc}/2$$

and the tension force T in the reinforcement is

$$T = f_{st}A_{sc}/2$$

where A_{sc} is the area of reinforcement placed symmetrically about the XX axis, f_{sc} is the stress in the compression steel and f_{st} is the stress in the tension steel. The sum of the internal forces is

$$N = C_c + C_s - T$$

The sum of the moments of the internal forces about the centreline of the column is

$$M = C_c\left(\frac{h}{2} - k_2x\right) + C_s\left(\frac{h}{2} - d'\right) + T\left(d - \frac{h}{2}\right)$$

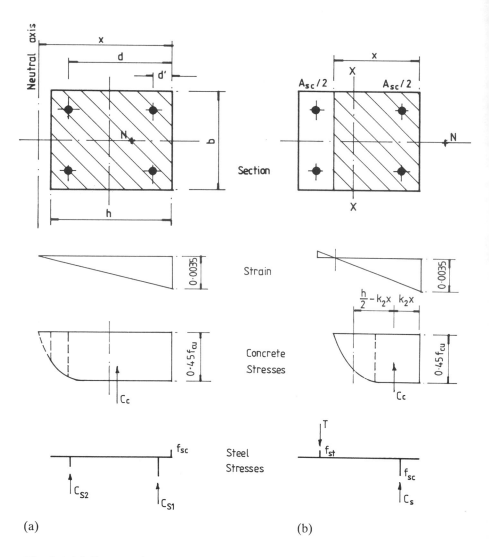

Fig. 9.6 (a) Compression over whole section; (b) compression over part of section, tension in steel.

Note that a given section subjected to an ultimate load N less than the capacity of the section under axial load only is able to support N and a determinable maximum ultimate moment M when the concrete is at its maximum strain and design strength. The steel stresses depend on the location of the neutral axis. If the moment is large the steel strength in tension will determine the moment capacity. The section can also be considered to support N at a maximum eccentricity $e = M/N$.

A given section can be analysed to see whether it can carry a given load or moment. The values of N and M can be found for a first value of x, say $x = d'$. Then x is increased until N equals the applied load. The coexisting value of M is compared with the applied moment. To design a section to carry a given load and moment a trial section must be selected, analysed as just discussed and then altered and re-analysed until an economic solution is found. The procedure is tedious and is not a practical manual design method. The problem can be solved more easily by constructing design charts or using a computer program.

☐ Example 9.3 Short column subjected to axial load and moment about one axis

Determine the ultimate axial load and moment about the XX axis that the column section shown in Fig. 9.7(a) can carry when the depth to the neutral axis is 250 mm. The materials are grade 30 concrete and grade 460 reinforcement.

The strain diagram is shown in Fig. 9.7(b). The concrete strain at failure is 0.0035. The strains in the reinforcement are as follows:

$$\text{Compression} \quad \varepsilon_{sc} = 0.0035 \times 200/250 = 0.0028$$
$$\text{Tension} \quad \varepsilon_{st} = 0.0035 \times 100/250 = 0.0014$$

The steel stresses from the stress diagram in Fig. 4.6 are

$$\text{Compression} \quad f_{sc} = 0.87f_y$$
$$\text{Tension} \quad f_{st} = 0.87f_y \times 0.0014/0.002$$
$$= 0.609f_y$$

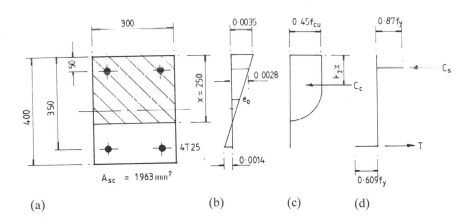

Fig. 9.7 (a) Section; (b) strain diagram; (c) concrete stresses; (d) steel stresses.

The steel forces arc

Compression $C_s = 0.87 \times 460 \times 981.5/10^3 = 392.8\,\text{kN}$
Tension $T = 0.609 \times 460 \times 981.5/10^3 = 274.9\,\text{kN}$

For grade 30 concrete (section 4.4.3)

$$\varepsilon_0 = 2.4 \times 10^{-4}(30/1.5)^{1/2} = 0.00107$$

$$C = k_1 bx$$

$$= \frac{0.45 \times 30 \times 300 \times 250}{0.0035 \times 10^3}\left(0.0035 - \frac{0.00107}{3}\right)$$

$$= 909.3\,\text{kN}$$

The location of the force C is given by

$$k_2 x = \frac{(2 - 0.00107/0.0035)^2 + 2}{4(3 - 0.00107/0.0035)}\,250 = 112.9\,\text{mm}$$

The ultimate axial force is

$$N = 909.3 + 392.7 - 274.9 = 1027.1\,\text{kN}$$

The ultimate moment is found by taking moments of the internal forces about the centre of the column:

$$M = [909.3(200 - 112.9) + (329.7 + 274.9)150]/10^3$$
$$= 179.3\,\text{kN m}$$ ∎

9.3.3 Construction of design chart

A design curve can be drawn for a selected grade of concrete and reinforcing steel for a section with a given percentage of reinforcement, $100A_{sc}/bh$, symmetrically placed at a given location d/h. The curve is formed by plotting values of N/bh against M/bh^2 for various positions of the neutral axis x. Other curves can be constructed for percentages of steel ranging from 0.4% to a maximum of 6% for vertically cast columns. The family of curves forms the design chart for that combination of materials and steel location. Separate charts are required for the same materials for different values of d/h which determines the location of the reinforcement in the section. Groups of charts are required for the various combinations of concrete and steel grades. Design charts are given in Part 3 of the code. The process for construction of a design chart is demonstrated below.

1. Select materials:

    Concrete $f_{cu} = 30\,\text{N/mm}^2$
    Reinforcement $f_y = 460\,\text{N mm}^2$

    The stress–strain curves for the materials are shown in Fig. 9.8(a).
2. Select a value of $d/h = 0.85$, $d = 0.85h$. Select a steel percentage

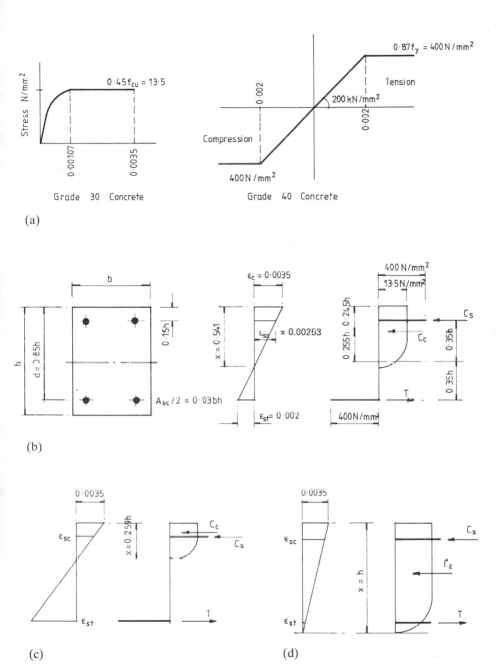

Fig. 9.8 (a) Materials – stress-strain curves; (b) yield in reinforcement; (c) moment only; (d) neutral axis at edge.

$100A_{sc}/bh = 6$. The steel area $A_{sc} - 0.06bh$. The column section is shown in Fig. 9.8(b).

3. Calculate the point on the design curve when the moment is zero, i.e. the axial load is

$$N = 13.5bh + 400 \times 0.06bh = 37.5bh$$

4. Calculate the value of the axial load and moment when the tension steel is at yield at strain 0.002 and a stress of $400\,N/mm^2$. The strain diagram for this case is shown in Fig. 9.8(b). From this

$$\frac{0.0035}{x} = \frac{0.002}{0.85h - x}$$

$$x = 0.541h$$

The strain in the compression steel is

$$\varepsilon_{sc} = (0.541 - 0.15) \times 0.0035/0.541 = 0.00253$$

The stress in the compression steel is $400\,N/mm^2$. The stress diagram and the internal forces are shown in Fig. 9.8(b).

Referring to section 4.4.3, the compression force in the concrete for $x = 0.541h$ is

$$C_c = 12.12 \times b \times 0.541\,h = 6.56bh$$
$$k_2x = 0.452 \times 0.541\,h \qquad = 0.45h$$

The sum of the internal forces is

$$N = 6.17bh \quad \text{or} \quad N/bh = 6.17$$

The forces in the steel in tension and compression are equal:

$$C_s = T = 400 \times 0.03bh = 12bh$$

The sum of the moments about the centre of the column is

$$M = 6.56bh \times 0.255h + 2 \times 12bh \times 0.35h$$
$$= 10.07bh^2$$

or

$$M/bh^2 = 10.07$$

5. Calculate the value of the moment when the axial load is zero. The value of x can be determined by successive trials to give the case when the sum of the internal forces is zero. Say

$$x = 0.31d = 0.264h$$
$$C_c = 12.12xb = 3.19bh$$
$$\varepsilon_{sc} = \frac{0.264h - 0.15h}{0.264h} 0.0035 = 0.00151$$

$$f_{sc} = \frac{0.00151 \times 400}{0.002} = 302.3 \, \text{N/mm}^2$$

$$C_s = 0.03bh \times 302.3 = 9.07bh$$

$$T = 400 \times 0.03bh = 12bh$$

Note that the strain in the tension steel exceeds 0.002.

$$C_c + C_s - T = (3.19 + 9.07 - 12)bh = 0.26bh$$

For $x = 0.305d = 0.259h$,

$$C_c + C_s - T = 3.14 + 8.84bh - 12bh = 0.02bh$$

Take moments about the centre of the column:

$$k_2x = 0.452 \times 0.259h = 0.117h$$

$$M = 3.14bh(0.5h - 0.117h) + (8.84 + 12)0.35bh^2$$

$$= (1.2 + 7.29)bh^2$$

$$= 8.49bh^2$$

$$M/bh^2 = 8.49$$

6. Calculate the value of the moment and axial load when the neutral axis lies at the edge of the column (Fig. 9.8(d)). For $x = h$

$$C_c = 12.12bh$$

$$k_2x = 0.452h$$

$$\varepsilon_{sc} = 0.85 \times 0.0035 = 0.00297$$

$$f_{sc} = 400 \, \text{N/mm}^2$$

$$C_s = 12bh$$

$$\varepsilon_{st} = 0.15 \times 0.0035 = 0.000525$$

$$f_{st} = 0.000525 \times 400/0.002 = 105 \, \text{N/mm}^2$$

$$T = 105 \times 0.03bh = 3.15bh$$

$$N = 12.12 + 12 + 3.15 = 27.27bh$$

$$M = 12.12(0.5 - 0.452)bh^2 + (12 - 3.15)0.35bh^2$$

$$= (0.58 + 3.09)bh^2$$

$$= 3.67bh^2$$

$$M/bh^2 = 3.67$$

7. One point is calculated where the neutral axis lies outside the section and part of the parabolic portion of the stress diagram lies off the column. The strain and stress diagrams for this case are shown in Figs 9.9(a) and 9.9(b) respectively. The load due to compression in the concrete can be taken as a uniform load C and a negative load C'. Referring to Fig. 9.9(c) the equation of the parabola is

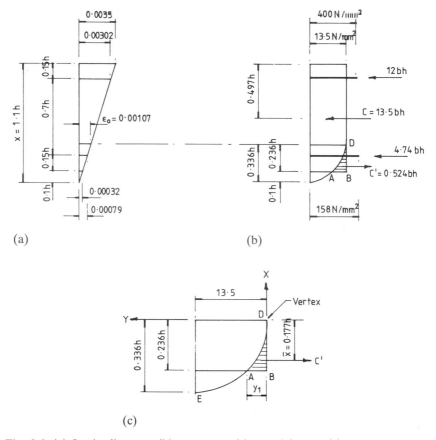

Fig. 9.9 (a) Strain diagram; (b) stresses and internal forces; (c) parabola ABD.

$$y_1 = K^1 x_1^2$$

At E

$$13.5 = K^1(-0.336h)^2$$
$$K^1 = 119.58/h^2$$

At A

$$y_1 = 119.58(-0.236h)^2/h^2 = 6.66 \, \text{N/mm}^2$$
$$C^1 = 6.66 \times 0.236hb/3 = 0.524bh$$
$$x_1 = -0.75 \times 0.236h = -0.177h$$

The standard properties of the parabola have been used. For the column section

$$N = (13.5 + 12 + 4.74 - 0.52)bh = 29.72bh$$
$$M = 13.5(0.5 - 0.497)bh^2 + (12 - 4.74)0.35bh^2$$
$$+ 0.524(0.5 - 0.236 + 0.177)bh^2$$
$$= (0.04 + 2.54 + 0.23)bh^2$$
$$= 2.81bh^2$$
$$M/bh^2 = 2.81$$

8. Further points can be calculated for the 6% steel curve by taking other values for the depth x of the neutral axis.
9. Curves for steel percentages 0.4, 1, 2, 3, 4 and 5 can be plotted. The design chart is shown in Fig. 9.10. The various zones which depend on location of the neutral axis are shown in the chart.
10. Other charts are required for different values of the ratio d/h to give a series of charts for a given concrete and steel strength. A separate series of charts is required for each combination of materials used.

□ Example 9.4 Short column subjected to axial load and moment using design chart.

A short braced column is subjected to an ultimate load of 1480 kN and an ultimate moment of 54 kN m. The column section is 300 mm × 300 mm. Determine the area of steel required. The materials are grade 30 concrete and grade 460 reinforcement.

Assume 25 mm diameter bars for the main reinforcement and 8 mm diameter links. The cover on the links is 25 mm.

$$d = 300 - 25 - 8 - 12.5 = 254.5 \text{ mm}$$
$$d/h = 254.5/300 = 0.85$$

Use the chart shown in Fig. 9.10 where $d/h = 0.85$.

$$\frac{N}{bh} = \frac{1480 \times 10^3}{300^2} = 16.4$$
$$\frac{M}{bh^2} = \frac{54 \times 10^6}{300^3} = 2.0$$
$$100A_{sc}/bh = 2.0$$
$$A_{sc} = 2.0 \times 300^2/100 = 1800 \text{ mm}^2$$

Provide four 25 mm diameter bars to give an area of 1963 mm². ∎

9.3.4 Further design chart

The design chart shown in Fig. 9.10 strictly applies only to the case where the reinforcement is placed on two opposite faces. Charts can be constructed for other arrangements of reinforcement. One such case is

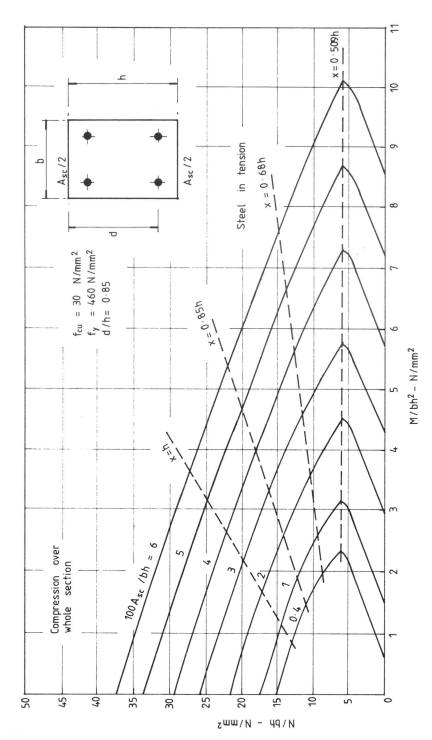

The chart contains the following labels:

$f_{cu} = 30$ N/mm^2
$f_y = 460$ N/mm^2
$d/h = 0.85$

Compression over whole section

$100 A_{sc}/bh = 6$
5
4
3
2
1
0.4

$x = h$
$x = 0.85h$
$x = 0.68h$
$x = 0.509h$

Steel in tension

$A_{sc}/2$
$A_{sc}/2$

$N/bh - $ N/mm^2
$M/bh^2 - $ N/mm^2

Fig. 9.10

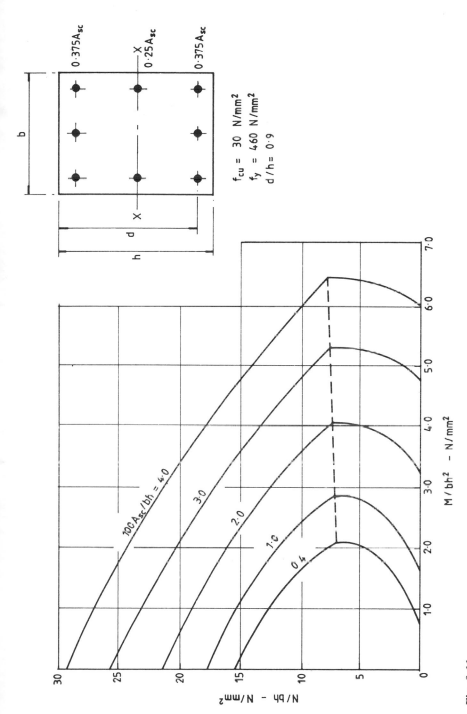

f_{cu} = 30 N/mm²
f_y = 460 N/mm²
d/h = 0·9

0·375 A_{sc}

X
0·25 A_{sc}

0·375 A_{sc}

100 A_{sc}/bh = 4·0

3·0

2·0

1·0

0·4

M / bh² – N / mm²

N/bh – N/mm²

Fig. 9.11

shown in Fig. 9.11 where eight bars are spread evenly around the perimeter of the column.

9.4 SHORT COLUMNS SUBJECTED TO AXIAL LOAD AND BENDING ABOUT ONE AXIS – UNSYMMETRICAL REINFORCEMENT

9.4.1 Design methods

An unsymmetrical arrangement of reinforcement provides the most economical solution for the design of a column subjected to a small axial load and a large moment about one axis. Such members occur in single-storey reinforced concrete portals.

Three methods of design are discussed:

1. general method using successive trials
2. use of design charts
3. approximate method

In these cases steel is in tension on one side and the neutral axis lies between the rows of steel.

9.4.2 General method

An unsymmetrically reinforced column section is shown in Fig. 9.12(a) where the area of reinforcement in compression A_s' is larger than the area A_s in tension. The strain diagram and internal stresses and forces in the concrete and steel are shown in 9.12(b) and 9.12(c) respectively. The neutral axis lies within the section.

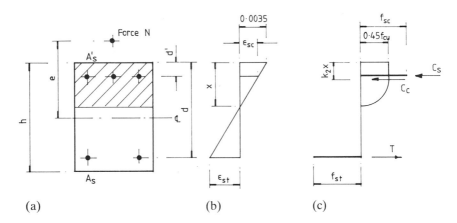

Fig. 9.12 (a) Section; (b) strain diagram; (c) stresses and internal forces.

The section is subjected to an axial load N and moment M, i.e. the force N acts at an eccentricity $e = M/N$ from the centre of the section. The steel area for any given depth to the neutral axis x is determined as follows.

1. For the depth to the neutral axis x determine the strain ε_{sc} in the compression steel and the strain ε_{st} in the tension steel (Fig. 9.12(b)).
2. Determine the steel stresses f_{sc} in compression and f_{st} in tension from the stress–strain diagram (Fig. 4.6(b)). The forces in the steel are $C_s = f_{sc}A_s'$ in compression and $T = f_{st}A_s$ in tension.
3. The force in the concrete in compression is $C_c = k_1bx$ acting at k_2x from the top face. Expressions for k_1, and k_2 from BS 8110: Part 2, Appendix A, are given in section 4.4.3.
4. Take moments about the centre of the steel in tension:

$$N(e - h/2 + d) = C_c(d - k_2x) + C_s(d - d')$$

Solve for the area A_s' of steel in compression.
5. The sum of the external and internal forces is zero, i.e.

$$N = C_c + C_s - T$$

The area A_s of steel in tension can be found from this equation.

Successive trials are made with different values of x to determine minimum total area of reinforcement to resist the external axial load and moment.

□ Example 9.5 Column section subjected to axial load and moment – unsymmetrical reinforcement

The column section shown in Fig. 9.13 is subjected to an ultimate axial load of 230 kN and an ultimate moment of 244 kN m. Determine the reinforcement required using an unsymmetrical arrangement. The concrete is grade 30 and the reinforcement is grade 460.

Assume the depth x to the neutral axis is 175 mm. The strain in the compression reinforcement is

$$\varepsilon_{sc} = 0.0035(175 - 50)/175 = 0.0025$$

The stress in the compression steel is

$$f_{sc} = 400 \, \text{N/mm}^2 \qquad \text{(Fig. 4.5)}$$

The stress in the tension steel is

$$f_{st} = 400 \, \text{N/mm}^2$$

Referring to section 4.4.3 for grade 30 concrete the force in the concrete is

$$C_c = 12.12 \times 300 \times 175 = 6.36 \times 10^5 \, \text{N}$$

and the location of C_c is given by

$$k_2x = 0.452 \times 175 = 79.1 \, \text{mm}$$

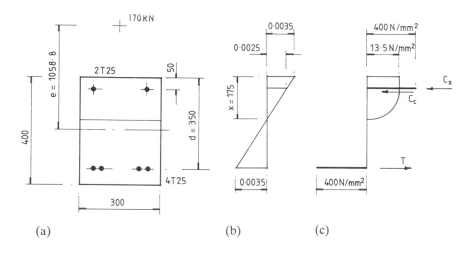

Fig. 9.13 (a) Section; (b) strain diagram; (c) internal stresses and forces.

The eccentricity of the applied load is

$$e = 244 \times 10^3/230 = 1060.9 \, \text{mm}$$

Take moments about the centre of the tension steel:

$$230 \times 10^3(1060.9 - 200 + 350)$$
$$= 6.36 \times 10^5(350 - 79.1) + 400A_s' \times 300$$

This gives $A_s' = 885.1 \, \text{mm}^2$. Sum the internal forces:

$$230 \times 10^3 = 6.38 \times 10^5 + 885.1 \times 400 - A_s \times 400$$

This gives $A_s = 1900.1 \, \text{mm}^2$. The total area of steel is $885.1 + 1900.1 = 2785.2 \, \text{mm}^2$. The minimum steel area is given when $x = 221 \, \text{mm}$, i.e. when

$$A_s' = 646 \, \text{mm}^2$$
$$A_s = 2080 \, \text{mm}^2$$

and

$$A_s' + A_s = 2726 \, \text{mm}^2$$

The best solution in this case could be to provide two 25 mm diameter bars, $A_s' = 981 \, \text{mm}^2$, compression reinforcement, and four 25 mm diameter bars, $A_s = 1963 \, \text{mm}^2$, tension reinforcement, giving a total area of 2944 mm². This is not the theoretical minimum. The simplified stress block could have been used. ∎

□ Example 9.6 Column section subjected to axial load and moment – symmetrical reinforcement

Redesign the above column section assuming symmetrical reinforcement.

$$d/h = 350/400 = 0.875$$

Use the chart shown in Fig. 9.10.

$$\frac{N}{bh} = \frac{230 \times 10^3}{300 \times 400} = 1.92$$

$$\frac{M}{bh^2} = \frac{240 \times 10^6}{300 \times 400^2} = 5.0$$

$$100A_s/bh = 3.1$$

$$A_{sc} = 3.1 \times 300 \times 400/100 = 3720\,\text{mm}^2$$

Provide eight 25 diameter bars to give a total area of 3927 mm². This is 33% more steel than is required for the unsymmetrically reinforced column. ∎

9.4.3 Design charts

Sets of design charts can be constructed for given combinations of materials and for given locations of the reinforcement. A separate chart is drawn for each area of compression reinforcement, i.e. each value of $100A_s'/bd$. Curves are drawn on the separate charts for various areas of tension reinforcement, i.e. values of $100A_s/bd$. Each curve is a plot of axial load capacity N/bd against moment of resistance M/bd^2. The chart construction process is the same as that given for the column design chart in section 9.3.3.

Charts for grade 30 concrete and grade 460 reinforcement are shown in Fig. 9.14. The area of compression reinforcement can be assumed and the area of tension reinforcement can be read off from the appropriate chart. Alternatively, suitable bars can be selected for compression reinforcement, $100\,A_s'/bd$ can be calculated and the area of tension reinforcement would then be interpolated from the charts.

□ Example 9.7 Column section subjected to axial load and moment – design chart

Redesign the column steel for Example 9.5 in section 9.4.2 using the charts in Fig. 9.14 (see Fig. 9.13).

$$\text{section } b \times d = 300\,\text{mm} \times 350\,\text{mm}$$

$$\text{axial load } N = 230\,\text{kN}$$

$$\text{moment } M = 244\,\text{kN m}$$

Assume that the compression reinforcement is to consist of two 25 mm diameter bars of area 981 mm².

$$\frac{100A_s'}{bd} = \frac{100 \times 981}{300 \times 350} = 0.934$$

Use the chart for $100A_s'/bd = 1.0$.

$$\frac{N}{bd} = \frac{230 \times 10^3}{600} = 2.19$$

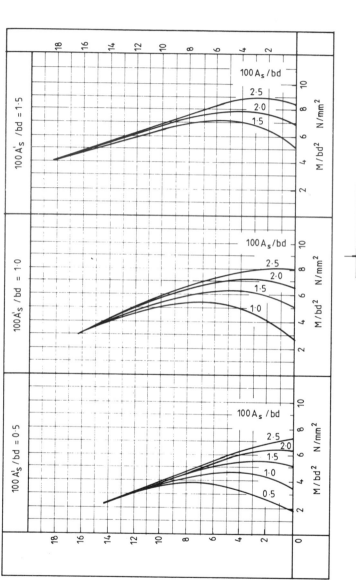
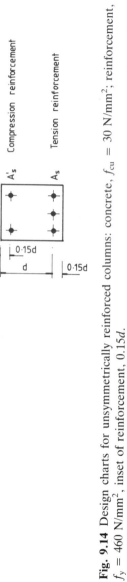

Fig. 9.14 Design charts for unsymmetrically reinforced columns: concrete, $f_{cu} = 30$ N/mm²; reinforcement, $f_y = 460$ N/mm², inset of reinforcement, 0.15d.

$$\frac{M}{bd^2} = \frac{244 \times 10^6}{300 \times 350^2} = 6.63$$

$$100A_s/bd = 1.75 \qquad \text{(Fig. 9.14)}$$

$$A_s = 1.75 \times 300 \times 350/100 = 1837.5 \, \text{mm}^2$$

Provide four 25 mm diameter bars to give $A_s = 1963 \, \text{mm}^2$. This is the solution recommended in the example above. ■

9.4.4 Approximate method from CP 110

An approximate method for the design of unsymmetrically reinforced columns is given in CP 110. The method can be used when

$$e = M/N \not< h/2 - d_2$$

where N is the axial load due to ultimate loads, M is the moment about the centre of the section due to ultimate loads, h is the depth of the section in the plane of bending and d_2 is the depth from the tension face to the reinforcement in tension. The load, moment and dimensions for a typical section are shown in Fig. 9.15(a).

The axial force N and moment M at the centre of the section are replaced by the equivalent system where the axial force N is applied at the centre of the tension steel and the moment is increased to

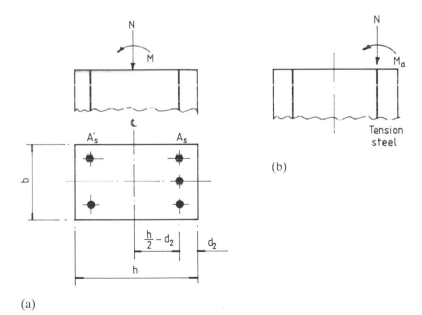

(a)

Fig. 9.15 (a) Section, load and moment; (b) load and equivalent moment.

$$M_a - M + N(h/2 - d_2)$$

where $h/2 - d_2$ is the distance from the centre of the column to the tension steel. The member is designed as a doubly reinforced beam to resist the moment M_a. The area of tension reinforcement required to resist M_a is reduced by $N/0.87f_y$, the axial compressive load applied to the tension steel. If compression steel is not required theoretically, suitable bars must be provided on the face to support the links.

☐ Example 9.8 Column section subjected to axial load and moment – unsymmetrical reinforcement. Approximate method from CP 110

Redesign the column steel for Example 9.5 in section 9.4.2 using the approximate method from CP 110 (see Fig. 9.13).

$$\text{section } b \times h = 300\,\text{mm} \times 400\,\text{mm}$$
$$d_2 = 50\,\text{mm}$$
$$\text{axial load } N = 230\,\text{kN}$$
$$\text{moment } M = 244\,\text{kN m}$$
$$\text{eccentricity } e = 244 \times 10^3/230 = 1060.9\,\text{mm}$$
$$h/2 - d_2 = 400/2 - 50 = 150\,\text{mm}$$
$$< e$$

The approximate method can be applied.
The enhanced moment for design is

$$M_A = 244 + 230 \times 150/10^3 = 278.5\,\text{kN m}$$

Refer to section 4.5.1. The moment of resistance of the concrete for $x = d/2 = 175\,\text{mm}$ is

$$M_{RC} = 0.156 \times 30 \times 300 \times 350^2/10^6 = 171.9\,\text{kN m}$$
$$d'/x = 50/175 = 0.29 < 0.43$$

The stress in the compression steel is $0.87f_y$.

$$A_s' = \frac{(278.5 - 171.9)10^6}{300 \times 0.87 \times 460} = 887.9\,\text{mm}^2$$

$$A_s = \frac{0.205 \times 30 \times 300 \times 350}{0.87 \times 460} + 887.9 - \frac{230 \times 10^3}{0.87 \times 460}$$

$$= 1597.8 + 887.9 - 574.7$$
$$= 1911\,\text{mm}^2$$

This gives the same solution as the methods above.   ■

9.5 COLUMN SECTIONS SUBJECTED TO AXIAL LOAD AND BIAXIAL BENDING

9.5.1 Outline of the problem

A given section with steel area A_{sc} subjected to biaxial bending is shown in Fig. 9.16(a). The strain diagram and the stresses and internal forces based on the assumptions set out in clause 3.4.4.1 of the code for resistance moment of beams are shown in Figs 9.16(b) and 9.16(c).

For the given location and direction of the neutral axis the strain diagram can be drawn with the maximum strain in the concrete of 0.0035. The strains in the compression and tension steel can be found and the corresponding stresses determined from the stress–strain diagram for the reinforcement. The resultant forces C_s and T in the compression and tension steel and the force C_c in the concrete can be calculated and their locations determined. The net axial force is

$$N = C_c + C_s - T$$

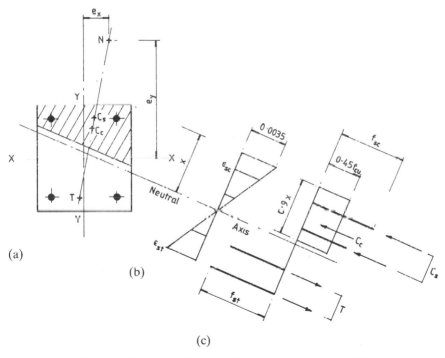

(a)

(b)

(c)

Fig. 9.16 (a) Section; (b) strain diagram; (c) stresses and internal forces.

Moments of the forces C_c, C_s and T are taken about the XX and YY axes to give

$$M_{xx} = Ne_y$$
$$M_{yy} = Ne_x$$

The eccentricities e_x and e_y can be calculated and the position of the force N found. At equilibrium the forces N, the resultant of C_s, C_c and T, lie in one plane.

Thus a given section can be analysed for a given location and direction of the neutral axis, and the axial force and biaxial moments that it can support can be determined.

The design of a section to determine the size and reinforcement required would require successive trials. A direct accurate design method is not possible but close approximations can be formulated.

9.5.2 Failure surface method

The axial load–moment failure curve for single-axis bending was determined in section 9.3.3. The curves for bending about the XX and YY axes are shown in Fig. 9.17(a). The failure surface theory extends the load–moment failure curve for single-axis bending into three dimensions as shown in Fig. 9.17(b). The following terms are defined:

N axial load on the section subjected to biaxial bending
N_{uz} capacity of the section under axial load only, $0.45f_{cu}A_c + 0.75f_yA_s'$
A_c area of concrete
A_s' area of longitudinal steel
M_x moment about the XX axis
M_y moment about the YY axis
M_{ux} moment capacity for bending about the XX axis only when the axial load is N
M_{uy} moment capacity for bending about the YY axis only when the axial load is N

At an axial load N the section can support uniaxial moments M_{ux} and M_{uy}. If it is subjected to moments M_x and M_y simultaneously which are such as to cause failure, then the failure point is at P which lies on the curve of intersection APB of the failure surface and the horizontal plane through N. This curve is defined by the expression

$$\left(\frac{M_x}{M_{ux}}\right)^{\alpha_n} + \left(\frac{M_y}{M_{uy}}\right)^{\alpha_n} = 1$$

The shape of the curve APB depends on the value of N/N_{uz}. It is an ellipse when $\alpha_n = 2$ and a straight line when $\alpha_n = 1$. This is the expression given in

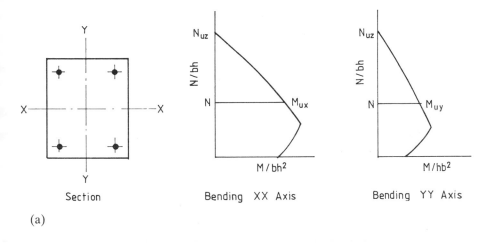

(a)

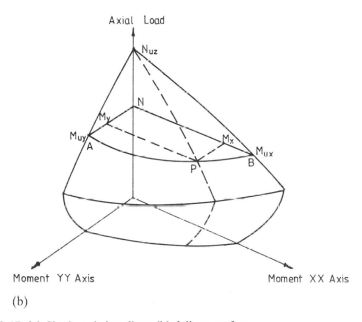

(b)

Fig. 9.17 (a) Single-axis bending; (b) failure surface.

CP 110. A safe combination of moment results if the left-hand expression is less than unity, i.e. when P lies inside the failure curve. Values of α_n are given in CP 110 Table 16, and are reproduced in Table 9.1.

A given column section can be checked by the method. To design a section to resist axial load and biaxial bending successive trials are necessary.

Table 9.1 Values of α_n

N/N_{uz}	<0.2	0.4	0.6	>0.8
α_n	1.0	1.33	1.67	2.0

☐ Example 9.9 Column section subjected to axial load and biaxial bending

Check that the section shown in Fig. 9.18 can resist the following actions:

$$\text{ultimate axial load } N = 950\,\text{kN}$$
$$\text{ultimate moment } M_x \text{ about XX axis} = 95\,\text{kN m}$$
$$\text{ultimate moment } M_y \text{ about YY axis} = 65\,\text{kN m}$$

The materials are grade 30 concrete and grade 460 reinforcement.

The capacity N_{uz} of the section under pure axial load is

$$[0.45 \times 30(400 \times 300 - 1963) + (0.87 \times 460 \times 1963)]/10^3 = 2270.7\,\text{kN}$$

$$\frac{N}{N_{uz}} = \frac{950}{2379.1} = 0.42$$

$$\alpha_n = 1.33 \qquad \text{(from Table 9.1)}$$

The bending about the XX axis is

$$\frac{d}{h} = \frac{350}{400} = 0.875$$

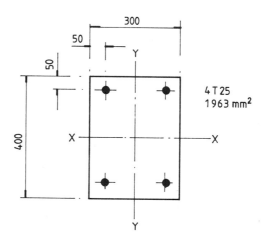

Fig. 9.18

Use BS 8110: Part 3, Chart 28:

$$\frac{N}{bh} = \frac{950 \times 10^3}{300 \times 400} = 7.91$$

$$\frac{100 A_{sc}}{bh} = \frac{100 \times 1963}{300 \times 400} = 1.64$$

$$M_{ux}/bh^2 = 3.7 \qquad \text{(from Chart 28)}$$

$$M_{ux} = 3.7 \times 300 \times 400^2/10^6 = 177.6 \, \text{kN m}$$

The bending about the YY axis is

$$\frac{d}{b} = \frac{250}{300} = 0.83$$

Use BS 8110: Part 3, Chart 28:

$$M_{uy}/hb^2 = 3.7$$

$$M_{uy} = 3.7 \times 400 \times 300^2/10^6 = 133.2 \, \text{kN m}$$

Substitute into the interaction expression and obtain

$$\left(\frac{95}{177.6}\right)^{1.33} + \left(\frac{65}{133.2}\right)^{1.33} = 0.82 < 1.0$$

The section is satisfactory.   ■

9.5.3 Method given in BS 8110

A direct design method is given in BS 8110, Part 1, clause 3.8.4.5. The method is derived from the failure surface theory and consists in designing a section subjected to biaxial bending for an increased moment about one axis. The main design axis depends on the relative values of the moments and the column section dimensions. The amount of increase depends on the ratio of the axial load to the capacity under axial load only. The code procedure is set out.

Define the following terms:

M_x design ultimate moment about the XX axis
M_x' effective uniaxial design moment about the XX axis
M_y design ultimate moment about the YY axis
M_y' effective uniaxial design moment about the YY axis
h overall depth perpendicular to the XX axis
h' effective depth perpendicular to the XX axis
b overall width perpendicular to the YY axis
b' effective width perpendicular to the YY axis

The applied moment and dimensions are shown in Fig. 9.19.

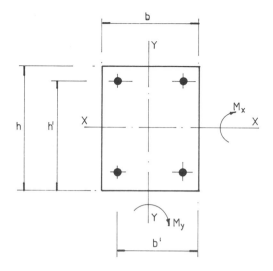

Fig. 9.19

If $M_x/h' > M_y/b'$

$$M_x' = M_x + \beta \frac{h'}{b'} M_y$$

If $M_x/h' < M_y/b'$

$$M_y' = M_x + \beta \frac{h'}{b'} M_x$$

The coefficient β is taken from Table 3.24 of the code. It depends on the value of N/bhf_{cu}, e.g. for $N/bhf_{cu} = 0, 0.3, > 0.6$, $\beta = 1.0, 0.65, 0.3$ respectively.

☐ Example 9.10 Column section subjected to axial load and biaxial bending – BS8110 method

Design the reinforcement for the column section shown in Fig. 9.20 which is subjected to the following actions:

ultimate axial load $N = 950\,kN$

ultimate moment M_x about XX axis $= 95\,kN\,m$

ultimate moment M_y about YY axis $= 65\,kN\,m$

The materials are grade 30 concrete and grade 460 reinforcement.

Assume the cover is 25 mm, links are 8 mm in diameter and main bars are 32 mm in diameter. Then

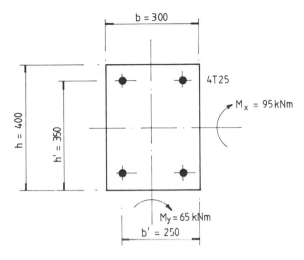

Fig. 9.20

$$h' = 400 - 25 - 8 - 16 = 351\,\text{mm, say } 350\,\text{mm}$$
$$b' = 300 - 25 - 8 - 16 = 251\,\text{mm, say } 250\,\text{mm}$$

The dimensions for design are shown in Fig. 9.20.

$$M_x/h' = 95/0.35 = 271.4$$
$$M_y/b' = 65/0.25 = 260$$
$$M_x/h' > M_y/b'$$
$$\frac{N}{bhf_{cu}} = \frac{950 \times 10^3}{400 \times 300 \times 30} = 0.264$$
$$\beta = 0.693 \qquad \text{(Table 3.24 of the code)}$$
$$M_x' = 95 + 0.693 \times 350 \times 65/250 = 158.1\,\text{kN m}$$
$$\frac{N}{bh} = \frac{950 \times 10^3}{300 \times 400} = 7.92$$
$$\frac{M_x'}{bh^2} = \frac{158.1 \times 10^6}{300 \times 400^2} = 3.29$$
$$\frac{d}{h} = \frac{350}{400} = 0.875$$

Use BS 8110: Part 3, Chart 28, where $d/h = 0.85$:

$$100A_{sc}/bh = 1.4$$
$$A_{sc} = 1.4 \times 400 \times 300/100 = 1680\,\text{mm}^2$$

Provide 4T25 bars to give an area of 1963 mm². The reinforcement is shown in Fig. 9.20. ∎

9.6 EFFECTIVE HEIGHTS OF COLUMNS

9.6.1 Braced and unbraced columns

An essential step in the design of a column is to determine whether the proposed dimensions and frame arrangement will make it a short or a slender column. If the column is slender additional moments due to deflection must be added to the moments from the primary analysis. In general columns in buildings are 'short'.

Clause 3.8.1.3 of the code defines short and slender columns as follows:

1. For a **braced structure**, the column is considered as short if both the slenderness ratios l_{ex}/h and l_{ey}/b are less than 15. If either ratio is greater than 15 the column is considered as slender.
2. For an **unbraced structure**, the column is considered as short if both the slenderness ratios l_{ex}/h and l_{ey}/b are less than 10. If either ratio is greater than 10 the column is considered as slender.

Here h is the column depth perpendicular to the XX axis, b is the column width perpendicular to the YY axis, l_{ex} is the effective height in respect of the XX axis and l_{ey} is the effective height in respect of the YY axis.

The code states that the columns can be considered braced in a given plane if the structure as a whole is provided with stiff elements such as shear walls which are designed to resist all the lateral forces in that plane. The bracing system ensures that there is no lateral displacement between the ends of the columns. If the above conditions are not met the column should be considered as unbraced. Examples of braced and unbraced columns are shown in Fig. 9.21.

9.6.2 Effective height of a column

The effective height of a column depends on

1. the actual height between floor beams, base and floor beams or lateral supports
2. the column section dimensions $h \times b$
3. the end conditions such as the stiffness of beams framing into the columns or whether the column to base connection is designed to resist moment
4. whether the column is braced or unbraced

The effective height of a pin-ended column is the actual height. The effective height of a general column is the height of an equivalent pin-ended column of the same strength as the actual member. Theoretically the effective height is the distance between the points of inflexion along the

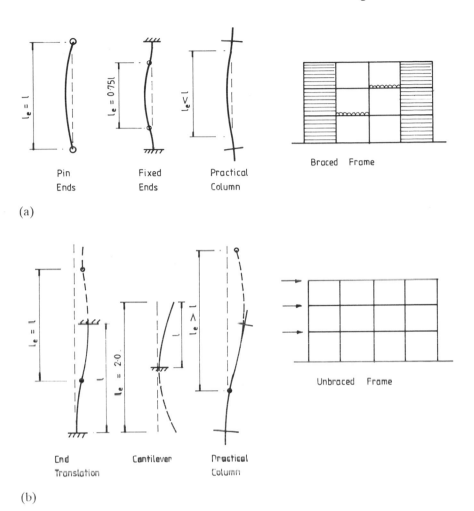

Braced   Frame

(a)

Unbraced   Frame

(b)

Fig. 9.21 (a) Braced columns; (b) unbraced columns.

member length. These points may lie within the member as in a braced column or on an imaginary line outside the member as in an unbraced column. Some effective heights for columns are shown in Fig. 9.21.

For a braced column the effective height will always be less than or equal to the actual height. In contrast, the effective height of an unbraced column will always be greater than the actual height except in the case where sway occurs without rotation at the ends (Fig. 9.21). The effective heights of a column in two plan directions may be different. Also, the column may be braced in one direction but unbraced in the other direction.

9.6.3 Effective height estimation from BS 8110

Two methods are given in the code to determine the effective height of a column:

1. simplified recommendations given in BS 8110: Part 1, clause 3.8.1.6, that can be used in normal cases
2. a more rigorous method given in BS 8110: Part 2, section 2.5

Clause 3.8.1.6.1 gives the following general equation for obtaining effective heights:

$$l_e = \beta l_0$$

where l_0 is the clear height between end restraints and β is a coefficient from Tables 3.21 and 3.22 of the code for braced and unbraced columns; β is a function of the end condition. In Tables 3.21 and 3.22 the end conditions are defined in terms of a scale from 1 to 4. An increase in the scale corresponds to a decrease in end fixity. The four end conditions are as follows.

Condition 1 The end of the column is connected monolithically to beams on either side which are at least as deep as the overall dimension of the column. When the column is connected to a foundation structure this should be designed to carry moment.

Condition 2 The end of the column is connected monolithically to beams or slabs on either side which are shallower than the overall dimension of the columns.

Condition 3 The end of the column is connected to members that, while not designed specifically to provide restraint, do provide nominal restraint.

Condition 4 The end of the column is unrestrained against both lateral movement and rotation, i.e. it is the free end of a cantilever.

Some values of β from Tables 3.21 and 3.22 of the code are as follows:

> Braced column
> > Top end,   condition 1 $\beta = 0.75$
> > Bottom end,   condition 1   Fixed ends
>
> Unbraced column
> > Bottom end,   condition 4 $\beta = 2.2$
> > Top end,   condition 1   Cantilever

The more accurate assessment of effective heights from BS 8110: Part 2, section 2.5, is set out. The derivation of the equations is based on a limited frame consisting of the columns concerned, column lengths above and below if they exist and the beams top and bottom on either side if they exist. The symbols used are defined as follows:

I second moment of area of the section

l_e effective height in the plane considered

l_0 clear height between end restraints

α_{c1} ratio of the sum of the column stiffnesses to the sum of the beam stiffnesses at the lower end

α_{c2} ratio of the sum of the column stiffnesses to the sum of the beam stiffnesses at the upper end

$\alpha_{c\,min}$ the lesser of α_{c1} and α_{c2}

Only members properly framed into the column are considered. The stiffness is I/l_0.

In specific cases the following simplifying assumptions may be made:

1. In the flat slab construction the beam stiffness is based on the section forming the column strip;
2. For simply supported beams framing into a column, $\alpha_c = 10$;
3. For the connection between column and base designed to resist only nominal moment, $\alpha_c = 10$;
4. For the connection between column and base designed to resist column moment, $\alpha_c = 1.0$.

The effective heights for framed structures are as follows:

1. For braced columns the effective height is the lesser of

$$l_e = l_0[0.7 + 0.05(\alpha_{c1} + \alpha_{c2})] < l_0$$
$$l_e = l_0(0.85 + 0.05\alpha_{c\,min}) < l_0$$

2. For unbraced columns the effective height is the lesser of

$$l_e = l_0[1.0 + 0.15(\alpha_{c1} + \alpha_{c2})]$$
$$l_e = l_0(2.0 + 0.3\alpha_{c\,min})$$

9.6.4 Slenderness limits for columns

The slenderness limits for columns are specified in clauses 3.8.1.7 and 3.8.1.8, as follows.

1. Generally the clear distance l_0 between end restraints is not to exceed 60 times the minimum thickness of the column;
2. For unbraced columns, if in any given plane one end is unrestrained, e.g. a cantilever, its clear height l_0 should not exceed

$$l_0 = \frac{100b'^2}{h'} \leq 60b'$$

where h' and b' are the larger and smaller dimensions of the column.

□ Example 9.11 Effective heights of columns – simplified and rigorous methods

(a) Specification

The lengths and proposed section dimensions for the columns and beams in a multi-storey building are shown in Fig. 9.22. Determine the effective lengths and slenderness ratios for the XX and YY axes for the lower column length AB, for the two cases where the structure is braced and unbraced. The connection to the base and the base itself are designed to resist the column moment. Use both the rigorous and the simplified methods.

(b) Simplified method

(i) YY axis buckling   End conditions: the top end is connected monolithically to beams with a depth (500 mm) greater than the column dimension (400 mm), i.e. condition 1; the base is designed to resist moment i.e. condition 1.

Braced column slenderness: $\beta = 0.75$ (Table 3.21 of the code) and l_0, the clear height between end restraints, is 4750 mm; $l_{ey}/h = 0.75 \times 4750/400 = 8.9 < 15$, i.e. the column is 'short'.

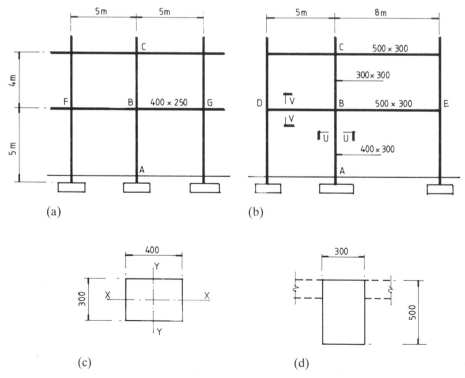

(a)   (b)

(c)   (d)

Fig. 9.22 (a) Side elevation; (b) transverse frame; (c) column UU; (d) beam VV.

Unbraced column slenderness: $\beta = 1.2$ (Table 3.22); $l_{ey}/h = 1.2 \times 4750/400 = 14.25 > 10$, i.e. the column is 'slender'.

(ii) XX axis buckling End conditions: top, condition 1; base, condition1.
Braced column slenderness: $l_{ex}/b = 0.75 \times 4750/300 = 11.9 < 15$; the column is 'short'.
Unbraced column slenderness: $l_{ex}/b = 1.2 \times 4750/300 = 19 > 10$; the column is 'slender'.

(c) Rigorous method

(i) YY axis buckling   The stiffness I/L of column AB is

$$\frac{300 \times 400^3}{12 \times 5000} = 3.2 \times 10^5$$

and of column BC is

$$\frac{300^4}{12 \times 4000} = 1.69 \times 10^5$$

It is conservative practice to base beam moments of inertia on the beam depth multiplied by the rib width. For beam BD

$$\frac{300 \times 500^3}{12 \times 5000} = 6.25 \times 10^5$$

and for beam BE

$$\frac{300 \times 500^3}{12 \times 8000} = 3.91 \times 10^5$$

The coefficient α_c for joint A is

$$\alpha_{c1} = 1.0 \qquad \text{(fixed end)}$$

and for joint B is

$$\alpha_{c2} = \frac{3.2 + 1.69}{6.25 + 3.91} = 0.48$$

Braced column slenderness: l_0, the clear height between end restraints, is 4750 mm and l_{ey} is the lesser of

$$4750[0.7 + 0.05(1.0 + 0.48)] = 3676.5 \text{ mm}$$
$$4750(0.85 + 0.05 \times 0.48) = 4151.5 \text{ mm}$$

but must be less than l_0; thus

$$\frac{l_{ey}}{h} = \frac{3676.5}{400} = 9.19 < 15$$

The column is 'short'.
Unbraced column slenderness: l_{ey} is the lesser of

$$4750[1.0 + 0.15(1.0 + 0.48)] = 5804.5 \text{ mm}$$
$$4570(2.0 + 0.3) = 9500 \text{ mm}$$

$$\frac{l_{ey}}{h} = \frac{5804.5}{400} = 14.5 > 10.0$$

The column is 'slender'.

(ii) XX axis buckling The stiffness I/L of column AB is 1.8×10^5 and of column BC is 1.69×10^5.

Stiffness I/L of beams BF and BG is 2.67×10^5.

The coefficient α_c for joint A is

$$\alpha_{c1} = 1.0$$

and for joint B is

$$\alpha_{c2} = 0.65$$

Braced column slenderness: $l_{ex} = 3716.9$ mm and $l_{ex}/b = 3716.9/300 = 12.4 <$ 15, i.e. the column is 'short'.

Unbraced column slenderness: $l_{ex} = 5925.6$ and $l_{ex}/b = 5925.6/300 = 19.8 > 10$, i.e. the column is 'slender'.

(d) Comment and summary

The two methods give the same results. These may be summarized as

Braced column   'short' with respect to both axes
Unbraced column   'slender' with respect to both axes

The maximum slenderness ratio is 19.8.   ■

9.7 DESIGN OF SLENDER COLUMNS

9.7.1 Additional moments due to deflection

In the primary analysis of the rigid frames the secondary moments due to deflection are ignored. This effect is small for short columns but with slender columns significant additional moments occur. The method for calculating the additional moments was derived by Cranston [10] of the Cement and Concrete Association. A simplified discussion is given.

If the pin-ended column shown in Fig. 9.23(a) is bent such that the curvature $1/r$ is uniform, the deflection at the centre can be shown to be $a_u = l^2/8r$. If the curvature is taken as varying uniformly from zero at the ends to a maximum of $1/r$ at the centre, $a_u = l^2/12r$. For practical columns a_u is taken as the mean $l_e^2/10r$. The same value is used for the unbraced column at the centre of the buckled length, as shown in Fig. 9.23(b).

The curvature at the centre of the buckled length of the column is assessed when the concrete in compression and steel in tension are at their maximum strains. This is the balance point on the column design chart in Fig. 9.10.

The curvature for this case is shown in Fig. 9.23(c). The concrete strain shown is increased to allow for creep and a further increase is made to take

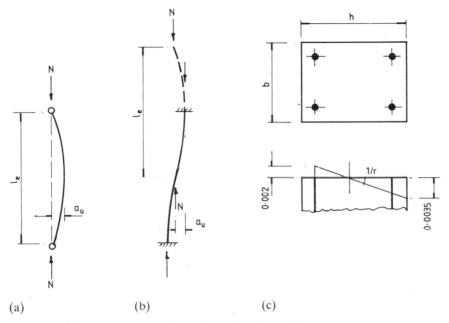

Fig. 9.23 (a) Braced column; (b) unbraced column; (c) curvature at centre.

account of slenderness. The maximum deflection for the case set out above is given in the code by the expression

$$a_u = \beta_a K h$$

where

$$\beta_a = \frac{1}{2000}\left(\frac{l_e}{b'}\right)^2$$

and b' is the smaller dimension of the column, equal to b if b is less than h. K is a reduction factor that corrects the curvature and so the resulting deflection for the cases where steel strain in tension is less than its maximum value of 0.002 or where compression exists over the whole section. The value of K is

$$K = \frac{N_{uz} - N}{N_{uz} - N_{bal}} \leq 1$$

where $N_{uz} = 0.45f_{cu}A_c + 0.87f_yA_{sc}$ is the capacity under pure axial load, A_c is the net area of concrete, A_{sc} is the area of longitudinal steel and N_{bal} is the design axial load capacity when the concrete strain is 0.0035 and the steel strain is 0.002 and is equal to $0.25f_{cu}bd$ (given in the code). N_{uz} and

N_{bal} can also be read off the design chart (Fig. 9.10). The design is first made with $K = 1$ and then K is corrected and a second design is made. The value of K converges quickly to its final result.

Referring to Fig. 9.23, the deflection causes an additional moment in the column given by

$$M_{\text{add}} = Na_{\text{u}}$$

The additional moment is added to the initial moment M_i from the primary analysis to give the total design moment M_t:

$$M_t = M_i + M_{\text{add}}$$

In a braced column the maximum additional moment occurs in the centre of the column whereas in the unbraced column it occurs at the end of the column.

9.7.2 Design moments in a braced column bent about a single axis

The distribution of moments over the height of a typical braced column in a concrete frame from Fig. 3.20 in the code is shown in Fig. 9.24. The maximum additional moment occurs at the centre of the column where the deflection due to buckling is greatest. The initial moment at the point of maximum additional moment is given in clause 3.8.3.2 of the code by

$$M_i = 0.4M_1 + 0.6M_2 \geqslant 0.4M_2$$

where M_1 is the smaller initial end moment and M_2 is the larger initial end moment.

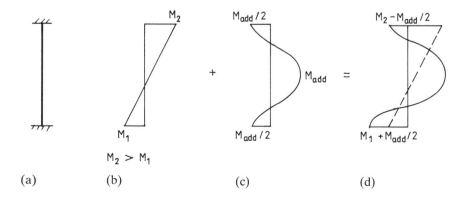

Fig. 9.24 (a) End conditions; (b) initial moments; (c) additional moments; (d) design moments.

The column will normally be bent in double curvature in a building frame and M_1 is to be taken as negative and M_2 as positive. The code states that the maximum design moment is the greatest of the following (Fig. 9.24): M_2; $M_i + M_{add}$; $M_1 + M_{add}/2$; $e_{min} N$, where e_{min} is $0.05h$ or $20\,mm$ maximum.

9.7.3 Further provisions for slender columns

Further important provisions regarding the design of slender columns set out in BS 8110: Part 1, clauses 3.8.3.3 – 3.8.3.6, are as follows.

(a) Slender columns bent about a single axis (major or minor)

If the longer side h is less than three times the shorter side b for columns bent about the major axis and $l_e/h \not> 20$, the design moment is $M_i + M_{add}$ as set out above.

(b) Columns where $l_e/h > 20$ bent about the major axis

The section is to be designed for biaxial bending. The additional moment occurs about the minor axis.

(c) Columns bent about their major axis

If $h > 3b$ (see 9.7.3(a) above), the section is to be designed for biaxial bending as in 9.7.3(b) above.

(d) Slender columns bent about both axes

Additional moments are to be calculated for both directions of bending. The additional moments are added to the initial moments about each axis and the column is designed for biaxial bending.

9.7.4 Unbraced structures

The distribution of moments in an unbraced column is shown in Fig. 3.21 of the code (see Fig. 9.25). The additional moment is assumed to occur at the stiffer end of the column. The additional moment at the other end is reduced in proportion to the ratio of joint stiffnesses at the ends.

☐ Example 9.12 Slender column

(a) Specification

Design the column length AB in the building frame shown in Fig. 9.22 for the two cases where the frame is braced and unbraced. The bending moment diagrams for the column bent about the YY axis and the axial loads for dead, imposed and wind loads are shown in Fig. 9.26. The materials are grade 30 concrete and grade 460 reinforcement.

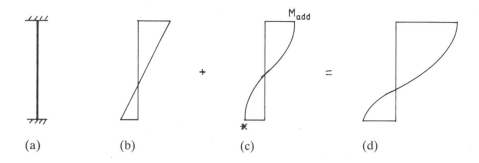

(a)   (b)   (c)   (d)

Fig. 9.25 (a) End conditions; (b) initial moments; (c) additional moments; (d) design moments. The asterisk indicates that M_{add} is reduced in proportion to the ratio of end stiffnesses.

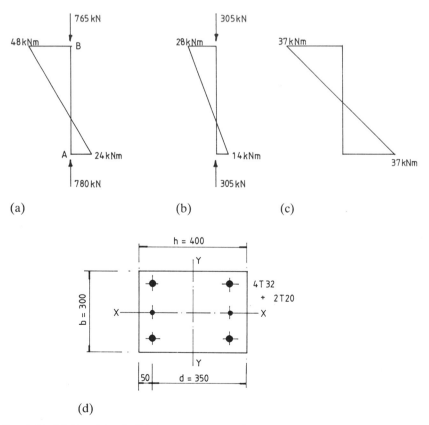

Fig. 9.26 (a) Dead load; (b) imposed load; (c) wind load; (d) column section.

(b) Braced column

For a braced column the wind load is resisted by shear walls. Referring to the example above the column is short with respect to both axes.

The design loads and moments at the top of the column are

$$N = (1.4 \times 765) + (1.6 \times 305) = 1559\,\text{kN}$$
$$M = (1.4 \times 48) + (1.6 \times 28) = 112\,\text{kN\,m}$$

The cover is 25 mm, the links are 8 mm and the bars are 25 mm in diameter. The inset of the bars is 50 mm.

$$\frac{d}{h} = \frac{350}{400} = 0.875$$

Use BS 8110: Part 3, Chart 28 (see Fig. 8.6).

$$\frac{N}{bh} = \frac{1559 \times 10^3}{300 \times 400} = 13.0$$

$$\frac{M}{bh^2} = \frac{112 \times 10^6}{300 \times 400^2} = 2.33$$

$$100 A_{sc}/bh - 1.6\%$$

$$A_{sc} = 1.6 \times 300 \times 400/100 = 1920\,\text{mm}^2$$

Provide 4T25 bars of area 1963 mm^2.

(c) Unbraced column

Calculate the design loads and moments taking wind load into account.

$$N = 1.2(765 + 305) \qquad = 1284\,\text{kN}$$
$$M = 1.2(48 + 28 + 37) - 135.6\,\text{kN\,m}$$

The column must be checked for the following. In case 1, dead I imposed load,

$$N = 1559\,\text{kN}$$
$$M = 112\,\text{kN\,m}$$

In case 2, dead + imposed + wind load,

$$N - 1284\,\text{kN}$$
$$M = 135.6\,\text{kN\,m}$$

The column is slender with respect to both axes. The maximum slenderness ratio $l_{ex}/b = 19.8$.

The column is bent about the major axis and l_e/h does not exceed 20. Assume the factor $K = 1$ initially. The deflection is

$$a_u = \frac{19.8^2 \times 400}{2000} = 79.41\,\text{mm}$$

(i) Case 1: dead + imposed load

$$\text{additional moment } M_{add} = \frac{1559 \times 79.41}{10^3}$$

$$= 123.8\,kN\,m$$

$$\text{design moment } M_t = 112 + 123.8 = 235.8\,kN\,m$$

$$\frac{N}{bh} = \frac{1559 \times 10^3}{300 \times 400} = 13.0$$

$$\frac{M}{bh^2} = \frac{235.8 \times 10^6}{300 \times 400^2} = 4.91$$

$$100A_{sc}/bh = 3.4$$

$$A_{sc} = 3.4 \times 300 \times 400/100 = 4080\,mm^2$$

Calculate the reduction factor K:

$$\begin{aligned}
N_{uz} &= 0.45 \times 30(400 \times 300 - 4080)/10^3 \\
&\quad + (0.87 \times 460 \times 4080)/10^3 \\
&= 3197.7\,kN
\end{aligned}$$

$$N_{bal} = 0.25 \times 30 \times 300 \times 350/10^3 = 787.5\,kN$$

$$K = \frac{3197.7 - 1559}{3197.7 - 787.5} = 0.68$$

$$M_t = 112 + (0.68 \times 123.8) = 196.2\,kN\,m$$

$$N/bh = 13.0$$

$$M/bh^2 = 4.09$$

$$100A_{sc}/bh = 2.9$$

$$A_{sc} = 3480\,mm^2$$

$$N_{uz} = 2965.7\,kN$$

$$K = 0.65$$

Provide 4T32 + 2T20, to give an area of $3843\,mm^2$.

(ii) Case 2: dead + imposed + wind load

$$M_{add} = \frac{1284 \times 79.41}{10^3} = 101.9\,kN\,m$$

$$M_t = 135.6 + 101.9 = 237.5\,kN\,m$$

$$N/bh = 10.7$$

$$M/bh^2 = 4.94$$

$$100A_{sc}/bh = 3.0$$

Case 1 gives the more severe design condition. The column reinforcement is shown in Fig. 9.26. ∎

10

Walls in buildings

10.1 FUNCTIONS, TYPES AND LOADS ON WALLS

All buildings contain walls the function of which is to carry loads, enclose and divide space, exclude weather and retain heat. Walls may classified into the following types:

1. internal non-loadbearing walls of blockwork or light movable partitions that divide space only
2. external curtain walls that carry self-weight and lateral wind loads
3. external and internal infill walls in framed structures that may be designed to provide stability to the building but do not carry vertical building loads; the external walls would also carry lateral wind loads
4. loadbearing walls designed to carry vertical building loads and horizontal lateral and in-plane wind loads and provide stability

Type 4 structural concrete walls are considered.

The role of the wall is seen clearly through the type of building in which it is used. Building types and walls provided are as follows:

(a) framed buildings – wall types 1, 2 or 3
(b) loadbearing and shear wall building with no frame – wall types 1, 2 and 4
(c) combined frame and shear wall building – wall types 1, 2 and 4

Type (c) is the normal multistorey building.

A wall is defined in BS 8110: Part 1, clause 1.2.4, as a vertical load-bearing member whose length exceeds four times its thickness. This definition distinguishes a wall from a column.

Loads are applied to walls in the following ways:

1. vertical loads from roof and floor slabs or beams supported by the wall
2. lateral loads on the vertical wall slab from wind, water or earth pressure
3. horizontal in-plane loads from wind when the wall is used to provide lateral stability in a building as a shear wall

10.2 TYPES OF WALL AND DEFINITIONS

Structural concrete walls are classified into the following two types defined in clause 1.2.4 of the code:

1. A **reinforced concrete wall** is a wall containing at least the minimum quantity of reinforcement given in clause 3.12.5 (section 10.3 below). The reinforcement is taken into account in determining the strength of the wall.
2. A **plain concrete wall** is a wall containing either no reinforcement or insufficient reinforcement to comply with clause 3.12.5. Any reinforcement in the wall is ignored when considering strength. Reinforcement is provided in most plain walls to control cracking.

Also in accordance with clause 1.2.4 mentioned above walls are further classified as follows:

1. A **braced wall** is a wall where reactions to lateral forces are provided by lateral supports such as floors or cross-walls;
2. An **unbraced wall** is a wall providing its own lateral stability such as a cantilever wall;
3. A **stocky wall** is a wall where the effective height divided by the thickness, l_e/h, does not exceed 15 for a braced wall or 10 for an unbraced wall;
4. A **slender wall** is a wall other than a stocky wall.

10.3 DESIGN OF REINFORCED CONCRETE WALLS

10.3.1 Wall reinforcement

(a) Minimum area of vertical reinforcement

The minimum amount of reinforcement required for a reinforced concrete wall from Table 3.27 of the code expressed by the term $100A_{sc}/A_{cc}$ is 0.4 where A_{sc} is the area of steel in compression and A_{cc} is the area of concrete in compression.

(b) Area of horizontal reinforcement

The area of horizontal reinforcement in walls where the vertical reinforcement resists compression and does not exceed 2% is given in clause 3.12.7.4 as

$$f_y = 250\,\text{N/mm}^2 \qquad 0.3\% \text{ of concrete area}$$
$$f_y = 460\,\text{N/mm}^2 \qquad 0.25\% \text{ of concrete area}$$

(c) Provision of links

If the compression reinforcement in the wall exceeds 2% links must be provided through the wall thickness (clause 3.12.7.5).

10.3.2 General code provisions for design

The design of reinforced concrete walls is discussed in section 3.9.3 of the code. The general provisions are as follows.

(a) Axial loads

The axial load in a wall may be calculated assuming the beams and slabs transmitting the loads to it are simply supported.

(b) Effective height

Where the wall is constructed monolithically with adjacent elements, the effective height l_e should be assessed as though the wall were a column subjected to bending at right angles to the plane of the wall.

If the construction transmitting the load is simply supported, the effective height should be assessed using the procedure for a plain wall (section 10.4.1(b)).

(c) Transverse moments

For continuous construction transverse moments can be calculated using elastic analysis. If the construction is simply supported the eccentricity and moment may be assessed using the procedure for a plain wall. The eccentricity is not to be less than $h/20$ or 20 mm where h is the wall thickness (section 10.4.1(g) below).

(d) In-plane moments

Moments in the plane of a single shear wall can be calculated from statics. When several walls resist forces the proportion allocated to each wall should be in proportion to its stiffness.

Consider two shear walls connected by floor slabs and subjected to a uniform horizontal load, as shown in Fig. 10.1. The walls deflect by the same amount

$$\delta = pH^3/8EI$$

Thus the load is divided between the walls in proportion to their moments of inertia: for wall 1

$$p_1 = \frac{pl_1^3}{l_1^3 + l_2^3}$$

and for wall 2

$$p_2 = p - p_1$$

A more accurate analysis for connected shear walls is given in Chapter 14.

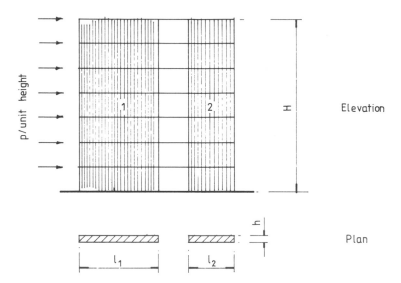

Fig. 10.1

(e) Reinforcement for walls in tension

If tension develops across the wall section the reinforcement is to be arranged in two layers and the spacing of bars in each layer should comply with the bar spacing rules in section 3.12.11 of the code.

10.3.3 Design of stocky reinforced concrete walls

The design of stocky reinforced concrete walls is covered in section 3.9.3.6 of the code. The provisions in the various clauses are as follows.

(a) Walls supporting mainly axial load

If the wall supports an approximately symmetrical arrangement of slabs, the design axial load capacity n_w per unit length of wall is given by

$$n_w = 0.35 f_{cu} A_c + 0.67 A_{sc} f_y$$

where A_c is the gross area of concrete per unit length of wall and A_{sc} is the area of compression reinforcement per unit length of wall. The expression applies when the slabs are designed for uniformly distributed imposed load and the spans on either side do not differ by more than 15%.

(b) Walls supporting transverse moment and uniform axial load

Where the wall supports a transverse moment and a uniform axial load, a unit length of wall can be designed as a column. The column charts from BS 8110: Part 3 can be used if symmetrical reinforcement is provided.

(c) Walls supporting in-plane moments and axial load

The design for this case is set out in section 10.3.4 below.

(d) Walls supporting axial load and transverse and in-plane moments

The code states that the effects are to be assessed in three stages.

(i) In-plane   Axial force and in-plane moments are applied. The distribution of force along the wall is calculated using elastic analysis assuming no tension in the concrete.

(ii) Transverse   The transverse moments are calculated using the procedure set out in section 10.3.2(c).

(iii) Combined   The effects of all actions are combined at various sections along the wall. The sections are checked using the general assumptions for beam design.

10.3.4 Walls supporting in-plane moments and axial loads

(a) Wall types and design methods

Some types of shear wall are shown in Fig. 10.2. The simplest type is the straight wall with uniform reinforcement as shown in 10.2(a). In practice the shear wall includes columns at the ends as shown in 10.2(e). Channel-shaped walls are also common as shown in 10.2(d), and other arrangements are used.

Three design procedures are discussed:

1. using an interaction chart
2. assuming a uniform elastic stress distribution
3. assuming that end zones resist moment

The methods are discussed briefly below. Examples illustrating their use are given.

(b) Interaction chart

The chart construction is based on the assumptions for design of beams given in section 3.4.4.1 of the code. A straight wall with uniform reinforcement is considered. For the purpose of analysis the vertical bars are replaced by uniform strips of steel running the full length of the wall as shown in Fig. 10.2(b). The chart is shown in Fig. 10.3.

A chart could also be constructed for the case where extra steel is placed in two zones at the ends of the walls as shown in Fig. 10.2(c). Charts could also be constructed for channel-shaped walls.

In design the wall is assumed to carry the axial load applied to it and the

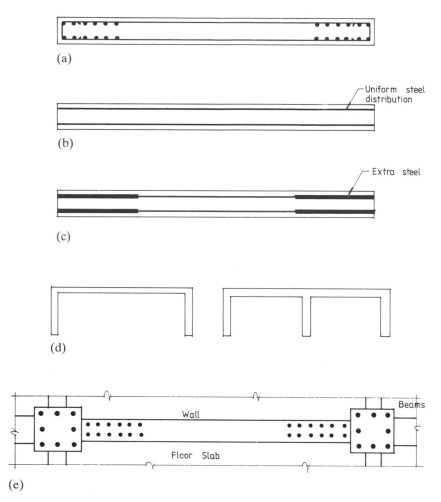

Fig. 10.2 (a) Wall reinforcement; (b) uniform strips of steel; (c) extra reinforcement in end zones; (d) channel-shaped shear wall; (e) shear wall between columns.

overturning moment from wind. The end columns, if existing, are designed for the loads and moments they carry.

(c) Elastic stress distribution

A straight wall section, including columns if desired, or a channel-shaped wall is analysed for axial load and moment using the properties of the gross concrete section in each case. The wall is divided into sections and each section is designed for the average direct load on it. Compressive forces are resisted by concrete and reinforcement. Tensile stresses are resisted by reinforcement only.

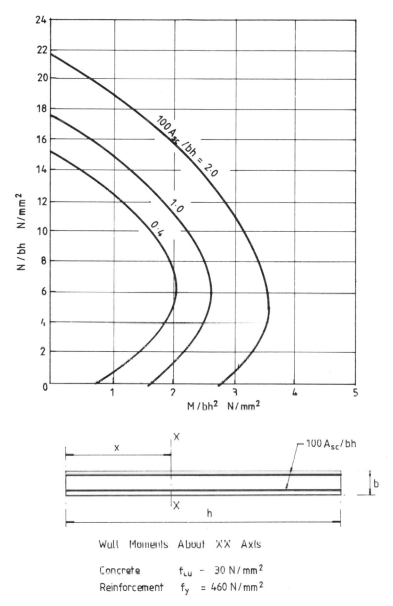

Fig. 10.3

(d) Assuming that end zones resist moment

Reinforcement located in zones at each end of the wall is designed to resist the moment. The axial load is assumed to be distributed over the length of the wall.

☐ Example 10.1 Wall subjected to axial load and in-plane moments using design chart

(a) Specification

The plan and elevation for a braced concrete structure are shown in Fig. 10.4(a). The total dead load of the roof and floors is $6\,kN/m^2$. The roof imposed load is $1.5\,kN/m^2$ and that for each floor is $3.0\,kN/m^2$. The wind speed is $45\,m/s$ and the building is located in a city centre. Design the transverse shear walls as straight walls without taking account of the columns at the ends. The wall is $160\,mm$ thick. The materials are grade 30 concrete and grade 460 reinforcement.

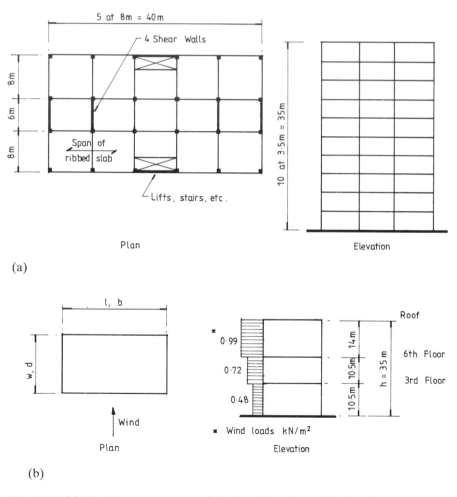

Fig. 10.4 (a) Framing arrangement; (b) estimation of wind loads.

(b) Type of wall – slenderness

The wall is 160 mm thick and is braced. Referring to Table 3.21 in the code the end conditions are as follows:

1. At the top the wall is connected to a ribbed slab 350 mm deep, i.e. condition 1;
2. At the bottom the connection to the base is designed to carry moment, i.e. condition 1.

From Table 3.21 $\beta = 0.75$. The clear height is 3150 mm, say. The slenderness is

$$0.75 \times 3150/160 = 14.8 < 15$$

The wall is 'stocky'.

(c) Dead and imposed loads on wall

The dead load on the wall, assuming that the wall is 200 mm thick including finishes, is as follows.

Roof and floor slabs	$10 \times 6 \times 8 \times 6 =$	2880 kN
Wall 200 mm thick	$0.2 \times 24 \times 6 \times 35 =$	1008 kN
Total load at base		3888 kN

The imposed load allowing 50% reduction in accordance with BS 6399: Part 1, Table 2, is

$$(0.5 \times 1.5 \times 6 \times 8) + (0.5 \times 3 \times 9 \times 6 \times 8) = 684\,kN$$

(d) Dead and imposed loads on the ends of the wall from the transverse beams

Roof and floor slabs	$4 \times 2880/6 =$	1920 kN
Column at wall ends, 400 mm $\times$ 400 mm $=$		134 kN
Imposed load	$4 \times 684/6 =$	456 kN

(e) Wind load

Refer to CP 3: Chapter V: Part 2. The ground roughness is category 3 and the building size is Class B. Wind pressures and loads are calculated for roof to sixth floor, sixth floor to third floor and third floor to base (Fig. 10.4(b)). The force coefficient from Table 10 in the wind code is estimated for the following parameters:

Table 10.1 Wind load values

	H (m)	S_2 (Table 3)	$V_s =$ $S_2 V$ (m/s)	$q = 0.613 V_s^2/10^3$ (kN/m²)
Roof to floor 6	35.0	0.89	40.1	0.99
Floor 6 to 3	21.0	0.76	34.2	0.72
Floor 3 to base	10.5	0.63	28.1	0.48

Table 3, CP3: Chapter V: Part 2

$$l/w - 10/22 = 1.8$$
$$b/d = 40/22 = 1.8$$
$$h/b = 35/22 = 1.6$$
$$C_f = 1.06$$

The heights, S_2 values, design wind speeds and dynamic pressures are given in Table 10.1. The wind pressures are shown in Fig. 10.4(b). The wind loads are resisted by four shear walls. The wind loads and moments at the base are as follows:

Roof to floor 6	Load	$0.99 \times 1.06 \times 10 \times 14 = 146.9\,\text{kN}$
	Moment	$= 146.9 \times 28 = 4113.2\,\text{kN}\,\text{m}$
Floor 6 to 3	Load	$0.72 \times 1.06 \times 10 \times 10.5 = 80.2\,\text{kN}$
	Moment	$= 80.2 \times 15.75 = 1263.2\,\text{kN}\,\text{m}$
Floor 3 to Base	Load	$0.48 \times 1.06 \times 10 \times 10.5 = 53.4\,\text{kN}$
	Moment	$= 53.4 \times 5.25 = 280.4\,\text{kN}\,\text{m}$

Thus the total load is 280.5 kN and the total moment is 5656.8 kN m.

(f) Load combination

(i) Case 1 1.2(Dead + Imposed + Wind)

$$N = 1.2[3888 + 648 + 2(1920 + 134 + 456)] = 11510.4\,\text{kN}$$
$$M = 1.2 \times 5656.8 = 6788.2\,\text{kN}\,\text{m}$$

(ii) Case 2 1.4(Dead + Wind)

$$N = 1.4[3888 + 2(1920 + 134)] = 11194.4\,\text{kN}$$
$$M = 1.4 \times 5656.8 = 7919.5\,\text{kN}\,\text{m}$$

(iii) Case 3 1.0 × Dead + 1.4 × Wind

$$N = 3888 + 2(1920 + 134) = 7996\,\text{kN}$$
$$M = 7919.5\,\text{kN}\,\text{m}$$

(g) Wall design for load combinations in (f)

The wall is 160 mm thick by 6000 mm long. The design is made using the chart in Fig. 10.3. The steel percentages for the three load cases are given in Table 10.2. The steel area in each of the two rows is

Table 10.2 Load combinations, column design

	Case 1	Case 2	Case 3
N/bh	11.99	11.66	8.32
M/bh^2	1.17	1.37	1.37
$100A_{sc}/bh$	0.4	0.6	0.4

$$A_{sc} = \frac{0.6 \times 160 \times 6000}{2 \times 100 \times 6} = 480\,\text{mm}^2/\text{m}$$

Provide two rows of 12 mm diameter bars at 200 mm centres to give a steel area of 565 mm²/m.

Note that a check shows that the wall just remains in compression over its full length for case 3. ∎

□ Example 10.2 Wall subjected to axial load and in-plane moments concentrating steel in end zones

The columns at the ends of the walls will be taken into account. The loads and moments are shown in Fig. 10.5.

Consider the load case 1.4(dead + wind). Assume that 1 m length at each end of the wall contains the steel to resist moment. The lever arm is 5.5 m. The force to resist moment is

$$1.4 \times 5656.8/5.5 = 1439.8\,\text{kN}$$

The steel area required is

$$1439.8 \times 10^3/0.87 \times 460 = 3597.9\,\text{mm}^2$$

One-half of this area, i.e. 1799 mm², is placed in the column and one-half in the wall end zone.

The capacity of the concrete alone in the column to resist an axial load is

$$0.4 \times 30(500^2 - 1799)/10^3 = 2978.4\,\text{kN}$$

The column axial load is

$$1.4(1920 + 134) = 2878.6\,\text{kN}$$

The concrete alone can support the axial load. Provide four 25 mm diameter bars to give an area of 1963 mm².

The end zone of the wall, 500 mm long, carries an axial load of

$$0.5 \times 1.4 \times 3888/5.5 = 494.8\,\text{kN}$$

The capacity of concrete alone in this position is

$$0.4 \times 30 \times 500 \times 200/10^3 = 1200\,\text{kN}$$

Provide six 20 mm diameter bars to give an area of 1884 mm².

The central zone of the wall, 4.5 mm long, carries an axial load of

$$4.5 \times 1.4 \times 3888/5.5 = 4453.5\,\text{kN}$$

The capacity of the concrete alone is

$$0.4 \times 30 \times 200 \times 4500/10^3 = 10800\,\text{kN}$$

Provide 0.4% minimum steel. The area required is $0.4 \times 1000 \times 160/100 = 640\,\text{mm}^2/\text{m}$. Provide 10 mm diameter bars at 200 mm centres in two rows to give an area of 784 mm²/m. The steel arrangement is shown in Fig. 10.5.

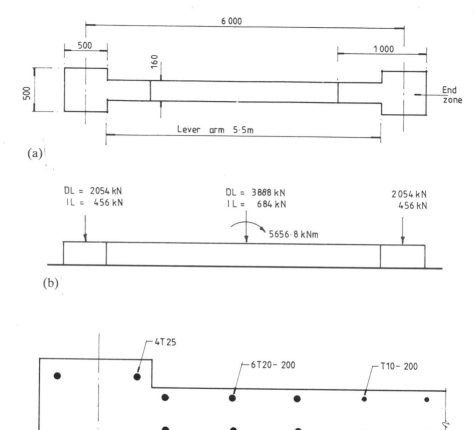

Fig. 10.5 (a) Plan; (b) loads at base; (c) steel arrangement.

■

☐ Example 10.3 Wall subjected to axial load, transverse and in-plane moments

(a) Specification

The section of a stocky reinforced concrete wall shown in Fig. 10.6 is subject to the following actions:

$$N = 4300\,\text{kN}$$
$$M_y = 2100\,\text{kN m}$$
$$M_x = 244\,\text{kN m}$$

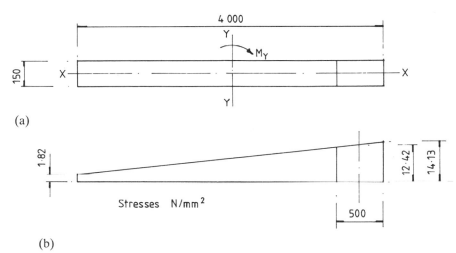

(a)

(b)

Fig. 10.6 (a) Wall section; (b) longitudinal stress distribution.

Design the reinforcement for the heaviest loaded end zone 500 mm long. The materials are grade 30 concrete and grade 460 reinforcement.

(b) Stresses

From an elastic analysis the stresses in the section due to moment M_y are calculated as follows.

$$A = 150 \times 500 = 6 \times 10^5 \, \text{mm}^2$$
$$I = 150 \times 4000^3/12 = 8 \times 10^{11} \, \text{mm}^4$$
$$\text{maximum stress} = \frac{4300 \times 10^3}{6 \times 10^5} + \frac{2100 \times 10^6 \times 2000}{8 \times 10^{11}}$$
$$= 7.17 + 5.25 = 12.42 \, \text{N/mm}^2$$

The stress at 250 mm from the end is

$$7.17 + 5.25 \times 1750/2000 = 11.76 \, \text{N/mm}^2$$

The load on the end zone is

$$11.76 \times 150 \times 500/10^3 = 882 \, \text{kN}$$

Design the end zone for an axial load of 882 kN and a moment of 224/8 = 28 kN m:

$$\frac{N}{bh} = 11.76$$
$$\frac{M}{bh^2} = \frac{28 \times 10^6}{500 \times 150^2} = 2.5$$
$$100 A_{sc}/bh = 1.2$$
$$A_{sc} = 900 \, \text{mm}^2$$

Provide four 20 mm diameter bars to give an area of 1263 mm². ∎

10.3.5 Slender reinforced walls

The following provisions are summarized from section 3.9.3.7 of the code.

1. The design procedure is the same as in section 10.3.3(d) above.
2. The slenderness limits are as follows:

braced wall, steel area $A_s < 1\%$, $l_e/h \not> 40$
braced wall, steel area $A_s > 1\%$, $l_e/h \not> 45$
unbraced wall, steel area $A_s > 0.4\%$, $l_e/h \not> 30$

10.3.6 Deflection of reinforced walls

The code states that the deflection should be within acceptable limits if the above recommendations are followed. The code also states that the deflection of reinforced shear walls should be within acceptable limits if the total height does not exceed 12 times the length.

10.4 DESIGN OF PLAIN CONCRETE WALLS

10.4.1 Code design provisions

A plain wall contains either no reinforcement or less than 0.4% reinforcement. The reinforcement is not considered in strength calculations.

The design procedure is summarized from section 3.9.4 of the code.

(a) Axial loads

The axial loads can be calculated assuming that the beams and slabs supported by the wall are simply supported.

(b) Effective height

(i) Unbraced plain concrete wall The effective height l_e for a wall supporting a roof slab spanning at right angles is $1.5l_0$, where l_0 is the clear height between the lateral supports. The effective height l_e for other walls, e.g. a cantilever wall, is $2l_0$.

(ii) Braced plain concrete wall The effective height l_e when the lateral support resists both rotation and lateral movement is 0.75 times the clear distance between the lateral supports or twice the distance between a support and a free edge. l_e is measured vertically where the lateral restraints are horizontal floor slabs. It is measured horizontally if the lateral supports are vertical walls.

The effective height l_e when the lateral supports resist only lateral movement is the distance between the centres of the supports or 2.5 times the distance between a support and a free edge.

The effective heights defined above are shown in Fig. 10.7.

The lateral support must be capable of resisting the applied loads plus 2.5% of the vertical load that the wall is designed to carry at the point of lateral support.

The resistance of a lateral support to rotation only exists where both the lateral support and the braced wall are detailed to resist rotation and for precast or *in situ* floors where the bearing width is at least two-thirds of the thickness of the wall.

(c) Slenderness limits

The slenderness ratio l_e/h should not exceed 30 whether the wall is braced or unbraced.

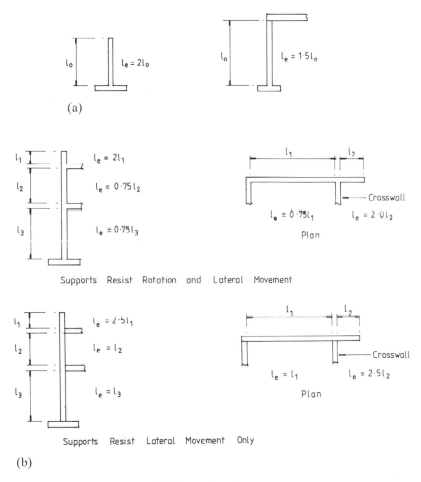

Fig. 10.7 (a) Unbraced walls; (b) braced walls.

(d) Minimum transverse eccentricity

The minimum transverse eccentricity should not be less than $h/20$ or 20 mm. Further eccentricity due to deflection occurs in slender walls.

(e) In-plane eccentricity

The in-plane eccentricity can be calculated by statics when the horizontal force is resisted by several walls. It is shared between walls in proportion to their stiffnesses provided that the eccentricity in any wall is not greater than one-third of its length. If the eccentricity is greater than one-third of the length the stiffness of that wall is taken as zero.

(f) Eccentricity of loads from a concrete floor or roof

The design loads act at one-third of the depth of the bearing from the loaded face. Where there is an *in situ* floor on either side of the wall the common bearing area is shared equally (Fig. 10.8). Loads may be applied through hangers at greater eccentricities (Fig. 10.8).

(g) Transverse eccentricity of resultant forces

The eccentricity of forces from above the lateral support is taken as zero. From Fig. 10.8 where the force R from the floor is at an eccentricity of $h/6$ and the force P from above is taken as axial, the resultant eccentricity is

$$e_R = \frac{Rh}{6(P + R)}$$

(h) Concentrated loads

Concentrated loads from beam bearings or column bases may be assumed to be immediately dispersed if the local stress under the load does not exceed $0.6f_{cu}$ for concrete grade 25 or above.

(i) Design load per unit length

The design load per unit length should be assessed on the basis of a linear distribution of load with no allowance for tensile strength.

(j) Maximum unit axial load for a stocky braced plain wall

The maximum ultimate load per unit length is given by

$$n_w = 0.3(h - 2e_x)f_{cu}$$

where e_x is the resultant eccentricity at right angles to the plane of the wall (minimum value $h/20$). In this equation the load is considered to be carried on part of the wall with the section in tension neglected. The stress block is rectangular with a stress value of $0.3f_{cu}$ (Fig. 10.9).

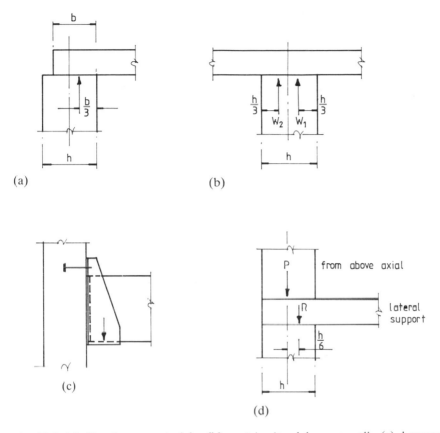

Fig. 10.8 (a) Simply support slab; (b) cast-*in-situ* slab over wall; (c) hanger; (d) resultant eccentricity.

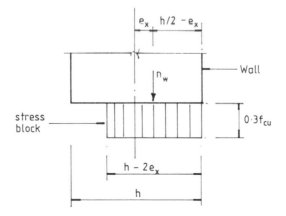

Fig. 10.9

(k) Maximum design axial load for a slender braced plain wall

The ultimate load per unit length is given by

$$n_w \leqslant 0.3(h - 1.2e_x - 2e_a)f_{cu}$$

where $e_a = l_e^2/2500h$ is the additional eccentricity due to deflection and l_e is the effective height of the wall.

(l) Maximum design axial load for unbraced plain walls

The ultimate load per unit length should satisfy the following:

$$n_w \leqslant 0.3(h - 2e_{x1})f_{cu}$$
$$n_w \leqslant 0.3(h - 2e_{x2} - e_a)f_{cu}$$

where e_{x1} is the resultant eccentricity at the top of the wall and e_{x2} is the resultant eccentricity at the bottom of the wall.

(m) Shear strength

The shear strength need not be checked if one of the following conditions is satisfied:

1. The horizontal design shear force is less than one-quarter of the design vertical load;
2. The shear stress does not exceed $0.45 \, \text{N/mm}^2$ over the whole wall cross-section.

(n) Cracking

Reinforcement may be necessary to control cracking due to flexure or thermal and hydration shrinkage. The quantity in each direction should be at least 0.25% of the concrete area for grade 460 steel and 0.3% of the concrete area for grade 250 steel. Other provisions regarding 'anticrack' reinforcement are given in the code.

(o) Deflection of plain concrete walls

The deflection should be within acceptable limits, if the preceding recommendations are followed.

The deflection of plain concrete shear walls should be within acceptable limits if the total height does not exceed ten times the length.

□ Example 10.4 Plain concrete wall

Check that the internal plain concrete wall BD in the braced building shown in Fig. 10.10 is adequate to carry the loads shown. The lateral supports resist lateral movement only. The concrete is grade 25.

$$\text{design load on BC} = (1.4 \times 6) + (1.6 \times 4) = 14.8 \, \text{kN/m}$$
$$\text{design load on AB} = 6 \, \text{kN/m} \qquad \text{(dead load only)}$$

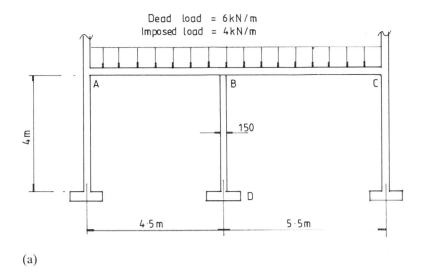

(a)

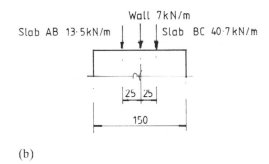

(b)

Fig. 10.10 (a) Section through building; (b) section at mid-height.

The reactions are as follows: for BC

$$14.8 \times 2.75 = 40.7 \, \text{kN}$$

and for AB

$$6 \times 2.25 = 13.5 \, \text{kN}$$

$$\text{self-weight} = 0.15 \times 23.5 = 3.5 \, \text{kN/m}$$

At mid-height, the weight of the wall is 7 kN/m; the effective height is 4000 mm and the slenderness ratio is $4000/150 = 26.6 < 30$.

The wall is slender and is checked at mid-height where the additional moment due to deflection is a maximum. The resultant eccentricity due to vertical load is

$$e_x = \frac{(40.7 - 13.5)25}{13.5 + 40.7 + 7} = 11.1 \, \text{mm}$$

The eccentricity due to slenderness is

$$e_a = 4000^2/2500 \times 150 = 42.7\,\text{mm}$$

The total eccentricity is not to be less than $h/20 = 7.5\,\text{mm}$ or $20\,\text{mm}$.
    The applied ultimate load must be less than

$$n_w = 0.3(150 - 1.2 \times 11.1 - 2 \times 42.7)25$$
$$= 384.6\,\text{N/mm or kN/m}$$
$$> \text{applied load of } 61.2\,\text{kN/m}$$

The maximum permissible slenderness ratio of 30 controls the thickness. The case where the imposed load covers the whole floor should also be checked. The total applied load then is $81\,\text{kN/m}$ and the wall is satisfactory.   ■

11

Foundations

11.1 GENERAL CONSIDERATIONS

Foundations transfer loads from the building or individual columns to the earth. Types of foundations are

1. isolated bases for individual columns
2. combined bases for several columns
3. rafts for whole buildings which may incorporate basements

All the above types of foundations may bear directly on the ground or be supported on piles. Only isolated and combined bases are considered.

The type of foundation to be used depends on a number of factors such as

1. the soil properties and conditions
2. the type of structure and loading
3. the permissible amount of differential settlement

The choice is usually made from experience but comparative designs are often necessary to determine the most economical type to be used.

The size of a foundation bearing directly on the ground depends on the safe bearing pressure of the soil, which is taken to mean the bearing pressure that can be imposed without causing excessive settlement. Values for various soil types and conditions are given in BS 8004: *Code of practice for foundations*. In general, site load tests and laboratory tests on soil samples should be carried out to determine soil properties for foundation design. Typical values are assumed for design in the worked examples in this chapter.

11.2 ISOLATED PAD BASES

11.2.1 General comments

Isolated pad bases are square or rectangular slabs provided under individual columns. They spread the concentrated column load safely to the ground and may be axially or eccentrically loaded (Figs 11.1 and 11.2). Mass concrete can be used for lighter foundations if the underside of the base lies inside a dispersal angle of 45°, as shown in Fig. 11.1(a). Otherwise a reinforced concrete pad is required (Fig. 11.1(b)).

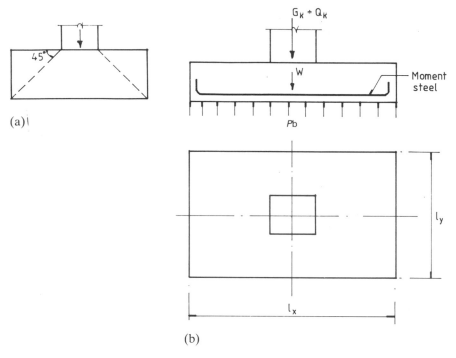

(a)|

(b)

Fig. 11.1 (a) Mass concrete foundation; (b) reinforced concrete foundation.

Assumptions to be used in the design of pad footings are set out in clause 3.11.2 of the code:

1. When the base is axially loaded the load may be assumed to be uniformly distributed. The actual pressure distribution depends on the soil type. Refer to soil mechanics textbooks;
2. When the base is eccentrically loaded, the reactions may be assumed to vary linearly across the base.

11.2.2 Axially loaded pad bases

Refer to the axially loaded pad footing shown in Fig. 11.1(b) where the following symbols are used:

G_k characteristic dead load from the column (kN)
Q_k characteristic imposed load from the column (kN)
W weight of the base (kN)
l_x, l_y base length and breadth (m)
p_b safe bearing pressure (kN/m^2)

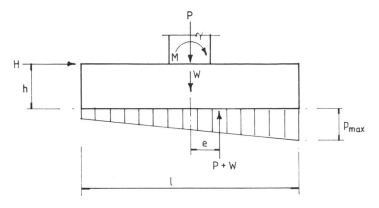

Fig. 11.2

The area required is found from the characteristic loads including the weight of the base:

$$\text{area} = (G_k + Q_k + W)/p_b = l_x l_y \, \text{m}^2$$

The design of the base is made for the ultimate load delivered to the base by the column shaft, i.e. the design load is $1.4G_k + 1.6Q_k$.

The critical sections in design are set out in clauses 3.11.2.2 and 3.11.3 of the code and are as follows.

(a) Bending

The critical section is at the face of the column on a pad footing or the wall in a strip footing. The moment is taken on a section passing completely across a pad footing and is due to the ultimate loads on one side of the section. No redistribution of moments should be made. The critical sections are XX and YY in Fig. 11.3(a).

(b) Distribution of reinforcement

Refer to Fig. 11.3(b). The code states that where l_c exceeds $(3c/4 + 9d/4)$, two-thirds of the required reinforcement for the given direction should be concentrated within a zone from the centreline of the column to a distance $1.5d$ from the face of the column (c is the column width, d is the effective depth of the base slab and l_c is half the spacing between column centres (if more than one) or the distance to the edge of the pad, whichever is the greater). Otherwise the reinforcement may be distributed uniformly over l_c.

The arrangement of reinforcement is shown in Fig. 11.3(b).

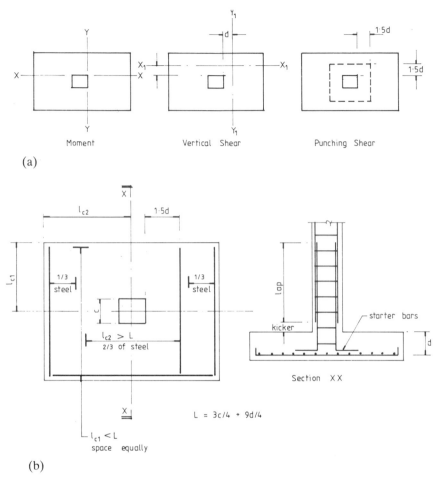

Fig. 11.3 (a) Critical sections for design; (b) base reinforcement.

(c) Shear on vertical section across full width of base

Refer to Fig. 11.3(a). The vertical shear force is the sum of the loads acting outside the section considered. The shear stress is

$$v = V/ld$$

where l is the length or width of the base.

Refer to clause 3.4.5.10 (Enhanced shear strength near supports, simplified approach). If the shear stress is checked at d from the support and v is less than the value of v_c from Table 3.9 of the code, no shear reinforcement is required and no further checks are needed. If shear reinforcement is required, refer to Table 3.17 of the code. It is normal practice to make the base sufficiently deep so that shear reinforcement is not required. The depth of the base is controlled by the design for shear.

(d) Punching shear around the loaded area

The punching shear force is the sum of the loads outside the periphery of the critical section. Refer to clause 3.7.7.6 of the code and section 8.7.6 here dealing with the design of flat slabs for shear. The shear stress is checked on the perimeter at $1.5d$ from the face of the column. If the shear stress v is less than the value of v_c in Table 3.9 no shear reinforcement is needed and no further checks are required. If shear reinforcement is required refer to clause 3.7.7.5 of the code. The critical perimeter for punching shear is shown in Fig. 11.3(a). The maximum shear at the column face must not exceed $0.8f_{cu}^{1/2}$ or $5\,\text{N/mm}^2$.

(e) Anchorage of column starter bars

Refer to Fig. 11.3(b). The code states in clause 3.12.8.8 that the compression bond stresses that develop on starter bars within bases do not need to be checked provided that

1. the starter bars extend down to the level of the bottom reinforcement
2. the base has been designed for the moments and shear set out above

(f) Cracking

See the rules for slabs in clause 3.12.11.2.7 of the code. The bar spacing is not to exceed $3d$ or $750\,\text{mm}$.

(g) Minimum grade of concrete

The minimum grade of concrete to be used in foundations is grade 35.

(h) Nominal cover

Clause 3.3.1.4 of the code states that the minimum cover should be 75 mm if the concrete is cast directly against the earth or 40 mm if cast against adequate blinding. Table 3.2 of the code classes non-aggressive soil as a moderate exposure condition.

□ Example 11.1 Axially loaded base

(a) Specification

A column 400 mm × 400 mm carries a dead load of 800 kN and an imposed load of 300 kN. The safe bearing pressure is 200 kN/m². Design a square base to resist the loads. The concrete is grade 35 and the reinforcement grade 460.

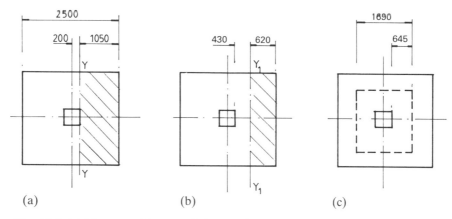

Fig. 11.4 (a) Moment; (b) vertical shear; (c) punching shear.

The condition of exposure is moderate from Table 3.2 for non-aggressive soil. The nominal cover is 40 mm for concrete cast against blinding.

(b) Size of base

Assume the weight is 80 kN.

$$\text{service load} = 800 + 300 + 80 = 1180 \, \text{kN}$$
$$\text{area} = 1180/200 = 5.9 \, \text{m}^2$$

Make the base 2.5 m × 2.5 m.

(c) Moment steel

$$\text{ultimate load} = (1.4 \times 800) + (1.6 \times 300) = 1600 \, \text{kN m}$$
$$\text{ultimate pressure} = 1600/6.25 = 256 \, \text{kN m}^2$$

The critical section YY at the column face is shown in Fig. 11.4(a).

$$M_{yy} = 256 \times 1.05 \times 2.5 \times 0.525 = 352.8 \, \text{kN m}$$

Try an overall depth of 500 mm with 20 mm bars. The effective depth of the top layer is

$$d = 500 - 40 - 20 - 10 = 430 \, \text{mm}$$

$$\frac{M}{bd^2 f_{cu}} = \frac{352.8 \times 10^6}{2500 \times 430^2 \times 35} = 0.022 < 0.042$$

Refer to the design chart in Fig. 4.14.

$$z = 0.95d$$

$$A_s = \frac{352.8 \times 10^6}{0.87 \times 460 \times 0.95 \times 430} = 2158 \, \text{mm}^2$$

Provide 13T16 bars, $A_s = 2613 \, \text{mm}^2$.

The distribution of the reinforcement is determined:

$$\frac{3c}{4} + \frac{9d}{4} = \frac{3 \times 100}{4} + \frac{9 \times 430}{4}$$
$$= 1267.5 \, \text{mm}$$
$$l_c = 1250 \, \text{mm}$$
$$< 1267.5 \, \text{mm}$$

The bars can be spaced equally at 200 mm centres.

The full anchorage length required past the face of the column is $37 \times 16 = 592 \, \text{mm}$. Adequate anchorage is available.

(d) Vertical shear

The critical section Y_1Y_1 at $d = 430 \, \text{mm}$ from the face of the column is shown in Fig. 11.4(b).

$$V = 256 \times 0.62 \times 2.5 = 396.9 \, \text{kN}$$
$$v = \frac{393.6 \times 10^3}{2500 \times 430} = 0.37 \, \text{N/mm}^2$$

The bars extend 565 mm, i.e. more than d, beyond the critical section and so the steel is effective in increasing the shear stress

$$\frac{100 A_s}{bd} = \frac{100 \times 2613}{2500 \times 430} = 0.24$$
$$v_c = 0.79(0.24)^{1/3}(35/35)^{1/3}/1.25$$
$$= 0.44 \, \text{N/mm}^2$$

The shear stress is satisfactory and no shear reinforcement is required.

(e) Punching shear

Punching shear is checked on a perimeter $1.5d = 625.5 \, \text{mm}$ from the column face. The critical perimeter is shown in Fig. 11.4(c).

$$\text{perimeter} = 1690 \times 4 = 6760 \, \text{mm}$$
$$\text{shear} = 256(2.5^2 - 1.69^2) = 868.8 \, \text{kN}$$
$$v = \frac{868.8 \times 10^3}{6760 \times 430} = 0.3 \, \text{N/mm}^2$$

The reinforcing bars extend 397.5 mm beyond the critical section. If the steel is discounted, $v_c = 0.34 \, \text{N/mm}^2$ from Table 3.9 of the code for $100 A_s/bd < 1.5$. The base is satisfactory and no shear reinforcement is required. The bars will be anchored by providing a standard 90° bend at the ends.

Check the maximum shear stress at the face of the column:

$$V = 256(2.5^2 - 0.4^2) = 1559 \, \text{kN}$$
$$v = \frac{1559 \times 10^3}{4 \times 400 \times 430} = 2.27 \, \text{N/mm}^2$$
$$< 0.8 \times 35^{1/2} = 4.73 \, \text{N/mm}^2$$

This is satisfactory.

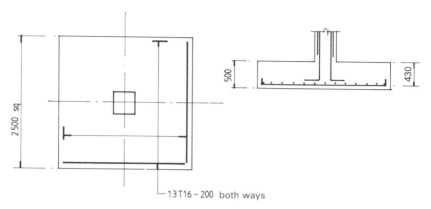

13T16 – 200 both ways

Fig. 11.5

(f) Cracking

The bar spacing does not exceed 750 mm and the reinforcement is less than 0.3%. No further checks are required.

(g) Reinforcement

The arrangement of reinforcement is shown in Fig. 11.5. Note that in accordance with clause 3.12.8.8 of the code the compression bond on the starter bars need not be checked. ■

11.3 ECCENTRICALLY LOADED PAD BASES

11.3.1 Vertical pressure

Clause 3.11.2 of the code states that the earth pressure for eccentrically loaded pad bases may be assumed to vary linearly across the base for design purposes.

The characteristic loads on the base are the axial load P, moment M and horizontal load H as shown in Fig. 11.2. The base dimensions are length l, width b and depth h.

$$\text{area } A = bl$$
$$\text{modulus } Z = bl^2/6$$

The total load is $P + W$ and the moment at the underside of the base is $M + Hh$. The maximum earth pressure is

$$p_{max} = \frac{P + W}{A} + \frac{M + Hh}{Z}$$

This should not exceed the safe bearing pressure. The eccentricity of the resultant reaction is

$$e = \frac{M + Hh}{P + W}$$

If $e < l/6$ there is pressure over the whole of the base, as shown in Fig. 11.2. If $e > l/6$ part of the base does not bear on the ground, as shown in Fig. 11.6(a). In this case

$$c = l/2 - e$$

and the length in bearing is $3c$. The maximum pressure is

$$p_{max} = \frac{2(P + W)}{3bc}$$

Sometimes a base can be set eccentric to the column by, say, e_1 to offset the moments due to permanent loads and give uniform pressure, as shown in Fig. 11.6(b):

$$\text{eccentricity } e_1 = (M + Hh)/P$$

11.3.2 Resistance to horizontal loads

Horizontal loads applied to bases are resisted by passive earth pressure against the end of the base, friction between the base and ground for cohesionless soils such as sand or adhesion for cohesive soils such as clay. In general, the load will be resisted by a combination of all actions. The ground floor slab can also be used to resist horizontal load. The forces are shown in Fig. 11.7(a).

Formulae from soil mechanics for calculating the resistance forces are given for the two cases of cohesionless and cohesive soils.

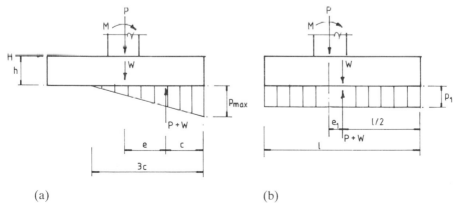

(a)   (b)

Fig. 11.6 (a) Bearing on part of base; (b) base set eccentric to column.

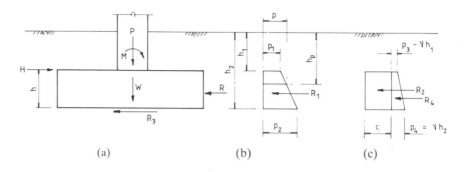

Fig. 11.7 (a) Base; (b) cohesionless soil; (c) cohesive soil.

(a) Cohesionless soils

Refer to Fig. 11.7(b). Denote the angle of internal friction ϕ and the soil density γ. The passive earth pressure p at depth h_p is given by

$$p = \gamma h_p(1 + \sin\phi)/(1 - \sin\phi)$$

If p_1 and p_2 are passive earth pressures at the top and bottom of the base, then the passive resistance

$$R_1 = 0.5bh(p_1 + p_2)$$

where

$$h \times b = \text{base depth} \times \text{base breadth}$$

If μ is the coefficient of friction between the base and the ground, generally taken as $\tan\phi$, the frictional resistance is

$$R_3 = \mu(P + W)$$

(b) Cohesive soils

Refer to Fig. 11.7(c). For cohesive soils $\phi = 0$. Denote the cohesion at zero normal pressure c and the adhesion between the base and the load β. The resistance of the base to horizontal load is

$$R = R_2 + R_4 + R_3$$
$$= 2cbh + 0.5bh(p_3 + p_4) + \beta lb$$

where the passive pressure p_3 at the top is equal to γh_1, the passive pressure p_4 at the bottom is equal to γh_2 and l is the length of the base. The resistance forces to horizontal loads derived above should exceed the factored horizontal loads applied to the foundation.

In the case of portal frames it is often helpful to introduce a tie between bases to take up that part of the horizontal force due to portal action from dead and imposed loads as in the pinned base portal shown in Fig. 11.8. Wind load has to be resisted by passive earth pressure, friction or adhesion.

Pinned bases should be used where ground conditions are poor and it would be difficult to ensure fixity without piling. It is important to ensure that design assumptions are realized in practice.

11.3.3 Structural design

The structural design of a base subjected to ultimate loads is carried out for the ultimate loads and moments delivered to the base by the column shaft. Pinned and fixed bases are shown in Fig. 11.9.

□ Example 11.2 Eccentrically loaded base

(a) Specification

The characteristic loads for an internal column footing in a building are given in Table 11.1. The proposed dimensions for the column and base are shown in Fig. 11.10. The base supports a ground floor slab 200 mm thick. The soil is a firm well-drained clay with the following properties:

Density	$18 \, kN/m^3$
Safe bearing pressure	$150 \, kN/m^2$
Cohesion	$60 \, kN/m^2$

The materials to be used in the foundation are grade 35 concrete and grade 460 reinforcement.

(b) Maximum earth pressure

The maximum earth pressure is checked for the service loads.

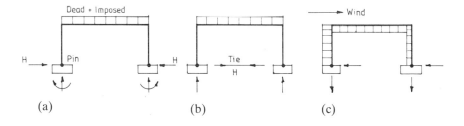

Fig. 11.8 (a) Portal base reaction; (b) force H taken by tie; (c) wind load and base reactions.

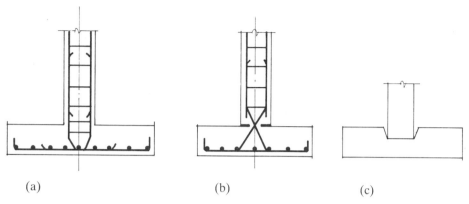

Fig. 11.9 (a) Fixed base; (b) pinned base; (c) pocket base.

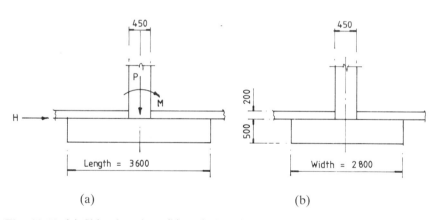

Fig. 11.10 (a) Side elevation; (b) end elevation.

Table 11.1 Column loads and moments

	Vertical load (kN)	Horizontal load (kN)	Moment (kNm)
Dead	770	35	78
Imposed	330	15	34

$$\text{weight of base} + \text{slab} = 0.7 \times 3.6 \times 2.8 \times 24 = 169.3\,\text{kN}$$

$$\text{total axial load} = 770 + 330 + 169.3 = 1269.3\,\text{kN}$$

$$\text{total moment} = 78 + 34 + 0.5(35 + 15) = 137\,\text{kN m}$$

$$\text{base area } A = 2.8 \times 3.6 = 10.1\,\text{m}^2$$

$$\text{modulus} = Z = 2.8 \times 3.6^2/6 = 6.05\,\text{m}^3$$

$$\text{maximum pressure} = \frac{1269.3}{10.1} + \frac{137}{6.05}$$

$$= 125.7 + 22.6 = 148.3\,\text{kN/m}^2$$

(c) Resistance to horizontal load

Check the passive earth resistance assuming no ground slab. The passive resistance is

$$(0.5 \times 18 \times 0.5 \times 0.5 \times 2.8) + (2 \times 60 \times 0.5 \times 2.8) = 6.3 + 168 = 174.3\,\text{kN}$$

$$\text{factored horizontal load} = (1.4 \times 35) + (1.6 \times 15)$$

$$= 73\,\text{kN}$$

The resistance to horizontal load is satisfactory.

The reduction in moment on the underside of the base due to the horizontal reaction from the passive earth pressure has been neglected. Adhesion has not been taken into account.

(d) Design of the moment reinforcement

The design is made for the ultimate loads from the column.

(i) Long-span moment steel

$$\text{axial load } N = (1.4 \times 770) + (1.6 \times 330) = 1598\,\text{kN}$$

$$\text{horizontal load } H = (1.4 \times 35) + (1.6 \times 15) = 73\,\text{kN}$$

$$\text{moment } M = (1.4 \times 78) + (1.6 \times 34) + (0.5 \times 73)$$

$$= 200.1\,\text{kN m}$$

$$\text{maximum pressure} = \frac{1598}{10.1} + \frac{200.1}{6.05}$$

$$= 158.2 + 33.1 = 191.3\,\text{kN/m}^2$$

The pressure distribution is shown in Fig. 11.11(a).

At the face of the column at section YY in Fig. 11.11(b) the shear is

$$V_y = (162.3 \times 1.57 \times 2.8) + (0.5 \times 29 \times 1.575 \times 2.8)$$

$$= 715.7 + 63.9 = 779.6\,\text{kN}$$

$$\text{moment } M_y = (715.7 \times 0.5 \times 1.575) + (63.9 \times 2 \times 1.575/3)$$

$$= 563.6 + 67.1 = 630.7\,\text{kN m}$$

If the cover is 40 mm and 20 mm diameter bars are used, the effective depth for the bottom layer is

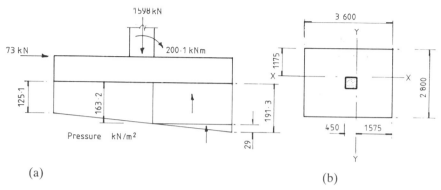

(a)

(b)

Fig. 11.11 (a) Earth pressures; (b) plan.

$$d = 500 - 40 - 10 = 450 \, \text{mm}$$

$$\frac{M}{bd^2 f_{cu}} = \frac{630.7 \times 10^6}{2800 \times 450^2 \times 35} = 0.032$$

From Fig. 4.14, $z/d = 0.95$ and

$$A_s = \frac{630.7 \times 10^6}{0.87 \times 460 \times 0.95 \times 450}$$

$$= 3686.5 \, \text{mm}^2$$

Adopt 16 mm diameter bars, area 201 mm² per bar. The number of bars required is 3686.5/201 = 18.3, say 19.

$$\frac{3c}{4} + \frac{9d}{4} = 3 \times \frac{450}{4} + 9 \times \frac{450}{4}$$

$$= 1350 \, \text{mm}$$

$$l_c = 2800/2 = 1400 \, \text{mm}$$

Provide 20 bars at 140 mm centres to give a total steel area of 4020 mm².

(ii) Short-span moment steel   Refer to Fig. 11.1(b)

$$\text{average pressure} = 158.2 \, \text{kN/m}^2$$

$$\text{moment } M_x = 158.2 \times 1.175 \times 3.6/1 = 334.6 \, \text{kN m}$$

$$\text{effective depth } d = 500 - 40 - 20 - 10 = 430 \, \text{mm}$$

$$\frac{M}{bd^2 f_{cu}} = \frac{334.6 \times 10^6}{3600 \times 430^2 \times 35} = 0.014$$

$$z/d = 0.95$$

$$A_s = \frac{334.6 \times 10^6}{0.87 \times 460 \times 0.95 \times 430}$$

$$= 2046.7 \, \text{mm}^2$$

The minimum area of steel from Table 3.27 of the code is 0.13%.

$$A_s = 0.13 \times 3600 \times 500/100 = 2340 \, mm^2$$

Adopt 12 mm diameter bars, area 113 mm². The number of bars needed is 21.

$$3c/4 + 9d/4 > l_c = 1800 \, mm$$

Place two-thirds of the bars in the central zone 1800 mm wide. More bars are to be placed in the half under heaviest pressure. The arrangement of bars is shown in Fig. 11.12.

(e) Vertical shear

The vertical shear stress is checked on section Y_1Y_1 shown in Fig. 11.13(a) at d from the face of the column. The average earth pressure on this part of the base is shown in the figure.

$$\text{vertical shear} = 180.9 \times 2.8 \times 1.125 = 569.8 \, kN$$

$$\text{shear stress } v = \frac{569.8 \times 10^3}{2800 \times 450} = 0.45 \, N/mm^2$$

$$\frac{100A_s}{bd} = \frac{100 \times 4020}{2800 \times 450} = 0.32$$

$$\text{design stress } v_c = 0.79(0.32)^{1/3}(35/25)^{1/3}/1.25$$
$$= 0.483 \, N/mm^2$$

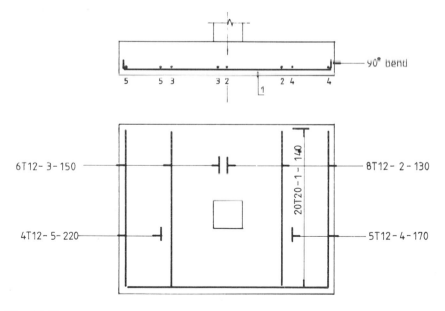

Fig. 11.12

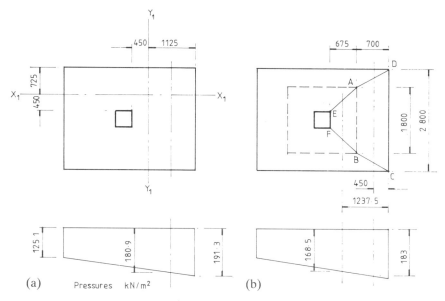

Fig. 11.13 (a) Vertical shear; (b) punching shear.

No shear reinforcement is required. The vertical shear stress on section X_1X_1 on the strip at the heaviest loaded end is less than on section Y_1Y_1.

(f) Punching shear and maximum shear

The punching shear is checked on a perimeter $1.5d$ from the face of the column. The stress is checked on AB, which is the heaviest loaded quadrant of the base because of the load on the trapezium ABCD, as shown in Fig. 11.13(b). The dimensions and average pressure are shown in the figure.

$$V = (1.8 + 2.8)0.9 \times 183/2 = 378.8 \, \text{kN}$$

$$v = \frac{378.8 \times 10^3}{1800 \times 450} = 0.47 \, \text{N/mm}^2$$

$$v_c = 0.483 \, \text{N/mm}^2 \qquad \text{(from (e) above)}$$

Note that both the effective depth and the steel area of the bars in the long span are used in the check.

The maximum shear stress is checked at the face of the column EF. The shear is due to the load on area EADCBF.

$$V = 378.8 + (1.8 + 0.45)0.675 \times 168.5/2$$

$$= 506.8 \, \text{kN}$$

$$v = \frac{506.8 \times 10^3}{450 \times 450} = 2.5 \, \text{N/mm}^2$$

The maximum shear stress is not to exceed

$$0.8 \times 35^{0.5} = 4.73 \, \text{N/mm}^2$$

(g) Sketch of reinforcement

The reinforcement is shown in Fig. 11.12.   ■

□ Example 11.3 Footing for pinned base steel portal

(a) Specification

The column base reactions for a pinned base rigid steel portal for various load cases are shown in Fig. 11.14. Determine the size of foundation for the two cases of independent bases and tied bases. The soil is a firm clay with the following properties:

Density	$18\,kN/m^3$
Safe bearing pressure	$150\,kN/m^2$
Cohesion and adhesion	$50\,kN/m^2$

(b) Independent base

The base is first designed for dead and imposed load. The proposed arrangement of the base is shown in Fig. 11.15(a). The base is 2 m long by 1.2 m wide by 0.5 m deep. The finished thickness of the floor slab is 180 mm.

$$\text{vertical load} = 103 + 84 + (0.68 \times 2 \times 1.2 \times 24)$$
$$= 226.2\,kN$$
$$\text{horizontal load} = 32.4 + 40.3 = 72.7\,kN$$
$$\text{moment} = 72.7 \times 0.5 = 36.4\,kN\,m$$

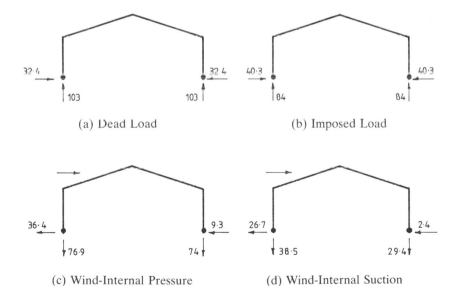

(a) Dead Load   (b) Imposed Load

(c) Wind-Internal Pressure   (d) Wind-Internal Suction

Fig. 11.14 (a) Dead load; (b) imposed load; (c) wind, internal pressure; (d) wind, internal suction.

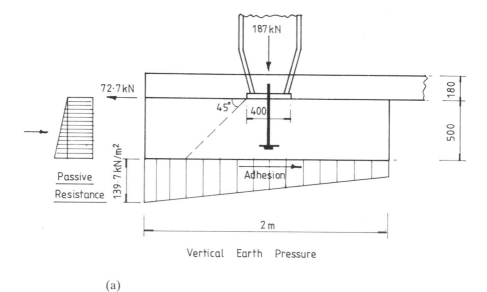

Vertical   Earth   Pressure

(a)

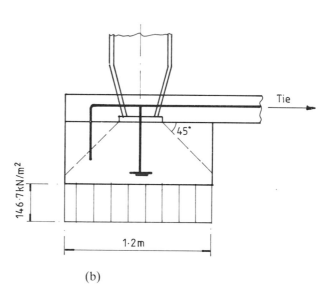

(b)

Fig. 11.15 (a) Independent base; (b) tied base.

For the base

$$\text{area} = 2 \times 1.2 = 2.4\,\text{m}^2$$
$$\text{modulus} = 1.2 \times 2^2/6 = 0.8\,\text{m}^3$$

The maximum vertical pressure is

$$\frac{226.2}{2.4} + \frac{36.4}{0.8} = 94.2 + 45.5 = 139.7\,\text{kN/m}^2$$

The resistance to horizontal load is

$$18 \times 0.5^2 \times 1.2/2 + (2 \times 50 \times 0.5 \times 1.2) + 2 \times 1.2 \times 50 = 2.7 + 60 + 120$$
$$= 182.7\,\text{kN}$$

The maximum factored horizontal load is

$$(1.4 \times 32.4) + (1.6 \times 40.3) = 109.9\,\text{kN}$$

The base is satisfactory with respect to resistance to sliding.
Check the dead + imposed + wind load internal suction at base B:

$$\text{vertical load} = 187 + 38.4 - 29.4 = 196\,\text{kN}$$
$$\text{horizontal load} = 72.7 + 2.4 = 75.1\,\text{kN}$$
$$\text{moment} = 75.1 \times 0.5 = 37.6\,\text{kN m}$$
$$\text{maximum pressure} = \frac{196}{2.4} + \frac{37.6}{0.8} = 128.7\,\text{kN/m}^2$$

The reinforcement for the base can be designed and the shear stress checked as in the previous example.

(c) Tied base

The proposed base is shown in Fig. 11.15(b). The trial size for the base is 1.2 m × 1.2 m × 0.5 m deep and tie rods are provided in the ground slab. The horizontal tie resists the reaction from the dead and imposed loads. For this case

$$\text{vertical load} - 187 + (24 \times 1.2^2 \times 0.7) - 211.2\,\text{kN}$$
$$\text{maximum pressure} - 211.2/1.44 - 146.7\,\text{kN/m}^2$$

The main action of the wind load is to cause uplift and the slab has to resist a small compression from the net horizontal load when the dead load and wind load internal pressure are applied at foundation A.
To find the steel area for the tie using grade 460 reinforcement,

$$\text{ultimate load} = (1.4 \times 32.4) + (1.6 \times 40.3)$$
$$= 109.9\,\text{kN}$$
$$A_s = 109.8 \times 1000/(0.87 \times 460)$$
$$= 274.6\,\text{mm}^2$$

Provide two 16 mm diameter bars to give an area of 402 mm².
If the steel column base slab is 400 mm square the underside of the base lies within the 45° load dispersal lines. Theoretically no reinforcement is required but 12 mm bars at 160 mm centres each way would provide minimum reinforcement.

■

11.4 WALL, STRIP AND COMBINED FOUNDATIONS

11.4.1 Wall footings

Typical wall footings are shown in Figs 11.16(a) and 11.16(b). In Fig. 11.16(a) the wall is cast integral with the footing. The critical section for moment is at Y_1Y_1, the face of the wall, and the critical section for shear is at Y_2Y_2, d from the face of the wall. A 1 m length of wall is considered and the design is made on similar lines to that for a pad footing.

If the wall is separate from the footing, e.g. a brick wall, the base is designed for the maximum moment at the centre and maximum shear at the edge, as shown in Fig. 11.16(b). The wall distributes the load W/t per unit length to the base and the base distributes the load W/b per unit length to the ground, where W is the load per unit length of wall, t is the wall thickness and b is the base width. The maximum shear at the edge of the wall is

$$w(b - t)/2b$$

The maximum moment at the centre of the wall is

$$\frac{w}{b}\frac{b}{2}\frac{b}{4} - \frac{w}{t}\frac{t}{2}\frac{t}{4} = \frac{w}{8}(b - t)$$

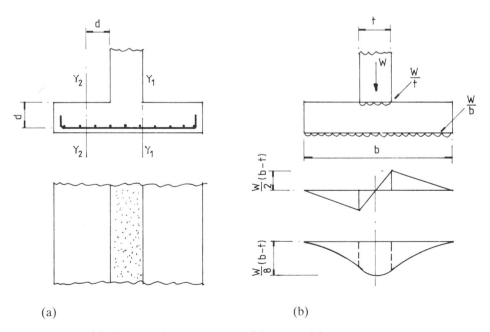

(a)   (b)

Fig. 11.16 (a) Wall and footing integral; (b) wall and footing separate.

11.4.2 Shear wall footing

If the wall and footing resist an in-plane horizontal load, e.g. when the wall is used as a shear wall to stabilize a building, the maximum pressure at one end of the wall is found assuming a linear distribution of earth pressure (Fig. 11.17). The footing is designed for the average earth pressure on, say, 0.5 m length at the end subjected to maximum earth pressure. Define the following variables:

W total load on the base
H horizontal load at the top of the wall
h height of the wall
b width of the base
l length of the wall and base

$$\text{area } A = bl$$
$$\text{modulus } Z = bl^2/6$$
$$\text{maximum pressure} = \frac{w}{A} + \frac{Hh}{Z}$$

If the footing is on firm ground and is sufficiently deep so that the underside of the base lies within 45° dispersal lines from the face of the wall, reinforcement need not be provided. However, it would be advisable to provide minimum reinforcement at the top and bottom of the footing to control cracking in case some settlement should occur.

11.4.3 Strip footing

A continuous strip footing is used under closely spaced rows of columns, as shown in Fig. 11.18 where individual footings would be close together or overlap.

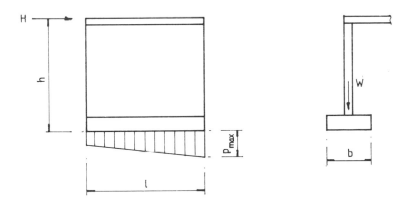

Fig. 11.17

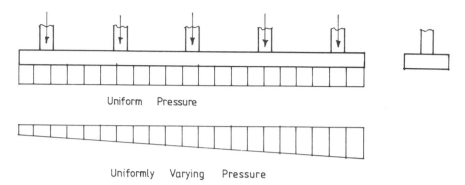

Fig. 11.18

If the footing is concentrically loaded, the pressure is uniform. If the column loads are not equal or not uniformly spaced and the base is assumed to be rigid, moments of the loads can be taken about the centre of the base and the pressure distribution can be determined assuming that the pressure varies uniformly. These cases are shown in Fig. 11.18.

In the longitudinal direction, the footing may be analysed for moments and shears by the following methods.

1. Assume a rigid foundation. Then the shear at any section is the sum of the forces on one side of the section, and the moment at the section is the sum of the moments of the forces on one side of the section;
2. A more accurate analysis may be made if the flexibility of the footing and the assumed elastic response of the soil is taken into account. The footing is analysed as a beam on an elastic foundation.

In the transverse direction the base may be designed along lines similar to that for a pad footing.

11.4.4 Combined bases

Where two columns are close together and separate footings would overlap, a combined base can be used as shown in Fig. 11.19(a). Again, if one column is close to an existing building or sewer it may not be possible to design a single pad footing, but if it is combined with that of an adjacent footing a satisfactory base can result. This is shown in Fig. 11.19(b).

If possible, the base is arranged so that its centreline coincides with the centre of gravity of the loads because this will give a uniform pressure on the soil. In a general case with an eccentric arrangement of loads, moments of forces are taken about the centre of the base and the maximum soil pressure is determined from the total vertical load and moment at the

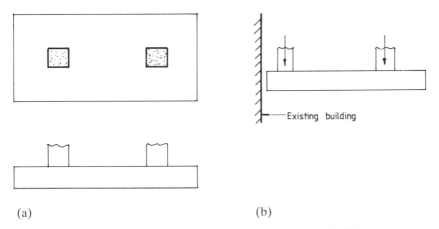

(a)   (b)

Fig. 11.19 (a) Combined base; (b) column close to existing building.

underside of the base. The pressure is assumed to vary uniformly along the length of the base.

In the longitudinal direction the actions for design may be found from statics. At any section the shear is the sum of the forces and the moment the sum of the moments of all the forces on one side of the section. In the transverse direction, the critical moment and shear are determined in the same way as for a pad footing. Punching shears at the column face and at 1.5 times the effective depth from the column face must also be checked.

□ Example 11.4 Combined base

(a) Specification

Design a rectangular base to support two columns carrying the following loads:

Column 1   Dead load 310 kN, imposed load 160 kN
Column 2   Dead load 430 kN, imposed load 220 kN

The columns are each 350 mm square and are spaced at 2.5 m centres. The width of the base is not to exceed 2.0 m. The safe bearing pressure on the ground is 180 kN/m². The materials are grade 35 concrete and grade 460 reinforcement.

(b) Base arrangement and soil pressure

Assume the weight of the base is 130 kN. Various load conditions are examined.

(i) Case 1: Dead + imposed load on both columns

$$\text{total vertical load} = 1250 \, \text{kN}$$
$$\text{area of base} = 1250/160 = 7.81 \, \text{m}^2$$
$$\text{length of base} = 7.81/2 = 3.91 \, \text{m}$$

The trial size is 4.5 m × 2.0 m × 0.6 m deep. The weight is 129.6 kN.

The base is arranged so that the centre of gravity of the loads coincides with the centreline of the base, in which case the soil pressure will be uniform. This arrangement will be made for the maximum ultimate loads.

The ultimate loads are

$$\text{column 1 load} = 1.4 \times 310 + 1.6 \times 160 = 690 \, kN$$
$$\text{column 2 load} = 1.4 \times 430 + 1.6 \times 220 = 954 \, kN$$

The distance of the centre of gravity from column 1 is

$$x = (954 \times 2.5)/(690 + 954) = 1.45 \, m$$

The base arrangement is shown in Fig. 11.20. The soil pressure is checked for service loads for case 1:

$$\text{base area} = 4.5 \times 2 = 9.0 \, m^2$$
$$\text{base modulus} = 2 \times 4.5^2/6 = 6.75 \, m^3$$
$$\text{direct load} = 310 + 160 + 430 + 220 + 129.6$$
$$= 1249.6 \, kN$$

The moment about the centreline of the base is

$$M = (430 + 220)1.05 - (310 + 160)1.45 = 1.0 \, kN \, m$$
$$\text{maximum pressure} = \frac{1249.6}{9} + \frac{1}{6.75}$$
$$= 138.9 \, kN/m^2$$

(ii) Case 2: Column 1, dead + imposed load; column 2, dead load

$$\text{direct load} = 1029.6 \, kN$$
$$\text{moment} = 230 \, kN \, m$$
$$\text{maximum pressure} = 114.4 + 34.1 = 148.5 \, kN/m^2$$

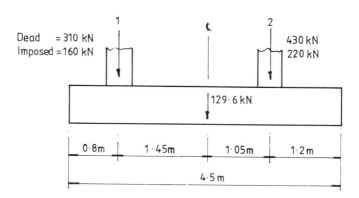

Fig. 11.20

(iii) Case 3: Column 1, dead load; column 2, dead + imposed load

$$\text{direct load} = 1089.6\,\text{kN}$$
$$\text{moment} = 233\,\text{kN m}$$
$$\text{maximum pressure} = 121.1 + 34.5 = 155.6\,\text{kN/m}^2$$

The base is satisfactory with respect to soil pressure.

(c) Analysis for actions in longitudinal direction

The design shears and moments in the longitudinal direction due to ultimate loads are calculated. The maximum moments are at the column face and between the columns, and maximum shears are at d from the column face.

The load cases are as follows (Fig. 11.20). For case 1

$$\text{column 1} = 1.4\,\text{dead} + 1.6\,\text{imposed} = 690\,\text{kN}$$
$$\text{column 2} = 1.4\,\text{dead} + 1.6\,\text{imposed} = 954\,\text{kN}$$

For case 2

$$\text{column 1} = 1.4\,\text{dead} + 1.6\,\text{imposed} = 690\,\text{kN}$$
$$\text{column 2} = 1.0\,\text{dead} = 430\,\text{kN}$$

For case 3

$$\text{column 1} = 1.0\,\text{dead} = 310\,\text{kN}$$
$$\text{column 2} = 1.4\,\text{dead} + 1.6\,\text{imposed} = 954\,\text{kN}$$

Moments and shears are calculated by statics. The calculations are tedious and are not given. The cover is 40 mm, and the bars, say, 20 mm in diameter. The effective depth d is 550 mm. The maximum shear at d from the column face is calculated. The shear force and bending moment diagrams for the three load cases are shown in Fig. 11.21.

(d) Design of longitudinal reinforcement

(i) Bottom Steel The maximum moment from case 3 is (Fig. 11.21)

$$M = 220.5\,\text{kN m}$$
$$\frac{M}{bd^2 f_{cu}} = \frac{220.5 \times 10^6}{2000 \times 550^2 \times 35} = 0.0104$$

Referring to Fig. 4.14, $z = 0.95d$ and

$$A_s = \frac{220.5 \times 10^6}{0.87 \times 460 \times 0.95 \times 550} = 1054.5\,\text{mm}^2$$

The minimum area of reinforcement is

$$0.13 \times 2000 \times 600/100 = 1560\,\text{mm}^2$$

Provide minimum reinforcement. Check that

$$l_c = 1000\,\text{mm}$$
$$< 3c/4 + 9d/4$$
$$< 3 \times 350/4 + 9 \times 550/4 = 1500\,\text{mm}$$

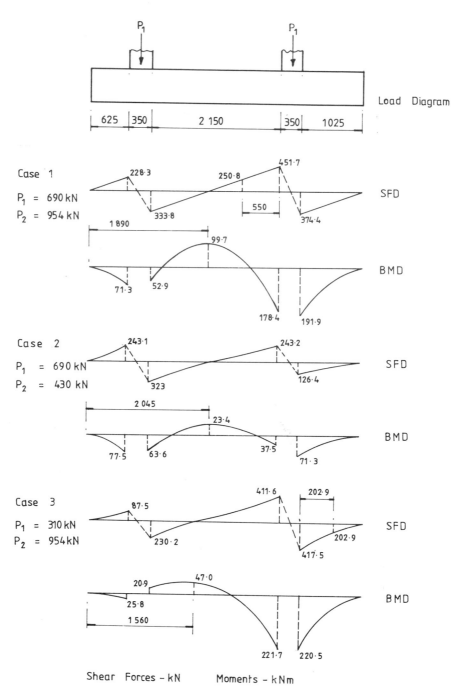

Fig. 11.21 Load diagram, shear force diagrams and bending moments diagrams for cases 1–3.

Provide 16 bars 12 mm in diameter at 125 mm centres to give a total area of 1808 mm².

(ii) Top steel   The maximum moment from case 1 is (Fig. 11.21)

$$M = 99.7 \, \text{kN m}$$

Provide minimum reinforcement as above in each direction.

(e) Transverse reinforcement

The pressures under the base for load cases 1 and 3 are shown in Figs 11.22(a) and 11.22(b) respectively. The moment on a 0.5 m length at the heaviest loaded end is

$$M = (222.3 + 204.1)0.5^3 \times 0.825^2$$

$$= 36.3 \, \text{kN m}$$

$$\frac{M}{bd^2 f_{cu}} = \frac{36.3 \times 10^6}{500 \times 550^2 \times 35} = 0.007$$

Provide minimum reinforcement in the transverse direction over the length of the base.

(f) Vertical shear

The maximum vertical shear from case 1 is

$$V = 250.8 \, \text{kN}$$

$$v = \frac{250.8 \times 10^3}{2000 \times 550} = 0.228 \, \text{N/mm}^2$$

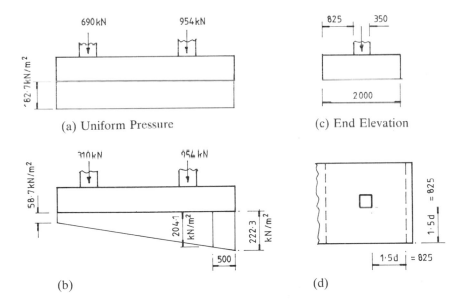

(a) Uniform Pressure   (c) End Elevation

(b)   (d)

Fig. 11.22 (a) Uniform pressure; (b) case 3, varying pressure; (c) end elevation; (d) punching shear.

$$v_c = 0.79\left(\frac{100 \times 1808}{2000 \times 550}\right)^{1/3}\left(\frac{35}{25}\right)^{1/3}\Big/1.25$$
$$= 0.39\,\text{N/mm}^2$$

No shear reinforcement is required.

(g) Punching shear

Punching shear is checked in a perimeter at $1.5d$ from the face of the column. The perimeter for punching shear which touches the sides of the base is shown in Fig. 11.22(d). The punching shear is less critical than the vertical shear in this case.

(h) Sketch of reinforcement

The reinforcement is shown in Fig. 11.23. A complete mat has been provided at the top and bottom. Some U-spacers are required to fix the top reinforcement in position.   ■

11.5 PILE FOUNDATIONS

11.5.1 General considerations

When a solid bearing stratum such as rock is deeper than about 3 m below the base level of the structure a foundation supported on bearing piles will provide an economical solution. Foundations can also be carried on fric-

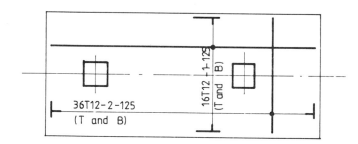

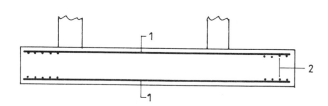

Fig. 11.23

tion piles by skin friction between the piles and the soil where the bedrock is too deep to obtain end bearing.

The main types of piles are as follows (Fig. 11.24(a)):

1. Precast reinforced or prestressed concrete piles driven in the required position;
2. Cast-*in-situ* reinforced concrete piles placed in holes formed either by

   (a) driving a steel tube with a plug of dry concrete or packed aggregate at the end into the soil or;
   (b) boring a hole and lowering a steel tube to follow the boring tool as a liner. (Other methods are also used [11].)

A reinforcement cage is inserted and the tube is withdrawn after the concrete is placed.

Short bored plain concrete piles are used for light loads such as carrying ground beams to support walls. Deep cylinder piles are used to carry large loads and can be provided under basement and raft foundations. A small number of cylinder piles can give a more economical solution than a large number of ordinary piles.

The safe load that a pile can carry can be determined by

1. test loading a pile
2. using a pile formula that gives the resistance from the energy of the driving force and the final set or penetration of the pile per blow

In both cases the ultimate load is divided by a factor of safety of from 2 to 3 to give the safe load. Safe loads depend on the size and depth and whether the pile is of the end bearing or friction type. The pile can be designed as a short column if lateral support from the ground is adequate. However, if ground conditions are unsatisfactory it is better to use test load results. The group action of piles should be taken into account because the group capacity can be considerably less than the total capacity of the individual piles.

The manufacture and driving of piles are carried out by specialist firms who guarantee to provide piles with a given bearing capacity on the site. Safe loads for precast and cast-*in-situ* piles vary from 100 kN to 1500 kN. Piles are also used to resist tension forces and the safe load in withdrawal is often taken as one-third of the safe load in bearing. Piles in groups are generally spaced at 0.8–1.5 m apart. Piles are driven at an inclination to resist horizontal loads in poor ground conditions. Rakes of 1 in 5 to 1 in 10 are commonly used in building foundations.

In an isolated foundation, the pile cap transfers the load from the column shaft to the piles in the group. The cap is cast around the tops of the piles and the piles are anchored into it by projecting bars. Some arrangements of pile caps are shown in Figs 11.24(b) and 11.24(c).

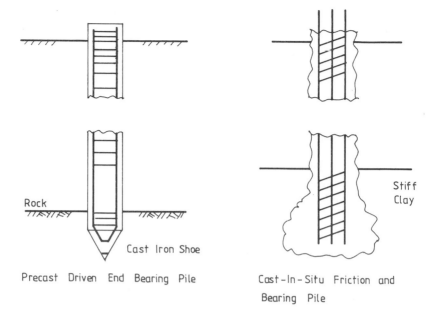

Rock

Cast Iron Shoe

Precast Driven End Bearing Pile

Stiff
Clay

Cast-In-Situ Friction and
Bearing Pile

(a).

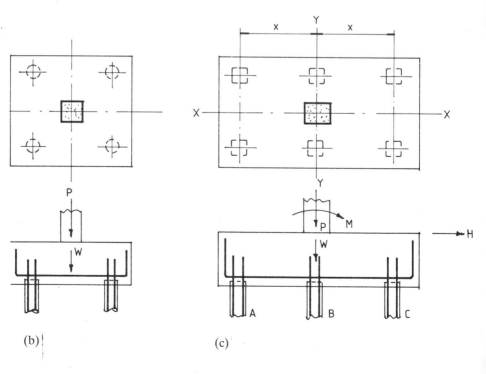

(b)

(c)

Fig. 11.24 (a) Pile types; (b) small pile cap, vertical load; (c) pile group resisting axial load and moment.

11.5.2 Loads in pile groups

In general pile groups are subjected to axial load, moment and horizontal load The pile loads are as follows.

(a) Axial load

When the load is applied at the centroid of the group it is assumed to be distributed uniformly to all piles by the pile cap, which is taken to be rigid. This gives the load per pile

$$F_a = (P + W)/N$$

where P is the axial load from the column, W is the weight of the pile cap and N is the number of piles (Fig. 11.24(b)).

(b) Moment on a group of vertical piles

The pile cap is assumed to rotate about the centroid of the pile group, and the pile loads resisting moment vary uniformly from zero at the centroidal axis to a maximum for the piles farthest away. Referring to Fig. 11.24(c), the moment of inertia about the YY axis is

$$I_y = 2(x^2 + x^2) = 4x^2$$

where x is the pile spacing. The maximum load due to moment on piles A in tension and C in compression is

$$F_m = \pm \frac{Mx}{I_y} = \pm \frac{M}{4x}$$

For a symmetrical group of piles spaced at $\pm x_1, \pm x_2, \ldots, \pm x_n$ perpendicular to the centroidal axis YY, the moment of inertia of the piles about the YY axis is

$$I_y = 2(x_1^2 + x_2^2 + \ldots + x_n^2)$$

and the maximum pile load is

$$F_m = \pm \frac{Mx_n}{I_y}$$

If the pile group is subjected to bending about both the XX and YY axes moments of inertia are calculated for each axis. The pile loads from bending are calculated for each axis as above and summed algebraically to give the resultant loads. The loads due to moment are combined with those due to vertical load.

(c) Horizontal load

In building foundations where the piles and pile cap are buried in the soil, horizontal loads can be resisted by friction, adhesion and passive resistance of the soil. Ground slabs that tie foundations together can be used to resist horizontal reactions due to rigid frame action and wind loads by friction and adhesion with the soil and so can relieve the pile group of horizontal load. However, in the case of isolated foundations in poor soil conditions where the soil may shrink away from the cap in dry weather or in wharves and jetties where the piles are clear between the deck and the sea bed, the piles must be designed to resist horizontal load.

Pile groups resist horizontal loads by

1. bending in the piles
2. using the horizontal component of the axial force in inclined piles

These cases are discussed below.

(d) Pile in bending

A group of vertical piles subjected to a horizontal force H applied at the top of the piles is shown in Fig. 11.25. The piles are assumed to be fixed at the top and bottom. The deflection of the pile cap is shown in 11.25(b).

$$\text{shear per pile } V = H/N$$

$$\text{moment } M_1 \text{ in each pile} = Hh_1/2N$$

where N is the number of piles and h_1 is the length of pile between fixed ends.

The horizontal force is applied at the top of the pile cap of depth h_2 and this causes a moment Hh_2 at the pile tops. When vertical load and moment

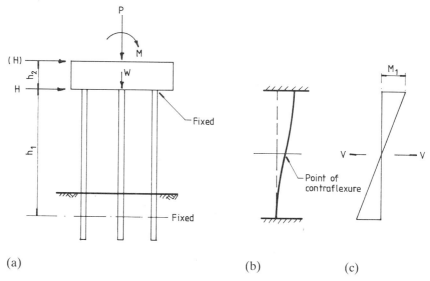

(a)   (b)   (c)

Fig. 11.25 (a) Pile group; (b) deflection; (c) moment diagram.

are also applied the resultant pile loads are a combination of those caused by the three actions. The total vertical load $P + W$ is distributed equally to the piles. The total moment $M + Hh_2$ is resisted by vertical loads in the piles and the analysis is carried out as set out in 11.5.2(b) above. The pile is designed as a reinforced concrete column subjected to axial load and moment. If the pile is clear between the cap and ground, additional moment due to slenderness may have to be taken into account. If the pile is in soil complete or partial lateral support may be assumed.

(e) Resistance to horizontal load by inclined piles

An approximate method used to determine the loads in piles in a group subjected to axial load, moment and horizontal load where the horizontal load is resisted by inclined piles is set out. In Fig. 11.26 the foundation carries a vertical load P, moment M and horizontal load H. The weight of the pile cap is W.

The loads F in the piles are calculated as follows.

(i) Vertical loads, pile loads F_v   The sum of the vertical loads is $P + W$.

$$F_{v2} = F_{v3} = (P + W)/8$$
$$F_{v1} = F_{v4} = \frac{P + W}{8} \frac{(R^2 + 1)^{1/2}}{R}$$

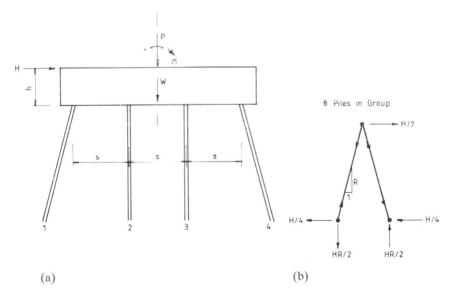

(a)   (b)

Fig. 11.26 (a) Pile group; (b) resistance to horizontal load.

(ii) *Horizontal loads, pile loads* F_H The horizontal load is assumed to be resisted by pairs of inclined piles as shown in Fig. 11.26(b). The sum of the horizontal loads is H.

$$-F_{H1} = F_{H4} = [H(R^2 + 1)^{1/2}]/4$$
$$F_{H2} = F_{H3} = 0$$

(iii) *Moments, pile loads* F_M The moment of inertia is

$$I_y = 2[(0.5S)^2 + (1.5S)^2]$$

The sum of the moments is

$$M^1 = M + Hh$$
$$-F_{M1} = F_{M4} = \frac{1.5SM^1}{I_y} \frac{(R^2 + 1)^{1/2}}{R}$$
$$-F_{M2} = F_{M3} = 0.5SM^1/I_y$$

The maximum pile load is $F_{v4} + F_{H4} + F_{M4}$.

□ Example 11.5 Loads in pile group

The analysis using the approximate method set out above is given for a pile group to carry the loads and moment from the shear wall designed in Example 10.1. The design actions for service loads are as follows:

Axial load	9592 kN
Moment	5657 kN m
Horizontal load	281 kN

The shear wall is 6 m long. The proposed pile group consisting of 18 piles inclined at 1 in 6 in shown in Fig. 11.27.

The weight of the base is 610 kN. For the vertical loads F_{v1} to F_{v6}

$$\frac{9592 + 610}{18} \frac{37^{1/2}}{6} = 574.6\,\text{kN}$$

For the horizontal loads

$$-F_{H1} = -F_{H2} = -F_{H3} = F_{H4} = F_{H5} = F_{H6}$$
$$= 281 \times 37^{1/2}/18 = 94.9\,\text{kN}$$

The moment of inertia is

$$I_y = 3 \times 2(0.6^2 + 1.8^2 + 3.0^2) = 76.6$$

The moment at the pile top is

$$5657 + (281 \times 1.2) = 5994\,\text{kN m}$$
$$-F_{M1} = F_{M6} = \frac{5994 \times 3 \times 37^{1/2}}{76.6 \times 6} = 238\,\text{kN}$$

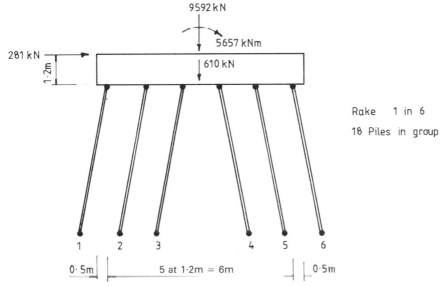

Fig. 11.27

$$-F_{M2} - F_{M5} - \frac{5994 \times 1.8 \times 37^{1/2}}{76.6 \times 6} - 142.8\,\text{kN}$$

$$-F_{M3} = F_{M4} - \frac{5994 \times 0.6 \times 37^{1/2}}{76.6 \times 6} - 47.6\,\text{kN}$$

The maximum pile load is

$$F_6 = 574.6 + 94.9 + 238 = 907.5\,\text{kN}$$

The method given in the *Reinforced Concrete Designers' Handbook* [6] gives a maximum pile load of 909 kN.

The pile group and pile cap shown in Fig. 11.27 can be analysed using a plane frame computer program. The large size of the cap in comparison with the pile ensures that it acts as a rigid member. The pile may be assumed to be pinned or fixed at the ends. ■

11.5.3 Design of pile caps

The design of pile caps is covered in section 3.11.4 of the code. The design provisions are as follows.

(a) General

Pile caps are designed either using bending theory or using the truss analogy. When the truss method is used, the truss should be of triangulated form with a node at the centre of the loaded area. The lower nodes are to lie at the intersection of the centrelines of the piles with the tensile

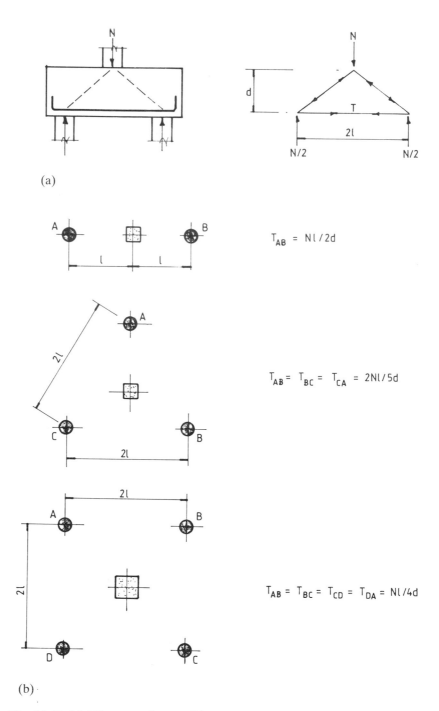

(a)

$T_{AB} = Nl/2d$

$T_{AB} = T_{BC} = T_{CA} = 2Nl/5d$

$T_{AB} = T_{BC} = T_{CD} = T_{DA} = Nl/4d$

(b)

Fig. 11.28 (a) Pile cap and truss; (b) tensile forces in pile caps.

reinforcement. Tensile forces in pile caps for some common cases are shown in Fig. 11.28.

(b) Truss method with widely spaced piles

Where the spacing exceeds 3 times the pile diameter only reinforcement within 1.5 times the diameter from the centre of the pile should be considered to form a tension member of a truss.

(c) Shear forces

The shear strength of a pile cap is normally governed by the shear on a vertical section through a full width of the cap. The critical section is taken at 20% of the pile diameter inside the face of the pile as shown in Fig. 11.29. The whole of the force from the piles with centres lying outside this line should be considered.

(d) Design shear resistance

The shear check may be made in accordance with provisions for the shear resistance of solid slabs given in clauses 3.5.5 and 3.5.6 of the code. The following limitations apply with regard to pile caps.

1. The distance a_v from the face of the column to the critical shear plane is as defined in 11.5.3(c) above. The enhanced shear stress is $2dv_c/a_v$

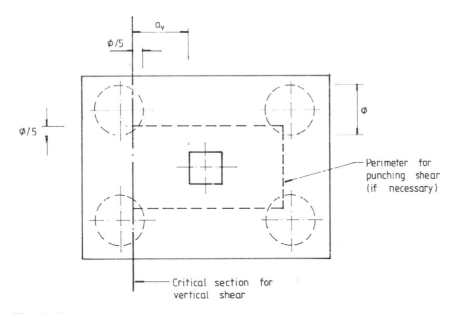

Fig. 11.29

where v_c is taken from Table 3.9 of the code. The maximum shear stress at the face of the column must not exceed $0.8f_{cu}^{1/2}$ or $5\,N/mm^2$.

2. Where the pile spacing is less than or equal to 3 times the pile diameter ϕ, the enhancement can be applied over the whole of the critical section. Where the spacing is greater, the enhancement can only be applied to strips of width equal to 3ϕ centred on each pile. Minimum stirrups are not required in pile caps where $v < v_c$ (enhanced if appropriate).

3. The tension reinforcement should be provided with a full anchorage in accordance with section 3.12.8 of the code. The tension bars must be anchored by bending them up the sides of the pile cap.

(e) Punching shear

The following two checks are required:

1. The design shear stress on the perimeter of the column is not to exceed $0.8f_{cu}^{1/2}$ or $5\,N/mm^2$;
2. If the spacing of the piles is greater than 3 times the pile diameter, punching shear should be checked on the perimeter shown in Fig. 11.29.

□ Example 11.6 Pile cap

Design a four-pile cap to support a factored axial column load of 3600 kN. The column is 400 mm square and the piles are 400 mm in diameter spaced at 1200 mm centres. The materials are grade 35 concrete and grade 460 reinforcement.

The pile cap is shown in Fig. 11.30. The overall depth is taken as 900 mm and the effective depth as 800 mm.

(a) Moment reinforcement

Refer to Fig. 11.28 for a four-pile cap.

$$\text{tension } T = \frac{3600 \times 600}{4 \times 800} = 675\,kN$$

$$A_s = \frac{675 \times 10^3}{0.87 \times 460} = 1686.6\,mm^2 \text{ per tie}$$

Provide 12T20 bars, area 3768 mm², for reinforcement across the full width for two ties.

The minimum reinforcement from Table 3.27 of the code is

$$0.13 \times 1900 \times 900/100 = 2223\,mm^2$$

$$< 3768\,mm \text{ provided}$$

The pile spacing is not greater than 3 times the pile diameter, and so the reinforcement can be spaced evenly across the pile cap. The spacing is 160 mm.

(b) Shear

The critical section for shear lies $\phi/5$ inside the pile as shown in Fig. 11.30, giving $a_v = 280$ mm. The shear is 1800 kN.

$$v = \frac{1800 \times 10^3}{1900 \times 800} = 1.18 \, \text{N/mm}^2$$

$$v_c = 0.79\left(\frac{100 \times 3768}{1900 \times 800}\right)^{1/3}\left(\frac{35}{25}\right)^{1/3} \Big/ 1.25$$

$$= 0.44 \, \text{N/mm}^2$$

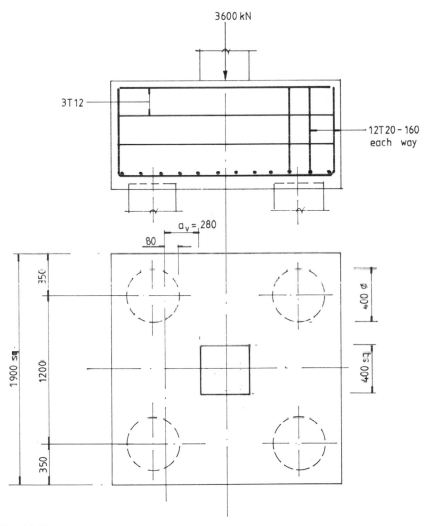

Fig. 11.30

The enhanced design shear stress is

$$0.44 \times 2 \times 800/280 = 2.53 \, \text{N/mm}^2$$

The shear stress at the critical section is satisfactory and no shear reinforcement is required.

Check the shear stress on the perimeter of the column:

$$v = \frac{3600 \times 10^3}{1600 \times 800} = 2.81 \, \text{N/mm}^2$$

$$< 0.8 \times 35^{1/2} = 4.73 \, \text{N/mm}^2$$

This is satisfactory. The pile spacing is not greater than 3 times the pile diameter and so no check for punching shear is required.

(c) Arrangement of reinforcement

The anchorage of the main bars is 34 diameters (680 mm), from Table 3.29 of the code.

The spacing of 160 mm does not exceed 750 mm and is satisfactory. Secondary steel, 12 mm diameter bars, is required on the sides of the pile cap. The reinforcement is shown in Fig. 11.30. ■

12

Retaining walls

12.1 TYPES AND EARTH PRESSURE

12.1.1 Types of retaining wall

Retaining walls are structures used to retain earth which would not be able to stand vertically unsupported. The wall is subjected to overturning due to pressure of the retained material.

The types of retaining wall are as follows:

1. In a **gravity wall** stability is provided by the weight of concrete in the wall;
2. In a **cantilever wall** the wall slab acts as a vertical cantilever. Stability is provided by the weight of structure and earth on an inner base or the weight of the structure only when the base is constructed externally;
3. In **counterfort and buttress walls** the slab is supported on three sides by the base and counterforts or buttresses. Stability is provided by the weight of the structure in the case of the buttress wall and by the weight of the structure and earth on the base in the counterfort wall.

Examples of retaining walls are shown in Fig. 12.1. Designs are given for cantilever and counterfort retaining walls.

12.1.2 Earth pressure on retaining walls

(a) Active soil pressure

Active soil pressures are given for the two extreme cases of a cohesionless soil such as sand and a cohesive soil such as clay (Fig. 12.2). General formulae are available for intermediate cases. The formulae given apply to drained soils and reference should be made to textbooks on soil mechanics for pressure where the water table rises behind the wall. The soil pressures given are those due to a level backfill. If there is a surcharge of $w \, \mathrm{kN/m^2}$ on the soil behind the wall, this is equivalent to an additional soil depth of $z = w/\gamma$ where γ is the density in kilonewtons per cubic metre. The textbooks give solutions for cases where there is sloping backfill.

(i) Cohesionless soil, c = 0 (Fig. 12.2(a))   The pressure at any depth z is given by

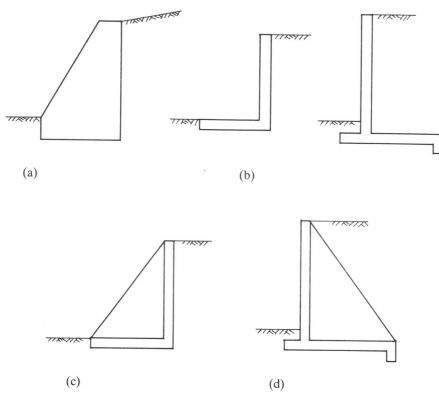

Fig. 12.1 (a) Gravity wall; (b) cantilever walls; (c) buttress wall; (d) counterfort wall.

$$p = \gamma z \frac{1 - \sin \phi}{1 + \sin \phi}$$

where γ is the soil density and ϕ is the angle of internal friction. The force on the wall of height H_1 is

$$P_1 = \frac{1}{2} \gamma H_1^2 \frac{1 - \sin \phi}{1 + \sin \phi}$$

(ii) Cohesive soil, $\phi = 0$ (Fig. 12.2(b))   The pressure at any depth z is given theoretically by

$$p = \gamma z - 2c$$

where c is the cohesion at zero normal pressure. This expression gives negative values near the top of the wall. In practice, a value for the active earth pressure of not less than $\frac{1}{4} \gamma z$ is used.

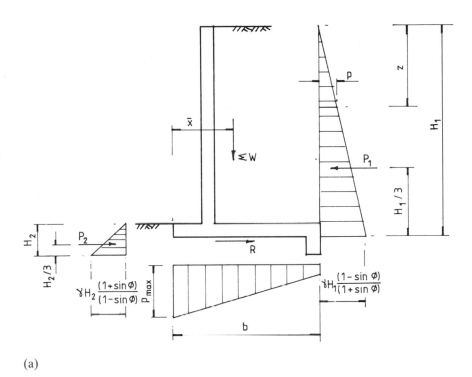

(a)

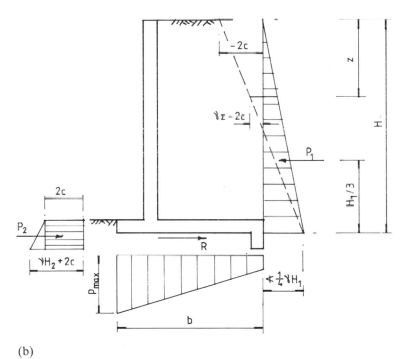

(b)

Fig. 12.2 (a) Cohesionless soil ($c = 0$); (b) cohesive soil ($\phi = 0$).

(b) Wall stability

Referring to Fig. 12.2 the vertical loads are made up of the weight of the wall and base and the weight of backfill on the base. Front fill on the outer base has been neglected. Surcharge would need to be included if present. If the centre of gravity of these loads is x from the toe of the wall, the stabilizing moment is ΣWx with a beneficial partial safety factor $\gamma_f = 1.0$. The overturning moment due to the active earth pressure is $1.4 P_1 H_1/3$ with an adverse partial safety factor $\gamma_f = 1.4$. The stabilizing moment from passive earth pressure has been neglected. For the wall to satisfy the requirement of stability

$$\Sigma Wx \geqslant 1.4 P_1 H_1/3$$

(c) Vertical pressure under the base

The vertical pressure under the base is calculated for service loads. For a cantilever wall a 1 m length of wall with base width b is considered. Then

$$\text{area } A = b \, \text{m}^2$$
$$\text{modulus } Z = b^2/6 \, \text{m}^3$$

If ΣM is the sum of the moments of all vertical forces ΣW about the centre of the base and of the active pressure on the wall then

$$\Sigma M = \Sigma W(x - b/2) - P_1 H_1/3$$

The passive pressure in front of the base has been neglected again. The maximum pressure is

$$P_{\max} = \frac{\Sigma W}{A} + \frac{\Sigma M}{Z}$$

This should not exceed the safe bearing pressure on the soil.

(d) Resistance to sliding (Fig. 12.2)

The resistance of the wall to sliding is as follows.

(i) Cohesionless soil   The friction R between the base and the soil is $\mu \Sigma W$ where μ is the coefficient of friction between the base and the soil ($\mu = \tan \phi$). The passive earth pressure against the front of the wall from a depth H_2 of soil is

$$P_2 = 0.5 \gamma H_2^2 \frac{1 + \sin \phi}{1 - \sin \phi}$$

(ii) Cohesive soils   The adhesion R between the base and the soil is βb where β is the adhesion in kilonewtons per square metre. The passive earth pressure is

$$P_2 = 0.5\gamma H_2{}^2 + 2cH_2$$

A nib can be added, as shown in Fig. 12.2, to increase the resistance to sliding through passive earth pressure.

For the wall to be safe against sliding

$$1.4P_1 < P_2 + R$$

where P_1 is the horizontal active earth pressure on the wall.

12.2 DESIGN OF CANTILEVER WALLS

12.2.1 Design procedure

The steps in the design of a cantilever retaining wall are as follows.

1. Assume a breadth for the base. This is usually about 0.75 of the wall height. The preliminary thicknesses for the wall and base sections are chosen from experience. A nib is often required to increase resistance to sliding.
2. Calculate the horizontal earth pressure on the wall. Then, considering all forces, check stability against overturning and the vertical pressure under the base of the wall. Calculate the resistance to sliding and check that this is satisfactory. A partial safety factor of 1.4 is applied to the horizontal loads for the overturning and sliding check. The maximum vertical pressure is calculated using service loads and should not exceed the safe bearing pressure.
3. Reinforced concrete design for the wall is made for ultimate loads. The partial safety factors for the wall and earth pressure are each 1.4. Surcharge if present may be classed as either dead or imposed load depending on its nature. Referring to Fig. 12.3 the design consists of the following.
   (a) For the *wall*, calculate shear forces and moments caused by the horizontal earth pressure. Design the vertical moment steel for the inner face and check the shear stresses. Minimum secondary steel is provided in the horizontal direction for the inner face and both vertically and horizontally for the outer face.
   (b) The net moment due to earth pressure on the top and bottom faces of the *inner footing* causes tension in the top and reinforcement is designed for this position.
   (c) The moment due to earth pressure causes tension in the bottom face of the *outer footing*.

   The moment reinforcement is shown in Fig. 12.3.

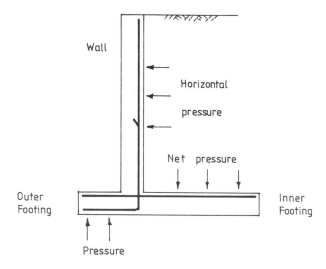

Fig. 12.3

□ Example 12.1 Cantilever retaining wall

(a) Specification

Design a cantilever retaining wall to support a bank of earth 3.5 m high. The top surface is horizontal behind the wall but it is subjected to a dead load surcharge of 15 kN/m². The soil behind the wall is a well-drained sand with the following properties:

$$\text{density } \gamma = 1800 \text{ kg/m}^3 = 17.6 \text{ kN/m}^3$$
$$\text{angle of internal friction } \phi = 30°$$

The material under the wall has a safe bearing pressure of 100 kN/m². The coefficient of friction between the base and the soil is 0.5. Design the wall using grade 30 concrete and grade 460 reinforcement.

(b) Wall stability

The proposed arrangement of the wall is shown in Fig. 12.4. The wall and base thickness are assumed to be 200 mm. A nib has been added under the wall to assist in the prevention of sliding. Consider 1 m length of wall. The surcharge is equivalent to an additional height of 15/17.6 = 0.85 m. The total equivalent height of soil is

$$3.5 + 0.25 + 0.85 = 4.6 \text{ m}$$

The horizontal pressure at depth y from the top of the surcharge is

$$17.6y(1 - 0.5)/(1 + 0.5) = 5.87y \text{ kN/m}^2$$

The horizontal pressure at the base is

$$5.87 \times 4.6 = 27 \text{ kN/m}^2$$

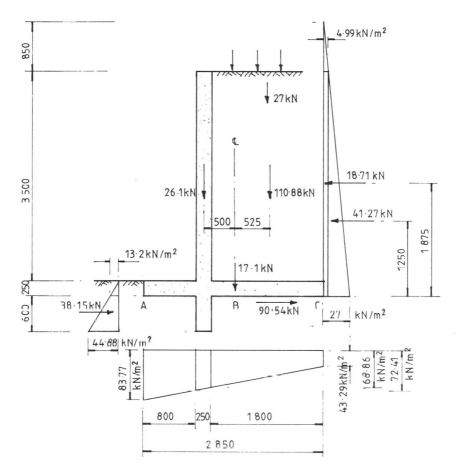

Fig. 12.4

The weight of wall, base and earth and the moments for stability calculations are given in Table 12.1.

(i) Maximum soil pressure   The base properties are

$$\text{area } A = 2.85\,\text{m}^2$$
$$\text{modulus } Z = 2.85^2/6 - 1.35\,\text{m}^3$$

The maximum soil pressure at A calculated for service load is

$$\frac{181.08}{2.85} + \frac{86.67 - 59.34}{1.35} = 63.53 + 20.24 = 83.77\,\text{kN/m}^2$$

The maximum soil pressure is satisfactory.

(ii) Stability against overturning   The stabilizing moment about the toe A of the wall for a partial safety factor $\gamma_f = 1.0$ is

Table 12.1 Stability calculations

Load	Horizontal load (kN)		Distance from C (m)	Moment about C (kN m)
Active pressure	4.99×3.75	$= 18.71$	1.875	-35.08
	$0.5 \times 22.01 \times 3.75$	$= 41.27$	1.25	-51.59
Total		59.98		-86.67

	Vertical load (kN)		Distance from B (m)	Moment about B (kN m)
Wall + nib	$4.35 \times 0.25 \times 24 =$	26.1	-0.5	-13.05
Base	$2.85 \times 0.25 \times 24 =$	17.1	0	0
Backfill	$1.8 \times 3.5 \times 17.6 =$	110.88	0.525	58.21
Surcharge	$1.8 \times 15 \qquad =$	27.0	0.525	14.18
Total		181.08		59.34

$$59.34 + (181.08 \times 1.425) = 317.4 \, \text{kN m}$$

The overturning moment for a partial safety factor $\gamma_f = 1.4$ is

$$1.4 \times 86.67 = 121.34 \, \text{kN m}$$

The stability of the wall is adequate.

(iii) Resistance to sliding   The forces resisting sliding are the friction under the base and the passive resistance for a depth of earth of 850 mm to the top of the base:

$$0.5 \times 181.08 + \frac{17.6 \times 0.85^2(1 + 0.5)}{1 - 0.5} = 90.54 + 38.15 = 128.69 \, \text{kN}$$

For the wall to be safe against sliding

$$128.69 > 1.4 \times 59.98 = 83.97 \, \text{kN}$$

The resistance to sliding is satisfactory.

(iv) Overall comment   The wall section is satisfactory. The maximum soil pressure under the base controls the design.

(c) Structural design

The structural design is made for ultimate loads. The partial safety factor for each pressure and surcharge is $\gamma_f = 1.4$.

(i) *Wall reinforcement*   The pressure at the base of the wall is

$$1.4 \times 5.89 \times 4.35 = 35.7\,\text{kN/m}^2$$

The pressure at the top of the wall is

$$1.4 \times 4.99 = 6.99\,\text{kN/m}^2$$
$$\text{shear} = (6.99 \times 3.5) + (0.5 \times 3.5 \times 28.76)$$
$$= 24.47 + 50.33 = 74.8\,\text{kN}$$
$$\text{moment} = (24.47 \times 0.5 \times 3.5) + (50.33 \times 3.5/3)$$
$$= 101.51\,\text{kN m}$$

The cover is 40 mm; assume 20 mm diameter bars. Then

$$d = 250 - 40 - 10 = 200\,\text{mm}$$
$$\frac{M}{bd^2} = \frac{101.51 \times 10^6}{1000 \times 200^2} = 2.54$$
$$100A_s/bd = 0.7 \quad \text{(Fig. 4.13)}$$
$$A_s = 0.7 \times 200 \times 1000/100$$
$$= 1400\,\text{mm}^2/\text{m}$$

Provide 16 mm diameter bars at 140 mm centres to give a steel area of 1435 mm²/m.
  Determine the depth y_1 from the top where the 16 mm diameter bars can be reduced to a diameter of 12 mm.

$$A_s = 807\,\text{mm}^2/\text{m}$$
$$100A_s/bd = 100 \times 807/(1000 \times 200) = 0.4$$
$$M/bd^2 = 1.6 \quad \text{(Fig. 4.13)}$$
$$M = 1.5 \times 1000 \times 200^2/10^6$$
$$= 64\,\text{kN m}$$

The depth y_1 is given by the equation

$$64 = 6.99y_1^2/2 + 1.4 \times 5.87y_1^3/6$$

or

$$y_1^3 + 2.55y_1^2 - 46.73 = 0$$

Solve to give $y_1 = 2.92\,\text{m}$.
  Referring to the anchorage requirements in BS 8110: Part 1, clause 3.12.9.1, bars are to extend an anchorage length beyond the theoretical change point. The anchorage length from Table 3.29 of the code for grade 30 concrete is (section 5.2.1)

$$37 \times 16 = 595\,\text{mm}$$

Stop bars off at $2920 - 592 = 2328\,\text{mm}$, say 2000 mm from the top of the wall.
  The shear stress at the base of the wall is

$$\frac{74.8 \times 10^3}{100 \times 200} = 0.374\,\text{N/mm}^2$$

The design shear stress is

$$v_c = 0.79\left(\frac{100 \times 1436}{1000 \times 200}\right)^{1/3}\left(\frac{400}{200}\right)^{1/4}\left(\frac{30}{25}\right)^{1/3}\bigg/1.25 = 0.71\,\text{N/mm}^2$$

The shear stress is satisfactory.

The deflection need not be checked.

For control of cracking the bar spacing must not exceed 3 times the effective depth, i.e. 600 or 750 mm. The spacing at the bars in the wall is 140 mm. This is less than the 160 mm clear spacing given in Table 3.30 of the code for crack control.

For distribution steel provide the minimum area of 0.13% from Table 3.27 of the code:

$$A = 0.13 \times 1000 \times 250/100 = 325\,\text{mm}^2/\text{m}$$

Provide 10 mm diameter bars at 240 mm centres horizontally on the inner face.

For crack control on the outer face provide 10 mm diameter bars at 240 mm centres each way.

(ii) Inner footing   Referring to Fig. 12.4 the shear and moment at the face of the wall are as follows:

$$\begin{aligned}
\text{shear} &= 1.4[110.88 + 27 + (17.1 \times 1.8/2.85)\\
&\quad -(43.29 \times 1.8) - (0.5 \times 25.57 \times 1.8)\\
&= 1.4(110.88 + 27 + 10.8 - 77.92 - 23.01)\\
&= 66.85\,\text{kN}\\
\text{moment} &= 1.4[(70.76 \times 0.9) - (23.01 \times 0.6)]\\
&= 1.4 \times 49.87 = 69.82\,\text{kN m}
\end{aligned}$$

$$\frac{M}{bd^2} = \frac{69.82 \times 10^6}{1000 \times 200^2} = 1.75$$

$$100A_s/bd = 0.45 \quad \text{(Fig. 4.13)}$$

$$A_s = 0.45 \times 1000 \times 200/100 = 900\,\text{mm}^2/\text{m}$$

Provide 12 mm diameter bars at 120 mm centres to give 942 mm²/m.

$$\text{shear stress} = \frac{66.85 \times 10^3}{10^3 \times 200} = 0.334\,\text{N/mm}^2$$

This is satisfactory. For the distribution steel, provide 10 mm bars at 240 mm centres.

(iii) Outer Footing   Referring to Fig. 12.4 the shear and moment at the face of the wall are as follows:

$$\begin{aligned}
\text{shear} &= 1.4(72.41 \times 0.8 + 11.36 \times 0.8/2 - 17.1 \times 0.8/2.85)\\
&= 1.4(57.93 + 4.54 - 4.8)\\
&= 80.74\,\text{kN}\\
\text{moment} &= 1.4[(57.93 - 4.8)0.4 + 4.54 \times 2 \times 0.8/3]\\
&= 33.13\,\text{kN m}
\end{aligned}$$

Note that the sum of the moments at the bottom of the wall and at the face of the wall for the inner and outer footing is approximately zero.

Reinforcement from the wall will be anchored in the outer footing and will provide the moment steel here. The anchorage length required is 592 mm and this will be provided by the bend and a straight length of bar along the outer footing. The radius of the bend is determined to limit the bearing stress to a safe value. The permissible bearing stress inside the bend is

$$\frac{2 \times 30}{1 + 2(16/140)} = 48.84 \, \text{N/mm}^2$$

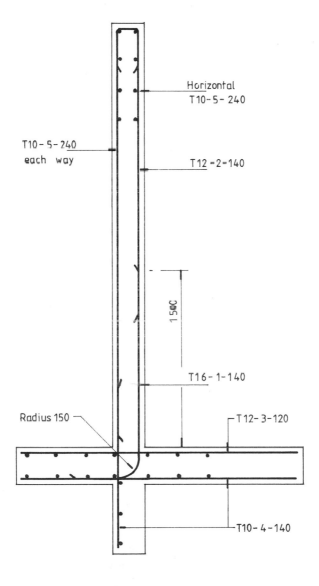

Fig. 12.5

where a_b is the bar spacing, 140 mm. The internal radius of the bend is

$$r = \frac{0.87 \times 460 \times 201}{16 \times 48.84} = 102.9\,\text{mm}$$

Make the radius of the bend 150 mm:

$$\text{shear stress} = \frac{80.74 \times 10^3}{1000 \times 200} = 0.404\,\text{N/mm}^2$$

This is satisfactory. See the wall design above. The distribution steel is 10 mm diameter bars at 240 mm centres.

(iv) Nib   Referring to Fig. 12.4 the shear and moment in the nib are as follows:

$$\text{shear} = 1.4(13.2 \times 0.6 + 31.68 \times 0.6/2)$$
$$= 24.39\,\text{kN}$$
$$\text{moment} = 1.4(7.9 \times 0.3 + 9.5 \times 0.4)$$
$$= 8.65\,\text{kN\,m}$$

The minimum reinforcement is 0.13% or 325 mm²/m. For crack control the maximum spacing is to be limited to 160 mm as specified in Table 3.30 of the code. Provide 10 mm diameter bars at 140 mm centres to lap onto the main wall steel. The distribution steel is 10 mm diameter bars at 240 mm centres.

(v) Sketch of the wall reinforcement   A sketch of the wall with the reinforcement designed above is shown in Fig. 12.5.   ■

12.3 COUNTERFORT RETAINING WALLS

12.3.1 Stability and design procedure

A counterfort retaining wall is shown in Fig. 12.6. The spacing is usually made equal to the height of the wall. The following comments are made regarding the design.

(a) Stability

Consider as one unit a centre-to-centre length of panels taking into account the weight of the counterfort. The earth pressure under this unit and the resistance to overturning and sliding must be satisfactory. The calculations are made in a similar way to those for a cantilever wall.

(b) Wall slab

The slab is much thinner than that required for a cantilever wall. It is built in on three edges, free at the top, and is subjected to a triangular load due to the active earth pressure. The lower part of the wall cantilevers vertically from the base and the upper part spans horizontally between the counterforts. A load distribution commonly adopted between vertically

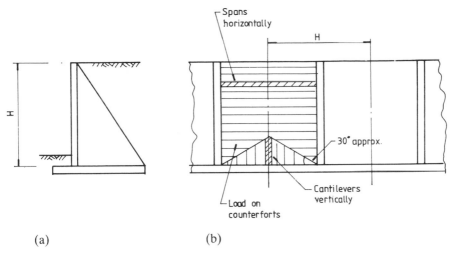

Fig. 12.6 (a) Section; (b) back of wall.

and horizontally spanning elements is shown in Fig. 12.6. The finite element method could be used to analyse the wall to determine the moments for design. The yield line method is used in the example that follows.

The yield line pattern for the wall is shown in Fig. 12.7(a). Reinforcement for the sagging moments on the outside of the wall covers the whole wall. Reinforcement for the hogging moments extends in a band around the three side supports as shown in the figure.

(c) Base

The inner footing is a slab built in on three sides and free on the fourth. The loading is trapezoidal in distribution across the base due to the net effect of the weight of earth down and earth pressure under the base acting upwards. The base slab can be analysed by the yield line method. The yield line pattern is shown in Fig. 12.7(b). The outer footing, if provided, is designed as a cantilever.

(d) Counterforts

Counterforts support the wall and base slab and are designed as vertical cantilevers of varying T-beam section. It is usual to assume the distribution of load between counterforts and base shown in Fig. 12.6. A design is made for the base section and one or more sections in the height of the counterfort. Links must be provided between the wall slab and inner base and the counterfort to transfer the loading. Reinforcement for the counterfort is shown in Fig. 12.7(c).

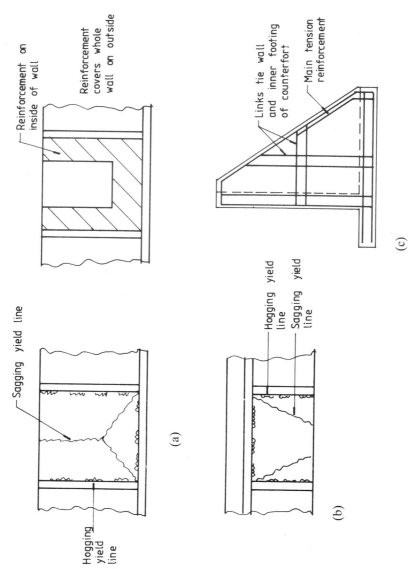

Fig. 12.7 (a) Yield line pattern and reinforcement in wall; (b) yield line pattern in base slab; (c) reinforcement of counterfort.

☐ Example 12.2 Counterfort retaining wall

(a) Specification

A counterfort retaining wall has a height from the top to the underside of the base of 5 m and a spacing of counterfoils of 5 m. The backfill is level with the top of the wall. The earth in the backfill is granular with the following properties:

Density	$15.7 \, \text{kN/m}^3$
Angle of internal friction	$30°$
Coefficient of friction between the soil and concrete	0.5

The safe bearing pressure of the soil under the base is $150 \, \text{kN/m}^2$.

The construction materials are grade 35 concrete and grade 460 reinforcement. Set out a trial section for the wall and base and check stability. Design the wall slab.

(b) Trial section

The proposed section for the counterfort retaining wall is shown in Fig. 12.8. The wall slab is made 180 mm thick and the counterfort and base slab is 250 mm thick.

(c) Stability

Consider a 5 m length of wall centre to centre of counterforts. The horizontal earth pressure at depth y is

$$15.7y(1 - 0.5)/(1 + 0.5) = 5.23y \, \text{kN/m}^2$$

The stability calculations are given in Table 12.2. The loads are shown in Fig. 12.8.

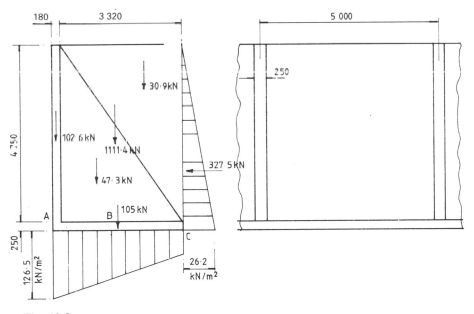

Fig. 12.8

Table 12.2 Stability calculations

Load	Horizontal load (kN)		Distance from C (m)	Moment about C (kNm)
Active pressure	$0.5 \times 26.2 \times 5 \times 5 = 327.5$		1.67	−546.9

	Vertical load (kN)			Distance from B (m)	Moment about B (kNm)
Wall	$5 \times 0.18 \times 4.75 \times 24$	=	102.6	−1.66	−170.3
Base	$5 \times 0.25 \times 3.5 \times 24$	=	105.0	0	0
Counterfort	$0.5 \times 4.75 \times 3.32 \times 0.25 \times 24$	=	47.3	−0.46	−21.8
Earth	$4.5 \times 4.75 \times 3.32 \times 15.7$	=	1114.2	+0.09	100.3
	$0.5 \times 3.32 \times 4.75 \times 0.25 \times 15.7$	=	30.9	+0.64	19.8
Total			1400.0		72.0

(i) *Maximum soil pressure*   The properties of the base are as follows:

$$\text{area } A = 3.5 \times 5 = 17.5 \, \text{m}^2$$
$$\text{modulus } Z = 5 \times 3.5^2/6 = 10.21 \, \text{m}^3$$

The maximum soil pressure is

$$\frac{1400}{17.5} + \frac{546.9 - 72}{10.21} = 80 + 46.5 = 126.5 \, \text{kN/m}^2$$

The pressure under the base is shown in Fig. 12.8. The maximum soil pressure is satisfactory.

(ii) *Stability against overturning*   The stabilizing moment about the toe A of the wall for a partial safety factor $\gamma_f = 1.0$ is

$$(1400 \times 1.75) + 72 = 2522 \, \text{kN m}$$

The overturning moment for a partial safety factor $\gamma_f = 1.4$ is

$$1.4 \times 546.9 = 765.7 \, \text{kN m}$$

The stability of the wall is adequate.

(iii) *Resistance to sliding*   The friction force resisting sliding is

$$0.5 \times 1400 = 700 \, \text{kN}$$

For the wall to be safe against sliding

$$700 > 1.4 \times 327.5 = 458.5 \, \text{kN}$$

The resistance to sliding is satisfactory.

(iv) *Overall comment*   The wall section is satisfactory. The maximum soil pressure under the base controls the design.

(d) Wall design

The yield line solution is given for a square wall with a triangular load with the yield line pattern shown in Fig. 12.9(a). One parameter z, locating F, controls the pattern.

Expressions for values and locations of the centroids of loads on triangular plates are shown in Fig. 12.10(a). The expressions for the loads and deflections of the centroids of the loads for the various parts of the wall slab are shown in Figs 12.10(b), 12.10(c) and 12.10(d) respectively.

Formulae for the work done by the loads found by multiplying each load by its appropriate deflection from Fig. 12.10 are given in Table 12.3(a). The work done by the load is given by the expression

$$\frac{wz^3\theta}{24} - \frac{waz^2\theta}{6} + \frac{wa^2z\theta}{4}$$

The slab is to be reinforced equally in both directions and the reinforcements for sagging and hogging moments will be made equal. The ultimate resistance moment in all yield lines is taken as m kN m/m. The work done in the yield lines is given by the expression

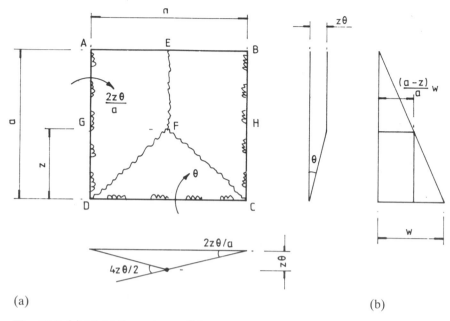

(a)   (b)

Fig. 12.9 (a) Yield line pattern; (b) pressure.

$$2ma\theta + 8mz\theta$$

and formulae are given in Table 12.3(b). Equate the work expressions to give

$$m = \frac{wz^3/24 - waz^2/6 + wa^2z/4}{2a + 8z}$$

Put $dM/dz = 0$ and reduce to give

$$\frac{2wz^3}{3} - \frac{13waz^2}{12} - \frac{2wa^2z}{3} + \frac{wa^3}{2} = 0$$

The maximum pressure w on the wall slab is

$$1.4 \times 26.2 = 36.7 \, \text{kN/m}^2$$

and the dimension $a = 5 \, \text{m}$. The equation becomes

$$z^3 - 8.12z^2 - 25z + 93.75 = 0$$

Solve to give $z = 2.43 \, \text{m}$. Then $m = 13.54 \, \text{kN m/m}$. Increase the moment by 10% to allow for the formation of corner levers. The design moment is

$$m = 14.89 \, \text{kN m/m}$$

Use 10 mm diameter bars and 40 mm cover.

$$d = 180 - 40 - 10 - 5 = 125 \, \text{mm}$$

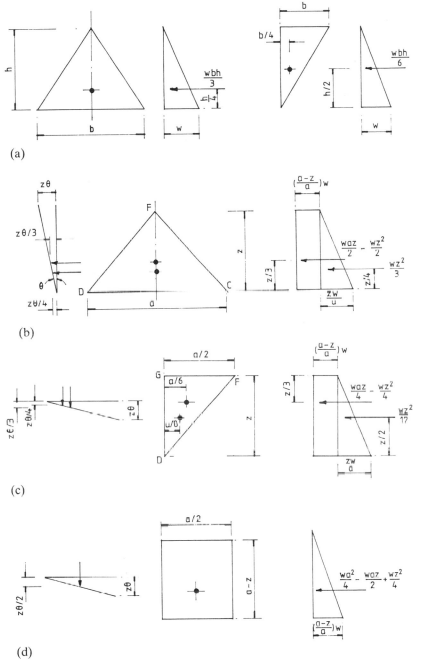

Fig. 12.10 (a) Plates subjected to triangular loads; (b) plate DFC; (c) plate GFD; (d) plate AEFG.

Table 12.3(a) Work done by loads

Area	Load	Deflection	Work = load × deflection
DFC	$\dfrac{waz}{2} - \dfrac{wz^2}{2}$	$\dfrac{z\theta}{3}$	$\dfrac{waz^2\theta}{6} - \dfrac{wz^3\theta}{6}$
	$\dfrac{wz^2}{3}$	$\dfrac{z\theta}{4}$	$+\dfrac{wz^3\theta}{12}$
GFD	$\dfrac{waz}{2} - \dfrac{wz^2}{2}$	$\dfrac{z\theta}{3}$	$\dfrac{waz^2\theta}{6} - \dfrac{wz^3\theta}{6}$
FHC	$\dfrac{wz^2}{6}$	$\dfrac{z\theta}{4}$	$+\dfrac{wz^3\theta}{24}$
AEFG EBHF	$\dfrac{wa^2}{2} - waz + \dfrac{wz^2}{2}$	$\dfrac{z\theta}{2}$	$-\dfrac{waz^2\theta}{2} + \dfrac{wz^3\theta}{4} + \dfrac{wa^2z\theta}{4}$
		Σ	$-\dfrac{waz^2\theta}{6} + \dfrac{wz^3\theta}{24} + \dfrac{wa^2z\theta}{4}$

Table 12.3(b) Work done in yield lines

Line	Length L	Rotation ϕ in yield line	No. off	Work = $mL\phi$ × no.
DC	a	θ	1	$ma\theta$
AD BC	a	$\dfrac{2z\theta}{a}$	2	$4mz\theta$
EF	$a - z$	$\dfrac{4z\theta}{a}$	1	$4mz\theta - \dfrac{4m^2z^2\theta}{a}$
DF	z	$\dfrac{2z\theta}{a}$ (on AD)	2	$+\dfrac{4mz^2\theta}{a}$
EC	$\dfrac{a}{2}$	θ (on DC)	2	$ma\theta$
			Σ	$2\,ma\theta + 8mz\theta$

$$\frac{m}{bd^2f_{cu}} = \frac{14.89 \times 10^6}{1000 \times 125^2 \times 35} = 0.027$$

Referring to Fig. 4.14, $z/d = 0.95$ and

$$A_s = \frac{14.89 \times 10^6}{0.87 \times 460 \times 0.95 \times 125} = 313.3 \text{ mm}^2/\text{m}$$

Provide 10 mm diameter bars at 240 mm centres to give a steel area of 327 mm^2/m. The same steel is provided in each direction on the outside and inside of the wall.

The steel on the outside of the wall covers the whole area. On the inside of the wall the steel can be cut off at 0.3 times the span from the bottom and from each counterfort support in accordance with the simplified rules for curtailment of bars in slabs.

Alternatively, the points of cut-off of the bars on the inside of the wall may be determined by finding the size of a simply supported slab that has the same ultimate moment of resistance $m = 13.54$ kN m/m as the whole wall. This slab has the same yield line pattern as the wall slab.

The clear spacing of the bars does not exceed $3d$ and the slab depth is not greater than 200 mm and so the slab is satisfactory with respect to cracking.   ■

13

Reinforced concrete framed buildings

13.1 TYPES AND STRUCTURAL ACTION

Commonly used single-storey and medium-rise reinforced concrete framed structures are shown in Fig. 13.1. Tall multistorey buildings are discussed in Chapter 14. Only cast-*in-situ* rigid jointed frames are dealt with, but the structures shown in the figure could also be precast.

The loads are transmitted by roof and floor slabs and walls to beams and to rigid frames and through the columns to the foundations. In cast-*in-situ* buildings with monolithic floor slabs the frame consists of flanged beams and rectangular columns. However, it is common practice to base the analysis on the rectangular beam section, but in the design for sagging moments the flanged section is used. If precast slabs are used the beam sections are rectangular.

Depending on the floor system and framing arrangement adopted the structure may be idealized into a series of plane frames in each direction for analysis and design. Such a system where two-way floor slabs are used is shown in Fig. 13.2; the frames in each direction carry part of the load. In the complete three-dimensional frame, torsion occurs in the beams and biaxial bending in the columns. These effects are small and it is stated in BS 8110: Part 1, clause 3.8.4.3, that it is usually only necessary to design for the maximum moment about the critical axis. In rectangular buildings with a one-way floor system, the transverse rigid frame across the shorter plan dimension carries the load. Such a frame is shown in the design example in section 13.5.

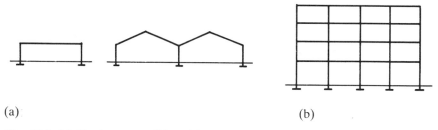

(a)   (b)

Fig. 13.1 (a) Single storey; (b) multistorey.

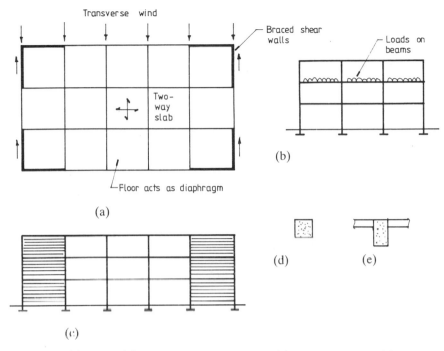

Fig. 13.2 (a) Plan; (b) rigid transverse frame; (c) side elevation; (d) column; (e) T-beam.

Resistance to horizontal wind loads is provided by

1 braced structures – shear walls, lift shaft and stairs
2. unbraced structures – bending in the rigid frames

The analysis for combined shear wall, rigid frame systems is discussed in Chapter 14.

In multistorey buildings, the most stable arrangement is obtained by bracing with shear walls in two directions. Stairwells, lift shafts, permanent partition walls as well as specially designed outside shear walls can be used to resist the horizontal loading. Shear walls should be placed symmetrically with respect to the building axes. If this is not done the shear walls must be designed to resist the resulting torque. The concrete floor slabs act as large horizontal diaphragms to transfer loads at floor levels to the shear walls. BS 8110: Part 1, clause 3.9.2.2, should be noted: it is stated that the overall stability of a multistorey building should not depend on unbraced shear walls alone. Shear walls in a multistorey building are shown in Fig. 13.2.

Foundations for multistorey buildings may be separate pad or strip type. However, rafts or composite raft and basement foundations are more usual. For raft type foundations the column base may be taken as fixed for frame analysis. The stability of the whole building must be considered and the stabilizing moment from dead loads should prevent the structure from overturning.

Separate pad type foundations should only be used for multistorey buildings if foundation conditions are good and differential settlement will not occur. For single-storey buildings, separate foundations are usually provided and, in poor soil conditions, pinned bases can be more economical than fixed bases. The designer must be satisfied that the restraint conditions assumed for analysis can be achieved in practice. If a fixed base settles or rotates a redistribution of moments occurs in the frame.

13.2 BUILDING LOADS

The load on buildings is due to dead, imposed, wind, dynamic, seismic and accidental loads. In the UK, multistorey buildings for office or residential purposes are designed for dead, imposed and wind loads. The design is checked and adjusted to allow for the effects of accidental loads. The types of load are discussed briefly.

13.2.1 Dead load

Dead load is due to the weight of roofs, floors, beams, walls, columns, floor finishes, partitions, ceilings, services etc. The load is estimated from assumed section sizes and allowances are made for further dead loads that are additional to the structural concrete.

13.2.2 Imposed load

Imposed load depends on the occupancy or use of the building and includes distributed loads, concentrated loads, impact, inertia and snow. Loads for all types of buildings are given in BS 6399: Part 1.

13.2.3 Wind loads

Wind load on buildings is estimated in accordance with CP 3: Chapter V: Part 2. The following factors are taken into consideration:

1. The basic wind speed V depends on the location in the country.
2. The design wind speed V_s is $VS_1S_2S_3$ where S_1 is a topography factor normally taken as 1, S_2 depends on ground roughness, building size and height above the ground and S_3 is a statistical factor, normally taken as 1.

    The ground roughness is in four categories in which category 3 is a location in the suburbs of a city. The building size is in three classes.

Class B refers to a building where neither the greatest horizontal dimension nor the greatest vertical dimension exceeds 50 m. Class C buildings are larger.

The height may refer to the total height of the building or the height of the part under consideration. In a multistorey building the wind load increases with height and the factor S_2 should be increased at every floor or every three or four floors (Fig. 13.3(b)).

3. The dynamic pressure $q = 0.613 V_s^2\,N/m^2$ is the pressure on a surface normal to the wind and is modified by the dimensions of the building and by openings in the building.
4. Pressure coefficients are given for individual surfaces. External pressure coefficients C_{pe} that depend on dimensions and roof angles are estimated for external surfaces. Depending on whether openings occur on the windward or leeward sides, internal pressure or suction exists inside the building. Tables and guidance are given in the code for evaluating external and internal pressure coefficients C_{pe} and C_{pi}.
5. The wind force F on a surface is

$$F = (C_{pe} - C_{pi})qA$$

where A is the area of the surface and C_{pe} and C_{pi} are added algebraically. The force acts normal to the surface. Distributed wind loads on the surfaces of a building are shown in Fig. 13.3(a).
6. Force coefficients C_f are given to find the wind load on the building as a whole. The wind load is given by

$$F = C_f q A_e$$

C_f is the force coefficient and A_e is the effective frontal area of the building. The use of force coefficients is an alternative to determining wind loads on individual surfaces. This method is used for multistorey buildings. See Fig. 3.13(b) where the wind load is applied as point loads at the floor levels.

Wind loads should be calculated for lateral and longitudinal directions to obtain loads on frames or shear walls to provide stability in each direction. In asymmetrical buildings it may be necessary to investigate wind from all directions.

13.2.4 Load combinations

Separate loads must be applied to the structure in appropriate directions and various types of loading combined with partial safety factors selected to cause the most severe design condition for the member under consideration. In general the following load combinations should be investigated.

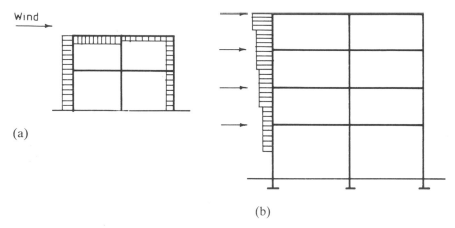

(a)

(b)

Fig. 13.3 (a) Loads distributed on surfaces; (b) loads applied at floor levels.

(a) Dead load G_k + imposed load Q_k

1. All spans are loaded with the maximum design load of $1.4G_k + 1.6Q_k$;
2. Alternate spans are loaded with the maximum design load of $1.4G_k + 1.6Q_k$ and all other spans are loaded with the minimum design load of $1.0G_k$.

(b) Dead load G_k + wind load W_k

If dead load and wind load act in the same direction or their effects are additive the load combination is $1.4(G_k + W_k)$. However, if the effects are in opposite directions, e.g. wind uplift, the critical load combination is $1.0G_k - 1.4W_k$.

(c) Dead load G_k + imposed load Q_k + wind load W_k

The structure is to be loaded with $1.2(G_k + Q_k + W_k)$.

13.3 ROBUSTNESS AND DESIGN OF TIES

Clause 2.2.2.2 of the code states that situations should be avoided where damage to a small area or failure of a single element could lead to collapse of major parts of the structure. The clause states that provision of effective ties is one of the precautions necessary to prevent progressive collapse. The layout also must be such as to give a stable and robust structure.

The design of ties set out in section 3.12.3 of the code is summarized below.

13.3.1 Types of tie

The types of tie are

1. peripheral ties
2. internal ties
3. horizontal ties to columns and walls
4. vertical ties

The types and location of ties are shown in Fig. 13.4.

13.3.2 Design of ties

Steel reinforcement provided for a tie can be designed to act at its characteristic strength. Reinforcement provided for other purposes may form the whole or part of the ties. Ties must be properly anchored and a tie is considered anchored to another at right angles if it extends 12 diameters or an equivalent anchorage length beyond the bar forming the other tie.

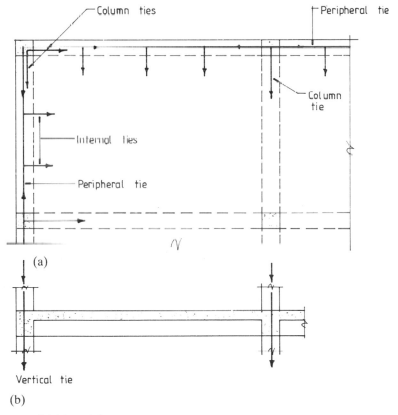

Fig. 13.4 (a) Plan; (b) section.

13.3.3 Internal ties

Internal ties are to be provided at the roof and all floors in two directions at right angles. They are to be continuous throughout their length and anchored to peripheral ties. The ties may be spread evenly in slabs or be grouped in beams or walls at spacings not greater than $1.5l_r$ where l_r is defined below. Ties in walls are to be within $0.5\,\mathrm{m}$ of the top or bottom of the floor slab.

The ties should be capable of resisting a tensile force which is the greater of

$$\frac{g_k + q_k}{7.5}\frac{l_r}{5}F_t$$

or $1.0F_t$, where $g_k + q_k$ is the characteristic dead plus imposed floor load $(\mathrm{kN/m^2})$, F_t is the lesser of $(20 + 4n_0)$ or $60\,\mathrm{kN}$, n_0 is the number of storeys and l_r is the greater of the distance in metres between the centres of columns, frames or walls supporting any two adjacent floor spans in the direction of the tie.

13.3.4 Peripheral ties

A continuous peripheral tie is to be provided at each floor and at the roof. This tie is to resist F_t as defined above and is to be located within $1.2\,\mathrm{m}$ of the edge of the building or within the perimeter wall.

13.3.5 Horizontal ties to columns and walls

Each external column and, if a peripheral tie is not located within the wall, every metre length of external wall carrying vertical load should be tied horizontally into the structure at each floor and at roof level. The tie capacity is to be the greater of $2F_t$ or $(l_s/2.5)F_t$ if less or 3% of the ultimate vertical load carried by the column or wall where l_s is the floor-to-ceiling height in metres.

Where the peripheral tie is located within the walls the internal ties are to be anchored to it.

13.3.6 Corner column ties

Corner columns are to be anchored in two directions at right angles. The tie capacity is the same as specified in section 13.3.5 above.

13.3.7 Vertical ties

Vertical ties are required in buildings of five or more storeys. Each column and loadbearing wall is to be tied continuously from foundation to roof.

The tie is to be capable of carrying a tensile force equal to the ultimate dead and imposed load carried by the column or wall from one floor.

13.4 FRAME ANALYSIS

13.4.1 Methods of analysis

The methods of frame analysis that are used may be classified as

1. manual methods such as moment distribution or using solutions for standard frames
2. simplified manual methods of analysing subframes given in section 3.2.1 of the code (these are set out in section 3.4.2 here and are shown in Fig. 3.3)
3. computer plane frame programs based on the matrix stiffness method of analysis (refer to standard textbooks on structural analysis [12, 13])

All methods are based on elastic theory. BS 8110 permits redistribution of up to 30% of the peak elastic moment to be made in frames up to four storeys. In frames over four storeys in height where the frame provides the lateral stability, redistribution is limited to 10%.

In rigid frame analysis the sizes for members must be chosen from experience or established by an approximate design before the analysis can be carried out because the moment distribution depends on the member stiffness. Ratios of stiffnesses of the final member sections should be checked against those estimated and the frame should be re-analysed if it is found necessary to change the sizes of members significantly.

It is stated in BS 8110: Part 1, clause 2.5.2, that the relative stiffness of members may be based on one of the following sections:

1. the gross concrete section ignoring the steel
2. the gross concrete section including the reinforcement on the basis of modular ratio, i.e. the transformed section that includes the whole of the concrete
3. the transformed section consisting of the compression area of concrete and the reinforcement on the basis of modular ratio

A modular ratio of 15 can be assumed. The code states that a consistent approach should be used throughout. It is usual to use the first method because only gross section sizes have to be assumed and if these prove satisfactory the design is accepted.

As noted previously in beam – slab floor construction it is normal practice to base the beam stiffness on a uniform rectangular section consisting of the beam depth by the beam rib width. The flanged beam section is taken into account in the beam design for sagging moments near the centre of spans.

☐ Example 13.1 Simplified analysis of concrete framed building – vertical load

The application of the various simplified methods of analysis given in section 3.2 of the code is shown in the following example.

(a) Specification

The cross-section of a reinforced concrete building is shown in Fig. 13.5(a). The frames are at 4.5 m centres, the length of the building is 36 m and the column bases are fixed. Preliminary sections for the beams and columns are shown in Fig. 13.5(b). The floor and roof slabs are designed to span one way between the frames. Longitudinal beams are provided between external columns of the roof and floor levels only.

The loading is as follows: for the roof

$$\text{total dead load} = 4.3 \, \text{kN/m}^2$$
$$\text{imposed load} = 1.5 \, \text{kN/m}^2$$

and for the floors

$$\text{total dead load} = 6.2 \, \text{kN/m}^2$$
$$\text{imposed load} = 3.0 \, \text{kN/m}^2$$

The wind load is according to CP3: Chapter V: Part 2. The location is on the outskirts of a city in the northeast of the UK.

The materials are grade 30 concrete and grade 460 reinforcement. Determine the design actions for the beam BFK and column length FE for an internal frame for the two cases where the frame is braced and unbraced. Results for selected cases using only the simplified method of analysis from BS 8110: Part 1, section 3.2, are given.

(b) Loading

The following load cases are required for beam BFK for the braced frame.

Case 1 $1.4G_k + 1.6 Q_k$ on the whole beam
Case 2 $1.4G_k + 1.6Q_k$ on BF and $1.0G_k$ on FK
Case 3 $1.0G_k$ on BF and $1.4G_k + 1.6Q_k$ on FK

For the unbraced frame, an additional load case is required:

Case 4 $1.2(G_k + Q_k)$ on the whole beam

The characteristic loads are as follows. For the dead load,

Roof $4.3 \times 4.5 = 19.4 \, \text{kN/m}$
Floors $6.2 \times 4.5 = 27.9 \, \text{kN/m}$

For the imposed load,

Roof $1.5 \times 4.5 = 6.8 \, \text{kN/m}$
Floors $3.0 \times 4.5 = 13.5 \, \text{kN/m}$

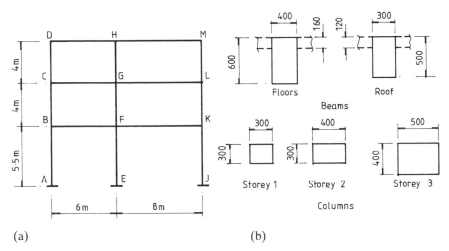

(a)   (b)

Fig. 13.5 (a) Cross-section; (b) assumed member sections.

The dead load on column GF just above first floor level is

$$7 \times 4.5 \, (4.3 + 6.2) + (0.3 \times 0.44 + 0.3 \times 0.38)$$
$$\times 7 \times 24 + (0.3^2 + 0.3 \times 0.4)4 \times 24 = 392.3 \text{kN}$$

and the imposed load is

$$7 \times 4.5(1.5 + 3) = 141.8 \text{ kN}$$

In accordance with BS 6399, Table 2, the axial load in the column due to imposed load may be reduced by 30% for a column carrying three floors including the roof. The design loads for beam BFK for case 1 are shown in Fig. 13.6.

The wind loads are calculated using CP 3: Chapter 5: Part 2:

Basic wind speed $V_s = 45 \text{ m/s}$
Topography factor S_1 and statistical factor S_2 both   1.0
Ground roughness 3
Building size Class B

The heights for estimating S_2, the S_2 factors, the design wind speeds and the dynamic pressures are shown in Table 13.1. The force coefficient for the wind blowing laterally for

$$l/w = 36/14 = 2.6 = b/d$$
$$h/w = 13.5/14 = 0.97$$

is $C_f = 1.13$, from CP 3: Chapter V: Part 2, Table 10. The wind pressures and characteristic wind loads for the frame are shown in Fig. 13.7.

(c) Section properties

The beam and column properties are given in Table 13.2. Distribution factors are calculated for the particular analysis.

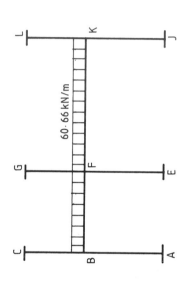

A	B			C	E	F				G	J	K			L
AB	BA	BF	BC	CB	EF	FE	FB	FG	FK	GF	JK	KJ	KF	KL	LK
	0·32	0·51	0·17			0·23	0·37	0·12	0·28			0·37	0·44	0·19	
	58·2	−181·9 92·8	30·9			32·5	181·9 52·3	16·9	−323·2 39·6			−119·6	323·2 −142·2	−61·4	
29·1	−8·3	26·2 −13·4	−4·5	15·5	16·3	5·7	46·4 9·1	3·0	−71·1 6·9	8·5	−59·8	−7·3	19·8 −8·7	−3·8	−30·7
−4·2	−1·5	4·6 −2·3	−0·8	−2·3	2·9	2·6	−6·7 4·1	1·3	−4·4 3·1	1·5	−3·7	−1·3	3·5 −1·5	−0·7	−1·9
24·9	48·4	−74·0	25·6	13·3	19·2	40·8	287·1	21·2	−349·1	10·0	−63·5	−128·2	194·1	−65·9	−32·6

Fig. 13.6

Table 13.1 Wind load data

Location	H (m)	S_2	$V_s = S_2V$ (m/s)	$q = 0.613V_s^2/10^3$ (kN/m²)
Roof	13.5	0.8	36	0.79
Second floor	11.5	0.77	34.7	0.74
First floor	7.5	0.7	31.5	0.61

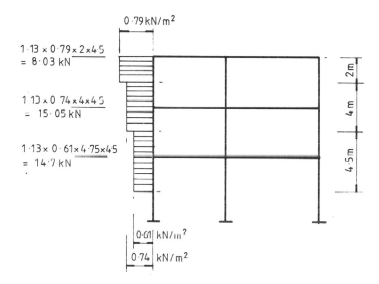

Fig. 13.7

Table 13.2 Section properties

Member	Length l (mm)	Moment of intertia I (mm⁴)	Stiffness $K\alpha I/l$
Column FE	5500	4.17×10^9	7.55×10^5
Column GF	4000	$1.6 \ \times 10^9$	$4.0 \ \times 10^5$
Beam FK	8000	$7.2 \ \times 10^9$	$9.0 \ \times 10^5$
Beam BF	6000	$7.2 \ \times 10^9$	$12.0 \ \times 10^5$

(d) Subframe analysis for braced frame

The subframe consists of the beams at first floor level and the columns above and below that level with ends fixed. The frame is analysed for the dead and imposed load cases given in (b) above.

The distribution factors at the joints of the subframe are, for joint B

$$BC : BF : BA = \frac{4 : 12 : 7.58}{23.58}$$

$$= 0.17 : 0.51 : 0.32$$

for joint F

$$FB : FG : FK : FE = 0.37 : 0.12 : 0.28 : 0.23$$

and for joint K

$$KL : KF : KJ = 0.19 : 0.44 : 0.37$$

The design loads are

$$1.4G_k + 1.6Q_k = 1.4 \times 27.9 + 1.6 \times 13.5 = 60.66 \, \text{kN/m}$$
$$1.0G_k = 27.9 \, \text{kN/m}$$

The fixed end moments are, for case 1 ($1.4G_k + 1.6Q_k$ on the whole beam),

$$\text{span BF} = 60.66 \times 6^2/12 = 181.98 \, \text{kN m}$$
$$\text{span FK} = 60.66 \times 8^2/12 = 323.2 \, \text{kN m}$$

The moment distribution for case 1 is shown in Fig. 13.6. The shear force and bending moment diagram for beam BFK and the bending moment diagram for column FE are shown in Fig. 13.8. Analyses are also required for cases 2 and 3.

(e) Continuous beam simplification

The beam BFK can be taken as a continuous beam over supports that provide no restraint to rotation. The load cases are the same as for the subframe analysis above. The shear force and bending moment diagrams for the beam are shown in Fig. 13.8(b). Analyses are also required for cases 2 and 3.

The moments for column FE are calculated assuming that column and beam ends remote from the junction considered are fixed and that beams have one-half their actual stiffness. The bending moment diagram for the column for case 1 loads is also shown in Fig. 13.8.

Referring to Fig. 13.8(b), the beam ends B and K must be designed for hogging moments that will arise from the monolithic construction of the beams and columns. These moments should be taken to be equal to those found from the subframe analyses for the asymmetrically loaded outer columns. ∎

□ Example 13.2 Wind load analysis – portal method

The analysis for vertical loads can be made in the same way as for the braced frames using any of the subframe methods given. The load in this case is $1.2(G_k + Q_k)$.

The analysis for the wind load is made for the whole frame assuming points of

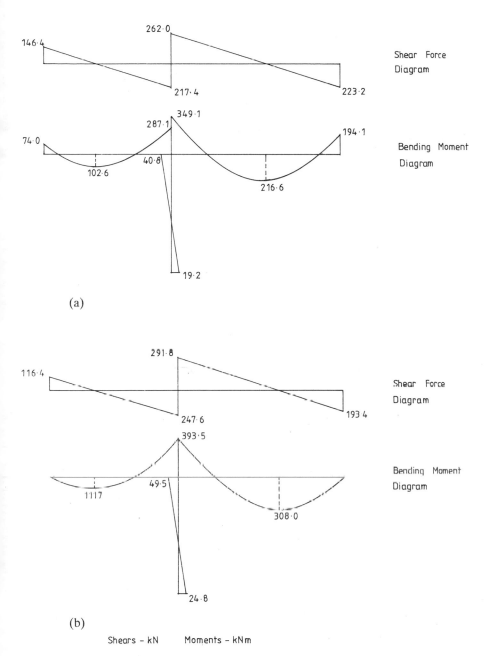

Shear Force Diagram

Bending Moment Diagram

(a)

Shear Force Diagram

Bending Moment Diagram

(b)

Shears – kN   Moments – kNm

Fig. 13.8 (a) Subframe analysis; (b) continuous beam simplification.

contraflexure at the centres of columns and beams. In the portal method the shear in each storey is assumed to be divided between the bays in proportion to their spans. The shear in each bay is then divided equally between the columns. The column end moments are the column shear multiplied by one-half the column height. Beam moments balance the column moments. The external columns only resist axial load which is found by dividing the overturning moment at any level by the width of the building. The application of the method is shown in the analyses of the frame for wind loads shown in Fig. 13.7.

The moments in the first and second storey only are calculated (Fig. 13.9). The wind loads from Fig. 13.7 have been multiplied by 1.2 to give shears in Fig. 13.9.

For the second storey the shear is $9.7 + 18.1 = 27.8 \, \text{kN}$. Divide between bays in proportion to spans:

$$\text{Bay BF} \quad \text{shear} = 6 \times 27.8/14 = 11.9 \, \text{kN}$$
$$\text{Bay FK} \quad \text{shear} = 15.9 \, \text{kN}$$

The column shears are as follows:

$$\text{Column BC} \quad 5.95 \, \text{kN}$$
$$\text{Column FG} \quad 0.5(11.9 + 15.9) = 13.9 \, \text{kN}$$
$$\text{Column KL} \quad 7.95 \, \text{kN}$$

The column moments are as follows:

$$\text{Column BC} \quad 5.95 \times 2 = 11.9 \, \text{kN m}$$
$$\text{Column FG} \quad 13.9 \times 2 = 27.8 \, \text{kN m}$$
$$\text{Column KL} \quad 7.95 \times 2 = 15.9 \, \text{kN m}$$

The moments for columns in the first storey can be calculated in a similar way:

$$\text{Column AB} \quad 26.8 \, \text{kN m}$$
$$\text{Column EF} \quad 62.4 \, \text{kN m}$$
$$\text{Column JK} \quad 35.6 \, \text{kN m}$$

The beam moments balance the column moments:

Joint B   sum of column moments $= 26.8 + 11.9$
$$= 38.7 \, \text{kN m} = M_{BF}$$
Joint K   sum of column moments $= 51.5 \, \text{kN m} = M_{KF}$
Joint F   sum of column moments $= 27.8 + 62.4$
$$= 90.2 \, \text{kN m}$$
sum of beam moments $= 38.7 + 51.5$
$$= 90.2 \, \text{kN m}$$

The moments are shown in Fig. 13.9.   ■

□ Example 13.3 Wind load analysis – cantilever method

The axial loads in the column are assumed to be proportional to the distance from the centre of gravity of the frame. The columns are taken to be of equal area. Refer to Fig. 13.10. The centre of gravity of the columns is $(8 + 14)/3 = 7.33 \, \text{m}$ from column MJ. The column forces are

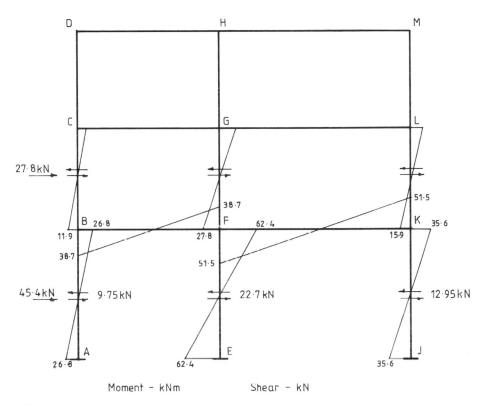

Fig. 13.9

at D, 6.67F;   at H, 0.67F;   at M, 7.33F

Take moments about X; $\Sigma M_x = 0$:

$$8.03 \times 2 + 0.67F \times 6.67 - 7.33F \times 14 = 0$$
$$F = 0.164\,\text{kN}$$

The separate column forces are

at D, 1.09 kN;   at H, 0.11 kN;   at M, 1.2 kN

The shear in beam DII is 1.09 kN and in beam HM 1.2 kN.

The shear in the column is found by taking moments about the centre of the beams, e.g.

Column D shear = 1.09 × 3/2 = 1.64 kN
Column M shear = 1.2 × 4/2 = 2.4 kN
Column H shear = 8.03 − 1.64 − 2.4 = 3.99 kN

The forces in the other two sections XY and YZ are found in the same way. These are shown in Fig. 13.10.

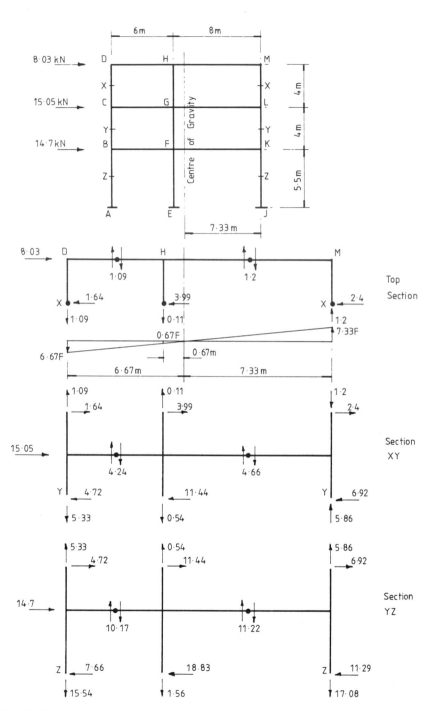

Fig. 13.10

The column and beam moments are found by multiplying the appropriate shear force by one-half the member length. For example,

Column FE $M_F = M_E = 18.83 \times 2.75 = 51.78 \times 1.2 = 62.1\,\text{kN m}$
Beam BF $M_B = M_F = 10.17 \times 3 = 30.51 \times 1.2 = 36.6\,\text{kN m}$
Beam FK $M_F = M_K = 11.22 \times 4 = 44.88 \times 1.2 = 53.8\,\text{kN m}$

The final moments are multiplied by 1.2 to give the design moments. Compare moments with those obtained by the portal method. ∎

13.5 BUILDING DESIGN EXAMPLE

☐ Example 13.4 Design of multi-storey reinforced concrete framed buildings

Specification

The framing plans for a multistorey building are shown in Fig. 13.11. The main dimensions, structural features, loads, materials etc. are set out below.

(a) Overall dimensions

The overall dimensions are $36\,\text{m} \times 22\,\text{m}$ in plan $\times$ 36 m high

Length, six bays at 6 m each   36 m
Breadth, three bays, 8 m, 6 m, 8 m   22 m
Height, ten storeys, nine at 3.5 m + one at 4.5 m

(b) Roof and floors

The floors and roof are constructed in one-way ribbed slabs spanning along the length of the building. Slabs are made solid for 300 mm on either side of the beam.

(c) Stability

Stability is provided by shear walls at the lift shafts and staircases in the end bays.

(d) Fire resistance

All elements are to have a fire resistance period of 2 h.

(e) Loading condition

Roof imposed load $1.5\,\text{kN/m}^2$
Floors imposed load $3.0\,\text{kN/m}^2$
Finishes – roof $1.5\,\text{kN/m}^2$
Finishes – floors, partitions, ceilings, services $3.0\,\text{kN/m}^2$

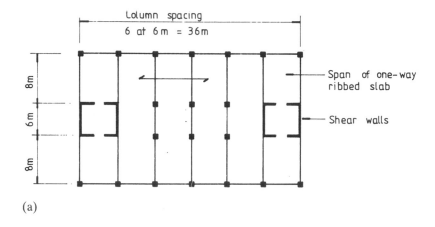

(a)

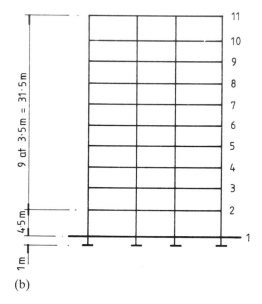

(b)

Fig. 13.11 (a) Floor and roof plan; (b) elevation.

Parapet	2.0 kN/m
External walls at each floor	6.0 kN/m

The load due to self-weight is estimated from preliminary sizing of members. The imposed load contributing to axial load in the columns is reduced by 50% for a building with ten floors including the roof.

(f) Exposure conditions

> External   moderate
> Internal   mild

(g) Materials

> Concrete   grade 30
> Reinforcement   grade 460

(h) Foundations

Pile foundations are provided under each column and under the shear walls.

Scope of the work

The work carried out covers analysis and design for

1. transverse frame members at floor 2 outer span only
2. an internal column between floors 1 and 2

The design is to meet requirements for robustness. In this design, the frame is taken as completely braced by the shear walls in both directions. A link-frame analysis can be carried out to determine the share of wind load carried by the rigid frames (Chapter 14). The design for dead and imposed load will be the critical design load case.

Preliminary sizes and self-weights of members

(a) Floor and roof slab

The one-way ribbed slab is designed first. The size is shown in Fig. 13.12. For design refer to Example 8.2. The weight of the ribbed slab is

$$2 \times 24[(0.5 \times 0.275) - (0.375 \times 0.215)] = 2.73 \, \text{kN/m}^2$$

(b) Beam sizes

Beam sizes are specified from experience:

> depth $-$ span/15 $-$ 500 mm, say
> width $= 0.6 \times$ depth $= 400$ mm, say

Preliminary beam sizes for roof and floors are shown in Fig. 13.12. The weights of the beams including the solid part of the slab are: roof beams, $24[(0.3 \times 0.45) + (0.6 \times 0.275)] = 7.2 \, \text{kN/m}$ and floor beams, 8.8 kN/m.

(c) Column sizes

Preliminary sizes are shown in Fig. 13.12. The self-weights are as follows.

> Floors 1 to 3 $0.55^2 \times 24 = 7.3 \, \text{kN/m}$

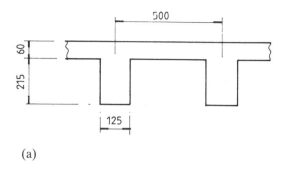

(a)

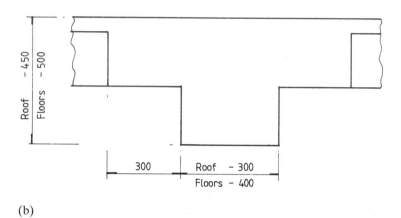

(b)

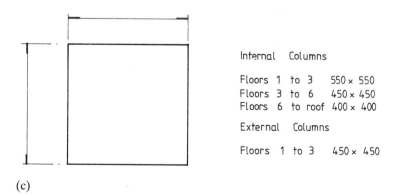

(c)

Fig. 13.12 (a) Roof and floor slab; (b) roof and floor beams; (c) columns.

Floors 3 to 7 $0.45^2 \times 24 = 4.9\,\text{kN/m}$
Floor 7 to roof $0.4^2 \times 24 = 3.8\,\text{kN/m}$

Vertical loads

(a) Roof beam

The dead load (slab, beam, finishes) is

$$(2.73 \times 5.1) + 7.2 + (1.5 \times 6) = 35\,\text{kN/m}$$

The imposed load is

$$6 \times 1.5 = 9\,\text{kN/m}$$

(b) Floor beams

The dead load is

$$(2.73 \times 5) + 8.8 + (3 \times 6) = 40.5\,\text{kN/m}$$

and the imposed load is

$$6 \times 3 = 18\,\text{kN/m}$$

(c) Internal column below floor 2

The dead load is

$$7[35 + (40.5 \times 9)] + 3.5[7.3 + 4(4.9 + 3.8)] = 2939.7\,\text{kN}$$

and the imposed load is

$$7 \times 0.5[9 + (18 \times 9)] = 598.5\,\text{kN}$$

The imposed load has been reduced 50%.

Subframe analysis

(a) Subframe

The subframe consisting of the beams and columns above and below the floor level 1 is shown in Fig. 13.13.

(b) Distribution factors

The distribution factors are

Joints B and M $K_{BA} : K_{BE} : K_{BC} = 0.43 : 0.23 : 0.34$
Joints E and H $K_{EB} : K_{ED} : K_{EH} : K_{EF} = 0.1 : 0.43 : 0.14 : 0.33$

The distribution factors are shown in the figure.

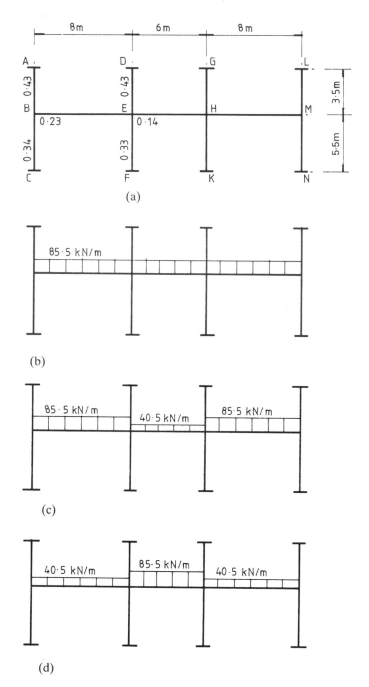

Fig. 13.13 (a) Subframe; (b) case 1, all spans $1.4G_k + 1.6Q_k$; (c) case 2A, maximum load on outer spans; (d) case 2B, maximum load on centre span.

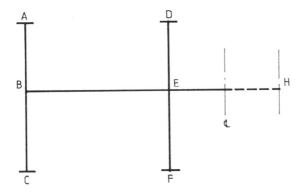

C	B			A	F	E				D
CB	BC	BE	BA	AB	FE	EF	EB	ED	EH	DE
	0.34	0.23	0.43			0.33	0.1	0.43	0.14	
	155.1	-456 104.8	196.1			-65.8	456 -20.0	-85.8	-256.5 -27.9	
77.6	3.4	-10.0 2.3	4.3	98.1	-32.9	21.9	52.4 -6.6	-28.5	13.9 -9.3	-42.9
1.7	1.1	-3.3 0.8	1.4	2.2	-10.9	-1.9	1.2 -0.6	-2.6	4.7 -0.8	-14.3
79.8	159.6	-361.4	201.8	100.3	-43.8	-89.6	482.4	-117.0	-275.8	-57.2

Fig. 13.14

(c) Loads and load combinations

(i) Case 1   All spans are loaded with the maximum design load $1.4G_k + 1.6Q_k$:

$$\text{design load} = (1.4 \times 40.5) + (1.6 \times 18)$$
$$= 85.5 \, \text{kN/m}$$

The fixed end moments are

Spans BE, HM $85.5 \times 8^2/12 = 456 \, \text{kN m}$
Span EH $256.5 \, \text{kN m}$

(ii) Case 2 Alternate spans are loaded with the maximum design load $1.4G_k + 1.6Q_k$ and the other spans are loaded with $1.0G_k$:

$$\text{design load} = 1.0G_k = 40.5\,\text{kN/m}$$

The design load cases are shown in Fig. 13.13. Case 2 involves two separate analyses (A and B).

(d) Analysis

The moment distribution for case 1 is shown in Fig. 13.14. The shear force and bending moment diagrams for the load cases are shown in Fig. 13.15.

Design of the outer span of beam BEH

(a) Design of moment reinforcement

(i) Section at mid-span, M = 267 kN m (Fig. 13.15)   The exposure is mild, and the fire resistance 2 h. Cover is 30 mm for a continuous beam. Refer to BS 8110: Part 1, Tables 3.4 and 3.5.

Assume 25 mm diameter bars and 10 mm diameter links:

$$d = 500 - 30 - 10 - 12.5 = 447.5\,\text{mm}$$
$$\frac{M}{f_{cu}bd^2} = \frac{267 \times 10^6}{30 \times 1000 \times 447.5^2}$$
$$= 0.044 < 0.156$$
$$z = 447.5[0.5 + (0.25 - 0.044/0.9)^{1/2}]$$
$$= 424.2 \not> 0.95d = 425.1\,\text{mm}$$
$$A_s = \frac{267 \times 10^6}{0.87 \times 460 \times 424.2} = 1572.8\,\text{mm}$$

Provide 4T25 to give an area of 1963 mm² (Fig. 13.16). This will provide for tie reinforcement.

(ii) Section at outer support, M = 367 kN m   The beam section is rectangular of breadth $b = 400$ mm. Provide for 25 mm bars in vertical pairs; $d = 435$ mm.

$$\frac{M}{f_{cu}bd^2} = \frac{367 \times 10^6}{30 \times 400 \times 435^2} = 0.161 > 0.156$$

Design as a doubly reinforced beam. $d' = 52.5$ mm; $d'/d = 0.121 < 0.213$ when the compressive stress in steel reaches yield.

$$A_s' = \frac{(0.161 - 0.156)400 \times 435^2 \times 30}{0.87 \times 460 \times 382.5}$$
$$= 74.2\,\text{mm}^2$$

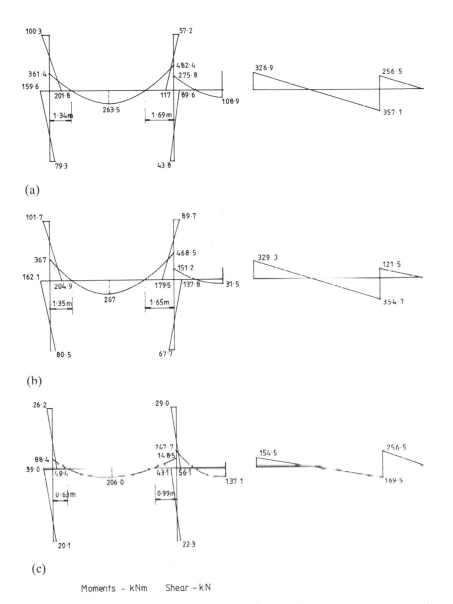

(a)

(b)

(c)

Moments - kNm   Shear - kN

Fig. 13.15 (a) Case 1, all spans $1.4G_k + 1.6Q_k$; (b) case 2A, maximum load on outer spans; (c) case 2B, maximum load on centre span.

$$A_s = \frac{0.156 \times 30 \times 400 \times 435^2}{0.87 \times 460 \times 0.775 \times 435} + 74.2$$
$$= 2625.5 + 74.2 = 2699.7 \, \text{mm}^2$$

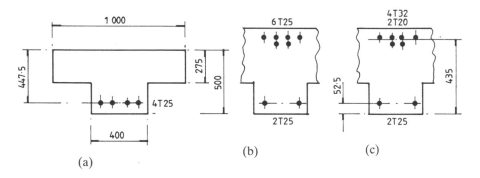

Fig. 13.16 (a) Mid-span; (b) outer column; (c) inner column.

For the compression steel, carry 2T25 through from the centre span. For the tension steel, provide 6T25 to give an area of 2944 mm². Refer to Fig. 13.16.

(iii) Section at inner support, M = 428.4 kN m

$$\frac{M}{f_{cu}bd^2} = \frac{482.4 \times 10^6}{30 \times 400 \times 435^2} = 0.212$$

$$A_s' = \frac{(0.212 - 0.156)400 \times 435^2 \times 30}{0.87 \times 460 \times 382.5}$$

$$= 830.7 \text{ mm}^2$$

$$A_s = 2625.5 + 830.7 = 3456.2 \text{ mm}^2$$

For the compression steel, carry 2T25 through from the centre span. For the tension steel, provide 4T32 + 2T20 to give an area of 3844 mm². The steel area is 1.92% of the gross concrete area. Refer to Fig. 13.16.

(b) Curtailment and anchorage

Because of the heavy moment reinforcement in the beam the cut-off points will be calculated in accordance with section 3.12.10 in the code.

(i) Top steel – outer support   Refer to Fig. 13.16. The section has 6T25 bars at the top and 2T25 bars at the bottom. Determine the positions along the beam where the two bars and four bars can be cut off.

The moment of resistance of the section with 4T25 bars ($A_s = 1963 \text{ mm}^2$) in tension and 2T25 bars ($A_s' = 981 \text{ mm}^2$) in compression is calculated (Fig. 13.17(a)). The strain in the compression steel is

$$\varepsilon_{sc} = \frac{x - 52.5}{x} 0.0035$$

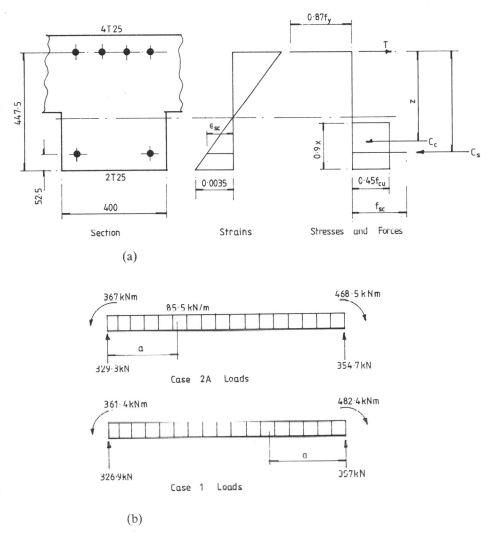

Fig. 13.17 (a) Sections at outer support; (b) load cases.

The stress in the compression steel is

$$f_{sc} = 200 \times 10^3 \times 0.0035 \frac{x - 52.5}{x}$$

$$= 700(x - 52.5)/x$$

Equate the forces in the section:

$$0.87 \times 460 \times 1963 = 0.45 \times 30 \times 400(0.9x) + 700(x - 52.5)981/x$$

Solve to give $x = 96.9$ mm and

$$z = 447.5 - 0.9 \times 96.9/2 = 403.9 \, \text{mm}$$
$$M_R = [(0.45 \times 30 \times 400 \times 0.9 \times 96.9 \times 403.9)$$
$$+700(96.9 - 52.5)981 \times 395/96.9]/10^6$$
$$= 314.5 \, \text{kN m}$$

Refer to the load diagram for case 2 loads for the end span shown in Fig. 13.17(b). The theoretical cut-off point for two bars is given by the solution of the equation

$$314.5 = 367 + 85.5a^2/2 - 329.3a$$

This is $a = 0.16$ m.

In accordance with the general rules for curtailment of bars in the tension zone given in clause 3.12.9.1, the code states that one of the following requirements should be satisfied:

(c) The bar must continue for an anchorage length (37 diameters) beyond the point where it is no longer required to resist bending moment;
(e) The bar must reach a point where other bars continuing past provide double the area required to resist moment at the section.

Note that (c) and (e) are the code designation. Requirement (e) will be satisfied.

In a similar manner to the above, the point where a second pair of 25 mm bars can be cut off can be determined. The theoretical cut off is at 0.68 m, say 0.7 m, from the centreline of the support. Hence, this is the point where the first 2T25 bars can be cut off.

Again, the point where 1T25 bar can be cut off is calculated. This is at 0.98 m, say 1.0 m, from the support. The second 2T25 bars can be cut off at this point.

Continue the remaining bars to say 1.6 m from support and lap 2T25 bars on to carry links. This satisfies the requirement that 20% of the inner support steel should run through as set out in the simplified rules. The point of contraflexure, at its furthest extent, is 1.35 m from the support.

(ii) Top steel – inner support

The section has 4T32 + 2T20 bars at the top and 2T25 bars at the bottom. The calculations are similar to those above. The compression steel is at yield at the point where the 2T20 bars can be cut off. The case 1 loads shown in Fig. 13.17(b) apply. The theoretical cut off point is at 0.11 m from the support.

A further 2T32 bars may be cut off at 0.65 m from the support. Thus the 2T20 bars can be cut off at 650 mm from the centre of the support.

1T32 bar can be cut off at 1.11 m from the support. The 2T32 bars can be cut off at 1150 mm from the support.

The remaining 2T32 bars are lapped onto 2T25 bars to support the links. The point of contraflexure is at 1.69 m from the support. See section (e), p. 424.

(iii) Bottom steel – outer support

The bottom steel consists of 4T25 bars. The point where two bars can be cut off will be determined. Assume that at the theoretical cut off points the effective top steel consists of 2T25 bars. The beam section is shown in Fig. 13.16 with a flange breadth of 1000 mm.

Neglect the compression steel and equate forces in the section:

$$0.87 \times 460 \times 981 = 0.43 \times 30 \times 1000 \times 0.9x$$
$$x = 32.3 \text{ mm}$$
$$z = 447.5 - 0.5 \times 0.9 \times 32.3 = 432.9 \text{ mm}$$
$$\not< 0.95d = 425.1 \text{ mm}$$

The steel at the top actually has a small tensile stress, which is neglected.

$$M_R = 0.87 \times 460 \times 981 \times 425.1/10^3$$
$$= 166.9 \text{ kN m}$$

Consider case 2A loads shown in Fig. 13.17(b) and solve the following equation to give the theoretical cut off points:

$$166.9 = 329.9a - 367 - 85.5a^2/2$$

where $a = 2.35$ m or $a = 5.35$ m from the outer column centreline.

The points where a further 1T25 bars can be cut off are at 1.77 m and 5.93 mm. The actual cut off points for the 2T25 bars are at 1700 mm from the outer support and 2000 from the inner support. Note that these cut off points will be re-examined when cracking is checked.

(iv) Outer support – anchorage of top bars 6T25 bars which include two pairs are to be anchored. The arrangement for anchorage is shown in Fig 13.18. The anchorage length is calculated for pairs of bars.

A larger steel area has been provided than is required (section 13.5.6(a)(ii)). The stress in the bars at the start of the bend is

$$\frac{0.87 \times 460 \times 2699.7}{2944} = 367 \text{ N/mm}^2$$

From Table 3.28 of the code $\beta = 0.5$ for type 2 deformed bars in tension:

$$\text{anchorage bond stress } f_{bu} = 0.5 \times 30^{1/2}$$
$$= 2.74 \text{ N/mm}^2$$

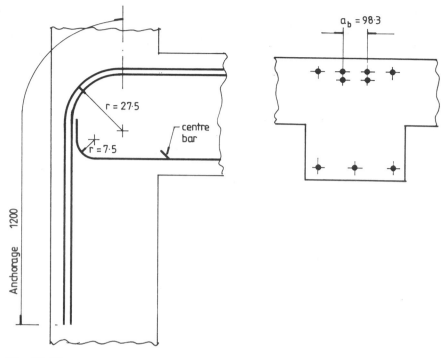

Fig. 13.18

$$\text{effective bar size } \phi_e = (4 \times 981/\pi)^{1/2}$$
$$= 35.4 \, \text{mm}$$
$$\text{anchorage length} = \frac{367 \times 981}{2.74 \times \pi \times 35.4}$$
$$= 1182.1 \, \text{mm}$$

The bearing stress is checked at the centre of the bend with an average radius of 275 mm for the pairs of bars.

The centre of the bend is at 107.9 mm from the start. The stress at the centre of the bend is

$$\frac{367 \times (1182.1 - 107.9)}{1182.1} = 333.5 \, \text{N/mm}^2$$

The bearing stress is

$$\frac{333.5 \times 981}{275 \times 35.4} = 33.6 \, \text{N/mm}^2$$

$$< \frac{2 \times 30}{1 + 2(35.4/98.3)} = 34.9\,\text{N/mm}^2$$

where the centre-to-centre distance of the bars is 98.3 mm. The bend radius is satisfactory. The top bars will extend to 1.6 m to lap on the beam reinforcement.

(v) Arrangement of longitudinal bars   The arrangement of the longitudinal bars is shown in Fig. 13.19.

(c) Design of Shear Reinforcement

The shear force envelope constructed from the shear force diagrams is shown in Fig. 13.20. Take account of the enhanced shear strength near the support using the simplified approach set out in clause 3.4.5.9 of the code.

(i) Inner support   The shear at d from the face of the support is 295.6 kN.

$$v = \frac{295.6 \times 10^3}{400 \times 444} = 1.66\,\text{N/mm}^2$$

The effective tension steel is 4T32 bars, $A_s = 3216\,\text{mm}^2$, $d = 444\,\text{m}$ (Fig. 13.19). The bars continue for 481 mm past the section.

$$v_c = 0.79\left(\frac{100 \times 3216}{400 \times 444}\right)^{1/3}\left(\frac{30}{25}\right)^{1/3}\Big/ 1.25$$
$$= 0.82\,\text{N/mm}^2$$

Use T10 links, $A_{sv} = 157\,\text{mm}^2$:

$$s_v = \frac{0.87 \times 460 \times 157}{400(1.66 - 0.82)} = 187\,\text{mm}$$
$$\not> 0.75d = 326.25$$

Provide links at 175 mm centres. The spacing for minimum links is

$$s_v = \frac{0.87 \times 460 \times 157}{0.4 \times 400} = 392.7\,\text{mm}$$

Adopt a minimum spacing of 300 mm.

Determine the distance from the centre of the inner support where links at 300 mm centres can be used. At this location the effective tension steel is 2T32 bars, $A_s = 1608\,\text{mm}^2$:

$$v_c = 0.65\,\text{N/mm}^2$$

Then taking account of the shear resistance of the T10 links at 300 mm centres, the average shear stress v in the concrete can be found:

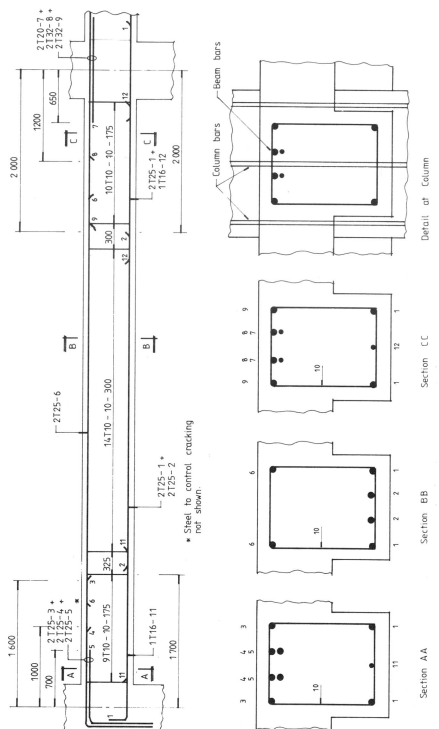

2T20-7 +
2T32-8 +
2T32-9

650

1200

2 000

10T10 - 10 - 175

2T25-1 +
1T16-12

2 000

C

C

12

7

8

9

6

300

2

12

2T25-6

14T10 - 10 - 300

B

B

2T25-1 +
2T25-2

* Steel to control cracking
not shown.

11

325

2

3

1 600

1000

700

2T25-3 +
2T25-4 +
2T25-5

*

5

4

6

3

9T10-10-175

1T16-11

A

A

11

11

1700

1

Beam bars

Column bars

Detail at Column

9

9

8

7

8

7

9

9

10

12

1

1

Section CC

6

6

2

2

1

1

10

Section BB

3

4

5

3

4

5

3

11

1

1

10

Section AA

Fig. 13.19

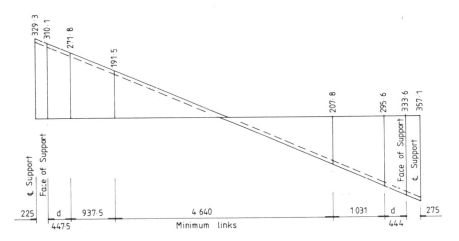

Fig. 13.20

$$v - 0.65 = \frac{0.87 \times 460 \times 157}{400 \times 300}$$

$$= 0.52 \, \text{N/mm}^2$$

and

$$v = 1.17 \, \text{N/mm}^2$$

The shear V at the section is

$$V = 1.17 \times 444 \times 400/10^3 - 207.8 \, \text{kN}$$

The distance a from the centre support where the shear is 207.8 kN is given by

$$a = \frac{357.1 - 207.8}{85.5} = 1.75 \, \text{m}$$

(II) Outer support, d — 447.5 mm The shear at d from the face of the support is 271.8 kN. The shear stress $v = 1.55 \, \text{N/mm}^2$. The design stress for 4T25 bars, $A_s = 1963 \, \text{mm}^2$, at the top gives $v_c = 0.69 \, \text{N/mm}^2$.

The spacing s_v for the T10 links is 182.6 mm. For a minimum spacing of 300 mm with $v_c = 0.55 \, \text{N/mm}^2$ for 2T25 bars, the shear $V = 191.5 \, \text{kN}$. This shear occurs at 1.61 m from the centre of the support.

(iii) Rationalization of link spacings The following rationalization of link spacings will be adopted:

Face of outer support, 1400 mm 9T10, 175
Centre portion T10, 300
Face of centre support, 1575 mm 10T10, 175

The link spacing is shown in Fig. 13.19.

(d) Deflection

Refer to Fig. 13.16.

$$\frac{b_w}{b} = \frac{400}{1000} = 0.4 > 0.3$$

Interpolating from Table 3.10 of the code the basic span/d ratio is

$$20.8 + (26 - 20.8)\left(\frac{0.4 - 0.3}{1.0 - 0.3}\right) = 21.5$$

$$\frac{M}{bd^2} = \frac{267 \times 10^6}{400 \times 447.5^2} = 3.33$$

$$f_s = \frac{5 \times 460 \times 1569.4}{8 \times 1963} = 229.9\,\text{N/mm}^2$$

The modification factor for tension reinforcement is

$$0.55 + \frac{277 - 229.9}{120(0.9 + 3.33)} = 1.04 < 2.0$$

The modification factor for compression reinforcement with 2T25 bars supporting the links is

$$1 + \frac{100 + 981}{1000 \times 447.5}\bigg/\left(3 + \frac{100 + 981}{1000 \times 447.5}\right) = 1.07$$

$$\text{allowable span/}d \text{ ratio} = 21.5 \times 1.04 \times 1.07 = 23.9$$

$$\text{actual span/}d \text{ ratio} = 8000/447.5 = 17.9$$

The beam is satisfactory with respect to deflection.

(e) Cracking

Referring to Table 3.20 in the code the clear spacing between bars in the tension zone for grade 460 steel and no redistribution should not exceed 160 mm. The cut-off points calculated above are re-examined. Refer to Figs 13.17 and 13.19.

(i) Outer support – top steel   The maximum distance of the point of contraflexure from the support is 1350 mm; 2T25–4 bars are cut off at 1000 mm giving a clear spacing between bars of 270 mm. A small bar must be added in the centre of the beam to control cracking.

(ii) Inner support – top steel   The point of contraflexure is 1690 mm from the support. The centre 2T32–8 bars are cut off at 1200 mm from the

support. A small bar is necessary in the centre of the beam to control cracking.

(iii) Outer support – bottom steel For case 3 loads the point of contra-flexure is 630 mm from the support. It is necessary to add a small bar in the centre of the beam to control cracking between the cut-off of the inner two bars and the column (Fig. 13.19, section AA).

(iv) Inner support – bottom steel For case 3 loads the point of contra-flexure is 990 mm from the support. A centre bar to control cracking is added (Fig. 13.19, section CC).

(f) Arrangement of reinforcement

The final arrangement of the reinforcement is shown in Fig. 13.19.

Design of centre column – lower length

(a) Design loads and moments

Referring to the section on vertical loads on p. 411 and Fig. 13.11, the axial load and moment at the column top are as follows. For case 1

$$\text{axial load} = (1.4 \times 2939.7) + (1.6 \times 598.5)$$
$$= 5073.2 \, \text{kN}$$
$$\text{moment} = 89.6 \, \text{kN m}$$

In case 2, at the first floor the centre beam carries dead load only:

$$\text{axial load} - 5073.2 - [(0.4 \times 40.5) + 18]3$$
$$= 4970.6$$
$$\text{moment} = 137.8 \, \text{kN m}$$

(b) Effective length and slenderness

Refer to BS 8110: Part 1, section 3.8.1.6. The column is square with assumed dimensions 550 mm × 550 mm. The restraining members are as follows:

Transverse direction   beam 500 mm deep
Longitudinal direction   ribbed slab 275 mm deep

Check the slenderness in the longitudinal direction. The end conditions for a braced column are (Table 3.21 of the code)

Top   Condition 3, ribbed slab
Bottom   Condition 1, moment connection to base

$$\beta - 0.9$$
$$\text{effective length } l_c = 0.9(5500 - 250) = 4725 \text{ mm}$$
$$\text{slenderness} = 4725/550 = 8.59$$
$$< 15$$

The column is short.

(c) Column reinforcement

The column reinforcement is designed for case 2A loads:

$$\frac{N}{bh} = \frac{4970.6 \times 10^3}{550^2} = 16.4$$

$$\frac{M}{bh^2} = \frac{137.8 \times 10^6}{550^3} = 0.83$$

Refer to Fig. 9.11 earlier.

$$100A_{sc}/bh = 1.4$$
$$A_{sc} = 1.4 \times 550^2/100 = 4235 \text{ mm}^2$$

Provide 6T25 + 2T32 to give an area of 4552 mm².

The links required are 8 mm in diameter at 300 mm centres. The reinforcement is shown in Fig. 13.21. Note that no bar must be more than 150 mm from a restrained bar. Centre links are provided.

Less steel is required for case 1 loads.

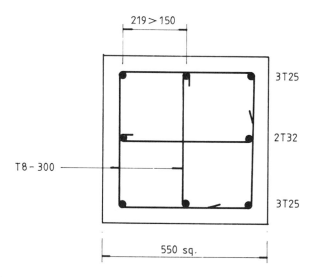

Fig. 13.21

Robustness – design of ties

The design must comply with the requirements of sections 2.2.2.2 and 3.12.3 of the code regarding robustness and the design of ties. These requirements are examined.

(a) Internal ties

(i) *Transverse direction*   The ties must be able to resist a tensile force in kilonewtons per metre width that is the greater of

$$\frac{g_k + q_k}{7.5} \frac{l_r}{5} F_t = \frac{7 + 3}{7.5} \frac{8}{5} = 2.13 F_t$$

where

$$g_k = 2.73 + 8.8/6 + 3.0 = 7 \, \text{kN/m}^2$$
$$q_k = 3.0 \, \text{kN/m}^2$$
$$l_r = 8.0 \, \text{m} \quad \text{(transverse direction)}$$

or

$$1.0 F_t$$

where

$$F_t = 20 + 4n_0 = 60 \, \text{kN}$$

and $n_0 = 10$ is the number of storeys.

$$\text{tie force} = 127.8 \, \text{kN/m}$$
$$\text{steel area} = \frac{127.8 \times 10^3}{0.87 \times 460} = 319.3 \, \text{mm}^2/\text{m}$$

Provide 3T12 bars, $A_s = 339 \, \text{mm}^2$, in the topping of the ribbed slab per metre width.

(ii) *Longitudinal direction*   The area of ties must be added to the area of steel in the ribs.

(b) Peripheral ties

The peripheral ties must resist a force F_t of 60 kN. This will be provided by an extra steel area in the edge L-beams running around the building.

(c) External column tie

The force to be resisted is the greater of

$$2.0 F_t = 120 \, \text{kN}$$

or

$$(l_s/2.5)F_t = 3 \times 60/2.5 = 72\,\text{kN}$$

where l_s is the floor to ceiling height (3.0 m), or 3% of the design ultimate vertical load at that level (p. 425) which is

$$3 \times 5264.4/100 = 157.9\,\text{kN}$$

$$\text{steel area} = \frac{157.9 \times 10^3}{0.87 \times 460} = 394.6\,\text{mm}^2$$

The moment reinforcement provided at the bottom of the beam is just adequate to resist this force. At the centre of the beam 1963 mm² are provided whereas 1569.4 mm² are required. The top reinforcement will also provide resistance. The bars are anchored at the external column.

The corner columns must be anchored in two directions at right angles.

(d) Vertical ties

The building is over five storeys and so each column must be tied continuously from foundation to roof. The tie must support in tension the design load of one floor (section on vertical loads, p. 411).

$$\text{design load} = (1.4 \times 7 \times 40.5) + (1.6 \times 7 \times 18)$$
$$= 598.5\,\text{kN}$$

The steel area required is 1495.5 mm².

The column reinforcement is lapped above floor level with a compression lap of 37 times the bar diameter (Table 3.29 of the code). This reinforcement is more than adequate to resist the code load. ∎

14

Tall buildings

14.1 INTRODUCTION

For the structural engineer the major difference between low and tall buildings is the influence of the wind forces on the behaviour of the structural elements. Generally, it can be stated that a tall building structure is one in which the horizontal loads are an important factor in the structural design. In terms of lateral deflections a tall concrete building is one in which the structure, sized for gravity loads only, will exceed the allowable sway due to additionally applied lateral loads. This allowable drift is set by the code of practice. If the combined horizontal and vertical loads cause excessive bending moments and shear forces the structural system must be augmented by additional bracing elements. These could take several forms. Cross-sections of existing beams and columns can be enlarged or efficient lateral-load-resisting bents such as concrete shear walls can be added to the structure.

The analysis of tall structures pertains to the determination of the influence of applied loads on forces and deformations in the individual structural elements such as beams, columns and walls. The design deals with the proportioning of these members. For reinforced concrete structures this includes sizing the concrete as well as the steel in an element. Structural analyses are commonly based on established energy principles and the theories developed from these principles assume linear elastic behaviour of the structural elements. Non-linear behaviour of the structure makes the problem extremely complex. It is very difficult to formulate, with reasonable accuracy, the problems involving inelastic responses of building materials. At present the forces in structural components and the lateral drift of tall structures can be determined by means of an elastic method of analysis regardless of the method of design. Non-linear methods of analysis for high-rise structures are not readily available.

This chapter is mainly concerned with the elastic static analysis of tall structures subject to lateral loads. An attempt is made to explain the complex behaviour of such structures and to suggest simplified methods of analysis including manual as well as computer procedures. Some design requirements such as common assumptions for the structural analysis of tall buildings and sway limitations are discussed. The behaviour of individual planar bents subjected to horizontal forces is then considered. The interaction between two types of bent will be examined in detail as it highlights the complexity involved in the analysis of three-dimensional structures. With that knowledge it is then possible to classify tall buildings into a few categories and explain how their analysis can be simplified. The chapter concludes with a section on framed tube structures for very tall buildings.

14.2 DESIGN AND ANALYSIS CONSIDERATIONS

14.2.1 Design

As stated in of BS 8110: Part 1, clause 2.1, the aim of design is the achievement of an acceptable probability that structures being designed will perform satisfactorily during their intended life. The horizontal and vertical loads to which framed structures are subjected have been discussed in Chapter 13. For multistorey structures the imposed floor loads can be substantially reduced in the design of columns, piers, walls, beams and foundations. Details are given in BS 6399: Part 1, clause 5. BS 8110 contains additional clauses for structures consisting of five storeys or more.

(a) Ultimate limit state

(i) Structural stability Recommendations for stability are given in BS 8110: Part 1, clause 2.2.2.1. The instability of individual structural members is well established and discussed in many textbooks [12, 13]. For tall structures, however, this problem has not been reduced to simple techniques suitable for the design office. Detailed discussion of the theory is beyond the scope of this chapter.

Tall slender frames may buckle laterally owing to loads that are much smaller than predicted by buckling equations applied to isolated columns. Instability may occur for a variety of reasons such as slenderness, excessive axial loads and deformations, cracks, creep, shrinkage, temperature changes and rotation of foundations. Most of these are ignored in a first-order analysis of tall structures but may cause lateral deflections that are much larger than initially expected. The increased deformations can induce substantial additional bending moments in axially loaded members as a result of the so-called P-delta effect. This will increase the probability of buckling failure. In principle the instability of a multistorey building structure is no different from that of a low structure but because of the great height of such buildings horizontal deflections must be computed with great accuracy. The deflected shapes of individual structural members should be taken into account in the final analysis of tall slender structures, i.e. a second-order analysis is required.

If lateral deflections in tall buildings are kept well within allowable limits, a first-order analysis combined with a check on the buckling of individual columns will be sufficient. This is usually the case with rein-forced concrete structures. More advanced textbooks discuss the condi-tions where a second-order analysis is necessary [14,15].

(ii) Robustness   Clause 2.2.2.2 requires that all structures be capable of safely resisting a notional horizontal load applied at each floor or roof level simultaneously equal to 1.5% of the characteristic dead weight of the structure between mid-height of the storey below and either mid-height of the storey above or the roof surface. In addition to horizontal ties around the periphery and between vertical structural elements vertical ties must also be applied (clause 3.12.3.7). In the design of tall structures it will also be necessary to identify key elements. These can be defined as important structural members whose failure will result in an extended collapse of a large part of the building. Their design recommendations are in BS 8110: Part 2, clause 2.6.2.

(b) Serviceability limit state – Response to wind loads

Ideally the limit states of lateral deflection should be concerned with cases where the side sway can

1. limit the use of the structure
2. influence the behaviour of non-loadbearing elements
3. affect the appearance of the structure
4. compromise the comfort of the occupants

The diversity of these situations makes it quite difficult to define the limit states. Deflection limits stated in codes of practice are usually represented as traditional values derived from experience and lead to acceptable condi-tions in normal circumstances. It is stated in BS 8110: Part 2, clause 3.2.2.2, that unless partitions, cladding and finishes etc. have been specifically detailed to allow for the anticipated deflections, relative lateral deflection in any one storey under the characteristic wind load should not exceed $H/500$ where H is the storey height. This limitation in the storey slope of $1/500$ requires the overall slope of the structure to be even smaller. Depend-ing on the type of lateral-load-resisting element used in the structure, the maximum storey slope will occur between about one-third up the height, as in rigid frame structures, and the top storey if the structure consists entirely of shear walls. The drift limitation set by the code of practice must there-fore be checked for a number of storeys.

14.2.2 Assumptions for analysis

The structural form of a building is inherently three dimensional. The development of efficient methods of analysis for tall structures is possible only if the usual complex combination of many different types of structural members can be reduced or simplified whilst still representing accurately the overall behaviour of the structure. A necessary first step is therefore the selection of an idealized structure that includes only the significant structural elements with their dominant modes of behaviour. Achieving a simplified analysis of a large structure such as a tall building is based on two major considerations:

1. *the relative importance of individual members contributing to the solution*

   This allows a member stiffness to be taken as infinity if the associated mode of behaviour is expected to yield a negligible deformation relative to that of other members in the structure. It also allows elements of minor influence on the final results to be given a zero stiffness.

2. *the relative importance of modes of behaviour of the entire structure*

   It is often possible to ignore the asymmetry in a structural floor plan of a building, thereby making a three-dimensional analysis unnecessary.

The user of a computer program, be it a simple plane frame or a general finite element program, can usually assign any value to the properties of an element even if these are inconsistent with the actual size of that member, e.g. it is quite acceptable for a structural element to be given true values for its flexural and shear stiffnesses, zero torsional stiffness and an infinite axial stiffness. Several simplifying assumptions are necessary for the analysis of tall building structures subject to lateral loading. The following are the most commonly accepted assumptions.

1. All concrete members behave linearly elastically and so loads and displacements are proportional and the principle of superposition applies. Because of its own weight the structure is subjected to a compressive prestress and pure tension in individual members is not likely to occur;
2. Floor slabs are fully rigid in their own plane. Consequently, all vertical members at any level are subject to the same components of translation and rotation in the horizontal plane. This does not hold for very long narrow buildings and for slabs which have their widths drastically reduced at one or more locations;
3. Contributions from the out-of-plane stiffness of floor slabs and structural bents can be neglected;
4. The individual torsional stiffness of beams, columns and planar walls can be neglected;
5. Additional stiffness effects from masonry walls, fireproofing, cladding and other non-structural elements can be neglected;

6. Deformations due to shear in slender structural members (length-to-width ratio larger than 5) can be neglected;
7. Connections between structural elements in cast-*in-situ* buildings can be taken as rigid;
8. Concrete structures are elastically stable.

One additional assumption that deserves special attention concerns the calculation of the structural properties of a concrete member. The cross-sectional area and flexural stiffness can be based on the gross concrete sections. This will give acceptable results at service loads but leads to underestimation of the deflections at yielding. In principle the bending stiffness of a structural member reflects the amount of reinforcing steel and takes account of cracked sections which cause variations in the flexural stiffness along the length of the member. These complications, however, are usually not taken into account in a first-order analysis.

14.3 PLANAR LATERAL-LOAD-RESISTING ELEMENTS

14.3.1 Rigid frames

The most common type of planar bent used for medium height structures is the rigid frame. Many methods of analysis are available for rigid frames subject to horizontal loading. They fall into two categroies: simplified manual methods and standard computer methods. After sizing the structure for gravity loads a simple manual lateral load analysis will yield additional forces in the individual members which might then require adjustments of the sectional properties. Once these have been established, either the sway of the building is calculated first using an approximate manual method again or a computer analysis is used immediately. The initial results of the manual method of analysis can be a useful check on the reasonableness of the final results from the computer analysis.

(a) Simplified manual methods of analysis

Several simplified manual methods of analysis for tall buildings subject to horizontal loading are available. Among these the portal and cantilever methods are the most popular; they are discussed in Chapter 13. A major advantage of both methods is that the initial sizes of the beams and columns are not required. This important simplification indicates that these techniques should only be used as a preliminary method of analysis where they can rapidly yield individual member forces. They are thus quite useful in obtaining trial sections for tall rigid frames.

An example in section 14.3.1(d) will give a general impression of the degree of accuracy of the two manual methods compared with a computer method of analysis.

(b) Standard computer analysis

Most standard computer programs are based on the matrix method of structural analysis and for the theory the reader should refer to books on structural mechanics. Commercially available interactive computer programs demand little more of the structural engineer then the keying in of specific structural data such as geometry, member sizes, material properties and loading. Some of these programs incorporate several different types of structural elements such as beam and truss elements. These are the so called general-finite-element programs. The size of the structure that can be analysed is dependent on the way that the program is structured and the type of computer used. For the analysis of less complicated structures like those described in this chapter, a computer program incorporating the use of just one type of element, i.e. the beam element, will be sufficient. Many simple plane frame programs have been published in engineering journals and can readily be used by anyone taking the time to enter the few hundred lines of such a program. The writers of these programs have all chosen their own favourite way of entering data into the computer and so reference should be made to the respective program guidelines.

A rigid frame comprises beams and columns with finite dimensions. In a simple plane frame analysis the dimensions of the cross-sections of the structural members are often ignored and the beams and columns are represented by line members as shown in Fig. 14.1. This is standard practice, but this aspect will be discussed in more detail later. The horizontal and vertical loads on the frame are usually replaced by end reactions on the members. A uniformly distributed gravity load on the girder will be represented by a vertical point load at both ends of the member augmented by fixed end moments. Modelling the wind load on a building is a little different. Here it is assumed that the wind is first resisted by the cladding on the side of the structure which transfers the load to the perimeter beams and subsequently to the columns. Thus the wind load on the structure is represented only by horizontal point loads at the exterior beam–column connections. Figure 14.1(a) shows a small segment of a rigid frame near the perimeter of a building with horizontal and vertical loading. In Fig. 14.1(b) the computer model of this area is displayed with nodes at the centres of beam–column joints, columns and beams represented by line members connecting the nodes, point loads acting at the nodes and fixed end moments on the beams at their end connections. The joints are treated as rigid, i.e. fully moment resisting. At the base of the structure the program user will probably have a choice between a hinged or fixed connection. The decision must be based on the type of foundation. However, there are several techniques for

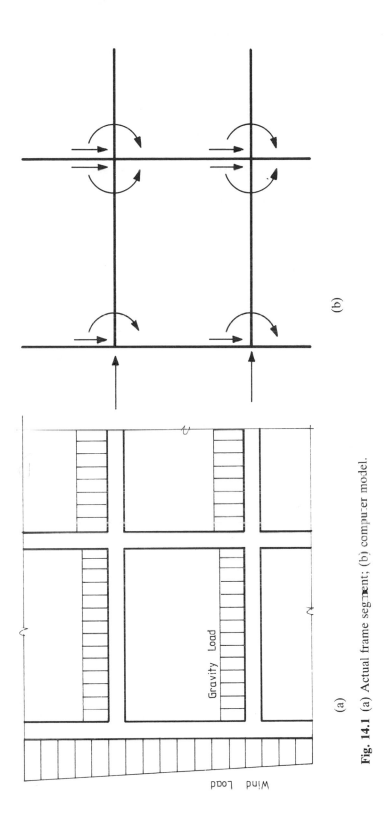

(a)

(b)

Fig. 14.1 (a) Actual frame segment; (b) computer model.

modelling partially fixed connections. Refer to research journals for further information.

(c) Half-frame analysis

The analysis of a symmetric rigid frame subject to lateral loads can be simplified by considering only one half of it. This might not be necessary when the analysis is of a single frame. In combination with other structural bents such as walls or frames with different geometry, the stiffness matrix representing the entire structure will become very large. If the lateral-load-resisting elements possess symmetry about their neutral axes, the size of the problem can be almost halved if the conditions at the neutral axis are properly modelled. In the frame shown in Fig. 14.2(a) the columns on lines 1 and 2 will lengthen owing to the horizontally applied load while the columns on lines 5 and 4 will undergo shortenings of magnitudes identical with those of 1 and 2 respectively. This is because of symmetry in geometry as well as stiffness. The centre points of the interior beams will only move laterally in the direction of the load because they are all situated on the neutral axis of the bent, i.e. they remain at floor level. These points of contraflexure can each be modelled by a roller. The simplified model is shown in Fig. 14.2(b). Here, both the rotational and translational degrees of freedom have been released at one end of a member. The structure now should be subjected to half the lateral load.

In a symmetric rigid frame with an even number of bays, the neutral axis will be on the centre column line. When subjected to lateral loading, the columns on the left-hand side will lengthen while the columns on the right will shorten. The column on the axis of symmetry will not change in length. This can be modelled by giving it an infinite axial stiffness. In the half-frame computer model the flexural stiffness of this column must be reduced by 50%.

(d) Lateral load analysis of a tall rigid frame

Fig. 14.3(a) shows an elevation of a tall reinforced concrete rigid frame. The columns of this three-bay 18-storey structure are assumed to be fixed at the base. Dimensions for beam and column sections are given in Fig. 14.3(b). The horizontal point loads up the height of the structure represent the wind force on one single frame. It follows a distribution that is outlined in CP 3: Chapter V: Part 2, Table 3. A total height of 63.0 m and a location in the city centre puts this structure in Group 4, Class C. A detailed procedure for the calculation of the individual horizontal point loads is given in Chapter 13. The self-weight of the structure is ignored in this analysis. The results for three methods of analysis are shown in Fig. 14.4. Since the structure is symmetrical it is sufficient to display the actions in the frame on one side only. The left-hand side of Fig. 14.4(a) shows the bending

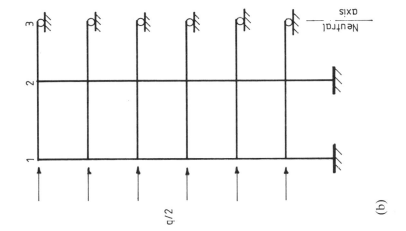

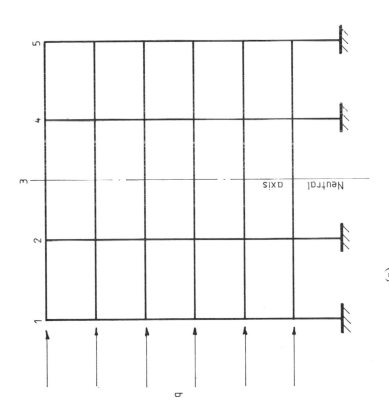

Fig. 14.2 (a) Rigid frame; (b) half-frame computer model.

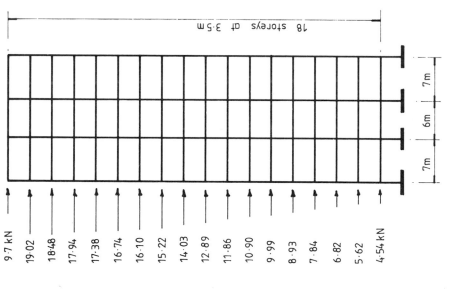

Storey	Exterior Column	Interior Column	Beam
18	40 × 40	50 × 50	30 × 40
17			
16			
15	40 × 40	50 × 50	40 × 50
14			
13			
12			
11			
10	40 × 50	50 × 60	40 × 50
9			
8			
7			
6			
5			
4	50 × 50	60 × 60	40 × 50
3			
2			
1			

All sizes in cm.

(b)

Elevation (a):

18 storeys at 3.5 m

7m 6m 7m

9·7 kN
19·02
18·48
17·94
17·38
16·74
16·10
15·22
14·03
12·89
11·86
10·90
9·99
8·93
7·84
6·82
5·62
4·54 kN

(a)

Fig. 14.3 (a) Elevation (b) member sizes.

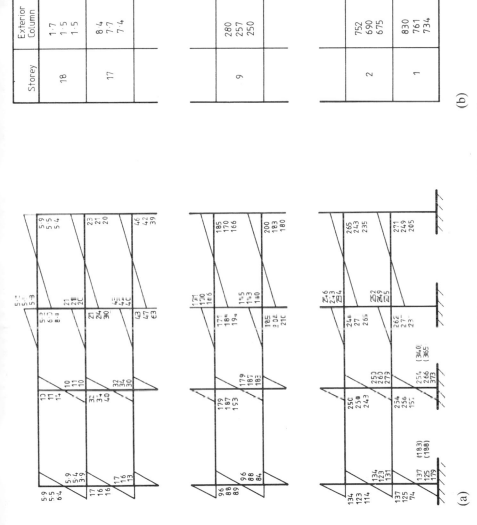

(a)

Storey	Exterior Column	Interior Column
18	1·7 1·5 1·5	0 0·4 1·4
17	8·4 7·7 7·4	0 2·3 5·6
9	280 257 250	0 77 104
2	752 690 675	0 207 247
1	830 761 734	0 228 265

(b)

Fig. 14.4 (a) Bending moments in kilonewton metres; (b) axial forces in kilonewtons.

moments in the columns while the right-hand side gives the bending
moments in the beams. The axial forces in the columns are shown in Fig.
14.4(b). Since the wind load can also be applied in the opposite direction,
all beam and column forces must be considered reversible, i.e. the axial
forces can be taken as tensile or compressive and the bending moments are
to be considered positive as well as negative. The values for the bending
moments and axial forces are given in groups of three. The first number is
derived from the portal frame method of analysis, the second is from the
cantilever method and the final number is obtained from a computer stiffness matrix analysis. The actions in the structural members are shown for
the top and bottom two storeys and for a single storey segment half-way up
the building.

Comparison of the two manual methods with the computer method
shows that the larger discrepancies occur near the interior columns, espe-
cially in the top storeys. Generally, if the overall bending action in the frame
is the dominant mode of behaviour, the cantilever method of analysis will
yield better results than the portal frame method. The latter is unable to
give values for the axial forces in the interior columns. Both methods,
however, are inadequate to predict reasonably accurate bending moments
for the first storey columns. This is because in both procedures it is
assumed that the points of contraflexure occur at mid-storey height. Since
the columns are fixed at the base these points will move higher up the
member depending on the relative stiffness of the adjacent beams and
columns. An improvement can be made by assuming that the points of
contraflexure in the base columns occur two-thirds up the height of the
member. The results of this are shown in parentheses in the diagram.

The bending moments and axial forces must be combined with the forces
from a gravity load analysis to obtain the total forces in the structural
members. It is at this point that the designer will find whether he has to
make adjustments to the individual beams and columns. If so, this will
usually be to the beams in the lower storeys of the structure where the
bending moments due to wind loading can be quite high.

14.3.2 Shear walls

The simplest form of bracing against horizontal loading is the plane cantilevered shear wall. For walls with total height-to-width ratios larger than 5
ordinary beam theory will yield acceptable results for stresses and deflections due to lateral loads. A computer model of a shear wall in a multistorey
structure consists of single-storey-height line elements stacked on top of
each other by means of rigid connections. The nodes at each floor level will
supply proper application points for the lateral and gravity loads. Figure
14.5(a) shows a cantilever shear wall structure subjected to a uniformly
distributed horizontal load. The computer model with horizontal point

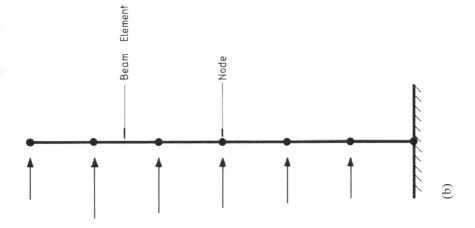

Beam Element

Node

(b)

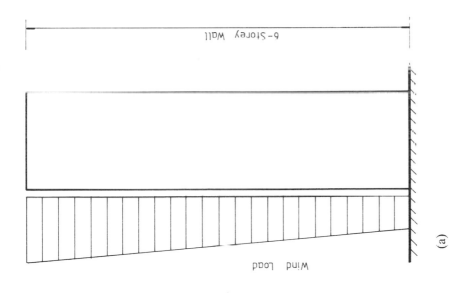

6-Storey Wall

Wind Load

(a)

Fig. 14.5 (a) Cantilever shear wall; (b) computer model.

loads representing the wind forces is shown in Fig. 14.5(b). If thc walls have very small height-to-width ratios or irregularly spaced openings for windows and doorways, the assumptions that plane sections remain plane is no longer valid and it will be necessary to use an improved model to take account of the more complicated behaviour.

14.3.3 Coupled shear walls

A coupled shear wall structure comprises two or more cantilever shear walls in a single plane which are connected by beams or slabs at each floor level. Figure 14.6(a) shows two connected shear walls subjected to a lateral load. If the flexural stiffness of the connecting members is very small compared with the flexural stiffness of the walls or if the stiffness of the beam–wall connections is low causing them to behave more like hinges, then the coupled shear wall structure can be considered as two individual cantilevers connected by links at each floor level. The connecting members only transfer axial loads, i.e. they behave like truss members. When subjected to lateral loading both walls will attain identical deflected profiles. The computer model in Fig. 14.6(b) shows the rigid column-to-column connections at each floor level while the horizontal elements are pin linked to these joints. Some standard plane frame computer programs do not allow the use of a truss element. A pin-ended member can still be modelled by using a beam element and releasing its end moments. Another possibility is to make the flexural stiffness of the connecting beam very small so that it will not attract any bending moments. This can be done by setting the moment of inertia equal to zero or a very small value. The cross-sectional area can be given its actual value. A third way of modelling a pin joint is by replacing it with a very short beam element, say 1 mm long, with a near zero value for its bending stiffness. Its axial stiffness will be identical to that of the connecting beam.

The situation is far more complicated if the beam and floor connections to the walls are considered to be moment resisting. The rigid connections will now cause full participation of the connecting elements. The behaviour of such coupled shear walls subject to lateral loads is partly as individual cantilevers, as discussed before, and partly as one single wall bending about a common neutral axis. The relative extent of these two actions depends upon the effectiveness of the connecting system. A computer model for this type of structure is more involved because of the rather complicated beam–wall connections. When the shear wall in Fig. 14.7(a) is subjected to lateral loading, the large width of the wall will cause point a on the windward side to move laterally as well as upwards while point b on the leeward side moves laterally and downwards, as shown in Fig. 14.7(b). Considering again that plane sections remain plane, the wide column behaviour of the walls can best be represented by a column, placed at the neutral axis of the

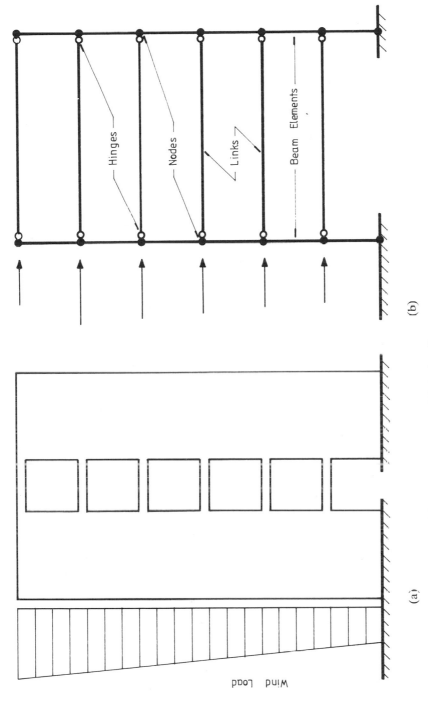

Fig. 14.6 (a) Shear wall structure; (b) computer model of linked walls.

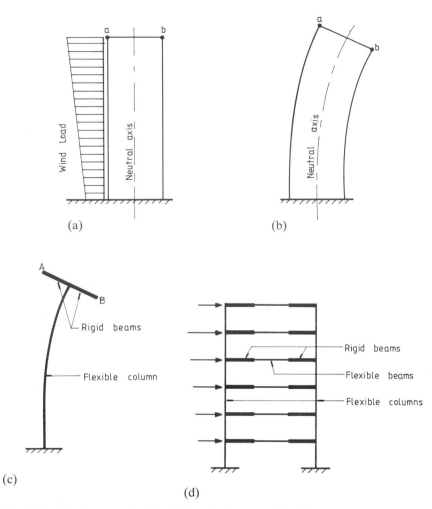

Fig. 14.7 (a) Shear wall; (b) deflected shape; (c) rigid-arm computer model; (d) computer model of coupled walls.

wall, and rigidly connected beams. These beams will have infinite bending stiffness and reach from the neutral axis of the wall to its exterior edges. They represent the plane sections in the wall and are shown in Fig. 14.7(c). The floor-to-floor columns are given the same flexural stiffness as the shear wall. When subjected to a horizontal load, point A in the computer model will undergo identical translations to point a in the actual structure. The process of adding rigid elements can be repeated at each floor level. The nodes at the ends of the 'arms' are used for rigid connections to the flexural coupling beams. The exterior parts of the rigid arms are not connected to any other structural element and thus can be omitted from the analysis. A complete computer model of a coupled wall structure can now be assembled and is shown in Fig. 14.7(d). In the case of symmetric coupled walls, only half the structure needs to be analysed, similarly to rigid frames.

14.3.4 Shear walls connected to columns

Rigid frames can be used very effectively for office buildings since they allow free use of movable partitions. Since framed structures depend on the rigidity of the beam–column connections for their resistance to horizontal loading, they may become uneconomic at heights above 20 storeys. Additional bracing in a concrete rigid frame can easily be achieved by widening one of the columns in such a way that it effectively becomes a shear wall which is connected by beams to the remaining columns of the bent (Fig. 14.8(a)). Architecturally these walls can be used to divide or enclose space. Depending on the bending stiffness of the beams and the rigidity of the beam–wall connections the wall can be represented by a wide column which is either rigidly or pin connected to the adjacent beams. Both models are shown in Fig. 14.8(b).

14.3.5 Wall frames

A wall frame can be considered as a wall with many regularly spaced openings or a rigid frame with wide columns and deep beams. In section 14.3.3 on coupled walls the behaviour of a wide column was discussed and for the purpose of a computer analysis was replaced by a combination of line members representing flexible columns and rigid beams. The same reasoning can be applied to the deep beams of the wall frame structure. Their behaviour can be modelled by line members representing flexible beams and rigid short columns, acting as the 'side arms' to the beams. The length of these columns extends from the bottom of the deep beam to the top. The computer model of a rigid connection of deep beams and wide columns is shown in Fig. 14.9. It requires a total of five nodes and four flexurally rigid beam elements and thus quite a lot of computer memory. A beam–column joint in a 'regular' rigid plane frame only requires a single node per connection and no additional short rigid beam elements. Ignoring the sizes of the structural members can lead to oversimplification and large errors in the analysis.

14.4 INTERACTION BETWEEN BENTS

The discussion of various structural models for different types of lateral-load-resisting elements has so far covered only the analysis of two-dimensional structures consisting of a single bent. The analysis of a tall building structure

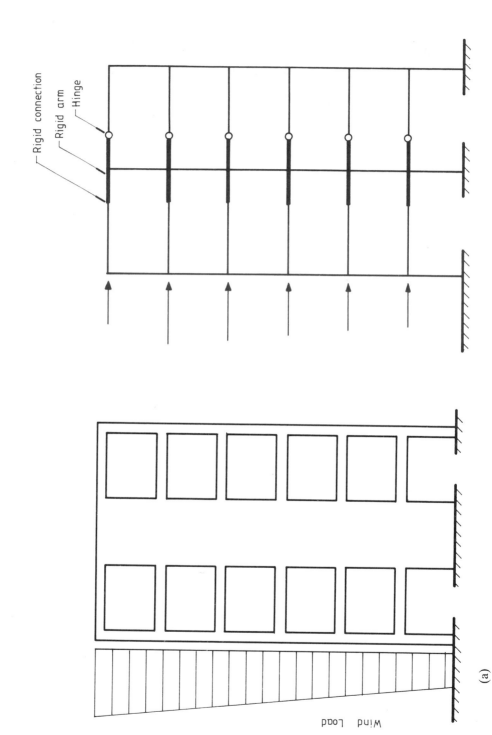

Fig. 14.8 (a) Shear wall and columns; (b) computer models.

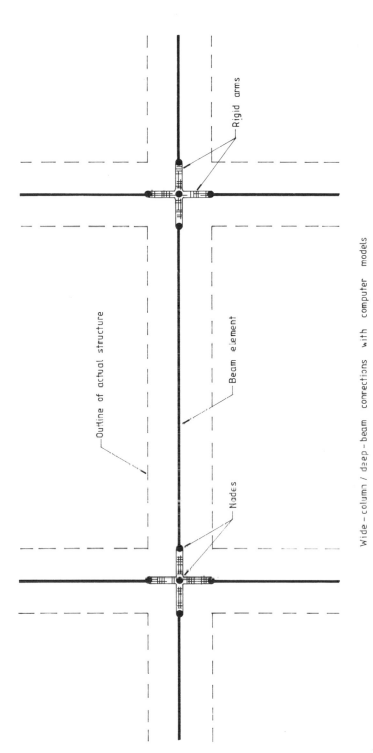

Wide-column / deep-beam connections with computer models

Fig. 14.9 Connections between wide columns and deep beams with computer models.

subject to horizontal and vertical loads is a three-dimensional problem. In many cases, however, it is possible to simplify and reduce this problem by splitting the structure into several smaller two-dimensional components which then allow a less complicated planar analysis to be carried out. The procedure for subdividing a three-dimensional structure requires some knowledge of the sway behaviour of individual bents subjected to lateral loads. A brief description of this kind of behaviour is given here for two distinctly different bents:

1. Rigid frames subject to wind load will mainly deflect in a shear configuration, i.e. with concave curvature in the upper part of the structure;
2. Shear walls will adopt a flexural configuration under identical loading conditions, i.e. convex curvature up the height of the structure.

Both deflection profiles are shown in Fig. 14.10. These types of behaviour describe extreme cases of deflected shapes along the height of the structures. All other bents such as coupled walls and wall frames will show a combination of the two deflection curves. In general they behave as flexural bents in the lower region of the structure and show some degree of shear behaviour in the upper storeys. Combining several bents with characteristically different types of behaviour in a single three-dimensional structure will inevitably complicate the lateral load analysis. It would be incorrect to isolate one of the bents and subject it to a percentage of the horizontal loading. A closer look at a mixed bent structure will demonstrate the complex interaction between different types of lateral-load-resisting elements.

A horizontally loaded building comprising a symmetric combination of frames and walls will deflect in the direction of the load. Owing to the high in-plane flexural stiffness of the floor elements, the rigid frames and shear walls are forced to adopt identical deflection profiles. The shapes of the curves in Fig. 14.10 show that a rigid frame can attract a large proportion of the wind force at the top while the shear wall will be the dominant load-resisting element near the base of the structure. This will cause a redistribution of the applied load between the individual bents with heavy interaction at the top and bottom. Thus frames and walls do not simply attract a fixed percentage of the applied load along the height of the structure. For this reason the bents cannot be separated and analysed as individual two-dimensional structures – they must be treated as one structure. This does not mean that a full three-dimensional analysis is required, however. This is discussed later.

Non-symmetric structural floor plans comprising rigid frames and shear walls will complicate the matter even further. The following example demonstrates the complexity of buildings that rotate about a vertical axis.

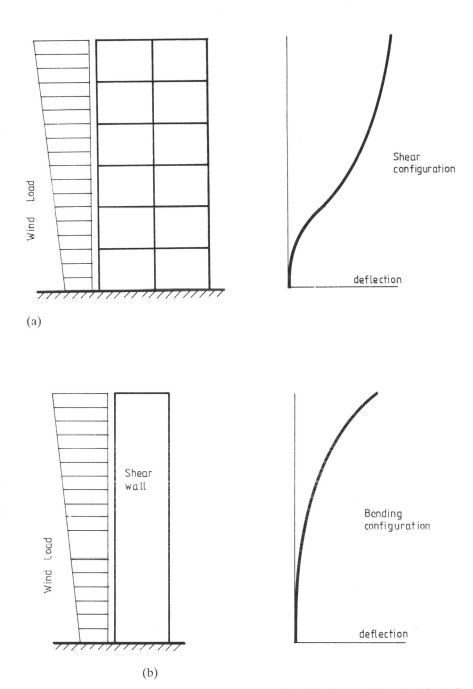

Fig. 14.10 (a) Rigid frame and deflected profile; (b) shear wall and deflected profile.

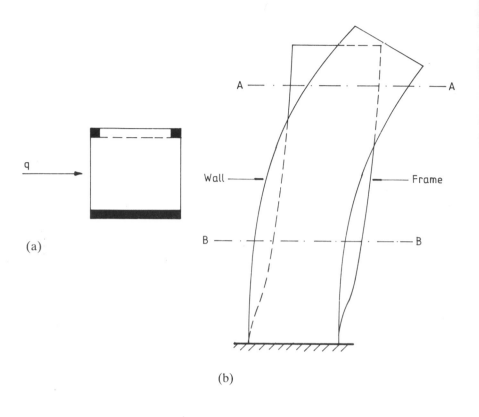

(a)

q

Wall

Frame

A — · — · A

B — · — · B

(b)

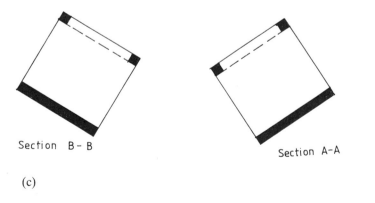

Section B – B

Section A-A

(c)

Fig. 14.11 (a) Structural floor plan; (b) deflected profiles; (c) floor rotations.

Figure 14.11(a) shows the structural floor plan of a multistorey building that consists of a single one-bay frame combined with a shear wall. The symmetrically applied lateral load will cause the structure to rotate owing to the distinctly different characteristics of the two bents. A side view of the deflections of both cantilevers is shown in Fig. 14.11(b). Sections taken at different levels show (Fig. 14.11(c)) that the rotation of the floor plans cannot be assumed to be continuously increasing along the height in one direction. Figure 14.11(c) also shows that it cannot be assumed that the structure has a single centre of rotation. This will be at a different location for each floor level. To deal with these complications a more sophisticated three-dimensional analysis will be necessary.

14.5 THREE-DIMENSIONAL STRUCTURES

14.5.1 Classification of structures (computer modelling)

In many cases it is possible to simplify the analysis of a three-dimensional tall building structure subject to lateral load by considering only small parts which can be analysed as two-dimensional structures. This type of reduction in the size of the problem can be applied to many different kinds of building. The degree of reduction that can be achieved depends mainly on the layout of the structural floor plan and the location, in plan, of the horizontal load resultant. The analysis of tall structures as presented here is divided into three main categories on the basis of the characteristics of the structural floor plan.

(a) Category 1: Symmetric floor plan with identical parallel bents subject to a symmetrically applied lateral load q

The structure shown in Fig. 14.12(a) comprises six rigid frames, four in the y direction and two in the x direction. Because of symmetry about the y axis, all beams and columns at a particular floor level will have identical translations in the y direction when subjected to load q. There will be no deflections in the x direction. Assumption 3 of section 14.2.2 allows the out-of-plane stiffness of rigid frames to be neglected, i.e. the flexural stiffness of the beams and columns in the x direction can be ignored. The resulting simplified structural floor plan is shown in Fig. 14.12(b). For the analysis of this model consisting of four rigid frames parallel to the applied load, it will be sufficient to consider only one lateral-load-resisting element. Since all four frames will deflect identically each bent can be assigned one-quarter of the total horizontal load. The frame and load are shown in Fig. 14.12(c). Structures in this category consisting entirely of rigid frames can be economically built to a height of about 20 storeys.

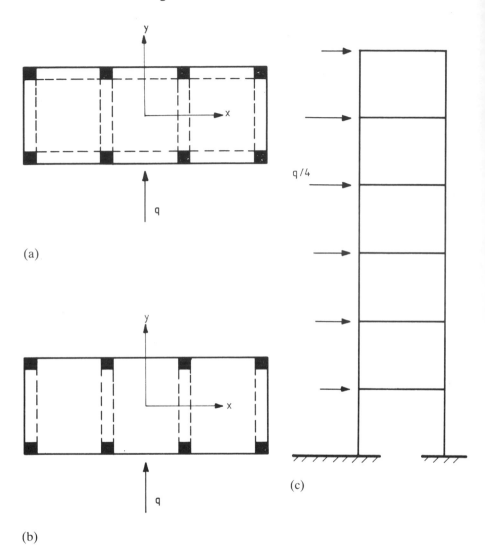

(a)

(b)

(c)

Fig. 14.12 (a) Structural floor plan of tall rigid frame building; (b) simplified floor plan; (c) one-bay rigid frame computer model.

(b) Category 2: Symmetric structural floor plan with non-identical bents, subject to a symmetric horizontal load *q*

The lateral load-resisting component of the structure shown in Fig. 14.13(a) comprises two rigid frames and two shear walls orientated parallel to the direction of the horizontal load *q*. Mixed bent structures like these allow economic construction of tall buildings up to 35 storeys. The floor

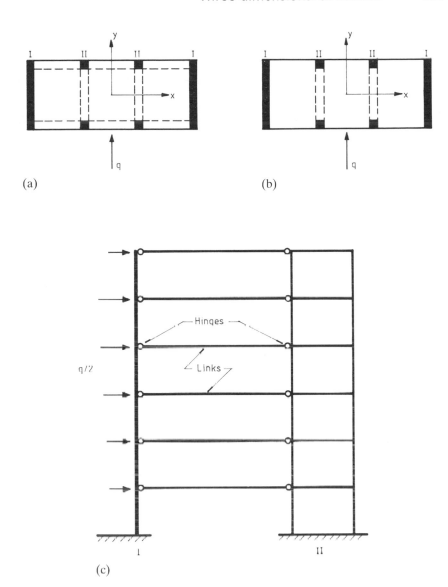

Fig. 14.13 (a) Structural floor plan of shear wall, rigid frame building; (b) simplified floor plan; (c) computer model of linked bents in a single plane.

plan has full symmetry about the y axis. The symmetrically applied load q will thus cause the structure to deflect in the y direction only, i.e. there will be no rotation in the horizontal plane. As before, the symmetric structural floor plan allows the behaviour of the bents oriented in the x direction to be neglected. The simplified floor plan of the structure can be reduced as shown in Fig. 14.13(b). The two different types of bent, I and II, will cause a redistribution of the horizontally applied load between the four bents along the height of the structure, i.e. it cannot be assumed that each bent will attract a fixed percentage of the load q at each floor level. It is still possible to perform a plane frame analysis and it is sufficient to consider only half the structure subjected to half the lateral force. If there also exists symmetry about the x axis then only one-quarter of the structure need be analysed by using half-bent models, as discussed in section 14.3.1(c). A two-dimensional model of half the structure is shown in Fig. 14.13(c) where one bent of each type is assembled in series with axially rigid pin-ended links which connect the bents at each floor level. This in-line structure is then subjected to one-half the lateral load. The links simulate the effect of the floor slabs causing identical deflection profiles in both bents.

For a tall building that has a symmetric structural floor plan comprising an odd number of lateral-load-resisting elements, the centre bent can be split in half, i.e. the computer model of this linked bent consists of structural members having only half the cross-sectional area and half the moment of inertia.

So far it has been assumed that all structures in the first two categories keep their symmetry up the height of the building, i.e. symmetry of geometry as well as stiffness is maintained. It is possible, however, to alter the geometry along the height and keep symmetry in the structural floor plan. A setback in the upper storeys for all exterior bays in the floor plan shown in Fig. 14.14(a) will still allow a plane frame analysis for the linked bents shown in Fig. 14.14(b). If the setback causes a loss of symmetry about the y axis, however, the structure will rotate in the horizontal plane and a full three-dimensional analysis will be necessary.

(c) Category 3: Non-symmetric structural floor plan with identical or non-identical bents, subject to a lateral load q

A category 3 structure, of which an example floor plan is shown in Fig. 14.15, will rotate in the horizontal plane regardless of the location of the lateral load q. It cannot be reduced to a plane frame problem and a complete three-dimensional analysis is required, i.e. all structural members in the y direction as well as in the x direction must be taken into account.

14.5.2 Non-planar shear walls

The shear walls introduced in section 14.3.2 can be expanded into three-dimensional shapes. The so-called concrete shear cores have several additional advantages in resisting lateral forces. They are very effective as bracing members because of the greatly increased flexural stiffness as the

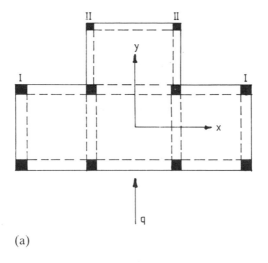

(a)

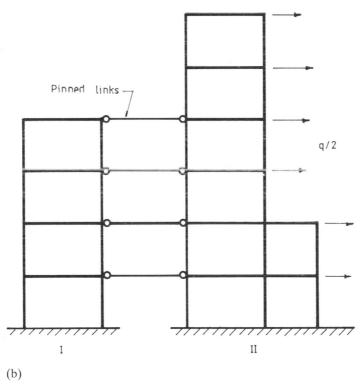

Pinned links

q/2

(b)

I   II

Fig. 14.14 (a) Structural floor plan of rigid frame building; (b) linked rigid frames in a single plane.

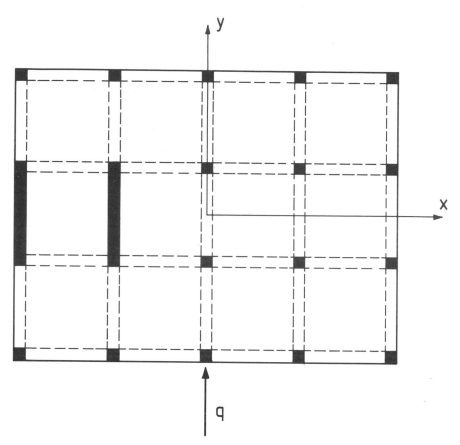

Fig. 14.15 Non-symmetric structural floor plan.

result of a more efficient distribution of material in the cross-section since they now offer increased moment-resisting capacity in two directions. They allow the creation of large open floor areas and can carry all essential services. An example of a structure incorporating a service core is shown in Fig. 14.16(a). The horizontally applied loads will mainly be shared by the interior core and the rigid frames parallel to the load. The distribution depends on the characteristics of the floor system connecting the vertical elements. Two assumptions about these connections can be made, resulting in different computer models.

(a) The interior beams and/or floors are effectively pin connected to the cores and columns

If the structural floor plan of this type of building is symmetric about the *y* axis, the structure can be classified under category 2 and a plane frame analysis is possible. Only half the structure needs to be considered. Half the core is bent B, i.e. one channel-shaped cantilever wall, is bundled with its exterior columns of the two exterior frames perpendicular to the direction of the load. Together they can be modelled as a single flexural cantilever with a combined bending stiffness represented by the wall and columns 1 and 2. One rigid frame parallel to the direction of the load, bent

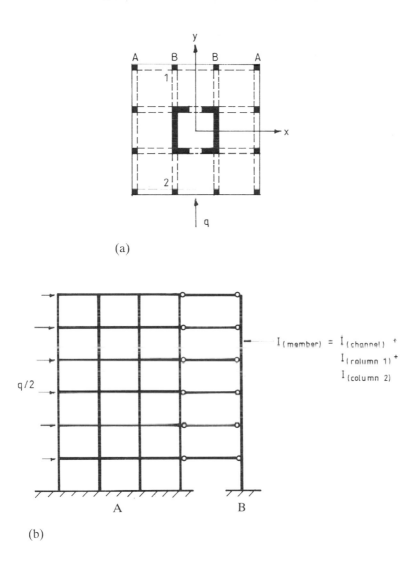

(a)

(b)

$$I_{(member)} = I_{(channel)} + I_{(column \ 1)} + I_{(column \ 2)}$$

Fig. 14.16 (a) Structural floor plan; (b) rigid frame linked to core and columns; (c) linked bents.

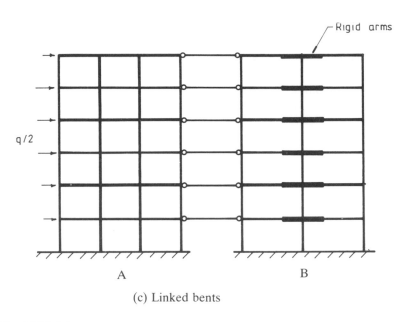

(c) Linked bents

Fig. 14.16 (c).

A, is then connected to it in a single plane by means of rigid links at each floor level. The two-dimensional model is to be subjected to half the lateral

(b) Beams spanning from the exterior columns to the cores can be considered rigidly connected

The channel-shaped shear wall which is parallel to the load and rigidly connected to floor beams will behave as a wide column and must be modelled as such. Flexural column elements are located on the neutral axis of the wall but in the plane of the bent. The moment of inertia of these members should represent the full section of the channel-shaped wall. Rigid arms are then attached in two directions at each floor level. Floor beams are rigidly connected to these arms and the columns of the perpendicular frames. The plane frame model of half the structure subjected to half the horizontal loading is shown in Fig. 14.16(c). The short deep beams connecting the shear walls at each floor level will not influence the deflection behaviour of the structure in the y direction since both walls adopt exactly the same deflection profile when subjected to lateral load.

When the core is turned through 90°, without loss of symmetry, a wide arm column model is still possible. The flexible column elements are to be placed on the neutral axis of the channel-shaped section but in the plane of the bent to be analysed. The moment of inertia of this element should represent only one-half of one channel-shaped section. The two unequal rigid arms at each floor level add up to the width of the 'flange' of the channel-shaped cantilever. Beams connecting the wide column to other walls or columns can then be rigidly jointed to the arms.

14.5.3 Framed tube structures

For tall buildings up to 55 storeys a framed tube structure will be able to supply efficient bracing in controlling the lateral deflections. This type of tall structure consists of perimeter frames with closely spaced columns and rigidly connected deep spandrel beams which form a perforated tube, as shown in the floor plan in Fig. 14.17(a). The gravity loading is shared between the perimeter columns and interior walls or columns. The lateral loads are usually considered to be entirely carried by the perimeter frames.

In a simple analysis the two frames parallel to the direction of the horizontal load can be taken as the principal load-carrying components and a plane frame analysis of one frame with 50% of the load could be sufficient. A more sophisticated analysis would also include the influence of the so-called 'flange effect' of the frames perpendicular to the wind load. This effect is not an out-of-plane contribution but the influence of the axial behaviour of the vertical members of that frame on the overall behaviour of the structure. The bending in the columns and girders of the frames parallel to the direction of the lateral load, the so called 'web' frames, will not be transferred to the flange frames. The interaction between the orthogonal frames is the vertical deformation of the corner columns only. This will rapidly decay away towards the centre of the flange frame as shown in Fig. 14.17(b). It is possible to analyse 'around' the corner in a two-dimensional computer model, as shown in Fig. 14.18(a). Symmetry allows the analysis of only one-quarter of the structure to be sufficient. The flexural cantilever A represents the transverse bending of one-half of one flange frame. The moment of inertia of this cantilever is obtained by summing the individual moments of inertia for the columns in the y direction. Since the flexural stiffness of the corner column will be taken into account in the web frame, it should be omitted here. Frame B represents half of one web frame parallel to the direction of the lateral loading. Frame C is half of the flange frame which interacts with the vertical deformations at the corner columns but is isolated from the bending of the columns and girders in frame B. The moments of inertia of the columns in frame C are taken in the x direction and the corner column is given a zero axial stiffness. The bending and translational isolation can be achieved by introducing fictitious short beams and releasing the translational and rotational degrees of freedom at one end. The centre of the flange frame is modelled by symmetric

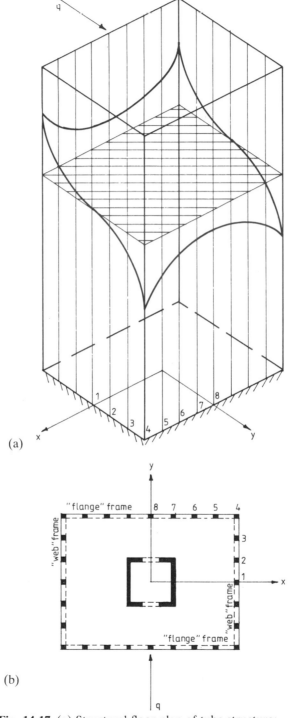

(a)

(b)

Fig. 14.17 (a) Structural floor plan of tube structure;
(b) stress distribution in tube structure subject

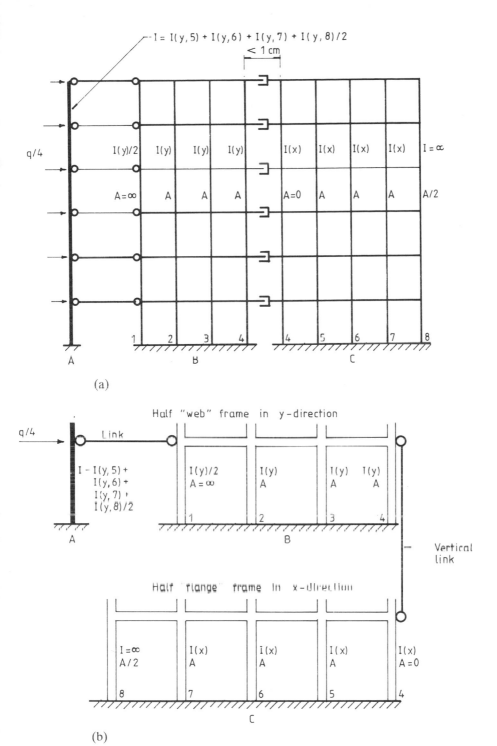

Fig. 14.18 (a) Computer model of tube structure; (b) pinned link computer model.

boundary conditions. If this is located on a column line, the column should be given an infinite bending stiffness. Symmetry at mid-span requires vertical rollers. As before the links represent the in-plane rigidity of the floor slabs.

If the standard plane frame program does not allow the releasing of specific degrees of freedom, the rather complicated connection at the corner can be modelled by vertical links. The corner columns 4x and 4y in the flange and web frames respectively are then located on the same line but offset in a vertical direction as shown for the bottom storey in Fig. 14.18(b). If necessary the links can be modelled by beams with zero bending stiffness and infinite axial stiffness.

If the framed tube is insufficiently stiff, additional stiffening can be obtained by combining the exterior tube with the interior shear core wall. This results in a tube in tube structure. The lateral load will now be shared by two tubes. This form of construction is applicable to structures up to 65 storeys. The plane frame computer model is obtained by adding a single flexural member, representing the core, to cantilever A of the frame structures shown in Fig. 14.18.

15

Programs for reinforced concrete design

15.1 INTRODUCTION

One of the main editorial changes in BS 8110 is in providing the mathematical expressions from which the various tables and graphical data given in the code are obtained. This is in recognition of the increase in the use of computers by practising engineers and students for the design of reinforced concrete structures. The provision of these expressions will enable designers to write simple programs to assist with their design calculations. Such programs, if properly planned, not only will speed up calculations but will ensure that designers consider all necessary aspects of design. A number of program packages, ranging in sophistication, are available commercially. The more comprehensive and sophisticated programs enable the user to link results from structural analysis to detailed design programs as well as to produce engineering drawings. In this chapter the source listings are presented for

1. design of rectangular sections
2. design of simply supported beams subject to uniform loading
3. calculating the deflections of simply supported beams carrying uniformly distributed loads
4. analysis and design of column sections.

The programs are written in BBC BASIC since the the BBC microcomputer was widely available in many educational establishments in the UK at the time that the revision of this book was planned. The BBC microcomputer is no longer available on the market, but these programs will run on the Master series which has replaced it. Input data for the programs are to be supplied by the user in an interactive manner. Interactive design programs should incorporate the following features:

1. Error traps to prevent accidental entry of data which will cause the program either to fail or to turn out meaningless results. For example, entering values for the overall depth of a beam which is less than its effective depth should cause the program not only to reject both entries with the opportunity to re-enter sensible values but also to provide an explanation of the error;

2. The ability to save data for future use in a datafile named by the user or designer. Ideally this facility should be available at various stages in the use of the program. It is essential at the end of the program;
3. Example data to assist the first time user through the program;
4. Help routines which not only introduce the program but also provide useful background information to the user at critical stages. For example, when asking for the shrinkage coefficient, the help facility should provide the user with a short explanation on shrinkage and point the user to the appropriate clauses in BS 8110. If required by the user, the program should be able to suggest sensible design input data.

A listing of interactive programs which incorporate the above mentioned features would be beyond the scope of this book. The following programs for the design of rectangular sections and simply supported beams, and for calculating the deflections of simply supported beams with uniformly distributed loads, and for column design, provide the reader with an insight into one of the many ways in which programs for reinforced concrete design may be written.

BBC BASIC is one of the many extended versions of standard BASIC; it is probably the first version of BASIC to allow full procedure (i.e. subroutine) and function handling. This is one of the most useful features of BBC BASIC in that it permits the program to be structured in an orderly manner with the bulk of the coding tucked away in procedures. Hence the major steps can be presented within relatively few lines at the start of the program. The programs presented here make use of a number of procedures such as PROCspace which requires the user to hit the space bar for the program to continue. These useful procedures are grouped together after the main section of the program. In order to ensure that the programs may be easily adapted for other microcomputers, most of the special features of BBC BASIC have not been used.

15.2 PROGRAM: SECTION DESIGN

15.2.1 Program discussion

The design of rectangular sections based on the simplified stress block was presented in sections 4.4 and 4.5. This is usually the type of problem first encountered by students who are new to the subject. The steps to be taken are as follows:

1. Decide on the cross-sectional dimensions b and d;
2. Determine, using $M = 0.156f_{cu}bd^2$, whether the section is to be singly or doubly reinforced;
3. If the section is to be designed for balanced conditions or to be singly reinforced then determine the required tensile steel area A_s;

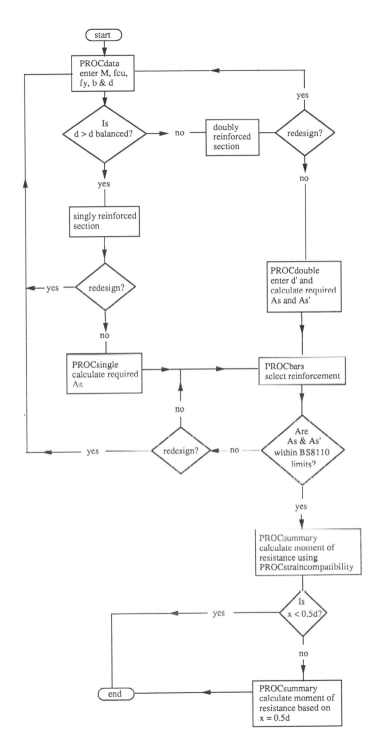

Fig. 15.1 Flow chart for section design

4. If the section is to be doubly reinforced then determine the required compressive and tensile steel areas A_s and A_s';
5. Select the number and diameters of the bars;
6. Check that the selected reinforcement complies with the minimum and maximum reinforcement areas specified in BS 8110: Part 1, clauses 3.12.5 and 3.12.6;
7. Check, using the procedures described in section 4.6, that the selected cross-section and reinforcement provide an ultimate moment of resistance which is at least equal to the applied ultimate moment. This is particularly important if the steel areas provided (step 5 above) are significantly different from the calculated steel areas (steps 3 and 4). This check calculation will also indicate whether the actual depth of compression x is larger than the limiting value required by BS 8110, i.e. $(\beta_b - 0.4)d$. Where redistribution of moments is less than 10%, this implies that the compressive depth should not be greater than half the effective depth d. Hence it is essential to ensure that the applied ultimate moment is less than the section's ultimate moment of resistance based on the limiting value.

A flow chart illustrating the relationships between the above steps with the opportunity to redesign the section at various stages is shown in Fig. 15.1. These steps can easily be computerized and the source listing for such a program is given in section 15.2.2.

At the start of the program, the procedure PROCdata (listed between lines 550 and 1230) is called at line 80 to enable entry of basic data such as design ultimate moment, material characteristic strengths, beam breadth and effective depth. After entering values for the design moment and characteristic strengths the program (lines 810 and 920) offers the user the opportunity to fix either

(a) the beam breadth b

or

(b) the beam breadth-to-effective depth ratio b/d

If the first option is selected, then the effective depth for balanced conditions is given by

$$d_{balanced} = \left(\frac{\text{design moment}}{0.156bf_{cu}}\right)^{1/2}$$

However, some designers may wish to end up with a rectangular section of fixed b/d ratio. In this case, the effective depth for balanced conditions is obtained from

$$d_{\text{balanced}} = \left(\frac{\text{design moment}}{0.156(bd\text{-ratio})f_{\text{cu}}}\right)^{1/3}$$

where bd-ratio is the required b/d. This is achieved for both options between lines 930 and 960. The actual effective depth for design purposes is then entered in line 1130.

The program then calls PROCreintype at line 90. This procedure (listed between lines 1300 and 1510) informs the program user whether a singly or doubly reinforced section will be required to resist the design ultimate moment, after comparing the selected effective depth value and the calculated value for balanced conditions. At this juncture (line 1500) the designer may decide either to proceed or to redesign the section. If the redesign option is selected then the program returns to the start via line 100. Otherwise either PROCsingle (lines 1700–1950) or PROCdouble (lines 2020–2590) is called at line 110.

Within PROCsingle the required steel area A_s is calculated (lines 1780–1830) using

$$M = f_y A_s z$$

where

$$z = d\left[0.5 + \left(0.25 - \frac{K}{0.9}\right)^{1/2}\right]$$

and $K = 0.156$.

Thereafter PROCbars (lines 2870–3490) is used to select the number of reinforcing bars and their diameters. The selected reinforcement is then checked for compliance with clauses 3.12.5 and 3.12.6 (i.e. for limiting values of minimum and maximum steel areas). If compliance is not achieved, the user may choose to reselect a different set of reinforcements or to redesign the beam (lines 3340–3480). In a similar manner, PROCdouble calculates (lines 2050–2420) the required compression steel areas A_s' and calls PROCbars at line 2370. It then calculates (lines 2430–2590) the required tensile steel area A_u and calls PROCbars at line 2540.

As pointed out in item 7 above, if the reinforcement provided is not approximately equal to the required steel areas it is prudent to check that the capacity of the section exceeds the applied ultimate moment. This check is carried out at line 130 which calls PROCsummary (lines 3550–4120). The first step is to determine the depth of compression at which there is equilibrium of compressive and tensile forces. This is achieved in PROC-straincompatibility (lines 4180–4420) by an iterative process which compares the relative magnitudes of compressive and tensile forces in the section for assumed depths of compression until equilibrium is achieved.

Having determined the depth of compression x, the moment of resistance of the section is calculated from

$$M_R = 0.402f_{cu}bx(d - 0.45x) + A_s'f_y'(d - d')$$

However, where x is greater than $d/2$ and where less than 10% redistribution of bending moments has been carried out, the resisting moment of the section is limited to

$$M_R = 0.156f_{cu}bd^2 + A_s'f_y'(d - d')$$

15.2.2 Source listing of program Section Design

```
 10 REM Program "Section-Design"
 20 REM for the design of rectangular reinforced concrete sections
 30 :
 40 REM *************************
 50 REM Main program starts here
 60 REM *************************
 70 :
 80 PROCdata
 90 PROCreintype
100 IF a$="R" OR a$="r" THEN GOTO 80
110 IF D>=dB THEN PROCsingle ELSE PROCdouble
120 IF STCK$="R" THEN GOTO 80
130 PROCsummary
140 GOTO 80
150 END
160 REM ***********************
170 REM Main program stops here
180 REM ***********************
190 :
200 REM *********************
210 REM Some useful procedures
220 REM *********************
230 :
240 DEF PROCspace
250 PRINT TAB(4,23)"Press space bar to continue"
260 REPEAT
270    UNTIL GET=32
280 ENDPROC
290 :
300 DEF PROCchange
310 PRINT TAB(1,23)"Change the above input ? Type Y or N"
320 REPEAT
330    a$ = GET$
340    UNTIL a$="Y" OR a$="N" OR a$="y" OR a$="n"
350 ENDPROC
360 :
370 DEF PROCab
380 PRINT "Select option A or B"
390 REPEAT
400    a$ = GET$
410    UNTIL a$="A" OR a$="B" OR a$="a" OR a$="b"
420 ENDPROC
430 :
440 DEF PROCpr
450 PRINT TAB(1,23)"Proceed or Redesign ? Type P or R"
460 REPEAT
470    a$ = GET$
480    UNTIL a$="P" OR a$="R" OR a$="p" OR a$="r"
490 ENDPROC
```

```
 500 :
 510 REM ************************
 520 REM Procedure for data entry
 530 REM ************************
 540 :
 550 DEF PROCdata
 560 CLS
 570 PRINT
 580 PRINT
 590 PRINT"Enter the following:-"
 600 INPUT"1) the design moment (kNm) = " DM
 610 INPUT"2) fcu (N/mm2)            = " FC
 620 INPUT"3) fy (N/mm2)            = " FY
 630 IF FY<>250 AND FY<>460 THEN GOTO 620
 640 PRINT
 650 KD = .156
 660 PRINT
 670 PRINT"The limiting value of k is "; KD
 680 PRINT"(see clause 3.4.4.4)"
 690 PROCchange
 700 IF a$="Y" OR a$="y" THEN GOTO 560
 710 CLS
 720 PRINT
 730 PRINT"At balanced conditions, the moment"
 740 PRINT"of resistence is given by"
 750 PRINT
 760 PRINT"Mu = ";KD;" fcu bd2"
 770 PRINT"where fcu = charac. concrete strength"
 780 PRINT"      b   = breadth of section"
 790 PRINT"      d   - effective depth"
 800 PRINT
 810 PRINT"To calculate d for balanced design,"
 820 PRINT"do you wish to :-"
 830 PRINT"A) fix the breadth b"
 840 PRINT"B) select the b/d ratio"
 850 PRINT
 860 PROCab
 870 IF a$="A" OR a$="a" THEN AB$="A" ELSE AB$="B"
 880 PRINT"Selected option ";AB$
 890 IF AB$="A" THEN INPUT"section breadth (mm) - " TEMP
 900 IF AB$="A" AND TEMP<50 THEN GOTO 890
 910 IF AB$="B" THEN INPUT"b/d ratio = " TEMP
 920 IF AB$="B" AND TEMP<0.01 THEN GOTO 910
 930 IF AB$="A" THEN B=TEMP ELSE BDR=TEMP
 940 Q=1E6*DM/(KD*FC*TEMP)
 950 IF AB$="A" THEN dB=SQR(Q) ELSE dB=Q^(1/3):B=BDR*dB
 960 PRINT"d = balanced condition = ";dB;" mm"
 970 PROCchange
 980 IF a$="Y" OR a$="y" THEN 710
 990 CLS
1000 PRINT
1010 PRINT"Given:"
1020 PRINT"Mu  = ";DM;" kNm"
1030 PRINT"fcu = ";FC;" N/mm2"
1040 PRINT"fy  = ";FY;" N/mm2"
1050 PRINT"For balanced design, b = ";B;" mm"
1060 PRINT"                     d = ";dB;" mm"
1070 PRINT
1080 PRINT"You may select :-"
1090 PRINT"A) d > ";dB" mm"
1100 PRINT"B) d = ";dB" mm"
1110 PRINT"C) d < ";dB" mm"
```

```
1120 PRINT
1130 INPUT"Required d (mm) = " D
1140 IF D<50 THEN GOTO 1130
1150 IF D=dB THEN GOTO 1190
1160 IF AB$="B" THEN B=BDR*D : dB=SQR(1E6*DM/(KD*FC*B))
1170 IF AB$="B" THEN PRINT:PRINT"In order to maintain the b/d ratio"
1180 IF AB$="B" THEN PRINT"of ";TEMP;", the beam breadth = ";B;" mm"
1190 PROCchange
1200 IF a$="Y" OR a$="Y" THEN 990
1210 IF D=dB THEN K=KD:GOTO 1230
1220 K=1E6*DM/(FC*B*D*D)
1230 ENDPROC
1240 :
1250 REM ***************************************
1260 REM Procedure to determine if the section is
1270 REM singly or doubly reinforced
1280 REM ***************************************
1290 :
1300 DEF PROCreintype
1310 Mbal=KD*FC*B*D*D/1E6
1320 CLS
1330 PROCgiven
1340 PRINT
1350 PRINT"Hence, Mu/(fcu bd2)    = ";K
1360 PRINT"and     Mu/bd2         = ";K*FC
1370 PRINT
1380 PRINT
1390 PRINT"For balanced design,"
1400 PRINT"    Mu = ";KD;"fcu bd2"
1410 PRINT"       = ";Mbal;" kNm"
1420 PRINT" & d  = ";dB;" mm"
1430 PRINT
1440 IF D>=dB THEN PRINT"Since selected d >= ";dB;" mm"
1450 IF D>=dB THEN PRINT"and Mu/(fcu bd2) <= ";KD
1460 IF D>=dB THEN PRINT"section will be singly reinforced."
1470 IF D<dB THEN PRINT"Since selected d < ";dB;" mm"
1480 IF D<dB THEN PRINT"and Mu/(fcu bd2) > ";KD
1490 IF D<dB THEN PRINT"a doubly reinforced section is required."
1500 PROCpr
1510 ENDPROC
1520 :
1530 REM *****************************
1540 REM Procedure to print input data
1550 REM *****************************
1560 :
1570 DEF PROCgiven
1580 PRINT
1590 PRINT"Given:"
1600 PRINT"Mu  = ";DM;" kNm"
1610 PRINT"fcu = ";FC;" N/mm2" TAB(20) "b  = ";B;" mm"
1620 PRINT"fy  = ";FY;" N/mm2" TAB(20) "d  = ";D;" mm"
1630 ENDPROC
1640 :
1650 REM ********************************
1660 REM Procedure for obtaining steel area
1670 REM for a singly reinforced section
1680 REM ********************************
1690 :
1700 DEF PROCsingle
1710 SD$="S"
1720 sd$=" Singly Reinforced Section"
1730 CD=0
```

```
1740 CA=0
1750 FYD1=0
1760 D1=0
1770 D1XM=0
1780 Z=D*(.5+SQR(.25-K/.9))
1790 IF Z >= .95*D THEN Z = .95*D
1800 X=(D-Z)/.45
1810 XD=X/D
1820 FS=.87*FY
1830 AS=DM*1E6/FS/Z
1840 CLS
1850 PROCgiven
1860 PRINT"Z   = ";Z;" mm"TAB(20)"fs = ";FS" N/mm2"
1870 PRINT"Required As  = ";AS;" mm2"
1880 PROCspace
1890 ST$="Tensile"
1900 PROCbars(AS,FS)
1910 IF STCK$="P" THEN GOTO 1900
1920 TA=T
1930 TN=NOB
1940 TD=R
1950 ENDPROC
1960 :
1970 REM *********************************
1980 REM Procedure for obtaining steel areas
1990 REM for a doubly reinforced section
2000 REM *********************************
2010 :
2020 DEF PROCdouble
2030 SD$="D"
2040 sd$="Doubly reinforced section"
2050 X=0.5*D
2060 XD=0.5
2070 Z=D-.45*X
2080 D1XM=1-FY/805
2090 CLS
2100 PRINT
2110 PRINT
2120 PRINT"Depth to neutral axis = ";X" mm"
2130 PRINT
2140 PRINT"Enter effective depth to compression"
2150 PRINT"steel,"
2160 INPUT"ie d' (mm) = " D1
2170 IF D1<20 THEN GOTO 2160
2180 IF D1>=X THEN GOTO 2160
2190 PROCgiven
2200 PRINT TAB(20) "d'   ",D1;" mm"
2210 PRINT" Note: d'/x   limit   = 1 - fy/805"
2220 PRINT TAB(23) "=";D1XM
2230 D1X=D1/X
2240 FSD=0.87*FY
2250 IF D1X>D1XM THEN ESD=0.0035*(1-D1/D/XD):FSD=200000*ESD
2260 IF D1X>D1XM THEN PRINT"      actual d'/x    >";D1XM
2270 IF D1X>D1XM THEN PRINT"      Hence fs'     < .87 fy"
2280 IF D1X<=D1XM THEN PRINT"      actual d'/x   <=";D1XM
2290 IF D1X<=D1XM THEN PRINT"      Hence,fs'    = .87 fy"
2300 ASD=(K-KD)*FC*B*D*D/(FSD*(D-D1))
2310 PRINT"                      = ";FSD;" N/mm2"
2320 PRINT
2330 PRINT"Reqd steel area As'  = ";ASD;" mm2"
2340 PROCchange
2350 IF a$="Y" OR a$="y" THEN GOTO 2040
```

```
2360 ST$="Compression"
2370 PROCbars(ASD,FSD)
2380 IF STCK$="P" THEN GOTO 2370
2390 IF STCK$="R" THEN ENDPROC
2400 CA=T
2410 CN=NOB
2420 CD=R
2430 FS=0.87*FY
2440 AS=(KD*FC*B*D*D/Z+ASD*FSD)/FS
2450 CLS
2460 PRINT sd$
2470 PROCgiven
2480 PRINT" x    = ";X;" mm" TAB(20) "d' = ";D1;" mm"
2490 PRINT" Reqd. comp. steel     = ";ASD;" mm2"
2500 PRINT" Provided comp. steel  = ";CA" mm2"
2510 PRINT" Reqd. tensile steel   = ";AS;" mm2"
2520 PROCspace
2530 ST$="Tensile"
2540 PROCbars(AS,FS)
2550 IF STCK$="P" THEN GOTO 2540
2560 TA=T
2570 TN=NOB
2580 TD=R
2590 ENDPROC
2600 :
2610 REM **********************************
2620 REM Procedure to show reinforcement areas
2630 REM **********************************
2640 :
2650 DEF PROCareas
2660 CLS
2670 PRINT
2680 PRINT
2690 PRINT
2700 PRINT"No. of!       Bar Diameter (mm)"
2710 PRINT" Bars !  12    16    20    25    32    40   "
2720 PRINT"   1  ! 113   201   314   490   804  1256"
2730 PRINT"   2  ! 226   402   628   981  1608 2513"
2740 PRINT"   3  ! 339   603   942  1472  2412 3769"
2750 PRINT"   4  ! 452   804  1256  1963  3216 5026"
2760 PRINT"   5  ! 565  1005  1570  2454  4021 6283"
2770 PRINT"   6  ! 678  1206  1884  2945  4825 7539"
2780 PRINT"   7  ! 791  1407  2199  3436  5629 8796"
2790 PRINT"   8  ! 904  1608  2513  3926  6433 10053"
2800 PRINT"   9  ! 1017 1809  2827  4417  7238 11309"
2810 ENDPROC
2820 :
2830 REM **********************************************
2840 REM Procedure for selecting required number of bars
2850 REM **********************************************
2860 :
2870 DEF PROCbars(as,f)
2880 T=0
2890 PROCareas
2900 PRINT TAB(0,16) " Steel area provided = ";T;" mm2"
2910 PRINT TAB(0,17) " Required steel area = ";as;" mm2"
2920 INPUT" Number of bars      = "NOB
2930 INPUT" Bar diameter (mm)   = "R
2940  IF R<>12 AND R<>16 AND R<>20 AND R<>25 AND R<>32 AND R<>40 THEN  GOTO 2930
2950 TTEMP=3.142*R*R/4*NOB
2960 T=T + TTEMP
2970 PRINT" Steel area provided = ";T;" mm2"
```

```
2980 PRINT"Type A for more steel or B to proceed"
2990 PROCab
3000 IF a$="A" OR a$="a" THEN AB$="A" ELSE AB$="B"
3010 PRINT"Selected option ";AB$
3020 IF a$="A" OR a$="a" THEN GOTO 2890
3030 PROCchange
3040 IF a$="Y" OR a$="y" THEN GOTO 2880
3050 :
3060 REM ************************************************************
3070 REM The rest of this procedure checks for compliance with clauses
3080 REM 3.12.5 and 3.12.6 for minimum and maximum steel areas
3090 REM ************************************************************
3100 :
3110 AM=.04*B*(D+50)
3120 IF ST$="Compression" THEN AMIN=.002*B*(D+50):am$=" .2%"
3130 IF ST$="Tensile" AND FY=250 THEN AMIN=.0024*B*(D+50):am$=" .24%"
3140 IF ST$="Tensile" AND FY=460 THEN AMIN=.0013*B*(D+50):am$=" .13%"
3150 Amax$="     maximum allowable = 4% Ac"
3160 Amin$="     minimum allowable ="+am$+" Ac"
3170 IF T>AM THEN AMM=AM ELSE AMM=AMIN
3180 IF T>AM THEN Amm$=Amax$ ELSE Amm$=Amin$
3190 IF T>AM THEN ACL$=" exceeds maximum      allowable - see clause 3.12.6."
3200 IF T<AMIN THEN ACL$=" is less than minimum  requirement - see clause 3.12.5."
3210 IF T<= AM AND T>= AMIN THEN STCK$="C"
3220 IF T<= AM AND T>= AMIN THEN ENDPROC
3230 REM ****************************↑↑↑↑↑↑↑↑↑↑*************************
3240 REM If the selected steel area is within the code limits
3250 REM then 'end' the procedure,
3260 REM otherwise
3270 REM the procedure permits either:-
3280 REM 1) reselection of reinforcement or
3290 REM 2) redesign.
3300 REM ************************************************
3310 CLS
3320 PROCgiven
3330 IF ST$="Compression" THEN PRINT"              d1 = ";D1;" mm"
3340 PRINT
3350 PRINT"    reqd steel area  = ";as;" mm2"
3360 PRINT"    actual steel area = ",T," mm2"
3370 PRINTAmm$
3380 PRINT"              = ";AMM;" mm2"
3390 PRINT"NOTE:    "
3400 PRINT" Actual steel area"+ACL$
3410 PRINT
3420 PRINT
3430 PRINT" You should:"
3440 PRINT
3450 PRINT" P) Provide different steel area"
3460 PRINT" R) Redesign the beam"
3470 PROCpr
3480 IF a$="P" OR a$="p" THEN STCK$="P" ELSE STCK$="R"
3490 ENDPROC
3500 :
3510 REM *************************************************
3520 REM Procedure for presenting a summary of the design
3530 REM *************************************************
3540 :
3550 DEF PROCsummary
3560 PROCstraincompatibility
3570 XDM=0.5
3580 XM=XDM*D
3590 CLS
```

```
3600 PRINT
3610 PRINT
3620 PRINT sd$
3630 PROCgiven
3640 IF SD$="D" THEN PRINT" x   = ";X;" mm" TAB(20) "d' = ";D1;" mm"
3650 IF SD$="S" THEN PRINT" x   = ";X;" mm" TAB(20) "z  = ";Z;" mm"
3660 AFSD=CA*FYD1/1000
3670 AFS=TA*FYD2/1000
3680 CF=.402*FC*B*X/1000
3690 PRINT
3700 PRINT" Comp. concrete force  = ";CF;" kN"
3710 IF SD$="D" THEN PRINT:PRINT" Comp. stress fs'      = ";FYD1;" N/mm2"
3720 IF SD$="D" THEN PRINT" Comp. steel area As'  = ";CA" mm2"
3730 IF SD$="D" THEN PRINT" Hence, C' = As' * fs' = ";AFSD;" kN"
3740 PRINT
3750 PRINT" Tensile stress fs     = ";FYD2;" N/mm2"
3760 PRINT" Tensile steel area As = ";TA" mm2"
3770 PRINT" Hence, T  = As * fs   = ";AFS" kN"
3780 MU=(0.402*FC*B*D*D*XD*(1-.45*XD) + FYD1*CA*(D-D1)) / 1000000
3790 PRINT
3800 PRINT" Moment of resistence  = ";MU;" kN-m"
3810 IF XM>X THEN GOTO 4110
3820 PROCspace
3830 CLS
3840 :
3850 REM ****************************************************************
3860 REM BS 8110 limits x/d to 0.5
3870 REM The rest of this procedure calculates the resising moment for
3880 REM the section with x/d = 0.5
3890 REM ****************************************************************
3900 PRINT
3910 PRINT sd$
3920 PROCgiven
3930 IF SD$="D" THEN PRINT" x  = ";X;" mm" TAB(20) "d' = ";D1;" mm"
3940 IF SD$="S" THEN PRINT" x  = ";X;" mm" TAB(20) "z  = ";Z;" mm"
3950 PRINT" For equilibrium, x/d = "XD
3960 PRINT" & resisting moment   = ";MU;" kN-m"
3970 PRINT" but BS 8110 x/d limit = ";XDM
3980 XD=XDM
3990 X=XM
4000 D1X=D1/X
4010 IF D1X>D1XM THEN FYD1=700*(1-D1X) ELSE FYD1=.87*FY
4020 AFSD=CA*FYD1/1000
4030 CF=.402*FC*B*X/1000
4040 PRINT" Hence,"
4050 PRINT" comp. concrete force  = ";CF;" kN"
4060 IF SD$="D" THEN PRINT" comp. stress fs'      = ";FYD1;" N/mm2"
4070 IF SD$="D" THEN PRINT" comp. steel area      = ";CA" mm2"
4080 IF SD$="D" THEN PRINT" C'   =   As' * fs'    = ";AFSD;" kN"
4090 MU=(0.402*FC*B*D*D*XD*(1-.45*XD) + FYD1*CA*(D-D1)) / 1000000
4100 PRINT" & resisting moment    = ";MU;" kN-m"
4110 PROCspace
4120 ENDPROC
4130 :
4140 REM ********************************************************
4150 REM Procedure for equilibrium & compatibility checks
4160 REM ********************************************************
4170 :
4180 DEF PROCstraincompatibility
4190 CLS
4200 PRINT
4210 PRINT
```

```
4220 PRINT
4230 PRINT
4240 PRINT
4250 PRINT" Please wait - equilibrium and strain"
4260 PRINT"                     compatibility checks"
4270 YE=FY/230000
4280 XD=0.01
4290 PRINT
4300 PRINT
4310 REPEAT
4320   XD=XD+0.001
4330   X=XD*D
4340   Z=D-.45*X
4350   PRINT" Assuming x/d = ";XD
4360   E=0.0035*(1/XD-1)
4370   IF E<=YE THEN FYD2=200000*E ELSE FYD2=FY*.87
4380   IF SD$="S" THEN GOTO 4410
4390   ED=0.0035*(1-D1/D/XD)
4400   IF ED<=YE THEN FYD1=200000*ED ELSE FYD1=FY*.87
4410   UNTIL 0.402*FC*B*D*XD+CA*FYD1>=TA*FYD2
4420 ENDPROC
```

15.2.3 Sample runs

To illustrate the use of the program Section Design, consider the following example problem presented as Example 4.7 which results in a doubly reinforced section.

□ Example 15.1 Section design using computer program based on Example 4.7

A rectangular beam is 200 mm wide and has an effective depth of 300 mm. The depth to the compression steel is 40 mm. Design the section to resist an ultimate design bending moment of 123.3 kN m. Assume grade 30 concrete and a yield stress of 460 N/mm^2 for the main reinforcement.

The following information will be displayed on the screen as input data is entered:

```
Enter the following:-
1) the design moment (kNm) = 123.3
2) fcu (N/mm2)            = 30
3) fy (N/mm2)             = 460


The limiting value of K is 0.156
(see clause 3.4.4.4)
Change the above input ? Type Y or N

At balanced conditions, the moment
of resistence is given by

Mu = 0.156 fcu bd2
where fcu = charac. concrete strength
      b   = breadth of section
      d   = effective depth
```

```
To calculate d for balanced design,
do you wish to :-
A) fix the breadth b
B) select the b/d ratio

Select option A or B
Selected option A
section breadth (mm)  = 200
d - balanced condition = 362.947337 mm
Change the above input ? Type Y or N


Given:
Mu  = 123.3 kNm
fcu = 30 N/mm2
fy  = 460 N/mm2
For balanced design, b = 200 mm
                     d = 362.947337 mm

You may select :-
A) d > 362.947337 mm
B) d = 362.947337 mm
C) d < 362.947337 mm

Required d (mm) = 300
Change the above input ? Type Y or N


Given:
Mu  = 123.3 kNm
fcu = 30 N/mm2      b  = 200 mm
fy  = 460 N/mm2     d  = 300 mm

Hence, Mu/(fcu bd2)   = 0.228333333
and    Mu/bd2         = 6.85


For balanced design,
    Mu = 0.156fcu bd2
       = 84.24 kNm
 & d   = 362.947337 mm

Since selected d < 362.947337 mm
and Mu/(fcu bd2) > 0.156
a doubly reinforced section is required.
Proceed or Redesign ? Type P or R
```

The required compressive steel area is 375.4 mm^2 and two 16 mm diameter bars are selected as shown below:

```
Depth to neutral axis = 150 mm

Enter effective depth to compression
steel,
ie d' (mm) = 40

Given:
Mu  = 123.3 kNm
```

```
fcu = 30 N/mm2        b  = 200 mm
fy  = 460 N/mm2       d  = 300 mm
                     d' = 40 mm
  Note: d'/x   limit     = 1 - fy/805
                        =0.428571429
        actual d'/x    <=0.428571429
        Hence,fs'        = 0.87 fy
                        = 400.2 N/mm2

Reqd steel area As'   = 375.389228 mm2
Change the above input ? Type Y or N



No. of!          Bar Diameter (mm)
 Bars !   12    16    20    25    32    40
   1  !  113   201   314   490   804  1256
   2  !  226   402   628   981  1608  2513
   3  !  339   603   942  1472  2412  3769
   4  !  452   804  1256  1963  3216  5026
   5  !  565  1005  1570  2454  4021  6283
   6  !  678  1206  1884  2915  4825  7539
   7  !  791  1407  2199  3436  5629  8796
   8  !  904  1608  2513  3926  6433 10053
   9  ! 1017  1809  2827  4417  7238 11309
Steel area provided = 0 mm2
Required steel area = 375.389228 mm2
Number of bars       = 2
Bar diameter (mm)    = 16
 Steel area provided = 402.176 mm2
Type A for more steel or B to proceed
Select option A or B
Selected option B
Change the above input ? Type Y or N



Doubly reinforced section

Given:
Mu  = 123.3 kNm
fcu = 30 N/mm2        b  = 200 mm
fy  - 460 N/mm2       d  = 300 mm
 x  = 150 mm         d' = 40 mm
 Reqd. comp. steel     = 375.389228 mm2
 Provided comp. steel  = 402.176 mm2
 Reqd. tensile steel   = 1280.743 mm2
Press space bar to continue
```

The required tensile steel area is 1280.7 mm^2, and two 25 mm and two 16 mm diameter bars are selected as shown below:

```
No. of!          Bar Diameter (mm)
 Bars !   12    16    20    25    32    40
   1  !  113   201   314   490   804  1256
   2  !  226   402   628   981  1608  2513
   3  !  339   603   942  1472  2412  3769
   4  !  452   804  1256  1963  3216  5026
   5  !  565  1005  1570  2454  4021  6283
   6  !  678  1206  1884  2945  4825  7539
```

```
7  ! 791   1407 2199 3436 5629 8796
8  ! 904   1608 2513 3926 6433 10053
9  ! 1017 1809 2827 4417 7238 11309
Steel area provided = 0 mm2
Required steel area = 1280.743 mm2
Number of bars     = 2
Bar diameter (mm)  = 25
Steel area provided = 981.875 mm2
Type A for more steel or B to proceed
Select option A or B
Selected option A


 Steel area provided = 981.875 mm2
 Required steel area = 1280.743 mm2
 Number of bars     = 2
 Bar diameter (mm)  = 16
 Steel area provided = 1384.051 mm2
Type A for more steel or B to proceed
Select option A or B
Selected option B
Change the above input ? Type Y or N
```

The output from PROCsummary shows that for equilibrium of axial forces the depth of compression is 163 mm and the corresponding moment of resistance is 131 kN m. However, limiting the compressive depth to half the effective depth results in a resisting moment of 126 kN m as shown below:

```
Doubly reinforced section

Given:
Mu  = 123.3 kNm
fcu = 30 N/mm2      b  = 200 mm
fy  = 460 N/mm2     d  = 300 mm
x   = 163.200002 mm d' = 40 mm
 For equilibrium, x/d  = 0.544000007
 & resisting moment    = 131.029934 kN-m
but BS 8110 x/d limit  = 0.5
Hence,
comp. concrete force   = 361.8 kN
comp. stress fs'       = 400.2 N/mm2
comp. steel area       = 402.176 mm2
C'  =  As' * fs'       = 160.950835 kN
& resisting moment     = 125.965717 kN-m
Press space bar to continue
```

15.3 PROGRAM: RC BEAM

15.3.1 Program discussion

The program Section Design can easily be altered to allow the design of simply supported rectangular beams carrying a uniformly distributed load. This requires a different procedure (PROCdata) for data entry at the start of the program, and calls for additional procedures for checking the span-to-depth ratio of the beam (PROCspandepth) and for the design of shear reinforcement (PROClinks) after the main reinforcement has been selected.

BS 8110: Part 1, clauses 3.4.5.2 and 3.4.5.8, limits the shearing force in a beam to either $0.8f_{cu}^{1/2}$ or $5\,N/mm^2$, whichever is the larger. Hence it is prudent to check that this condition is being met as early as possible in the design process. This check is embodied in PROCshearcheck which is called immediately after PROCdata with the option to redesign the beam. The additional coding incorporating the above is given in section 15.3.2.

In PROCspandepth, calculation of the modification factors which account for the effects of both tensile and compressive reinforcement on the basic span-to-effective depth ratios (BS 8110: Part 1, clauses 3.4.6.3 and 3.4.6.4) is listed in lines 4950–5060. This procedure merely shows the actual and limiting values of span-to-depth ratios for the beam. If the actual value exceeds the permitted value, the user should redesign the beam. However, he/she may wish to calculate the actual deflection using the program 'beam deflection' presented in section 15.4.

The design of links for resisting shear forces in beams (carrying generally uniform loading) was presented in Chapters 5 and 7. According to clause 3.4.5.10 it is necessary firstly to check that the value of the shear stress at the support face does not exceed the permitted maximum value and secondly to design for the shear at a distance d from the face of the support. Hence, in PROClinks shear design is initially carried out for the beam section at the support face. Owing to curtailment of the main reinforcement, the effective depth d and the area of tensile steel A_s may not be the same as that provided for the section at mid-span where bending moment is at a maximum. Since these affect the magnitude of the design concrete shear stress v_c, correct values for these two parameters are entered in lines 5280–5490. Thereafter, in lines 5640–5840, the nominal shear stress v at the support face is compared with the design concrete shear stress v_c in accordance with Table 3.8 of the code. The maximum permitted spacing is then calculated for selected values of link diameter, number of legs and characteristic strength. The program also calculates the distance over which the links are required (line 6210). The procedure repeats the above design steps for the section at a distance d from the support face (lines 6310–6550).

15.3.2 Source listing of program RC Beam

```
10 REM Program "RC-Beam"
20 REM for the design of simply supported reinforced concrete beams
25 :
30 REM ************************
40 REM Main program starts here
50 REM ************************
60 :
70 PROCdata
75 PROCshearcheck
80 IF a$="R" OR a$="r" THEN GOTO 70
90 PROCreintype
```

```
100 IF a$="R" OR a$="r" THEN GOTO 70
110 IF D>=dB THEN PROCsingle ELSE PROCdouble
120 IF STCK$="R" THEN GOTO 70
130 PROCsummary
135 PROCspandepth
140 PROClinks
145 GOTO 70
150 END
160 REM **********************
170 REM Main program ends here
180 REM **********************
190 REM:
200 REM ***********************************************
210 REM This program makes use of the useful procedures
220 REM listed between lines 200 and 500
230 REM in program "section design"
490 REM ***********************************************
500 :
510 REM ***********************
520 REM Procedure for data entry
530 REM ***********************
540 :
550 DEF PROCdata
560 CLS
570 PRINT
580 PRINT
590 PRINT"Enter the following:-"
600 INPUT"- effective span (m)        = " S
610 INPUT"- effective depth (mm)      = " D
620 INPUT"- beam breadth (mm)         = " B
630 W=2400*9.81*B*(D+50)/1E9
640 PRINT
650 PRINT"Note, beam's self weight    = ";W;" kN/m"
660 PRINT
670 PRINT"- characteristic uniformly"
680 PRINT"  distributed dead load"
690 PRINT"  including self-weight"
700 INPUT"  ie GK (kN/m)             = " GK
710 PRINT"- characteristic uniformly"
720 PRINT"  distributed imposed load"
730 INPUT"  ie QK (kN/m)             = " QK
740 DL=1.4*GK+1.6*QK
750 DM=DL*S*S/8
760 SF=DL*S/2
770 PRINT
780 PRINT"DL = 1.4Gk + 1.6Qk = ";DL;" kN/m"
790 PRINT"Design moment        = ";DM;" kN m"
800 PRINT"Shear force          = ";SF;" kN"
810 INPUT"- fcu (N/mm2)             = " FC
820 K=1E6*DM/(FC*B*D*D)
830 KD = 0.156
840 dB=SQR(1E6*DM/(KD*FC*B))
850 INPUT"- fy (N/mm2)              = " FY
860 IF FY<>250 AND FY<>460 THEN GOTO 850
870 PRINT
880 PROCchange
890 IF a$="Y" OR a$="y" THEN GOTO 560
900 ENDPROC
1240 :
1250 REM ***********************************************
1260 REM This program makes use of the following procedures:-
1270 :
1300 REM PROCreintype
1570 REM PROCgiven
1700 REM PROCsingle
2020 REM PROCdouble
2650 REM PROCareas
```

```
2870 REM PROCbars
3540 REM PROCsummary
4170 REM PROCstraincompatibility
4180 :
4190 REM which are listed between lines 1250 and 4420
4200 REM in program "section design"
4400 :
4410 REM **************************************************
4420 :
4430 REM ****************************************
4440 REM Procedure for checking shear requirements
4450 REM ****************************************
4460 :
4470 DEF PROCshearcheck
4480 CLS
4490 PRINT
4500 PRINT
4510 V=SF*1000/(B*D)
4520 VM=.8*(SQR(FC))
4530 IF VM>5 THEN VM=5
4540 PROCgiven
4550 PRINT
4560 PRINT" Shear stress       = ";V;" N/mm2"
4570 PRINT" Maximum allowable = ";VM;" N/mm2"
4580 PRINT" shear stress"
1590 IF V>VM THEN GOTO 4680
4600 PRINT
4610 PRINT"NOTE:"
4620 PRINT" Maximum allowable shear stress exceeds"
4630 PRINT" actual shear stress, however shear"
1640 PRINT" reinforcement may be necessary"
4650 PRINT" - see clause 14.5.2."
4660 PROCspace
4670 ENDPROC
4680 PRINT
4690 PRINT"NOTE:"
4700 PRINT" Actual shear stress exceeds maximum"
4710 PRINT" allowable - see clause  14.5.2."
4720 PRINT" You should redesign the beam,"
4730 PRINT" increasing the cross-section and/or"
4740 PRINT" concrete grade."
4750 PROCpi
4760 ENDPROC
4770 :
4780 REM ****************************************
4790 REM Procedure for checking span/depth ratios
4800 REM ****************************************
4810 :
4820 DEF PROCspandepth
4830 CLS
4840 PRINT
4850 PRINT
4860 PRINT" Check span/depth  ratio"
4870 PROCgiven
4880 IF SD$="D" THEN PRINT" x    = ";X;" mm"TAB(20)"d' = ";D1;" mm"
4890 IF SD$="S" THEN PRINT" x    = ";X;" mm"
4900 SDR=S*1000/D
4910 PRINT
4920 PRINT" The beam span  S        = ";S;" m"
4930 PRINT" & the beam depth d      = ";D;" mm"
4940 PRINT" Hence, S/d  ratio       = ";SDR
4950 FSR=(5*FY*AS)/(TA*8)
4960 IF FSR>300 THEN FSR=300
4970 IF FSR<100 THEN FSR=100
4980 K=K*FC
4990 M1=.55+(477-FSR)/120/(.9+K)
5000 IF M1>2 THEN M1=2
```

```
5010 IF SD$="S" THEN M2=1:GOTO5050
5020 ASBD=100*CA/B/D
5030 M2=1+ASBD/(3+ASBD)
5040 IF M2>1.5 THEN M2=1.5
5050 IF S<=10 THEN SDM=20*M1*M2
5060 IF S>10 THEN SDM=200/S*(M1*M2)
5070 PRINT" but BS 8110 S/d limit = ";SDM
5080 PRINT" (see clause 3.4.6)"
5090 PRINT
5100 PRINT" where"
5110 PRINT" modification factor   = ";M1
5120 PRINT" (tensile steel)"
5130 PRINT
5140 PRINT" modification factor   = ";M2
5150 PRINT" (compressive steel)"
5160 PROCspace
5170 ENDPROC
5180 :
5190 REM *******************************************
5200 REM Procedure for design of shear reinforcement
5210 REM *******************************************
5220 :
5230 DEF PROClinks
5240 COUNTER%=1
5250 CLS
5260 PRINT
5270 PRINT
5280 PRINT"Check shear strength at support face"
5290 PRINT"Due to curtailment of tensile steel"
5300 PRINT"the As at support face may be less than"
5310 PRINT"that provided for maximum moment"
5320 PRINT"Hence, for section at support face, enter"
5330 PRINT
5340 INPUT"- effective depth d (mm) = " D
5350 V=SF*1000/(B*D)
5360 TA=0
5370 INPUT"- number of bars          = " NOB
5380 INPUT"- bar diameter (mm)       = " R
5390 IF R<>10 AND R<>12 AND R<>16 AND R<>20 AND R<>25 THEN  GOTO 5380
5400 TTEMP=3.142*R*R/4*NOB
5410 TA=TA + TTEMP
5420 PRINT"Steel area provided       = ";TA;" mm2"
5430 PRINT"Type A for more steel or B to proceed"
5440 PROCab
5450 IF a$="A" OR a$="a" THEN AB$="A" ELSE AB$="B"
5460 PRINT"Selected option ";AB$
5470 IF a$="A" OR a$="a" THEN GOTO 5370
5480 PROCchange
5490 IF a$="Y" OR a$="y" THEN GOTO 5250
5500 P=100*TA/(B*D)
5510 IF P>3 THEN P=3
5520 IF P<.15 THEN P=.15
5530 DVR=400/D
5540 IF DVR<1 THEN DVR=1
5550 VCR=1
5560 IF FC>25 THEN VCR=(FC/25)^(1/3)
5570 IF FC>40 THEN VCR=1.17
5580 VC=VCR*.79*(P^(1/3))*(DVR^(1/4))/1.25
5590 CLS
5600 PRINTsd$
5610 PROCgiven
5620 IF SD$="D" THEN PRINT " d' = ";D1;" mm"
5630 PRINT
5640 PRINT" Shear stress, V        = ";V;" N/mm2"
5650 PRINT" Conc shear stress, Vc = ";VC;" N/mm2"
5660 PRINT" (see Table 3.9)"
5670 PRINT"NOTE:   "
```

```
5680 IF V<(VC/2) THEN PRINT"Since V < .5*Vc, only minimum links are"
5690 IF V<(VC/2) THEN PRINT"required for beams of structural"
5700 IF V<(VC/2) THEN PRINT"importance - Table 3.8 & clause 3.12.7"
5710 IF V<(VC/2) THEN GOTO 6570
5720 :
5730 IF V>(VC/2) AND V<(VC+.4) THEN delv=.4
5740 IF V>(VC/2) AND V<(VC+.4) THEN PRINT"Since Vc/2 < V < Vc + .4, minimum links"
5750 IF V>(VC/2) AND V<(VC+.4) THEN PRINT"to provide a design shear resistance"
5760 IF V>(VC/2) AND V<(VC+.4) THEN PRINT"of 0.4 N/mm2 is required - Table 3.8)"
5770 :
5780 IF V>(VC+.4) AND V<VM THEN delv=V-VC
5790 IF V>(VC+.4) AND V<VM THEN PRINT"Since Vc + .4 < V < .8 SQR( Fcu) or 5,"
5800 IF V>(VC+.4) AND V<VM THEN PRINT" links or links + bent-up bars are"
5810 IF V>(VC+.4) AND V<VM THEN PRINT" required - Table 3.8"
5820 IF V>(VC+.4) AND V<VM THEN PRINT" See clause 3.4.5.6 on bent-up bars."
5830 PROCspace
5840 CLS
5850 PRINT
5860 PRINT
5870 PRINT" Enter the following:-"
5880 PRINT
5890 PRINT"- characteristic yield"
5900 PRINT"  strength for steel links"
5910 INPUT"  ie Fvy (250  or 460 N/mm2) = " FV
5920 IF FV<>250 AND FV<>460 THEN 5890
5930 INPUT"- the number of legs        = " L
5940 INPUT"- link diameter (mm)        = " J
5950 IF J<>8 AND J <>8 AND J<>10 AND J<>12 AND J<>16 AND J<>20 AND J<>25 THEN GOTO 5940
5960 IF J<(CD/4) AND SD$="D" THEN PRINT"Dia. less than 1/4 comp. dia. ?")
5970 IF J<(CD/4) AND SD$="D" THEN GOTO 5940
5980 PRINT
5990 PRINT" Max. spacing of links:-"
6000 S1=PI*L*J*J/4*0.87*FV/(B*delv)
6010 PRINT"- calculated spacing        = ";S1;" mm"
6020 SMAX=S1
6030 SMAX$="Spacing > than calculated maximum?"
6040 :
6050 S2=0.75*D
6060 PRINT"- 0.75 * effective depth    = ";S2;" mm"
6070 PRINT"   (see clause 3.4.5.5)."
6080 IF SMAX>S2 THEN SMAX=S2
6090 IF SMAX>S2 THEN SMAX$="Spacing > 0.75 * effective depth ?"
6100 :
6110 IF SD$="D" THEN S3=12*CD ELSE S3=SMAX
6120 IF SD$="D" THEN PRINT"- 12 * compressive bar diam. = ";S3;" mm"
6130 IF SD$="D" THEN PRINT"   (see clause 3.12.7.1)"
6140 :
6150 IF SD$="D" AND SMAX>S3 THEN SMAX=S3
6160 IF SD$="D" AND SMAX>S3 THEN SMAX$="  Spacing > than 12 comp. dia. ?"
6170 PRINT
6180 INPUT"Enter the required spacing (mm) = " LS
6190 IF LS>SMAX THEN PRINT SMAX$:GOTO 6180
6200 PRINT
6210 LL=(V-VC)*B*D/(1000*DL)
6220 PRINT"These links required for ";LL;" m"
6230 PROCchange
6240 IF a$="Y" OR a$="y" THEN GOTO 5840
6250 :
6260 IF COUNTER%>1 THEN GOTO 6580
6270 COUNTER%=2
6280 CLS
6290 PRINT
6300 PRINT
6310 PRINT"Check shear strength at distance d"
6320 PRINT"from support - clause 3.4.5.10"
6330 PRINT"Due to curtailment of tensile steel"
6340 PRINT"the As at distance d may be less than"
```

```
6350 PRINT"provided for maximum moment"
6360 PRINT
6370 PRINT
6380 TA=0
6390 PRINT"Hence, for section at distance d, enter"
6400 INPUT"- effective depth d (mm) = " D
6410 SFD=SF-D*DL/1000
6420 V=SFD*1000/(B*D)
6430 INPUT"- number of bars        = " NOB
6440 INPUT"- bar diameter (mm)      = " R
6450 IF R<>10 AND R<>12 AND R<>16 AND R<>20 AND R<>25 THEN  GOTO 6440
6460 TTEMP=3.142*R*R/4*NOB
6470 TA=TA + TTEMP
6480 PRINT"  Steel area provided    = ";TA;" mm2"
6490 PRINT"Type A for more steel or B to proceed"
6500 PROCab
6510 IF a$="A" OR a$="a" THEN AB$="A" ELSE AB$="B"
6520 PRINT"Selected option ";AB$
6530 IF a$="A" OR a$="a" THEN GOTO 6430
6540 PROCchange
6550 IF a$="Y" OR a$="y" THEN GOTO 6280 ELSE GOTO 5500
6560 :
6570 PROCspace
6580 ENDPROC
```

15.3.3 Sample runs

To illustrate the program RC Beam, consider Example 7.2.

☐ Example 15.2 Beam design using computer program based on Example 7.2

A rectangular beam is 300 mm wide by 450 mm effective depth with inset of 55 mm to the compression steel. The beam is simply supported and spans 8 m. The dead load including an allowance for self-weight is 20 kN/m and the imposed load is 11 kN/m. The materials to be used are grade 30 concrete and grade 460 reinforcement. Design the beam.

The beam dimensions, loading and material characteristic strengths are entered as follows:

```
Enter the following:-
- effective span (m)        = 8
- effective depth (mm)      = 450
- beam breadth (mm)         = 300

Note, beam's self weight    = 3.5316 kN/m

- characteristic uniformly
  distributed dead load
  including self-weight
  ie GK (kN/m)              = 20
- characteristic uniformly
  distributed imposed load
  ie QK (kN/m)              = 11

DL = 1.4Gk + 1.6Qk = 45.60000001 kN/m
Design moment       = 364.8000001 kN m
```

```
Shear force          = 182.4 kN
- fcu (N/mm2)                 = 30
- fy (N/mm2)                  = 460

Change the above input ? Type Y or N
```

The program then calls PROCshearcheck to ensure that the nominal shear stress does not exceed the maximum allowable value as shown below:

```
Given:
Mu  = 364.8000001 kNm
fcu = 30 N/mm2     b  = 300 mm
fy  = 460 N/mm2    d  = 450 mm

  Shear stress        = 1.351111112 N/mm2
  Maximum allowable  = 4.381780459 N/mm2
  shear stress

NOTE:
  Maximum allowable shear stress exceeds
  actual shear stress, however shear
  reinforcement may be necessary
  - see clause 14.5.2.
Press space bar to continue
```

In the same manner as in the program Section Design, the required compressive and tensile steel areas are found to be 509 mm^2 and 2564 mm^2 respectively. For compressive steel two 20 mm diameter bars are provided and for tensile steel six 25 mm diameter bars are provided. Based on this design, the depth of compression is 256.5 mm (which is greater than $d/2$) and the moment of resistance is 409.8 kN m. However, limiting the compression depth to half the effective depth results in a resisting moment of 383 kN m as shown below:

```
Doubly reinforced section

Given:
Mu  = 364.8000001 kNm
fcu = 30 N/mm2       b  = 300 mm
fy  = 460 N/mm2      d  = 450 mm
x   = 256.5000024 mmd' = 55 mm
For equilibrium, x/d  = 0.5700000052
& resisting moment    = 409.8281332 kN-m
but BS 8110 x/d limit = 0.5
Hence,
comp. concrete force  = 814.05 kN
comp. stress fs'      = 400.2 N/mm2
comp. steel area      = 628.4000001 mm2
C'  =  As' * fs'      = 251.48568 kN
& resisting moment    = 383.2367811 kN-m
Press space bar to continue
```

The actual span-to-effective depth ratio is found to be 17.8 and the limiting value allowed by the code is found to be 18.7. Hence the beam is satisfactory with respect to deflection requirements:

```
Check span/depth  ratio

Given:
Mu  = 364.8000001 kNm
fcu = 30 N/mm2        b  = 300 mm
fy  = 460 N/mm2       d  = 450 mm
x   = 225 mm          d' = 55 mm

The beam span  S      = 8 m
& the beam depth d     = 450 mm
Hence, S/d  ratio      = 17.77777778
but BS 8110 S/d limit  = 18.73323864
(see clause 3.4.6)

where
modification factor    = 0.825747943
(tensile steel)

modification factor    = 1.134319426
(compressive steel)
Press space bar to continue
```

In accordance with the simplified rules for curtailment, three 25 mm diameter tension bars may be cut off at a distance of 0.08 of the span from the support as shown in Fig. 15.2. Hence at a distance d from the face of the simple support the effective depth is 462.5 mm and the tensile steel area provided is 1473 mm^2. Before checking the shear requirements at the section, the above data is entered as below:

```
Check shear strength at distance d
from support - clause 3.4.5.10
Due to curtailment of tensile steel
the As at distance d may be less than
provided for maximum moment


Hence, for section at distance d, enter
- effective depth d (mm) = 462.5
- number of bars         = 3
- bar diameter (mm)      = 25
  Steel area provided    = 1472.8125 mm2
Type A for more steel or B to proceed
Select option A or B
Selected option B
Change the above input ? Type Y or N
```

The actual shear stress v is then shown to be less than the maximum permitted value but is greater than $v_c + 0.4$; thus shear reinforcement is required.

```
Doubly reinforced section

Given:
Mu  = 364.8000001 kNm
```

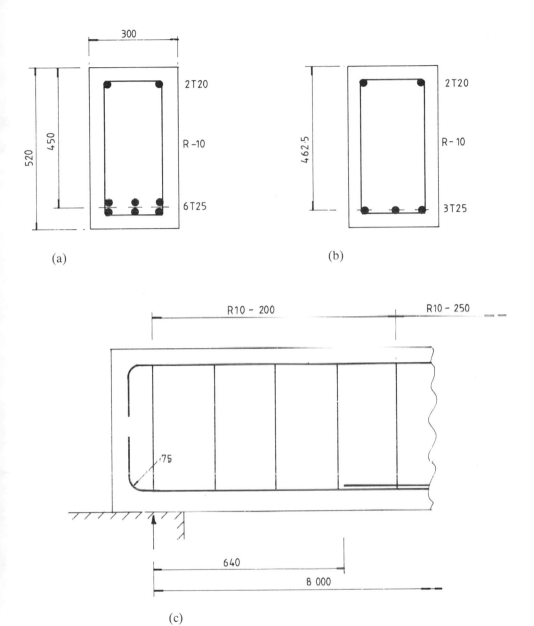

Fig. 15.2 (a) Section at centre; (b) end section; (c) part side elevation.

```
fcu - 30 N/mm2      b  - 300 mm
fy  = 460 N/mm2     d  = 462.5 mm
d'  = 55 mm

Shear stress, V         = 1.162594595 N/mm2
Conc shear stress, Vc = 0.6850921381 N/mm2
(see Table 3.9)
NOTE:
Since Vc + .4 < V < .8 SQR( Fcu) or 5,
links or links + bent-up bars are
required - Table 3.8
See clause 3.4.5.6 on bent-up bars.
Press space bar to continue
```

Using 10 mm diameter links (two legs) with a characteristic strength of 250 N/mm^2, the permitted spacing based on

$$A_{sv} > \frac{b_v s_v (v - v_c)}{0.87 f_{yv}}$$

is 238.5 mm. The link spacing is also limited to 0.75d and 12 times the diameter of the compressive bars, i.e. 347 mm and 240 mm respectively. Based on a spacing of 200 mm the links are required for a distance of 1.45 m, beyond which only minimum links are required. These design data are presented by the program as shown below:

```
Enter the following:-

- characteristic yield
    strength for steel links
    ie Fvy (250  or 460 N/mm2) = 250
- the number of legs        = 2
- link diameter (mm)        = 10

Max. spacing of links:-
- calculated spacing        = 238.4966448 mm
- 0.75 * effective  depth   = 346.875 mm
    (see clause 3.4.5.5).
- 12 * compressive bar diam. = 240 mm
    (see clause 3.12.7.1)

Enter the required spacing (mm) = 200

These links required for 1.452926882 m
Change the above input ? Type Y or N
```

15.4 PROGRAM BEAM DEFLECTION

15.4.1 Program discussion

The serviceability limit state of deflection is easily catered for by limiting the span-to-depth ratio. However, it is sometimes necessary to calculate deflection values from curvatures assuming either a cracked or an un-cracked section. Curvatures can be calculated for cracked sections, with little loss of accuracy, using the approximate method described in section 6.1.

In this section a program is presented for calculating the maximum deflection of simply supported rectangular or T-beams carrying uniformly distributed loads. Curvatures are calculated using the approximate method for cracked sections. The steps are as follows:

1. Enter the necessary data such as loading, beam dimensions and reinforcement. This is achieved using PROCdata (lines 1100–2020). In this procedure, $G\%$ is used to indicate whether the beam has a T or a rectangular cross-section;
2. Calculate, using PROCinstantcurvature (lines 2310–2640), the difference in instantaneous curvatures due to total and permanent loading;
3. Calculate, using PROClongtermcurvature (lines 2720–3060), the long-term curvature due to permanent loading;
4. Calculate the shrinkage curvature using PROCshrinkagecurvature (lines 3120–3390);
5. Calculate the beam deflection from

$$\delta = 0.104 \times \text{span}^2 \times \text{final curvature}$$

where final curvature is the instantaneous curvature under total load minus the instantaneous curvature under permanent load plus the long-term curvature under permanent load plus shrinkage curvature.

These calculations are performed in PROCdeflection (lines 3450–3920) which also compares the predicted deflection with the limiting values in BS 8110.

When calculating curvatures, it is necessary to determine the depth of the neutral axis for the transformed section. The coding for this operation is listed in PROCdepthNA (lines 560–1040). The calculations are initially performed assuming a rectangular cross-section (lines 580–790). The calculated neutral axis depth and second moments of area are also valid for a T-section provided that the neutral axis lies within the flange. If this is not so, the calculations have to be repeated using the appropriate expressions, as shown in lines 800–1040.

15.4.2 Source listing of program Beam Deflection

```
10 REM Program "Beam deflection"
20 REM for calculating the deflection of
30 REM Tee or rect reinforced concrete beam
40 :
50 REM ************************
60 REM Main program starts here
70 REM ************************
80 :
90 PROCdata
```

```
100 PROCinstantcurvature
110 PROClongtermcurvature
120 PROCshrinkagecurvature
130 PROCdeflection
140 GOTO90
150 END
160 :
170 REM ***********************
180 REM Main program stops here
190 REM ***********************
200 :
210 REM **********************
220 REM Some useful procedures
230 REM **********************
240 :
250 DEF PROCspace
260 PRINT TAB(4,23)"Press space bar to continue"
270 REPEAT
280    UNTIL GET=32
290 ENDPROC
300 DEF PROCchange
310 PRINT TAB(1,23)"Change the above input ? Type Y or N"
320 REPEAT
330    a$ = GET$
340    UNTIL a$="Y" OR a$="N" OR a$="y" OR a$="n"
350 ENDPROC
360 :
370 DEF PROCab
380 PRINT "Select option A or B"
390 REPEAT
400    a$ = GET$
410    UNTIL a$="A" OR a$="B" OR a$="a" OR a$="b"
420 ENDPROC
430 :
440 DEF PROCpr
450 PRINT TAB(1,23)"Proceed or Redesign ? Type P or R"
460 REPEAT
470    a$ = GET$
480    UNTIL a$="P" OR a$="R" OR a$="p" OR a$="r"
490 ENDPROC
500 :
510 REM *****************************************
520 REM Procedure for obtaining Neutral Axis depth
530 REM and Ixx
540 REM *****************************************
550 :
560 DEF PROCdepthNA
570 CLS
580 PRINT
590 PRINT"The neutral axis depth x of a cracked"
600 PRINT"section is obtained by solving the"
610 PRINT"quadratic equation"
620 PRINT
630 PRINT".5b(x^2) + (m-1)As'(x-d') =  As(d-x)m"
640 REM ie assuming a rectangular section
650 PRINT
660 QB=((modR-1)*ASD+modR*AS)/(.5*B)
670 QC=((modR-1)*ASD*D1+modR*AS*D)/(.5*B)
680 REM
690 REM In above equations the term (modR-1)
700 REM allows for the concrete area
710 REM displaced by compression steel
```

```
 720 REM
 730 X=(-QB+SQR(QB*QB+4*QC))/2
 740 IXX=B*X*X*X/3 + (modR-1)*ASD*(X-D1)*(X-D1) + modR*AS*(D-X)*(D-X)
 750 PRINT
 760 PRINT"Solving the above equation yields,"
 770 PRINT"x   = ";X;" mm"
 780 PRINT"Ixx = ";IXX;" mm4"
 790 PRINT
 800 IF G%=4 AND HF<X THEN PRINT"Note: hf =";HF;" mm"
 810 IF G%=4 AND HF<X THEN PRINT"Since x>hf, above solution is incorrect"
 820 PROCspace
 830 IF G%=4 AND HF<X THEN GOTO 840 ELSE GOTO 1040
 840 CLS
 850 PRINT
 860 PRINT"Hence, obtain the neutral axis depth"
 870 PRINT"by solving the quadratic equation:-"
 880 PRINT
 890 PRINT".5b(x^2) + (b-bw)hf(x-.5hf)  =  As(d-x)m"
 900 PRINT"+ (m-1)As'(x-d')"
 910 PRINT
 920 QB=((modR-1)*ASD+modR*AS+(B-BW)*HF)/(.5*BW)
 930 QC=((modR-1)*ASD*D1+modR*AS*D+(B-BW)*HF*HF/2)/(.5*BW)
 940 X=(-QB+SQR(QB*QB+4*QC))/2
 950 IXX=BW*X*X*X/3 + (modR-1)*ASD*(X-D1)*(X-D1)
 960 IXX=IXX + modR*AS*(D-X)*(D-X)
 970 IXX=IXX + (B-DW)*HF*(X-HF/2)*(X-HF/2)
 980 IXX=IXX + (B-BW)*HF*HF*HF/12
 990 PRINT
1000 PRINT"Solving the above equation yields,"
1010 PRINT"x   = ";X;" mm"
1020 PRINT"Ixx = "IXX;" mm4"
1030 PROCspace
1040 ENDPROC
1050 :
1060 REM ************************
1070 REM Procedure for data entry
1080 REM ************************
1090 :
1100 DEF PROCdata
1110 CLS
1120 PRINT
1130 PRINT
1140 PRINT"Note:- (A) for rectangular beam"
1150 PRINT"      (B) for Tee-beam"
1160 PROCab
1170 IF a$="A" OR a$="a" THEN AB$="A" ELSE AB$="B"
1180 PRINT"selected option = "(AB$
1190 IF a$="b" OR a$="B" THEN G%=4 ELSE G%=0
1200 PRINT
1210 PRINT"Enter the following:-"
1220 INPUT"- effective span (m)       = " S
1230 REM G%=4 represents a Tee-beam
1240 INPUT"- effective depth (mm)     = " D
1250 INPUT"- overall depth (mm)       = " H
1260 IF D > (H-30) THEN GOTO 1240
1270 IF G%=4 THEN GOTO 1330
1280 INPUT"- beam breadth (mm)        = " B
1290 W=2400*9.81*B*H/1E9
1300 HF=0
1310 BW=0
1320 GOTO 1380
1330 INPUT"- flange breadth (mm)      = " B
```

```
1340 INPUT"- flange thickness (mm)    - " HF
1350 INPUT"- web width (mm)           = " BW
1360 IF B>(1000*S/5 + BW) THEN B=(1000*S/5 + BW)
1370 W=2400*9.81*(B*HF + (H-HF)*BW) /1E9
1380 PRINT
1390 PRINT"Note: beam self weight     = ";W;" kN/m"
1400 PRINT
1410 INPUT"- char dead load (kN/m)    = " GK
1420 IF W>GK THEN GOTO 1410
1430 INPUT"- char imposed load (kN/m) = " QK
1440 PRINT"- percentage of imposed"
1450 PRINT"  load considered"
1460 INPUT"  as permanent load        = " PMR
1470 TK=GK+QK
1480 PK=GK+QK*PMR/100
1490 DMP=PK*S*S/8
1500 DMT=TK*S*S/8
1510 PRINT
1520 INPUT"- fy (N/mm2)               = " FY
1530 IF FY<>250 AND FY<>460 THEN GOTO 1520
1540 INPUT"- fcu (N/mm2)              = " FC
1550 EC=20+.2*FC
1560 PRINT
1570 PRINT"Concrete elastic modulus may be assumed"
1580 PRINT"as ";EC;" kN/mm2 - table 7.2"
1590 PRINT
1600 INPUT"- exact value             = " EC
1610 CLS
1620 PRINT
1630 PRINT" Enter the following:"
1640 PRINT
1650 AS=0
1660 ASD=0
1670 PRINT"- number of steel bars"
1680 INPUT"  in tension              = " TN
1690 INPUT"- bar diameter (mm)        = " TD
1700 IF TD<>12 AND TD<>16 AND TD<>20 AND TD<>25 AND TD<>32 AND TD<>40 THEN GOTO169
1710 Atemp=TN*PI*TD*TD/4
1720 AS=AS+Atemp
1730 PRINT"Type A for more steel or B to proceed"
1740 PROCab
1750 IF a$="A" OR a$="a" THEN AB$="A" ELSE AB$="B"
1760 PRINT"selected option = "+AB$
1770 IF a$="A" OR a$="a" GOTO 1670
1780 PRINT
1790 PRINT"- number of steel bars"
1800 INPUT"  in compression          = " CN
1810 IF CN=0 THEN CD=0:D1=0:ASD=0:GOTO 1970
1820 INPUT"- bar diameter (mm)        = " CD
1830 IF CD<>12 AND CD<>16 AND CD<>20 AND CD<>25 AND CD<>32 AND CD<>40 THEN GOTO182
1840 Atemp=CN*PI*CD*CD/4
1850 ASD=ASD+Atemp
1860 PRINT
1870 PRINT"Type A for more steel or B to proceed"
1880 PROCab
1890 IF a$="A" OR a$="a" THEN AB$="A" ELSE AB$="B"
1900 PRINT"selected option = "+AB$
1910 IF a$="A" OR a$="a" GOTO 1790
1920 PRINT
1930 PRINT"- depth to comp. steel"
1940 INPUT"  ie d' (mm)              = " D1
1950 IF D1>D/2 THEN GOTO 1930
```

```
1960 IF D1<20 THEN GOTO 1930
1970 CLS
1980 PRINT
1990 PROCgiven
2000 PROCchange
2010 IF a$="Y" OR a$="y" THEN GOTO 1110
2020 ENDPROC
2030 :
2040 REM ********************************
2050 REM Procedure for printing input data
2060 REM ********************************
2070 :
2080 DEF PROCgiven
2090 CLS
2100 PRINT" Given:"
2110 PRINT" span s              = ";S;" m"
2120 PRINT" effective depth d   = ";D;" mm"
2130 PRINT" overall depth h     = ";H;" mm"
2140 PRINT" beam breadth b      = ";B;" mm"
2150 IF G%=4 THEN PRINT" web width bw           = ";BW;" mm"
2160 IF G%=4 THEN PRINT" flange thickness hf   = ";HF;" mm"
2170 PRINT" dead load Gk        = ";GK;" kN/m"
2180 PRINT" imposed load Qk     = ";QK;" kN/m"
2190 PRINT" conc 28-day strength = ";FC;" N/mm2"
2200 PRINT" steel yield strength = ";FY;" N/mm2"
2210 PRINT" conc elastic modulus = ";EC;" kN/mm2"
2220 PRINT" tensile steel area  = ";AS;" mm2"
2230 PRINT" comp steel area     = ";ASD;" mm2"
2240 PRINT" depth to comp steel = ";D1;" mm"
2250 ENDPROC
2260 :
2270 REM *****************************************
2280 REM Procedure for calculating instantaneous curvatures
2290 REM *****************************************
2300 :
2310 DEF PROCinstantcurvature
2320 CLS
2330 modR=200/EC
2340 PROCdepthNA
2350 CLS
2360 PRINT
2370 PRINT"For the calculation of instantaneous"
2380 PRINT"curvature, the concrete tensile stress"
2390 PRINT"(fct) at depth d is 1 N/mm2"
2400 fCTS=(H-X)/(D-X)
2410 IF G%=4 THEN BTEMP=BW  ELSE BTEMP=B
2420 MCT=fCTS*BTEMP*(H-X)*(H-X)/3000000
2430 DMPN=DMP-MCT
2440 DMTN=DMT-MCT
2450 cti=DMTN/IXX/EC*1000000000
2460 cpi=DMPN/IXX/EC*1000000000
2470 PRINT"Hence,"
2480 PRINT
2490 PRINT"beam soffit tension  = ";fCTS;" N/mm2"
2500 PRINT"M - concrete tension = ";MCT;" kNm"
2510 PRINT"M - total load       = ";DMT;" kNm"
2520 PRINT"Thus M nett          = ";DMTN;" kNm"
2530 PRINT
2540 PRINT"And, curvature       = ";cti;" mm-1"
2550 PRINT"ie M/EI * 1E6"
2560 PRINT
2570 PRINT"M - permanent load   = ";DMP;" kNm"
```

```
2580 PRINT"Thus M nett        = ";DMPN;" kNm"
2590 PRINT
2600 PRINT"And, curvature     = ";cpi;" mm-1"
2610 PRINT"ie M/EI * 1E6"
2620 PRINT
2630 PROCspace
2640 ENDPROC
2650 :
2660 REM *********************************************
2670 REM Procedure for calculating long term curvature
2680 REM *********************************************
2690 :
2700 DEF PROClongtermcurvature
2710 CLS
2720 PRINT
2730 PRINT"In order to determine the long term"
2740 PRINT"curvature, it is necessary to the"
2750 PRINT"reduced concrete elastic modulus due to creep"
2760 PRINT
2770 PRINT"Enter the creep coefficient"
2780 PRINT"see  clause 3.6 of Part 2"
2790 INPUT"ie Cc  = " CF
2800 modR=200/EC*(1+CF)
2810 PRINT
2820 PRINT"Thus m = 200*(1+Cc)/Ec = "modR
2830 PROCchange
2840 IF a$="Y" OR a$="y" THEN GOTO 2730
2850 PROCdepthNA
2860 CLS
2870 PRINT"For the calculation of long term"
2880 PRINT"curvature, the concrete tensile"
2890 PRINT"stress (fct) at depth d is 0.55 N/mm2"
2900 fCTS=0.55*(H-X)/(D-X)
2910 IF G%=4 THEN BTEMP=BW  ELSE BTEMP=B
2920 MCT=fCTS*BTEMP*(H-X)*(H-X)/3000000
2930 DMPN=DMP-MCT
2940 cplt=DMPN/IXX/EC*1000000000*(1+CF)
2950 PRINT"Hence,"
2960 PRINT"beam soffit tension = ";fCTS;" N/mm2"
2970 PRINT"M - concrete tension = ";MCT;" kNm"
2980 PRINT"M - permanent load   = ";DMP;" kNm"
2990 PRINT"Thus M nett          = ";DMPN;" kNm"
3000 PRINT
3010 PRINT"And, curvature       = "cplt;" mm-1"
3020 PRINT"ie M/EI * 1E6"
3030 PRINT
3040 PRINT
3050 PROCspace
3060 ENDPROC
3070 :
3080 REM *********************************************
3090 REM Procedure for calculating shrinkage curvature
3100 REM *********************************************
3110 :
3120 DEF PROCshrinkagecurvature
3130 CLS
3140 PRINT
3150 PRINT"The shrinkage curvature is calculated"
3160 PRINT"from the expression:-"
3170 PRINT
3180 PRINT"   Fs x m x S / Ixx"
3190 PRINT
```

```
3200 PRINT"where Fs  = free shrinkage"
3210 PRINT"      m   = modular ratio Es*(1+Cc)/Ec"
3220 PRINT"      S   = 1st moment of reinforcement"
3230 PRINT"          area about centroid of"
3240 PRINT"          cracked section"
3250 PRINT
3260 PRINT"     Ixx  = 2nd moment of area of the"
3270 PRINT"          cracked section"
3280 PRINT
3290 PRINT"Enter the free shrinkage strain"
3300 PRINT"see   clause 7.4 of Part 2"
3310 INPUT"ie ecs (x 1E6)  = "fss
3320 Ss=AS*(D-X)+ASD*(X-D1)
3330 cs=modR*Ss*fss/IXX
3340 PRINT
3350 PRINT"Hence, curvature * 1E6 = ";cs;" mm-1"
3360 PRINT
3370 PROCchange
3380 IF a$="Y" OR a$="y" THEN GOTO 3320
3390 ENDPROC
3400 :
3410 REM ********************************************************
3420 REM Procedure for calculating totalcurvatures & deflection
3430 REM ********************************************************
3440 :
3450 DEF PROCdeflection
3460 ctt=cti-cpi+cplt+cs
3470 CLS
3480 PRINT
3490 PRINT"Total curvature x 1E6 = ";ctt;" mm-1"
3500 PRINT"ie It - Ip + Lp+ Sc"
3510 PRINT
3520 PRINT"where  It = instantaneous curvature"
3530 PRINT"          due to total load"
3540 PRINT"          = ";cti;" mm-1"
3550 PRINT
3560 PRINT"      Ip = instantaneous curvature"
3570 PRINT"          due to permanent load"
3580 PRINT"          = ";cpi;" mm-1"
3590 PRINT
3600 PRINT"      Lp = long term curvature"
3610 PRINT"          due to permanent load"
3620 PRINT"          = ";cplt;" mm-1"
3630 PRINT
3640 PRINT"      Sc = shrinkage curvature"
3650 PRINT"          = ";cs;" mm-1"
3660 PROCspace
3670 CLS
3680 df=.104*(S*1000)*(S*1000)*ctt/1E6
3690 PRINT
3700 PRINT"For a simply supported beam carrying"
3710 PRINT"uniform load, the deflection is given"
3720 PRINT"by:-"
3730 PRINT
3740 PRINT" delf  =  0.104 x L x L x C"
3750 PRINT"       = ";df;" mm"
3760 PRINT
3770 PRINT"where  L = effective span"
3780 PRINT"         = ";S" m"
3790 PRINT
3800 PRINT"      C = curvature at midspan"
3810 PRINT"         = ";ctt;"  mm-1"
```

```
3820 dmax=S*1000/250
3830 PRINT
3840 PRINT"Note: BS8110 limits deflection to"
3850 PRINT"       span/250 or 20 mm whichever"
3860 PRINT"       is the lesser."
3870 PRINT
3880 PRINT"Since, span/250 = ";dmax;" mm"
3890 IF dmax>20 THEN dmax=20
3900 PRINT"deflection is limited to ";dmax;" mm"
3910 PROCspace
3920 ENDPROC
>
```

15.4.3 Sample runs

To illustrate the use of the program Beam Deflection, consider Example 6.2 presented in section 6.1.3.

☐ Example 15.3 Beam deflection using computer program based on Example 6.2

A simply supported T-beam of 6 m span carries a dead load including self-weight of 14.8 kN/m and an imposed load of 10 kN/m. The permanent load is to be taken as the dead load plus 25% of the imposed load, the creep coefficient is 3.5 and the free shrinkage strain is 420×10^{-6}. The beam cross-section is shown in Fig. 15.3. Assuming grade 30 concrete and grade 460 steel, calculate the deflection of the beam at mid-span.

The beam dimensions, loading, characteristic strengths etc. are entered as follows:

```
Note:- (A) for rectangular beam
       (B) for Tee-beam
Select option A or B
selected option = B

Enter the following:-
- effective span (m)       = 6
- effective depth (mm)     = 300
- overall depth (mm)       = 350
- flange breadth (mm)      = 1450
- flange thickness (mm)    = 100
- web width (mm)           = 250

Note: beam self weight     = 4.88538 kN/m

- char dead load (kN/m)    = 14.8
- char imposed load (kN/m) = 10
- percentage of imposed
  load considered
  as permanent load        = 25

- fy (N/mm2)               = 460
- fcu (N/mm2)              = 30

Concrete elastic modulus may be assumed
as 26 kN/mm2 - table 7.2

- exact value              = 26
```

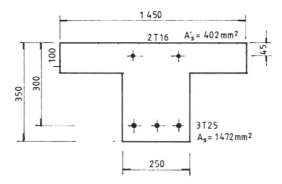

Fig. 15.3 T-beam section

```
Enter the following:

- number of steel bars
  in tension             = 3
- bar diameter (mm)      = 25
Type A for more steel or B to proceed
Select option A or B
selected option = B

- number of steel bars
  in compression         = 2
- bar diameter (mm)      = 16

Type A for more steel or B to proceed
Select option A or B
selected option = B

- depth to comp. steel
  ie d' (mm)             = 45
```

Assuming a rectangular section the program then calculates the neutral axis depth x as 60.7 mm and the second moment of area I_{xx} as 757×10^6 mm^4 as shown below. These values are acceptable since the neutral axis lies within the flange.

```
The neutral axis depth x of a cracked
section is obtained by solving the
quadratic equation

.5b(x^2) + (m-1)As'(x-d') =  As(d-x)m

Solving the above equation yields,
x   = 60.67304648 mm
Ixx = 757444077.7 mm4

Press space bar to continue
```

The instantaneous curvatures due to total and permanent loadings are respectively $5.24 \times 10^{-6}\,\text{mm}^{-1}$ and $3.52 \times 10^{-6}\,\text{mm}^{-1}$ as shown below:

```
For the calculation of instantaneous
curvature, the concrete tensile stress
(fct) at depth d is 1 N/mm2
Hence,

beam soffit tension  = 1.208919218 N/mm2
M - concrete tension = 8.433227647 kNm
M - total load       = 111.6 kNm
Thus M nett          = 103.1667723 kNm

And, curvature       = 5.238608234 mm-1
ie M/EI * 1E6

M - permanent load   = 77.85000002 kNm
Thus M nett          = 69.41677237 kNm

And, curvature       = 3.524848816 mm-1
ie M/EI * 1E6

Press space bar to continue
```

The creep coefficient of 3.5 results in a modular ratio of 34.6 as shown below:

```
In order to determine the long term
curvature, it is necessary to find the
reduced concrete elastic modulus due to creep

Enter the creep coefficient
see clause 3.6 of Part 2
ie Cc = 3.5

Thus m = 200*(1+Cc)/Ec = 34.61538461
Change the above input ? Type Y or N
```

Assuming a rectangular cross-section the neutral axis depth is found to be 110 mm, i.e. below the flange:

```
The neutral axis depth x of a cracked
section is obtained by solving the
quadratic equation

.5b(x^2) + (m-1)As'(x-d') =  As(d-x)m


Solving the above equation yields,
x   = 110.1525102 mm
Ixx = 2540633647 mm4

Note: hf =100 mm
Since x>hf, above solution is incorrect
Press space bar to continue
```

However, using the appropriate expression results in a similar value for the neutral axis depth and a second moment of area for the T-section as shown below:

```
Hence, obtain the neutral axis depth
by solving the quadratic equation:-

.5b(x^2) + (b-bw)hf(x-.5hf)  =  As(d-x)m
+ (m-1)As'(x-d')


Solving the above equation yields,
x   = 110.4441347 mm
Ixx = 2540197028 mm4
Press space bar to continue
```

This results in a long-term curvature of $5.08 \times 10^{-6} \, \text{mm}^{-1}$ as shown below:

```
For the calculation of long term
curvature, the concrete tensile
stress (fct) at depth d is 0.55 N/mm2
Hence,
beam soffit tension  = 0.6950759646 N/mm2
M - concrete tension = 3.32402776 kNm
M - permanent load   = 77.85000002 kNm
Thus M nett          = 74.52597228 kNm

And, curvature       = 5.077844681 mm-1
ie M/EI * 1E6


Press space bar to continue
```

Based on a free shrinkage strain of 420×10^{-6}, the shrinkage curvature is found as below:

```
The shrinkage curvature is calculated
from the expression:-

    Fs x m x S / Ixx

where Fs  = free shrinkage
      m   = modular ratio Es*(1+Cc)/Ec
      S   = 1st moment of reinforcement
            area about centroid of
            cracked section

      Ixx = 2nd moment of area of the
            cracked section

Enter the free shrinkage strain
see    clause 7.4 of Part 2
ie ecs (x 1E6)   = 420

Hence, curvature * 1E6 = 1.748261496 mm-1

Change the above input ? Type Y or N
```

Hence the final curvature and deflection are obtained as below:

```
For a simply supported beam carrying
uniform load, the deflection is given
by:-

   delf  =  0.104 x L x L x C
         = 31.97325679 mm

where  L  = effective span
          = 6 m

       C  = curvature at midspan
          = 8.539865594  mm-1

Note: BS8110 limits deflection to
      span/250 or 20 mm whichever
      is the lesser.

Since, span/250 = 24 mm
deflection is limited to 20 mm
Press space bar to continue
```

15.5 PROGRAM: COLUMN ANALYSIS

15.5.1 Program discussion

The procedure for analysing short column sections with symmetrical reinforcement carrying an axial load and bending moments has been presented in section 9.3. The expressions of axial and bending equilibrium for the section shown in Fig. 15.4 are

$$N = 0.45 f_{cu} b 0.9x + f_{sc} \frac{A_{sc}}{2} - f_{st} \frac{A_{sc}}{2}$$

and

$$M = 0.45 f_{cu} b 0.9x \left(\frac{h}{2} - \frac{0.9x}{2} \right) + f_{sc} \frac{A_{sc}}{2} \left(\frac{h}{2} - d' \right) + f_{st} \frac{A_{sc}}{2} \left(d - \frac{h}{2} \right)$$

since $\left(d - \frac{h}{2} \right) = \left(\frac{h}{2} - d' \right)$

$$M = 0.45 f_{cu} b d_c \left(\frac{h}{2} - \frac{d_c}{2} \right) + \frac{A_{sc}}{2} \left(\frac{h}{2} - d' \right) (f_{sc} + f_{st})$$

where $d_c = 0.9x$

The expressions are also valid for the case where the neutral axis depth x is outside the section as shown in Fig. 15.5, provided the depth of compression d_c is limited to the depth h of the column section.

It is sometimes necessary to analyse a given section (i.e. given $b, d, d', h,$ A_{sc}, f_{cu} and f_y) to see if it can carry a given combination of axial load and

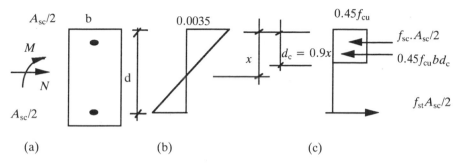

Fig. 15.4 (a) Column section; (b) strain distribution; (c) stress distribution

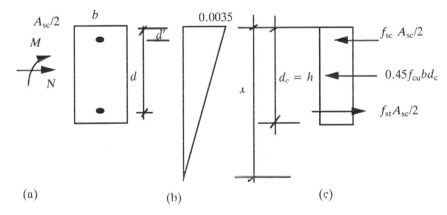

Fig. 15.5 (a) Column section; (b) strain distribution; (c) stress distribution

moment. Since the combined axial load and moment capacity of a given section is dependent on the neutral axis depth x, the procedure (described in section 9.3.2) is to iterate x until the calculated value of N equals the applied load and then to compare the corresponding moment capacity of the section with the applied moment. This procedure is illustrated in Fig. 15.6 and the source listing of a program to carry out this procedure is given in section 15.5.2.

The main steps in the program are

1. enter the data describing the column section
2. calculate the axial capacity of the section for various values of x until the value of the applied load is reached

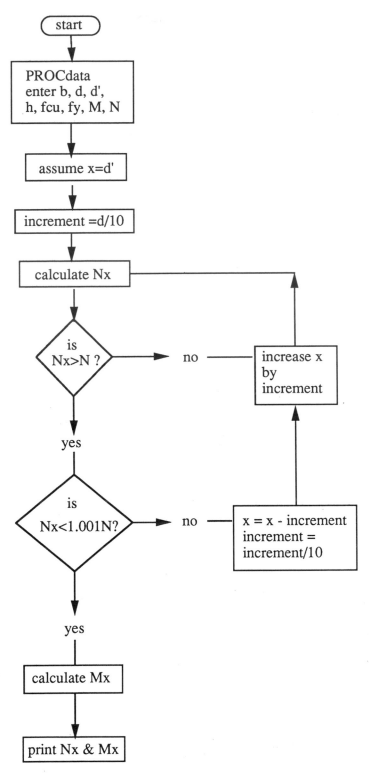

Fig. 15.6 Flow chart for column analysis

The program begins by calling PROCdata (lines 390–670) at line 90 for data entry purposes. After reading in the values of b, h, d' A_{sc}, f_{cu}, f_y and N a check is made (lines 580–610) to ensure that applied load N is less than the capacity of the section under only axial load. Where this is the case, the program then proceeds to PROCsummary (listed between lines 730 and 880) at line 100.

The first step in PROCsummary is to call PROCstraincompatibility which is listed between lines 940 and 1200. This procedure begins by assuming $x = d'$ (line 1010) before calculating

1. the depth of concrete compression d_c, which is limited to the overall depth h (lines 1070 to 1080)
2. the strains and stresses of the steel in compression and in tension (lines 1090 and 1120)
3. the corresponding values of axial and moment capacity (lines 1130 and 1140)

These calculations are repeated by increasing the assumed value of x by $d/10$ (lines 1020–1050) until the calculated value of axial capacity exceeds the axial load N (line 1150). However, if the calculated value exceeds N by more than 0.1% then the above calculations are repeated from the previous value of x with a smaller increment (lines 1170–1190). This increasingly finer increment of x enables the value of x, corresponding to the applied axial load N, to be determined rapidly. Thus the iterative process in PROCstraincompatability starts at $x = d'$ and ends when the value of x, corresponding to an axial load capacity between N and $1.001N$, has been obtained. The program ends by printing the combined axial and moment capacity of the section as well as the corresponding value of the neutral axis depth x.

15.5.2 Source listing of program Column Analysis

```
10 REM Program "Column-Analysis"
20 REM for the analysis of rectangular reinforced concrete
30 REM sections subjected to axial forces and bending moments.
40 :
50 REM ************************
60 REM Main program starts here
70 REM ************************
80 :
90 PROCdata
100 PROCsummary
110 GOTO 90
120 END
130 REM ************************
140 REM Main program stops here
150 REM ************************
160 :
170 REM ************************
180 REM Some useful procedures
190 REM ************************
```

```
200 :
210 DEF PROCspace
220 PRINT TAB(4,23)"Press space bar to continue"
230 REPEAT
240    UNTIL GET=32
250 ENDPROC
260 :
270 DEF PROCchange
280 PRINT TAB(1,23)"Change the above input ? Type Y or N"
290 REPEAT
300    a$ = GET$
310    UNTIL a$="Y" OR a$="N" OR a$="y" OR a$="n"
320 ENDPROC
330 :
340 :
350 REM ************************
360 REM Procedure for data entry
370 REM ************************
380 :
390 DEF PROCdata
400 CLS
410 PRINT
420 PRINT
430 PRINT    "Analysis of Rectangular Column Sections"
440 PRINT
450 PRINT"ie determine the moment capacity of a"
460 PRINT"   section for a given axial load"
470 PRINT
480 PRINT"Enter the following:-"
490 INPUT"1) section breadth b (mm)   = " B
500 INPUT"2) overall depth h (mm)     = " H
510 INPUT"3) depth d1 (mm) to steel   = " D1
520 D = H-D1
530 INPUT"4) total steel area (mm2)   = " AS
540 INPUT"5) fcu (N/mm2)              = " FC
550 INPUT"6) fy (N/mm2)               = " FY
560 IF FY<>250 AND FY<>460 THEN GOTO 550
570 INPUT"7) axial load (kN)          = " N
580 Nmax = 0.45*B*H*FC + AS*.87*FY
590 Nmax = Nmax/1000
600 IF N < Nmax THEN GOTO 640
610 PRINT "Note: axial capacity = " Nmax " kN"
620 PROCspace
630 GOTO 570
640 PROCchange
650 IF a$="Y" OR a$="y" THEN 400
660 N = N*1000
670 ENDPROC
680 :
690 REM ***************************************************
700 REM Procedure for presenting a summary of the design
710 REM ***************************************************
720 :
730 DEF PROCsummary
740 PROCstraincompatibility
750 CLS
760 PRINT
770 PRINT
780 PRINT
790 N = N/1000
800 Mbh = Mbh/1000000
810 PRINT"The column section's ultimate bending"
```

```
820 PRINT"capacity in combination with an axial"
830 PRINT"load of "; N " kN is " Mbh " kNm"
840 PRINT
850 PRINT
860 PRINT"The neutral axis depth = "; XD*D; " mm"
870 PROCspace
880 ENDPROC
890 :
900 REM **************************************************
910 REM Procedure for equilibrium & compatibility checks
920 REM **************************************************
930 :
940 DEF PROCstraincompatibility
950 CLS
960 YE=FY/230000
970 PRINT
980 PRINT
990 PRINT" Please wait - equilibrium and strain"
1000 PRINT"                compatibility checks"
1010 XD=D1/D
1020 INC=0.1
1030 XD=XD-INC
1040 REPEAT
1050    XD=XD+INC
1060    PRINT" Assuming x/d = ";XD
1070    dcH=.9*XD*D/H
1080    IF dcH>1 THEN dcH=1
1090    E=0.0035*(1/XD-1)
1100    IF E<=YE THEN FYD2=200000*E ELSE FYD2=(FY*.87)*SGN(E)
1110    ED=0.0035*(1-D1/D/XD)
1120    IF ED<=YE THEN FYD1=200000*ED ELSE FYD1=(FY*.87)*SGN(ED)
1130    Nbh = 0.45*FC*dcH*B*H + (FYD1-FYD2)*AS/2
1140    Mbh = .225*FC*dcH*(1-dcH)*B*H*H + (FYD2+FYD1)*AS*(H/2-D1)/2
1150    UNTIL Nbh >= N
1160 IF Nbh < 1.001*N THEN ENDPROC
1170 XD=XD-INC*1.1
1180 INC=INC/10
1190 GOTO 1040
1200 ENDPROC
```

15.5.3 Sample runs

To illustrate the use of this program, consider Example 9.3 in section 9.3.2.

□ Example 15.4 Column analysis using computer program based on Example 9.3

Calculate the ultimate moment of resistance of the column section ($b = 300\,\text{mm}$, $h = 400\,\text{mm}$, $d' = 50\,\text{mm}$) symmetrically reinforced with four 25 mm diameter bars when subjected to an ultimate axial load of 1020 kN. Assume grade 30 concrete and grade 460 steel.

The following information will be displayed on the screen after the data has been entered:

```
Analysis of Rectangular Column Sections

ie determine the moment capacity of a
   section for a given axial load

Enter the following:-
1) section breadth b (mm)    = 300
2) overall depth h (mm)      = 400
3) depth d1 (mm) to steel    = 50
4) total steel area (mm2)    = 1962
5) fcu (N/mm2)               = 30
6) fy (N/mm2)                = 460
7) axial load (kN)           = 1020
Change the above input ? Type Y or N
```

The neutral axis and ultimate moment capacity of the column section corresponding to the given axial load are found as shown below:

```
The column section's ultimate bending
capacity in combination with an axial
load of 1020 kN is 180.628325 kNm


The neutral axis depth = 248.8 mm
Press space bar to continue                              ■
```

15.6 PROGRAM COLUMN DESIGN

15.6.1 Program discussion

The program presented above may be modified for design purposes, i.e. to determine the required steel area for given values of column dimensions (b, h), reinforcement location $(d'$ or $d)$ and design ultimate axial load and bending moments. For given values of b, h, d, d', f_{cu}, f_y, M and N, the only unknowns in the equations for axial and moment equilibrium are the neutral axis depth x and the required steel area A_{sc}. Hence, the problem is to find values of x and A_{sc} which satisfy the two equations. It should be noted that direct solution of the equations is possible but is tedious and involves cubic expressions. This is because the steel stresses are also functions of the depth x and are dependent on whether the steel reinforcement has reached its yield value. A more straightforward approach is to assume a value of x, obtain the steel area A_{sc} which satisfies one of the two equilibrium equations and then to check that the other is also satisfied. The procedure is to iterate x until both equations are satisfied. In the program listed in section 15.6.2, the required steel area is obtained from the moment equilibrium equation and the iteration is carried out until a value of x is found which gives an axial load capacity within 0.1% of the design load N.

After calling PROCdata (lines 390–590) for entering values of b, h, d', f_{cu}, f_y, M and N, the program goes on to PROCstraincompatibility (lines

870–1150) which begins by assuming $x = d'$ and calculates the required steel area from the moment equilibrium equation at line 1070. The process is repeated by increasing the assumed value of x until the calculated value of axial capacity is between N and $1.001N$. The program ends by printing the steel area required to satisfy the design axial and moment forces, as well as the corresponding value of the neutral axis depth x.

The inclusion of procedures for selecting the number and size of reinforcement and for checking the maximum and minimum allowable steel areas (as provided in the Beam design programs) is left to the reader. The program may also be extended to include the various other checks required to satisfy BS 8110 and to take account of slender columns.

15.6.2 Source listing of program Column Design

```
10 REM Program "Column-Design"
20 REM for the design of symmetrically reinforced
30 REM rectangular concrete sections subjected
40 REM to axial forces and bending moments.
50 :
60 REM ***********************
70 REM Main program starts here
80 REM ***********************
90 :
100 PROCdata
110 PROCsummary
120 GOTO 100
130 END
140 REM ***********************
150 REM Main program stops here
160 REM ***********************
170 :
180 REM ***********************
190 REM Some useful procedures
200 REM ***********************
210 :
220 DEF PROCspace
230 PRINT TAB(4,23)"Press space bar to continue"
240 REPEAT
250    UNTIL GET=32
260 ENDPROC
270 .
280 DEF PROCchange
290 PRINT TAB(1,23)"Change the above input ? Type Y or N"
300 REPEAT
310    a$ = GET$
320    UNTIL a$="Y" OR a$="N" OR a$="y" OR a$="n"
330 ENDPROC
340 :
350 REM ***********************
360 REM Procedure for data entry
370 REM ***********************
380 :
390 DEF PROCdata
400 CLS
410 PRINT
420 PRINT
```

```
430 PRINT    "Design of Rectangular Column Sections"
440 PRINT
450 PRINT"Enter the following:-"
460 INPUT"1) section breadth b (mm)  = " B
470 INPUT"2) overall depth h (mm)    ≐ " H
480 INPUT"3) depth d1 (mm) to steel  = " D1
490 D = H-D1
500 INPUT"4) fcu (N/mm2)             = " FC
510 INPUT"5) fy (N/mm2)              = " FY
520 IF FY<>250 AND FY<>460 THEN GOTO 510
530 INPUT"6) design moment (kNm)     = " M
540 M = M*1000000
550 INPUT"7) axial load (kN)         = " N
560 N = N*1000
570 PROCchange
580 IF a$="Y" OR a$="y" THEN 400
590 ENDPROC
600 :
610 REM ************************************************
620 REM Procedure for presenting a summary of the design
630 REM ************************************************
640 :
650 DEF PROCsummary
660 PROCstraincompatibility
670 CLS
680 PRINT
690 PRINT
700 PRINT
710 PRINT"Total steel area of "; AS " mm2"
720 PRINT"is required to resist the"
730 PRINT"design axial load of "; N/1000 " kN"
740 PRINT"and design moment of "; M/1000000 " kNm"
750 PRINT
760 PRINT"Neutral axis depth  = "; XD*D " mm"
770 PRINT
780 PRINT"axial load capacity = "; Nbh/1000 " kN"
790 PRINT"moment capacity     = "; Mbh/1000000 " kNm"
800 PROCspace
810 ENDPROC
820 :
830 REM ************************************************
840 REM Procedure for equilibrium & compatibility checks
850 REM ************************************************
860 :
870 DEF PROCstraincompatibility
880 CLS
890 YE=FY/230000
900 PRINT
910 PRINT
920 PRINT
930 PRINT" Please wait - equilibrium and strain"
940 PRINT" ·                compatibility checks"
950 XD=D1/D
960 INC=0.1
970 XD=XD-INC
980 REPEAT
990    XD=XD+INC
1000   PRINT" Assuming x/d = ";XD
1010   dcH=.9*XD*D/H
1020   IF dcH>1 THEN dcH=1
1030   E=0.0035*(1/XD-1)
1040   IF E<=YE THEN FYD2=200000*E ELSE FYD2=(FY*.87)*SGN(E)
```

```
1050    ED=0.0035*(1-D1/D/XD)
1060    IF ED<=YE THEN FYD1=200000*ED ELSE FYD1=(FY*.87)*SGN(ED)
1070    AS=2*(M-.225*FC*dcH*(1-dcH)*B*H*H)/(FYD1+FYD2)/(H/2-D1)
1080    Nbh = 0.45*FC*dcH*B*H + (FYD1-FYD2)*AS/2
1090    Mbh = .225*FC*dcH*(1-dcH)*B*H*H + (FYD1+FYD2)*AS*(H/2-D1)/2
1100    UNTIL Nbh >= N
1110 IF Nbh < 1.001*N THEN ENDPROC
1120 XD=XD-INC*1.1
1130 INC=INC/10
1140 GOTO 980
1150 ENDPROC
```

15.6.3 Sample runs

To illustrate the use of this program, consider Example 9.4 in section 9.3.3.

☐ Example 15.5 Column design using computer program based on Example 9.4

Determine the required steel area for a symmetrically reinforced short braced column subjected to an ultimate load of 1480 kN and an ultimate moment of resistance of 54 kN m. The column section is 300 mm × 300 mm and the steel depth is 45.5 mm. Assume grade 30 concrete and grade 460 steel.

The following information will be displayed on the screen after the data has been entered:

```
Design of Rectangular Column Sections

Enter the following:-
1) section breadth b (mm)  = 300
2) overall depth h (mm)    - 300
3) depth d1 (mm) to steel  = 45.5
4) fcu (N/mm2)             = 30
5) fy (N/mm2)              = 460
6) design moment (kNm)     - 54
7) axial load (kN)         = 1480
Change the above input ? Type Y or N
```

The required steel area and neutral axis depth which satisfy the design loads are found as shown below:

```
Total steel area of 1856.24267 mm2
is required to resist the
design axial load of 1480 kN
and design moment of 54 kNm

Neutral axis depth  = 285.239 mm

axial load capacity = 1481.14411 kN
moment capacity     = 54 kNm
Press space bar to continue
```

15.7 CONCLUDING REMARKS

The above programs for the design of rectangular reinforced concrete sections, simply supported beams and columns have been based on the simplified stress block, thus enabling the results to be compared with those obtained in the earlier chapters. Both these programs can be extended to facilitate the design of rectangular sections and T-sections based on the exact stress block. For the purposes of this book RC Beam, Beam Deflection, Column Analysis and Column Design are presented as separate programs. However, it may be more convenient to link them together as one program or as a series of menu driven programs. This, and further development of the programs, are left to the reader.

References

British Standards

BS 12: 1978: *Specification for Ordinary and Rapid Hardening Portland Cement*
BS 882: 1983: *Specification for Aggregates from Natural Sources for Concrete*
BS 1881: *Methods of Testing Concrete*
  Part 108: Method for Making Test Cubes from Fresh Concrete
  Part 111: Method of Normal Curing of Test Specimens
  Part 116: Method for Determination of Compression Strength of Concrete Cubes
BS 5328: 1981: *Methods of Specifying Concrete including Ready-mixed Concrete
  ment for Concrete*
BS 4483: 1985: *Specification for Steel for the Reinforcement of Concrete*
BS 5328: *Methods of Specifying Concrete including Ready-mixed Concrete*
BS 6399: 1984: *Design Loading for Building*
  Part 1: *Code of Practice for Dead and Imposed Loads*
BS 8004: *Code of Practice for Foundations*
BS 8110: 1985: *Structural Use of Concrete*
  Part 1: *Code of Practice for Design and Construction*
  Part 2: *Code of Practice for Special Circumstances*
  Part 3: *Design Charts for Singly Reinforced Beams, Doubly Reinforced Beams
  and Rectangular Columns*
CP 3: 1972: Chapter V: *Loading.* Part 2: *Wind Loads*
CP 110: 1972: *Code of Practice for Structural Use of Concrete* (superseded by
  BS 8110 in 1985)

1. Concrete Society (1981) *Model Procedure for the Presentation of Calculations*,
   2nd edn, Technical Report 5, London.
2. Concrete Society and Institution of Structural Engineers (1989) *Joint Committee Report on Standard Method of Detailing Structural Concrete*, London
3. Teychenne, D.C. *et al.* (1988) *Design of Normal Concrete Mixes*, 2nd edn,
   Building Research Establishment.
4. Concrete Society and Institution of Structural Engineers (1983) *Standard
   Method of Detailing Reinforced Concrete*, London.
5. Timoshenko, S.P. and Goodier, J.N. (1970) *Theory of Elasticity*, 3rd edn,
   McGraw Hill, New York.
6. Reynolds, C.E. and Steedman, J.C. (1988) *Reinforced Concrete Designer's
   Handbook*, 10th edn, E & F N Spon, London.
7. Johansen, K.W. (1962) *Yield Line Theory*, Cement and Concrete Association,
   London.
8. Jones, L.L. and Wood, R.H. (1967) *Yield Line Analysis of Slabs*, Chatto and
   Windus, London. (New Edition to be published by E. & F.N. Spon, 1991.)
9. *Building Regulations and Associated Approved Documents*, HMSO, London,
   1985.
10. Cranston, W.B. (1972) *Analysis and Design of Reinforced Concrete Columns*,
    Cement and Concrete Association, Slough.
11. Chudley, R. (1976) *Construction Technology*, Longmans, London.
12. Coates, R.C., Coutie, M.G. and Kong, F.K. (1987) *Structural Analysis*, Van

Nostrand Reinhold, London.

13. Ghali, A. and Neville, A.M. (1989) *Structural Analysis: A Unified Classical and Matrix Approach*, 3rd edn, Chapman and Hall, London.

14. Council on Tall Buildings (1985) *Planning and Design of Tall Buildings*, 5 vols, American Society of Civil Engineers, New York.

15. Smolira, M. (1975) *Analysis of Tall Buildings by the Force–Displacement Method*, McGraw Hill, New York.

Further reading

Hodgkinson, A. (ed.) (1974) *Handbook of Building Structure*, Architectural Press, London.

Kong, F.K. (ed.) (1983) *Handbook of Structural Concrete*, McGraw Hill, New York.

Kong, F.K. and Evans, R.H. (1987) *Reinforced and Prestressed Concrete*, 3rd edn, Van Nostrand Reinhold, London.

Mosley, W.H. and Bungey, J.H. (1987) *Reinforced Concrete Design*, 3rd edn, Macmillan, London.

Neville, A.M. (1981) *Properties of Concrete*, 3rd edn, Pitman, London.

Rowe, R.E. *et al.* (1987) *Handbook to British Standard BS 8110: 1985: Structural Use of Concrete*, E & F N Spon, London.

Index